Word up

It's Got To Come Out Of Your Mouth!

Written By
William Thompson JR.

Table Of Contents

About The Author
WILLIAM (BILL) THOMPSON JR.

is the senior pastor of the Spoken Word Center, in Fort Worth, Texas.

Has been in the ministry of preaching the gospel since Feb. 7, 1982, and has engaged himself in much extensive studies and training of the word of God. He has been in the church all of his natural life and has the experience of a true churchman that lends the passion for which he ministers the gospel of God.

Pastor Thompson is an ordained elder of the "Churches of God In Christ", to which he is very thankful for all of the training and guidance beginning at 14' years of age.

Born March 12, 1961 in El'paso, Texas to the union of the late Rev. William Thompson Sr. & Rev. Daisy Y. Mclawler-Thompson; by the age of 3 years he had already began to express a passion to play the piano and to preach the Gospel.

The family later relocated to Fort Worth, Texas where he grew up in the Baptist church with his parents, sang in the choir and learned to study his own bible.

He attended the Fort Worth Independent School District through all of his primary education. His is a graduate of Dunbar Sr. High, class of 79'. He has attended Tarrant County Junior College, Dallas Theological Seminary, and Vogue Beauty College.

His uncle; the Late Apostle Russell Thompson, laid his hand on him at the age of 11, with which from that point on he knew that there was more for him in the Lord. He knew that he had to move to the next level in an effort to get to that which he desired most of the Lord.

He moved his experience of worship from the Baptist church to the Church of God in Christ where he further developed as a very talented singer and multi-talented musician. He has been skilled with talents to play 14 instruments, and has composed many songs.

Pastor Thompson has crossed the lines of the many denominational influences in his own local surroundings, enabling himself to become identified as a child of God and not Just a Baptist, a Methodist, a Pentecostal, or for that matter, just another member of the Church Of God In Christ!

Pastor Thompson has been the minister of music for many ministries in the DFW Metro-plex, and OKC, OK. In the past. He has traveled with evangelist, and has been the guest musician for many revivals, musicals, weddings, conferences, recordings and etc. He has also conducted many Revivals, Music Workshops, have spoken across the country, and Founded and established the Spoken Word Center, School of Prophetic Excellence.

Pastor Thompson hails from an extensive linage of dedicated ministers of the gospel of Jesus Christ. He is also a descendent of the Late; Great, Reverend Vol William McLawler of Louisville, Kentucky.

Pastor Thompson is also a descendent of the first generation Church of God In Christ. Through family research this discovery was made. By the grace of God and divine providence, Pastor Thompson found his way back to the grass roots of his own spiritual inheritance.

His endeavor is to serve the people of the Lord everywhere that will receive of the awesome gift of the Holy Ghost to which he has been endowed.

Pastor Thompson is also known and respected as a "_True Prophet_" of God, and a natural Evangelist at heart!

Pastor Thompson has been married to Sharon Renee for 22 years and is the father of four children, and have been blessed with 3 grandchildren.

V

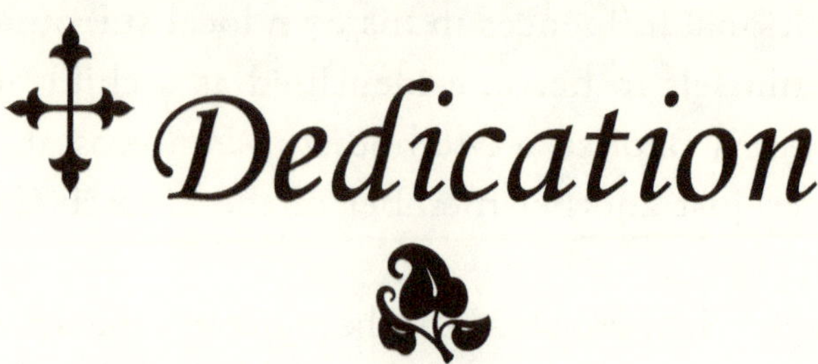 Dedication

Word Up, IS DEDICATED TO THE BODY OF CHRIST WORLD WIDE. I BELIEVE IN YOU, BECAUSE GOD BELIEVES IN YOU!

The COLLECTIVE IMPACT OF THE PEOPLE OF CHRIST'S CHURCH; THAT THEY MAY BE BROUGHT TO TOTAL FAITH AND TRUST IN JESUS CHRIST, IS WHAT I'M LOOKING FOR.

Finally; TO THE CLOSING AGE OF THE BODY OF CHRIST! JESUS IS COMING BACK VERY SOON! WHO WILL BE READY TO MEET HIM WHEN HE COMES BACK?

God Bless You!

Introduction

You may __be__ a Strong Talker! How Strong __is__ Your Listener?

In most of our lives, we have often had trying experiences that warrant being shared as a testimony of the grace and the power of God. It's a beautiful thing that God has intervened and changed the naturally expected outcomes of so many situations in the lives of people.

Alike myself, I know that you have also heard many testimonies that just brought chills up and down your spine.

Perhaps you have a testimony that would be a blessing to the body of Christ, that need to be shared with people. I could only wonder why you have never shared your testimony. I could never fathom in my mind why you would hold back on sharing the goodness of the Lord.

Some tell their testimonies every chance they get. Since God will never discriminate when helping us, no one is actually exempt from sharing what He's done for them.

In the inner church, many people have been closely evaluated and carefully considered for elevated positions of confidentiality as a result of their testimonies. Sometimes it may sound too good to be true being that the indiviual testify-

ING MIGHT HAVE ONLY BEEN IN THE CHURCH FOR A SHORT WHILE COMPARED TO OTHERS.

MANY PEOPLE DON'T LIKE TO SHARE THEIR TESTIMONIES FOR THE SAKE OF BEING DOUBTED AND DISCOUNTED AS UNRELIABLE. I FIND MYSELF WANTING TO ASK THE QUESTION AT TIMES, JUDGING THE DEMEANOR OF CERTAIN PERSON AS THEY SHARE THEIR TESTIMONIES; "DID YOU MEAN YOUR TESTIMONY; OR, ARE YOU INTENDING TO MARKET YOUR TESTIMONY!

I HOPE THAT PEOPLE WILL CONNECT WITH THE MESSAGE IN THE PAGES OF THIS BOOK SO THAT THEY WILL ALWAYS BE EVERYTHING TRUTHFUL AND HONEST WHEN THEY SPEAK, WHETHER IN CONVERSATION OR IN THE MIDST OF GIVING A TESTIMONY.

I AM SERIOUSLY PASSIONATE ABOUT INTELLIGENT HUMAN BEINGS EXERCISING VERBAL SKILLS, BECAUSE IT'S WHAT WE SAY THAT PEOPLE REMEMBER ABOUT US MOST OFTEN. YOU COULD BE *"tow up from the flo' up"*, BUT SPEAK LIKE A SENATOR, OR A KING, AND MOST PEOPLE THAT ARE WITNESSES OF YOUR CONVERSATION WILL REMEMBER THE SKILLFUL ARTICULATION IN YOUR VERBAL DIALOGUE.

TALKING IS A PRIVILEGE AND A GIFT TO EVERY HUMAN BEING ON THE EARTH. THE SOCIAL STATUS OF ONE INDIVIDUAL OVER AND AGAINST ANOTHER DOESN'T MATTER, AND IT DOESN'T CANCEL OUT THE ABILITY OF ANYONE ELSE TO SPEAK ON THE COMPREHENSIVE LEVEL OF THE NEXT PERSON.

GIVEN THE RIGHT CHANCE, THE AVERAGE HUMAN BEING WOULD DEFINITELY TALK WAY TOO MUCH, VERBALLY INTRUDING THE BUSINESS AFFAIRS OF OTHER PEOPLE, AS IS OFTEN THE CASE AND THE GRIM REALITY FOR MANY.

PEOPLE USUALLY DISCOVER THAT OTHERS SEEM TO SHOW AN INTEREST IN WHAT THEY HAVE TO SAY. SO THEY USUALLY DISREGARD THE RULES OF ENGAGEMENT THAT ARE NECESSARY FOR THE OBSERVANCE OF INTEGRITY IN THE MIDDLE OF A CONVERSATION.

VIII

It is one thing for people to question what you've said, but it is all together a totally different thing for people to regard you as a questionable individual!

Let's not take for granted that the persons we are talking to are really listening and often able to document our conversations verbatim. People can mentally document the date and the exact time that a particular statement was made.

We are not always as watchful of our words as we ought to be. When we feel comfortable with certain people, we allow too many unstable, non-profound statements, to come out of our mouths.

Your mouth was created to give wind to the wings of your words, to unlock the configurative combinations of your faith. What we say, should permanently set our faith in flight, to open the Heavens over our lives. You've never been so blessed, until the things verbally released from your mouth, brings the glory of God into your atmosphere.

This reading journey, will expose the ability or inability, the power or the lack of power, that may or may not be, flowing through you, based upon what, how, when, and where you do or do not say out of your mouth.

Come aboard this reading journey and allow your spirit to sore through the pages.

Say a prayer to open the channels of your heart and allow the information in this book to find it's way to the proper place of your spirit and intellect. My purpose is to help you to step up and bat 1,000 when speaking forth in obedience to God.

EXPECT CHANGE AND EFFECT, AND EXPERIENCE THE QUIETING OF STORMS IN YOUR LIFE!

WE NEED NOT ONLY TO BE IDENTIFIED WITH ANY PARTICULAR RELIGIOUS PERSUASION, TO DEVELOP AND MAINTAIN, WHAT I WILL CALL, *"corporate convictions."*

BELIEVING A PARTICULAR TEACHING OR PHILOSOPHY TO FIT IN TO A RELIGIOUS ENVIRONMENT OR A DENOMINATIONAL PERSUASION, IS WHAT CONSTITUTES THE ENTITLEMENT OF; **corporate convictions.**

IT'S NOT VERY WISE TO EMBRACE TEACHINGS AS A MATTER OF BELIEF WITHOUT EVER PERSONALLY EXAMINING THE DATA, AND BEGIN PASSING THE INFORMATION ALONG TO OTHERS.

EMBRACE THE KING JAMES VERSION OF THE BIBLE. STAND ON IT, EVEN IF YOU HAVE TO STAND, ALONE! GIVE GOD THE CHANCE TO BE THE MASTER OF YOUR THOUGHT PROCESS.

THERE WILL NEVER BE A DAY WHEN EVERYBODY WILL RECEIVE WHATEVER YOU SAY OUT OF YOUR MOUTH.

SO MANY PEOPLE FEEL THAT THEIR WORDS MAY NOT COME OUT RIGHT TO THE LORD, TO THE POINT THAT THEY RECEIVE THE HAND OF THE LORD MOVING OVER THEIR SITUATION.

FEELINGS AND EMOTIONS DON'T EVER, AND THEY WILL NEVER SUCCESSFULLY SPEAK TO THE LORD ON YOUR BEHALF! AS OF LATE WHILE FINISHING THIS BOOK, I READ IN THE FORT WORTH STAR TELEGRAM NEWSPAPER THAT APPROXIMATELY 700,000 PEOPLE IN THE COUNTRY, PER YEAR; OF ALL RACES, AGE GROUPS AND SOCIAL STATUS, SUFFER STROKES AT THE BRAIN!

IT IS EVIDENT TO ME THAT PEOPLE HAVE MANY DEADLY THINGS BOTTLED UP ON THE INSIDE OF THEMSELVES THAT NEED TO BE RELEASED TO THE LORD AND TO EVERYONE ELSE FOR THAT MATTER ALONE.

THE LORD KNOWS THAT YOU ARE FEELING VERY BADLY OVER YOUR SITUATIONS FROM THE PAST AND POS-

SIBLY PRESENT SITUATIONS ALIKE, BUT, THE RELEASE FOR THE PAINFUL FEELINGS THAT ARE ON THE INSIDE OF YOU, IS IN YOUR MOUTH.

OPEN YOUR MOUTH TO THE LORD!

YOU WILL DISCOVER READING THIS BOOK THAT YOU ARE NOT CRAZY AND YOU ARE REALLY NOT CONFUSED. YOU HAVE NEEDED ALL ALONG TO SAY SOMETHING AND DELIVER YOURSELF FROM THE SELF DESTRUCTION OF THE EXPLOSIVE INFORMATION LOCKED AWAY IN YOUR BELLY.

Journey the aisles of these pages to discover your verbal strength and authority, because,

It's Got To Come Out of Your Mouth*

Word up

The Mystery of My Mouth

> *And the Lord said unto him, who hath made mans mouth.*
>
> EXODUS 4:11

The Mouth!!!

YOU WILL NEVER KNOW HOW IMPORTANT IT IS TO TALK, UNTIL; IF YOU WERE TO LOSE THE ABILITY TO DO SO.

HOW IMPORTANT IS YOUR SPEAKING ABILITY TO YOU, AND WHAT ARE YOU DOING TO PROTECT YOUR GIVEN ABILITY TO SPEAK? NOT YOUR RIGHT AS A BELIEVER TO SPEAK, OR I^{ST} AMENDMENT RIGHT AS A VOTING AND TAX PAYING CITIZEN OF THE COUNTRY. BUT, YOUR ACTUAL PHYSICAL ABILITY TO VERBALLY SPEAK OUT OF YOUR MOUTH.

THERE IS ABSOLUTELY NO WAY TO SUCCESSFULLY EXERCISE THE NECESSARILY INTENDED USAGE OF THE VOCAL CHORDS IN THE THROAT, WITHOUT THE ATTACHED AID OF THE LIPS, TEETH, TONGUE AND THE CREATIVE SKILLFUL DYNAMIC MANEUVERING IN THE MOVEMENT OF THE JAWBONE FOR THE CREATION OF MULTIPLE TONES AND SOUNDS THAT COME OUT OF OUR MOUTHS TO SHAPE VERBAL UTTERANCES.

SOME PEOPLE HAVE BEEN PLAGUED WITH THE DISASTER OF DEAD VOCAL CHORDS IN THE THROAT, THAT ARE

INCAPABLE OF RESPONDING TO THE COMMANDED BREATH RELEASED INTO THE WIND PIPE, TO CREATE SOUND WAVES, HINDERING THE ABILITY OF THE MOUTH TO SOUND OUT THE ORAL ARTICULATIONS OF THEIR OWN ORIGINATED THOUGHTS, WHICH IS THE STARTING POINT AND THE VERY BEGINNING OF VERBAL UTTERANCES.

OTHERS HAVE HAD THEIR LARYNX (*"voice box"*) SURGICALLY REMOVED, HOWEVER RECONSTRUCTIVE SURGERY, AND MEDICAL TECHNOLOGIES, HAVE AGAIN GIVEN THEM THE RESTORED VOCAL ABILITY FOR THE PURPOSE OF COMMUNICATING, BUT A RESTORED VOCAL ABILITY IS NEVER COMPARABLE TO THE ORIGINATED VOICE GIVEN AT BIRTH.

IN THE LATTER CENTURIES OF THE LAST MILLENNIUM, EXTENSIVE EFFORTS WERE TAKEN TO PREVENT PTOMAINE POISONING WHICH WOULD RESULT IN WHAT WAS KNOWN TO THE AMERICAN POPULATION, AND PERHAPS TO THE WORLD, AS "LOCKJAW"; THE MOUTH WOULD BE PERMANENTLY SHUT IN SOME CASES.

A MUTE MOUTH, THOUGH IT MAY HAVE BEEN THE GRIM REALITY FOR SOME, IT IS NOT THE ACCEPTABLE PROFILE OF THE WORKING ORDER OF A MOUTH TO BE RECEIVED FROM THIS BOOK, ESPECIALLY IN THESE LATTER TIMES, AS YOU WILL SO AMAZINGLY DISCOVER THROUGH READING THIS ANOINTED WORK.

WHEN GOD SAID; "LET US MAKE MAN IN OUR LIKENESS, AND IN OUR OWN IMAGE", HE WAS VERY THOROUGH AND COMPLETE, SO HE CREATED A MOUTH FOR MANKIND THAT SPEAKS EXCLUSIVELY FROM ALL OTHER CREATED BEINGS IN THE EARTH, AS HE HIMSELF BEING GOD, ALSO SPEAK.

GOD KNOWS THE AWESOME POWER AND THE NECESSARY AUTHORITY THAT IS INGRAINED IN HAVING AN OPEN MOUTH THAT IS WORKING PROPERLY TO SPEAK FORTH THOSE THINGS THAT ARE NECESSARY AND OFTEN DESIRED! YOU HAVE TO SPEAK THE RIGHT THINGS FORTH OUT OF YOUR MOUTH! THE WHOLE WORLD WAS FRAMED BY THE SPO-

KEN WORDS OF GOD'S OWN MOUTH.

SOME PEOPLE SPEAK VERY SOFTLY, WHILE OTHERS SPEAK VERY LOUDLY WITH NO EFFORT INVOLVED. THEN THERE ARE THOSE INDIVIDUALS WHO ARE CLASSIFIED AS NORMAL, THEY SPEAK WITH VERY EVEN AND RATHER VERY NON-ATTENTION STIRRING TONES IN THEIR VOICE, UNLESS; WHENEVER THEY CHOOSE TO APPLY AN INCREASED VOLUME LEVEL TO GET THE ATTENTION OF THE PERSON THEY ARE SPEAKING TO.

SOME PEOPLE VERBALLY TAKE CHARGE BASED UPON A POSITION OF AUTHORITY OR AN AUTHORITATIVE ATTITUDE WHENEVER THEY SPEAK TO OTHER PEOPLE, HOWEVER, OTHERS HAVE AN AUTHORITATIVE TONE NATURALLY INGRAINED INTO THE RESONANCE IN THE SOUND OF THEIR VOICES AUTOMATICALLY.

WHETHER YOU SPEAK LOUDLY OR SOFTLY, VERY RASPY OR SMOOTHLY, THE FACT IS THAT YOU HAVE BEEN GIVEN THE ABILITY TO SPEAK FROM THE LORD, AND YOUR GIFT TO SPEAK IS AS IMPORTANT AS THE VERY NEXT PERSONS. EVERYONE'S VOICEPRINT IS IDENTIFIABLY, INDIVIDUALLY UNIQUE.

LET ME ENCOURAGE YOU TO NEVER GET CAUGHT UP INTO THE COMPARISON OF YOUR VOICE AGAINST ANOTHER PERSON'S, BECAUSE IT DOESN'T MATTER! JUST KNOW THAT GOD HAS GIVEN YOU THE ABILITY TO SPEAK WITH A TAILOR-MADE TONE TO ACCOMPANY YOUR SPEECH FOR THE SIGNATURE PURPOSE OF IDENTIFYING YOU IN THE EARTH.

IMAGINE THE TRAUMATIC DEVASTATION ONE MIGHT EXPERIENCE HAD THEY BEEN BORN WITHOUT A MOUTH ATTACHED TO THEIR BEAUTIFUL LITTLE BABY FACES?

SUPPOSE A MOTHER CARRIED HER BABY FOR THE FULL TERM IN HER WOMB, AND TIMELY DELIVERED A HEALTHY BABY, ONLY TO DISCOVER THAT HER BABY DIDN'T HAVE A MOUTH?

THAT BABY WOULD NOT BE ABLE TO CRY IN THE MIDDLE OF THE NIGHT WAKING UP IT'S PARENTS, BEING IN

NEED OF SOME SORT OF ATTENTION.

WITH NO MOUTH YOUR CUTE LITTLE TODDLER WOULD NOT HAVE BEEN ABLE TO LEARN TO SING OR EVEN TO SAY THE ALPHABETS, OR COUNT TO TEN VERBALLY WITH THEIR MOUTHS TO ESTABLISH THE BEGINNING OF THEIR EARLY "PRESCHOOL" DEVELOPMENTAL SKILLS FOR BEING PROPERLY EDUCATED.

WELL, PERHAPS YOU DIDN'T HAVE A MOUTH, BUT DIDN'T DIE AT BIRTH? COULD YOU BEAR THE FRUSTRATION OF NOT BEING ABLE TO PARTICIPATE IN ALL OF THE NOR-MAL BEHAVIORAL ACTIVITIES IN YOUR FAMILY HOME THAT REQUIRED THE AID OF YOUR MOUTH? YOU COULDN'T EN-JOY YOUR FAVORITE BEVERAGE, OR AN EYE OPENING HOT CUP OF COFFEE IN THE EARLY MORNING HOURS, HOT TEA OR ICED TEA, OR EVEN HOT CHOCOLATE.

PERHAPS YOU FREQUENT YOUR FAVORITE RESTAU-RANTS FOR A MEAL WITH YOUR FAMILY, FRIENDS, COWORK-ERS, OR CHURCH MEMBERS? COULD YOU IMAGINE BEING DEPRAVED OF THE DELIGHT OF RESTAURANT DINING NOW THAT YOU DO KNOW OF THE JOY?

FEEDING, FOR AN INFANT CHILD, WOULD HAVE BEEN VIRTUALLY IMPOSSIBLE, AND IT'S BREATHING WOULD HAVE BEEN SEVERELY HINDERED POSSIBLY TO THE POINT THAT THE CHILD MIGHT HAVE EVEN DIED SHORTLY AFTER BIRTH!

 PROTEIN AND VITAMINS THAT ARE TAKEN INTO OUR BODIES THROUGH THE AID OF OUR MOUTHS DURING A MEAL ARE NECESSARY FOR THE FURTHER DEVELOPMENT OF THE BODY AS THE BODY NEEDS ENERGY IN ORDER TO HELP US STAY UP ON OUR FEET, AND ALSO TO ENABLE US TO GET UP FROM OUR BEDS WHENEVER WE HAD BEEN LYING DOWN ASLEEP.

WELL NOT ONLY WOULD YOU BE DENIED THE DE-LIGHTFUL INTAKE OF THE MOUTH, AS FOOD IS FOR NOUR-ISHING THE BODY, BUT LIFE WOULD BE VIRTUALLY MOST IMPOSSIBLE TO LIVE, BECAUSE WE MUST NOT ONLY GAIN A CERTAIN AMOUNT OF WEIGHT AS WE GROW, WE MUST ALSO

MAINTAIN THE WEIGHT WE HAVE GAINED.

Talking Back!

ALTHOUGH WE ARE NOW IN THE AGE OF THE COMPUTER, MOST, IF NOT ALL OF THE CHOSEN CAREERS REQUIRE THE ABILITY TO SPEAK FOR THE PURPOSE OF COMMUNICATING OUR SKILLS TO OUR FELLOW COLLEAGUES.

IMAGINE WHAT WOULD HAPPEN IF YOU WERE EVER TO BECOME ILL, OR DEPRESSED, OR IF YOU EVER WONDERED OFF AND HAD GOTTEN YOURSELF LOST AND COULD NOT COMMUNICATE EITHER SITUATION MENTIONED ABOVE TO ANYONE BECAUSE YOU DID NOT HAVE YOUR MOUTH TO TALK? SUCH A STATE WOULD BE TERRIFYING! SUPPOSED THE WOLVES WERE UPON YOU AND YOU COULD NOT EVEN CRY WOLF!!!

ANY DREAM OF BEING A SINGING MEMBER OF THE CHURCH CHOIR OR THE PRAISE TEAM, WOULD ONLY BE A NIGHTMARE! YOU COULD NOT VERBALLY TEACH A CLASS, PREACH A SERMON, PASTOR A CHURCH, EVANGELISE, PROPHESY, OR EVEN BECOME THE PRESIDENT OF THE UNITED STATES OF AMERICA FOR THAT MATTER! HAD YOUR ABILITY TO TALK BEEN DIMINISHED OR TOTALLY REMOVED.

YOU COULD BE A MIME MASTERING THE ART OF GESTURING BUT NEVER EVER BECOMING ORATORS, OR PUBLIC SPEAKERS. MIMES DON'T TALK OR EVER SPEAK WITH THEIR MOUTHS!

OUR SPEAKING ABILITIES ARE REALLY VERY IMPORTANT TO US, IN AN EFFORT TO SUCCESSFULLY COMMUNICATE TO ONE ANOTHER. A FEW YEARS AGO WHILE STUDYING, I GAINED AN UNDERSTANDING RELATIVE TO HAVING A CONVERSATION WITH OTHER INDIVIDUALS.

CONVERSATION: ACCORDING TO THE GREEK AND HEBREW DEFINITIONS, THE PREFIX "CON" BEING THE FIRST SYLLABLE OF THE WORD, MEANS-<u>WITH</u>, WHICH MEANS TO BE INVOLVED. WHILE, THE LAST TWO SYLLABLES IN CONJUNCTION TO EACH OTHER "SA-TION" (SAY-SHUN) MEANS-

TURN AROUND, OR IN MY OWN TERMINOLOGY IT MEANS TO COME BACK AT YOU.

THE ENGLISH LANGUAGE ADDED THE SECOND SYL-LABLE "-VER-", OF WHICH IS INDICATIVE OF SAYING; VER-SUS, OR VERBAL. SEE: WITH-VERSUS-VERBAL-TURN AROUND. WE HAVE *CON-VERSUS-SATION*.

"Verbal involvement-versus-a-verbal comeback; at you."

ONE MOUTH-VERSUS-ANOTHER MOUTH, AND/OR ONE PERSON-VERSUS-ANOTHER PERSON, IS THE ONLY MANNER OF WHICH A SUCCESSFUL CONVERSATION CAN HAPPEN. AS LONG AS ONE PERSON DOES ALL OF THE TALKING, THERE CAN BE ABSOLUTELY NO CONVERSATION GOING ON!

IN ORDER TO HAVE A CONVERSATION, IT IS NECES-SARY FOR BOTH OR ALL PARTIES INVOLVED TO BE RESPON-SIVE, OR RATHER TO VERBALLY BOUNCE BACK AT ONE AN-OTHER. WITHOUT THE SPEAKING ABILITY, ONE WOULD SIM-PLY HAVE TO BE LEFT OUT OF ALL CONVERSATIONS AND VER-BALIZATIONS OF THE MOUTH.

He Started It!!

GOD HAS GIVEN US THE NECESSARY SPEAKING SKILLS WE NEED IN ORDER TO RENDER ACCEPTABLY TO HIM, THAT WHICH HE REQUIRES OF HIS PEOPLE EVERYWHERE, WHICH IS PRAISE AND WORSHIP.

GOD HAS ALSO GIVEN A MOUTH TO EVERY OTHER CREATURE ON EARTH; EVEN TO THE TINIEST INSECTS. BUT, NO FISH, FOWL OF THE AIR OR BEAST OF THE FIELD, HAS GOT A MOUTH LIKE MINE, OR LIKE THAT OF MANKIND ANY-WHERE IN THE WORLD.

WHILE EVERY CREATURE MAY OBSERVE ONE OR TWO, OR MAYBE EVEN MORE CHARACTERISTICS OF THE MOUTH THAT ARE SIMILAR, THE MOUTH OF MAN WHILE SURREN-DERED TO THE POWER OF GOD, POSSESS GODLIKE CHAR-ACTERISTICS UNLIKE ANY OTHER CREATURE IN THE EARTH, SINCE FROM THE BEGINNING OF TIME.

TREE DWELLERS, SUCH AS ARE CALLED; "MONKEYS, AND APES", MISTAKENLY HAVE BEEN REFERRED TO AS THE ANCESTORS OF MANKIND. BUT THEY DO NOT, AND HAVE NEVER EVEN POSSESSED THE LIBERATED MEASURE OF SPECTACULAR UTTERANCES OF WORDS, AND THE WORD USAGE TO CONSTRUCT SENTENCES FOR THE PURPOSE OF COMMUNICATING, LIKE THAT OF MANKIND.

SPEAKING, SAYING, AND DECLARING BEGAN WITH THE FATHER AND CREATOR OF THIS NOW EXISTING WORLD, AS WE KNOW OF IT TODAY.

GOD, SPOKE DIRECTLY MOUTH TO MOUTH, AND SPIRIT TO SPIRIT WITH MANKIND IN THE EARTH, WHO WERE ABLE TO VERBALLY RESPOND TO THEIR GOD HAVING BEEN EQUIPPED WITH A MOUTH TO DO SO.

MANY PEOPLE AND EVEN MANY THEOLOGIANS WILL ARGUE TODAY THAT GOD DOES NOT YET SPEAK MOUTH TO MOUTH WITH HIS PEOPLE, BUT HE *does* YET SPEAK IF YOU WILL ONLY LISTEN. YOU MUST LIVE CLOSE ENOUGH TO THE LORD IN EFFORT TO CLEARLY DISCERN HIS UNMISTAKABLE VOICE. HE COMMANDS US TO FOLLOW HIS LIKENESS AND ORDER.

GOD SPOKE WITH ADAM AND EVE, ABRAHAM, ISAAC, AND JACOB, ELIJAH, ELISHA, MOSES AND TO ALL OF THE OTHER MAJOR PROPHETS, KINGS, HIGH PRIEST AND SERVANTS.

OUR MOUTHS MUST OPEN UP AND SOUND OUT UNTO THE LORD AND SPEAK UP TO HIM, WHILE SIMULTANEOUSLY KNOWING WHEN TO TURN DOWN OR TO TURN OFF THE VOLUME OF OUR SPEECH! WE NEED TO KNOW WHEN TO BE SILENT BEFORE THE LORD ALSO.

Not Like Mine!

MANKIND HOLDS THE EXCLUSIVE POWER OF CREATION TO SPONTANEOUSLY WORSHIP GOD AND TO CHOOSE WHICH ABILITIES OF THE MOUTH WILL BE USED. SUCH AS, READING THE WORD OF GOD OUT ALOUD, SINGING, PRAYING, SPEAKING SEVERAL DIVERSE LANGUAGE DIALECTS, AND

SPEAKING IN AN UNKNOWN TONGUE, ETC. WE ARE ABLE TO MAKE VERY DISTINCT SOUNDS AND TO BLOW MUSICAL INSTRUMENTS.

OTHER CREATED SPECIES HAVE ONLY THE ABILITY TO REPEAT WHATEVER HAS BEEN SPOKEN IN THEIR EARS BY ANOTHER SOURCE, LIKE AS UNTO CERTAIN SPECIES OF BIRDS AND SOME DOGS; FOR THE SAKE OF SOME PEOPLE THAT WOULD HAVE GIVEN EQUAL RECOGNITION TO THE ANIMATED SPEAKING ABILITY OF NONHUMAN MAMMALS.

MANKIND HAS THE CREATIVE ABILITY TO IMITATE AND TO DUPLICATE THE VOICES OF OTHER MEN AND MANY ANIMALS ALIKE, HOWEVER WE HAVE THE EXCLUSIVE ABILITY TO VERBALLY SPEAK OUR OWN ORIGINATED THOUGHTS.

EXTEMPORANEOUSLY; TOPICS, RANGING FROM AN INNUMERABLE DIVERSITY OF SUBJECT IMPUTATIONS BEING MANY, MAY ALL BE UTTERED FROM OUR MOUTHS AT AN INSTANCE. OUR CONVERSATIONAL CHOICES MAY ALSO INCLUDE DECEPTIONS, FALSE TEACHINGS, AND A WIDE RANGE OF DISCUSSIONS.

THE ARTISTIC ABILITY OF THE VENTRILOQUIST IS TO ILLUSIVELY PROJECT THEIR OWN VOICE TO ANOTHER PLACE OTHER THAN WHERE THEY ARE PRESENTLY STANDING. THIS ART USE TO BE VERY POPULAR DURING THE EARLY-TO-MID YEARS OF THE TWENTIETH CENTURY, AND EVEN BEFORE THAT PARTICULAR TIME. IN THIS CENTURY, VENTRILOQUISTS ARE NOT AS POPULAR AS THEY USED TO BE, BUT THEY DO STILL EXIST AND PRACTICE.

I Choose to Say!

YOU TELL YOUR MOUTH WHAT TO SAY, SO YOU ARE RESPONSIBLE FOR HOW, WHEN, AND WHERE TO SAY IT. HAVE YOU EVER UTTERED THE WORDS, "I DIDN'T MEAN TO SAY THAT, IT JUST LEAPED OUT OF MY MOUTH?" THE REAL FACT IS, THOSE WORDS WERE ONLY AN EXCUSE FOR WHAT WAS SAID OUT OF YOUR MOUTH. DON'T EVER HESITATE TO TAKE CONTROL OF YOUR MOUTH.

THE MOST POWERFUL ABILITY THAT MANKIND WILL EVER POSSESS RELATIVE TO THE MOUTH, IS THE ABILITY TO SPEAK WHICH HAS THE INGRAINED POWER TO <u>SAY</u>!

NO BLAME COULD EVER BE PLACED ON ANYONE ELSE ON THE OUTSIDE OF YOUR BODY OR YOUR OWN MIND, FOR WHAT YOU SAY. NO ONE CAN FORCE US TO EVER SAY ANYTHING! NOT EVEN AT GUNPOINT!

IT IS VERY IMPORTANT TO BE KNOWLEDGEABLE AND RESOURCEFUL IN ONES OWN INTELLECT, AS A RESULT OF STUDIES, MAINTAINING REGARD AND REVERENTIAL ESTEEM FOR THE KNOWLEDGE OBTAINED. YET, THE REAL PERSONAL POWER IS NOT BASED PRIMARILY ON WHAT IS KNOWN, BUT RATHER ON WHAT IS SAID AS A RESULT OF WHAT IS KNOWN, CITING THE SKILLFUL MANNER VERBALLY MAINTAINED IN A CONVERSATIONAL DIALOGUE.

WE SHOULD NEVER AFFORD OURSELVES THE IRRESPONSIBILITY TO UTTER THINGS FROM OUR MOUTHS OF WHICH WE HAVE NO BUSINESS, SIMPLY BECAUSE WE FAILED TO BRUSH UP ON THE VERBAL SKILLS THAT WOULD HAVE EMPOWERED OUR CHOICE OF SAYING. WE MUST OBTAIN AND MAINTAIN VERBAL CONTROL IF WE ARE GOING TO BE RESPONSIBLE FOR WHAT WE CHOOSE TO SAY.

NOT VERY MANY PEOPLE SEEM TO CARE THAT THEIR WORDS CAN BE VERY DESTRUCTIVE AND IRRETRIEVABLE, TO THE POINT THAT THE VERBAL BLADES OF THEIR TONGUE, COULD CUT RIGHT TO THE HEART OF AN INDIVIDUAL.

> *"Life and death are in the power of the tongue."*
> PROVERBS 18:21

SO, WHAT WE CHOOSE TO SAY SHOULD BE VERY CAREFULLY THOUGHT OUT AS BECOMING CHILDREN OF THE MOST HIGH GOD, BEFORE SPEAKING.

> *But the tongue can no man tame, it is an unruly evil, full of deadly poison.*   JAMES 3:8

MOST LIKELY AT ONE TIME OR ANOTHER, WE HAVE ALL SAT DOWN TO DISCUSS A PARTICULAR SUBJECT OR TOPIC,

ONLY TO BE MADE AWARE THAT BASED ON WHAT WAS SAID OR THE LACK OF WHAT WAS ACTUALLY SAID ON THE TOPIC, THAT PERSON, OR THE PERSONS TALKING, REALLY DID NOT POSSESS THE ACCURATE KNOWLEDGE REQUIRED FOR KNOWING WHAT THEY'VE JUST SPENT HOURS TRYING TO CONVINCE US THAT THEY REALLY KNEW.

THE ABSENCE OF TRUE FACTUAL INFORMATION IN YOUR HEART AND IN YOUR MIND ON A SUBJECT OR A TOPIC ALLEVIATES THE ACTUAL POWER OF RELIABILITY TO WHAT YOU SAY CONCERNING THE MATTER. TO THE LIKES OF A PERSON ALWAYS GIVING AN OPINION BASED ON A FEELING, OR A THOUGHT AT THE TIME OF SPEAKING, BUT NOT REALLY KNOWING FOR A FACT.

YOUR ATTITUDE, RELATIVE TO ALL NEGATIVE EMOTIONS, PLAY AN EXTREME ROLE IN CHOOSING WHAT YOU WILL SAY. WHENEVER YOU ARE ANGRY OR IN A VERY NEGATIVE MOOD, OR MAYBE EVEN IN A SPIRIT OF DISCOURAGEMENT, YOU SHOULD BE CAREFUL TO SCRUTINIZE YOUR THOUGHTS BEFORE THEY ARE UTTERED FROM YOUR LIPS, SO THAT YOUR WORDS WILL POSITIVELY PRODUCE THE FAITHFUL, LIFE YIELDING RESULTS OF THE WORD OF GOD.

HAVE YOU EVER NOTICED HOW ECSTATIC WE BECOME, WHENEVER IT HAS BEEN DISCOVERED THAT A TODDLER HAS DEVELOPED THE ABILITY TO SPEAK COMPLETED WORDS AND PHRASES, OFTEN SOUNDING OUT THE NAMES OF THEIR PARENTS AND SIBLINGS?

 THIS EXCITEMENT IS SO, BECAUSE THE DEVELOPMENT OF SPEAKING; IS MORE OF A SPIRITUAL MATTER THAN IT IS A NATURAL OCCURANCE. THEREFORE, THE ACTUAL EXCITEMENT IS REALLY DEEPLY SPIRITUAL. EVEN IN THE LIGHT OF THOSE INDIVIDUALS WHO REFUSE TO BE CHRISTIANS, THEIR SPIRITS ARE OVERJOYED, WHICH CAUSES THEM TO BUBBLE OVER IN THEIR NATURAL BODIES. WE WERE GIVEN MOUTHS TO GLORIFY GOD!

WE ARE VERY HAPPY TO REALIZE, THAT THE CHILD HAS LEARNED TO SPEAK, BUT, ONLY LATER TO FEEL AS IF

THE SAME CHILD IS WRECKING OUR NERVES SOMETIMES, BECAUSE THEY ASK SO MANY QUESTIONS.

THE CHILD ITSELF IS ALSO OVERWHELMED WITH THE ABILITY TO SPEAK, SO AS A RESULT, WHENEVER THE OPPORTUNITY ARRIVES, THEY OPEN THEIR MOUTHS, BECAUSE THEY ARE EXCITED ABOUT THEIR GIFT OF GAB! HAS ANY CHILD EVER REPEATED WHATEVER YOU HAVE SAID?

THE TRUTH IS THAT THE CHILD IS DETERMINED TO MIMIC THE BIGGER PEOPLE IN ITS OWN CIRCLE OF LIFE, SO NATURALLY THEY BEGIN TO SPEAK WHAT THEY ARE HEARING IN THEIR EARS.

JUST AS HEAVEN REJOICES WHEN ONE SOUL REPENTS AND CONFESSES JESUS CHRIST AS LORD AND SAVIOR; OUR SPIRITS ARE OVERJOYED KNOWING THAT THE NEW SOUL THAT HAS ENTERED INTO THE WORLD IS ACTUALLY WORKING ITS WAY TO PROPERLY OPENING ITS MOUTH TO ACKNOWLEDGE THE FINISHED WORK OF THE CROSS, SPEAKING ACCORDING TO THE DESIGNED PLAN OF THE *CREATOR*; WHO ALSO SPEAK.

ARE YOU THE GREATEST PERSON IN YOUR OWN CIRCLE OF LIFE? IF SO; IT IS UNDERSTANDABLE THAT YOU HAVE NEVER CHOSEN TO SPEAK A MORE ELEVATING DIALOGUE THAN THAT TO WHICH YOU DO SPEAK. LIKE THE CHILD'S CIRCLE OF LIFE, WHEN GOD IS THE GREATER PERSON IN OUR CIRCLE OF LIFE, WE ARE DETERMINED TO MIMIC WHAT HE SAYS AND THE WAY THAT HE SAYS IT. WE ARE DETERMINED TO TALK JUST LIKE HIM!

No Reason!

YOU HAVE TO BE WATCHFUL OF WHAT YOU SAY, BECAUSE SOME PEOPLE; WHO BEING AS IMMATURE AS THE LITTLE CHILD TODDLER, HAVE POOR UNDERSTANDINGS WHEN THEY HEAR YOU. THE INTENTIONAL MEANING OF WHAT YOU SAID, IS TOTALLY DIFFERENT FROM WHAT YOU MEANT, IN THEIR HEARING. I GREW UP ON THE *"sticks and stones may break my bones, but words can never hurt me"*

PRINCIPLE, AS DID MANY OF YOU.

WHAT A LYING PRINCIPLE THAT ONE IS!

YOUR MOUTH REALLY CAN SAVE YOU OR IF AND WHENEVER YOU CHOOSE TO NEGLECT TO PUT A GUARD BEFORE YOUR OWN MOUTH, IT CAN AND WILL DESTROY YOU. YOU MIGHT WANT TO SAY TO YOURSELF, MY MOUTH CAN HELP ME OR HURT ME! MY MOUTH CAN BRING HEALING TO ME OR CAUSE ME TO REMAIN SICK EVEN LONGER THAN I SHOULD HAVE BEEN, BECAUSE OF FAILURE TO PRONOUNCE FAITH FILLED WORDS OF HEALING OVER MY BODY.

MY MOUTH CAN ESTEEM ME, OR CONDEMN ME, AND LAST BUT NOT LEAST, MY MOUTH CAN CAUSE ME TO BE SET IN EXALTED PLACES, OR CAUSE ME TO BE BURIED DEEP DOWN WITHIN THE DARK, COLD RUINS OF THE SOCIETY THIS NOW HUMAN LIFE.

WHATEVER I SAY OUT OF MY MOUTH, MAY ALSO EVENTUALLY CAUSE ME TO DWELL IN THE ETERNAL PRESENCE OF GOD'S GLORY, OR ALLOW HELL TO CLAIM MY SOUL ETERNALLY, BECAUSE OF THE JUDGMENT OF GOD.

SET YOUR AFFECTIONS UPON ELEVATING YOUR THOUGHT PROCESS TO THE POINT OF LIFTING THE DIALOGUE OF YOUR SPEECH, IN EFFORT NOT TO SUBJUGATE YOUR TOTAL CHARACTER SKETCH TO THE CONDESCENDING LOWS OF YOUR PRESENT SURROUNDINGS, OR DURING ETERNITY AFTER YOUR LIFE HAS ENDED.

SOME PEOPLE ARE LOCKED AWAY IN MENTAL INSTITUTIONS, OR SERVING TIME IN THE PENITENTIARY FOR CRIMINALS, BASED ON CONVERSATIONAL MATTERS TO WHICH THEY WERE NOT VERY CAREFUL OF. THEY WEREN'T WATCHFUL OF THE WORDS FROM THEIR MOUTHS. THEY THOUGHT THAT WHAT THEY SAID DIDN'T MATTER, BECAUSE THEY WERE BIG ENOUGH TO SAY WHATEVER THEY CHOSE TO SAY.

THE GRAVE HOLDS MANY RIGHT TODAY WHO HAVE UTTERED THE WRONG WORDS FROM THEIR MOUTHS, THAT WERE SPOKEN OUT OF SYNC WITH THE PROPER TIMING ON

A PARTICULAR ISSUE. *(be it they were true or false)* AND EVEN THOUGH THE TIMING WAS ON CUE FOR SOME AT OTHER TIMES, THEY'RE STILL DEAD AS A RESULT OF HAVING THEIR WORDS JUDGED.

THE CAUSE MAY HAVE BEEN FOR ANGER, FEAR, PAIN, HEARTACHE, EXCITEMENT, ANXIETY OR DOUBT AND UNBELIEF, THESE ARE NO REASONS TO JUST SAY WHATEVER YOU CHOOSE AT ANY GIVEN MOMENT WITHOUT THINKING FIRST.

Be Careful, Don't Bite!! Be Honest!!

YES, IT IS YOUR MOUTH! YOU ARE SO RIGHT ABOUT THAT FACT, AND YOU DO HOLD THE EXCLUSIVE RIGHT TO SAY WHATEVER, WHENEVER, AND HOWEVER YOU CHOOSE TO SAY WHATEVER YOU CHOOSE TO SAY IT, NO MATTER OF THE OUTCOME. YOUR APOLOGY FOR HAVEN BEEN SO FORWARD AND UNRESTRAINED WHILE SPEAKING, WON'T NECESSARILY CAUSE PEOPLE TO FORGET WHAT YOU HAVE SAID. THE MANNER IN WHICH YOU SAY THINGS AT TIMES, LEAVES A MORE INDELIBLE IMPRESSION EVEN MORE THAN WHAT WAS ACTUALLY SAID.

I'M SURE YOU'VE BEEN TOLD BEFORE, THAT IT IS NOT WHAT YOU SAID, BUT IT WAS THE SPIRIT AND THE MANNER IN WHICH YOU SAID IT, BECAUSE THERE ARE TIMES WHEN WHAT YOU SAY IS ACTUALLY OK. THERE IS FAR TOO MANY PEOPLE THINKING WITHOUT TALKING AND TALKING WITHOUT THINKING TO RELAY THEIR NECESSARY THOUGHTS, AS IT IS. YOU DON'T HAVE TO BE CHARACTERIZED AS AN IRRATIONAL SILLY HUMAN BEING.

HAVE YOU EVER BEEN CONFRONTED BY ANYONE, WHO WAS LOUD AND RAGING, AND JUST GOING OFF AT THE MOUTH? SHOUTING AT THE TOP OF THEIR VOICE ABOUT MATTERS TO WHICH YOU FELT WAS ACTUALLY NO REASON FOR THEIR VERBAL BEHAVIOR? DIDN'T YOU FEEL AS IF YOUR HEAD WAS JUST BITTEN OFF, CHEWED UP AND SPIT OUT? SUCH VERBAL ATTACKS CAN SPERN FEELINGS OF INFERIORITY.

ROUGH VERBAL MISHANDLING OF PEOPLE, BY A PASTOR, A JOB SUPERVISOR, PARENTS, SPOUSES, FRIENDS, OR LOVED ONES COULD CAUSE THE SELF ESTEEM OF THE PEOPLE ATTACKED TO BE SEVERELY CRUSHED! HOWEVER, "TAKE HEED (*be careful*) THAT YOU BE NOT CONSUMED (*swallowed up or rather completely taken in and verbally destroyed*) OF ONE ANOTHER."

<u>BITE</u>- TO SEIZE WITH THE TEETH, AS IF TO TEAR OFF A PIECE OF SOMETHING, OR TO CUT THROUGH OR EVEN RIP OUT A CHUNK. BITING, WHILE NECESSARY FOR DIGESTION DURING MEALS (AS FOOD MUST BE INGESTED BY THE BITE SIZE) HAS A WIDE RANGE OF MEASUREMENTS, RANGING FROM ANNOYING, TO SERIOUS, AND EVEN DEADLY BITES OF WHICH IS MEASURED BY THE INTENT OF IT'S PURPOSE . EMPHASIS- WILLIAM THOMPSON JR.

But if ye bite and devour one another, take heed that ye be not consumed one of another.

GALATIANS 5:15

YOU BE VERY SURE, AND FOR CERTAIN, THAT YOU ARE NOT THE ONE BITING AND DEVOURING PEOPLE EVERYWHERE YOU GO. TO PROJECT SUCH BEHAVIOR, OPENLY DISPLAYS THE ATTRIBUTES OF A BAD ATTITUDE, SUGGEST A LACK OF UNDERSTANDING AND SELF-DISCIPLINE, WHEREAS OUTRAGEOUS EMOTIONAL OUTBREAKS YIELD NON-DEFIANT EVIDENCE OF AN UNCONTROLLED BAD TEMPER.

NOT ONLY ARE YOU OUT OF CONTROL, BUT YOU JUST LET EVERYBODY KNOW IT! IT WOULD REALLY BE BENEFICIAL FOR YOU TO DEVELOP THE NECESSARY CONTROL OF YOUR MOUTH PREVENTING EVERYONE ELSE FROM BEING A WITNESS OF YOUR TEMPERAMENTAL STRUGGLES, WHICH HAS THE POWER TO SHAME AND TO DEFAME THE NAME OF JESUS CHRIST.

A good man out of the good treasure of the heart bringeth forth good things; and an evil man out of the evil treasure bringeth forth evil things. But I

*say unto you, that every idle word that men shall
speak, they shall give account thereof.*
ST. MATTHEW 12: 35-36

To give absolutely no thought to whatever you might say while blurting out unnecessarily or to be a person that will thoroughly consider what is said, clearly gives a very strong indication and a high probability of just who you are to the people that really matter most, in terms of making a difference in your life.

Be mindful of the scripture, to verbally conduct yourself accordingly, and you won't have as many problems as people that disregard the word of God.

Acting Like An Animal!!

It is not good to attack issues only, because in doing so, the surrounding circumstances and important details, *most times hidden details,* that shed more light on the matter to determine the actuality of reliability, or false hood of the stated report, are disregarded and overlooked.

Whenever we hunt facts of negative matters, and chase down the persons of whom the matters concern, we behave ourselves like nothing more than wild predators, whose territory has been evaded.

To attack and tear down one another is just what the Devil wants from the people of the Lord. You play right into the hands of the enemy whenever you refuse to follow after peaceful methods of dealing with situations, reluctant to be in harmony with persons of the body of Christ.

Do you even know the real status of that to which you are biting at and chasing after? Is it real, or is it a fake? Is it true or false?

It is animalistic to attack one another in a

MANNER OF VERBALLY BITING THE HEAD OFF OR BACKBIT-ING ANOTHER INDIVIDUAL. ANIMALS THEMSELVES, THEY CLAW AND SCRATCH WHICH IS IRRELEVANT TO THIS PRESENT SUBJECT MATTER, BECAUSE DEATH COMES ABOUT BY SOME-TIMES A SINGLE, BUT DEADLY BITE, OR MAYBE A SERIES OF BITES FROM THE MOUTH. BRUTALLY MAULING, THEY TEAR INTO PREY WITH THE FATAL INTENTIONS OF THEIR BITES.

I ONCE SAW A GROUP OF RESEARCHERS STUDYING A PRIDE OF LIONS IN THE WILD, WHILE WATCHING WILD DIS-COVERY. A REPLICA OF THE LIONS (A STUFFED ANIMAL), A FAKE, WAS PLACED OUT IN THE OPEN TERRITORY OF THE LION PRIDE. THIS PARTICULAR REPLICA, THOUGH CONVINCINGLY FEMILIAR TO THE LIONS, ONLY APPEARED TO BE A REAL THREAT TO THE OPEN TERRAIN, IN THE PRESENCE OF THESE LIONS.

ANIMALS, REALLY DON'T HAVE THE ABILITY TO KNOW TRUE FROM FALSE, AND HOW TO LOOK AT AN INTRUDER TO SEE THE TRUE LIFELESSNESS, BASED ON THE SKILLS OF VIS-IBILITY, AND DETERMINE THE ACTUAL STATUS, AS MANKIND DOES.

THE LIONS WOULD NOT HAVE BEEN ABLE TO DETER-MINE THAT FURTHER EXAMINATION WOULD BE TOTALLY UN-NECESSARY. THIS WOULD HAVE ALLOWED THEM TO TURN AWAY FROM THE INTRUDER WITHOUT EXERTING EVEN THE LEAST BIT OF THEIR ENERGY.

TWO DOMINANT MALES APPROACHED THE REPLICA TO CLOSELY INVESTIGATE THE INTRUDER. THEY STARED DOWN THE REPLICA, MONITORING THE INACTIVITY OF THE INTRUDING TRESPASSER IN THEIR TERRITORY. THE IN-TRUDER GAVE NO RESPONSE TO THEIR EXAMINATION WHICH INTRIGUED THE DOMINANT MALES TO MOVE IN FOR A CLOSER LOOK.

WITHOUT ANY WARNING THE TWO DOMINANT MALES LAUNCHED AN AWESOME ATTACK, BUT TO THEIR SURPRISE THERE WAS NO BLOOD, RETALIATION OR AN ATTEMPT TO FLEE THEIR AWESOME ASSAULT.

A SWIFT BITE TO THE SPINE OF THE REPLICA, DESIG-

NATED TO KILL AN OPPONENT, STILL DID NOT DOWN THE INTRUDER. THE <u>FACT</u> IS THAT THE INTRUDER WAS NOT EVEN REAL, <u>IT</u> WAS FAKE!

WHENEVER YOU ALLOW YOURSELF TO BITE, AND SEEK TO DEVOUR, AND TO VERBALLY CONSUME WITH THE INTENTIONS TO DEFAME THE NAME A BROTHER OR A SISTER IN THE LORD, YOU ARE DRIVEN, MOVED, AND MOTIVATED BY THE EVIL, UNGODLY WORKS OF THE FLESH.

> *"As we have therefore opportunity, let us do good unto all men, especially unto them who are of the household of faith.*　　　GALATIANS 6:10
> *Verily, Verily, I say unto thee, we speak that we do know, and testify, that we have seen;*
> 　　　　　　　　　　ST. JOHN 3:11

IT'S NOT NEAR AS COSTLY TO CONTROL THE WORDS THAT COME FROM YOUR MOUTH AS IT IS WHEN YOU IGNORE THE NEED TO BE WATCHFUL OF YOUR WORDS.

BE KIND AND BE CAREFUL TO EXERCISE DISCIPLINE OVER YOUR OWN MOUTH, AND PLEASE DON'T BITE AND DEVOUR ONE ANOTHER, EVEN IN THE PRESENCE OF TRUE FACTS WHERE THE TRUTH HAS BEEN ESTABLISHED.

JESUS PAID THE PRICE FOR US IN EFFORT THAT WE MIGHT HAVE A HOPE AND A FUTURE. SO RECEIVE THE SPIRIT OF GOD IN ORDER TO SHOW FORTH THE LOVE OF CHRIST WHENEVER WE SPEAK!

Word up

"Did I Say That?"

> *If I justify myself, mine own mouth shall condemn me: if I say I am perfect, it shall also provoke perverse.*
>
> JOB 9:20

Too Late! It's Set In Motion!

WORDS THAT ARE LEFT ON THE PAGES OF THE DICTIONARY IN THE LIBRARY, THAT ARE NOT OFTEN SELECTED TO BE USED IN SENTENCES OF GREAT RELEVANCE; ARE PACKED WITH EXPLOSIVE POWER, CAPABLE OF SETTLING THE SUBJECT MATTER WITH EXCELLENCE!

JUST SITTING ON THE SHELF PATIENTLY WAITING TO BE DISCHARGED TO EXPLODE INTO THE BATTLE REALM OF SPEAKING WARFARES.

SPOKEN WORDS, OFTEN SET FORTH A CERTAIN COURSE OF ACTION UNEXPECTEDLY, THAT CAN ENTRAP YOU AND CAUSE SITUATIONS TO DEVASTATINGLY BLOWUP IN REACTIONS TO WHAT HAS BEEN SAID. ONCE SET IN MOTION, THE REACTION TO WHAT HAS BEEN SAID MUST RUN IT'S PREVIOUSLY <u>UNDER-DETERMINED</u> COURSE TO THE BITTER END.

WORDS ONCE SPOKEN FROM YOUR MOUTH, SHOULD RETURN TO BLESS YOU, IF THEY DON'T COME BACK INSTEAD TO HAUNT YOU? THE ACTUAL POWER OF SPOKEN WORDS IS NOT JUST BECAUSE YOU SAID IT OUT OF YOUR MOUTH, WORDS ALONE ALL BY THEMSELVES ARE VERY POWERFUL EVEN IF THEY NEVER PROCEED FROM YOUR POWERFUL ABILITY TO SPEAK, BUT RATHER SOMEONE ELSE'S MOUTH.

IT IS MOST LIKELY, THAT MORE OFTEN THAN NOT, EVERY INDIVIDUAL WILL HAVE SAID SOMETHING THAT DID NOT SET WELL WITH THEIR OWN CONSCIOUS. THE REMEMBRANCE OF THOSE STATEMENTS ARE OFTEN DEEP DOWN WITHIN OUR SOULS GNAWING AT US LIKE CATERPILLARS ON A FRESH GREEN VINE, RELENTLESS TO RELIEVE US OF THE GUILT OF HAVING SAID THE WRONG THINGS.

SPOKEN WORDS MOVE INTO MOTION LIKE AN AUTOMOBILE TRANSMISSION THAT WILL ONLY SHIFT INTO DRIVE. NO MATTER HOW BAD WE MIGHT HAVE FELT ABOUT OUR COMMENTS, THERE IS NO REVERSE TO PUSH THE WORDS BACK TO THE ORIGINAL SOURCE OF IT'S INTENTIONAL RELEASE, OR NEUTRAL TO STOP THEM IN MIDAIR, WHICH MAKES IT LITERALLY FRIGHTENING TO REALIZE THAT CERTAIN THINGS WERE SAID OUT OF OUR MOUTHS, BUT, <u>THAT'S RIGHT</u>, <u>YOU SAID IT</u>!

YOU CAN NEVER "UNSAY" WHAT HAS ALREADY BEEN SAID; AND THIS IS REALLY THE TRUTH! IT IS A DREADFULLY TERRIFYING THING TO REALIZE YOU HAVE SAID SOMETHING TO WHICH YOU CANNOT TAKE BACK.

Thou art snared with the words of thy mouth,
thou art taken with the words of thy mouth.
PROVERBS 6:2

The Painful Course!

PEOPLE HAVE SPENT MONTHS AND YEARS TRYING TO CONVINCE OTHERS THAT WHAT THEY SAID WAS NOT REALLY WHAT THEY ACTUALLY INTENDED TO SAY!

We have to say what we mean, and mean exactly what we say! Some people get painfully scarred indefinitely as result of froward speaking mouths that talk without proper consideration. My good friend would always say, and I quote; "Words are cheap, but you cannot buy them back!"

An elderly woman I once knew, whenever I was about 25-26 years of age, she had to have been 60 years plus and definitely a senior grandmother! She needed landscaping done around her home now that her husband had recently passed away, of which I was very capable of doing.

I volunteered my services, and after talking for only a short while, she readily agreed to allow me to do the landscaping for her. Several days passed and she still had not given me direction concerning when to come and to do the landscaping, and/or even where she wanted the work done on her lawn.

I again inquired about the work and almost without thinking, she replied, "I don't know about you, I don't trust you!" My face dropped, and my mouth flew open, because she had only seen me at our place of employment.

Well, almost immediately she stopped whatever she was doing and made the statement; "I didn't mean that! That came out wrong!" She wanted to take back what she had said to me, but it was too late! Those words were destructively released to do all the damage they could do.

> *Let no corrupt communication proceed out of your mouth, but that which is good to the use of edifying, that it may administer grace unto the hearer. And grieve not the Holy Spirit of God, where by ye are sealed unto the day of redemption. Let all bitterness, and wrath, and*

> *anger, and clamour, be put away from you, with*
> *all malice: and be kind one to another, tender*
> *hearted, forgiving one another, even as God for*
> *Christ's sake hath forgiven you.*
>
> EPHESIANS:4:29-32

PERHAPS THE WOMAN SPOKE OUT OF BITTERNESS, ANGER, OR EVEN OUT OF THE PAIN OF HER GRIEF, DUE TO THE LOSS OF HER HUSBAND. SHE HAD LOST THE SECURITY OF HER ADULT LIFE, HAVING BEEN MARRIED FOR BETTER THAN FORTY YEARS? WHATEVER THE REASON, SHE SPOKE THOSE AWFULLY PAINFUL WORDS TO ME IN THE PRESENCE OF THE OTHER CO-WORKERS.

IT ACTUALLY TOOK ME A WHILE TO RELEASE THE PAINFUL MEMORY OF THAT DAY. EXAMINE YOUR REASONING AND YOUR MOTIVES BECAUSE YOU CAN NEVER REALLY KNOW THE DAMAGE THAT MAY BE DONE AS A RESULT OF WHAT YOU SAY.

EVEN IN A COURT OF LAW, A JUDGE MIGHT ORDER THE COURT REPORTER, TO STRIKE THE LAST STATEMENT FROM THE WITNESS' TRANSCRIBED CONFESSION. THE COURT REPORTER WILL MOST LIKELY DO SO, UPON COMMAND. BUT!! IN THE MINDS OF THE JURORS AND ALL OTHER ONLOOKERS, THE STATEMENT IS YET FRESH IN THEIR MINDS.

SOMETIMES IT TAKES ALL KINDS OF ACTS OF LOVE TO CONVINCE THE PERSON OR PERSONS SPOKEN TO, THAT WE ARE TRULY <u>SORRY</u> FOR SAYING THE WRONG THING.

Don't Talk Yet!

<u>STOP</u> THE MURDERING TONGUE IN YOUR OWN MOUTH BEFORE IT KILLS THE CHARACTER OF SOMEONE YOU REALLY DO LOVE.

DON'T ALLOW YOUR TONGUE TO BE <u>*loose*</u>, RUNNING WILD, LIKE A WILD BEAST WAITING TO DEVOUR AND KILL. NON-SURRENDERED TONGUES, WHICH ARE EQUIVALENT TO BEING WELL VERSED IN THE RELIGIOUS CHURCH DIALOGUE,

BUT, ARE NOT SURRENDERED TO THE WORD OF GOD, ARE ONE IN THE SAME AS BEING UNTAMED.

BEFORE ANY BEAST CAN BE TAMED, OR EVEN CONFINED TO A CAGE, THEY MUST FIRST BE CAPTURED. WE MUST SET OUR FOCUS ON THE MAGNETICALLY, PRESET TRAPS IN THE WORD OF GOD, TO CAPTURE THE WILD TALKING OF OUR TONGUES AND SWIFTLY GET THEM TAMED.

CAPTURED, BUT YET UNTAMED ANIMALS ARE STILL DANGEROUS, AND CAPABLE OF KILLING AND DEVOURING. LIKEWISE OUR CAPTIVATED, BUT ONLY RELIGIOUS TONGUES, ARE THE SAME AS BEING UNTAMED, AND ARE YET DANGEROUS AND DEADLY!

> *Even so the tongue is a little member, and boasteth great things behold how great a matter a little fire kindleth! And the tongue is a fire, a world of iniquity: so is the tongue among our members, that it defileth the whole body, and setteth on fire the course of nature; and it is set on fire of hell. For every kind of beast, and of birds, and of serpents, and of things in the sea, is tamed, and hath been tamed of mankind. But, the tongue can no man tame; it is an unruly evil, full of deadly poison.*
>
> JAMES 3:5-8

THE POWER YOU NEED FOR THE NECESSARY CONTROL OF YOUR OWN TONGUE, IS ON THE INSIDE OF YOU NOW THAT YOU ARE SAVED. BUT, YOU HAVE GOT TO SURRENDER YOUR WILL TO EXERCISE CONTROL.

IT IS LEFT UP TO YOU TO BE SURE THAT THE MESSAGE THAT YOU ARE CONVEYING TO ANOTHER INDIVIDUAL IS CLEAR, IN AN EFFORT TO PROTECT YOUR OWN INTEGRITY.

AS A <u>CHILD</u> I WAS ALWAYS TAUGHT, AS WERE MANY OF YOU, THAT IF YOU CANNOT SAY ANYTHING GOOD, DON'T SAY ANYTHING AT ALL, WHICH IS A POLICY THAT THIS LATE ARRIVING GENERATION NEED DESPERATELY TO RETURN TO! THE ELDERLY GENTLEMEN IN THE NEIGHBORHOOD, WHERE

I GREW UP USED TO SAY, "PUT A LID ON IT." SOMETIMES WE NEED TO JUST SHUT UP!!

SO MANY PEOPLE WILL LITERALLY TRY TO HANG YOU ON THE WORDS THAT ARE SPOKEN FROM YOUR MOUTH. PEOPLE WILL HOLD ON TO EVERY LITTLE SYLLABLE UTTERED FROM YOUR LIPS. THERE WILL BE TIMES WHEN A PARTICULAR LISTENER OF YOURS MAY HAVE AN UNDETERMINED MOTIVE WHILE IN CONVERSATION WITH YOU. REMAIN ON GUARD, AS PERTAINING TO HOW YOU VERBALLY HANDLE OTHER INDIVIDUALS DURING A CONVERSATION.

THERE WILL BE TIMES WHEN EVEN THE MOST HONEST DIALOGUE CAN BE TURNED INTO A TRAP OR A SETUP. IT MAY NOT ALWAYS BE YOUR OWN TONGUE IN NEED OF BEING TAMED, IT MAY BE THAT YOUR LISTENER IS IN NEED OF HAVING THEIR HEARING SPIRITUALLY EXERCISED OF THE EXTREME NEGATIVE ELEMENT THAT DRIVES THEM TO WANT TO HEAR SOMETHING ELSE OTHER THAN WHAT YOU ARE SAYING.

EVERYTHING THAT PASSES THROUGH THEIR HEARING CANAL IS DEMONICALLY FILTERED AND TURNED INSIDE OUT! WHEN YOU REALLY MEAN WELL AND ARE MOST CAREFUL, YOU YET MAY BE IN FOR A SURPRISE, AS YOUR LISTENER MAY BE IN OUTER SPACE MENTALLY, WHILE THEY SHOULD BE LISTENING TO YOUR CONVERSATION!

The Counselor Said!

PEOPLE HAVE RECEIVED THE WRONG ADVICE FROM INDIVIDUAL COUNSELORS. MOST PEOPLE DON'T EVEN REALIZE THEY HAVE BEEN GIVEN THE WRONG ADVICE UNTIL THEY HAVE ACTED UPON THE ADVICE THEY RECEIVED. CAUTION SHOULD BE APPLIED TO THE ADVICE THAT YOU GIVE TO A PERSON IN NEED OF COUNSEL.

CARELESSNESS CAN CAUSE THE WORD-OF-COUNSEL TO COME BACK IN A BAD WAY, WHEREAS YOU WILL FIND YOURSELVES ASKING THE QUESTION, "OH, DID I SAY THAT?" TOO LATE!! THE DAMAGE HAS ALREADY BEEN DONE!

Counselor, you must be wise enough to examine the listener, in an effort to evaluate the circumstantial evidence before giving directions.

You're The Parent!

Mom and dad, your words can be powerfully destructive, in a way that could even be incomprehensible to you many times. Even though you may not have meant for your words to be damaging, your words have the right punch at all times to damage the confidence of your child.

Enough people will do everything possible to damage the confidence of your child, without your help! Leave the destruction to those persons on the outside of your home and your family.

As a parent, your words are as training skills to the master builder. The master builder must be skillfully trained by a master technician in an effort to emerge from the training also as a master of the trade.

Children must come under the careful nurturing mannerisms of being properly spoken to by their parents, in an effort to develop the necessary skills of communicating, as they become adults and parents themselves one day.

People of God, to mean well is not good enough. It is a sorry attitude to face a situation all bottomed out as a result of your wrong advise, and then suggest as a statement of apology, "well, I meant well!" Too late! Far too many people are traveling the road of good intentions on a consistent whim, but falling way too short!

Those who are supposedly well-meaning are too often usually people who are supported greatly from the leadership platforms. Once it has been determined that they have indeed hurt others in

THE MINISTRY, THEY ARE NOT OFTEN REMOVED FROM BEING ABLE TO CAUSE MORE DAMAGE.

THESE INDIVIDUALS ARE NOT ALWAYS INSTRUCTED STERNLY TO JUST KEEP THEIR MOUTHS UNTIL THEY HAVE BEEN PROPERLY INSTRUCTED ON HOW TO SPEAK. SUCH DISCIPLINE MAY AID IN THE LIFE OF THE MINISTRY, OR THE CHURCH FAMILY.

MANY NEW BABES IN CHRIST HAVE OFTEN BEEN PUSHED AWAY SIMPLY BECAUSE THEY ENCOUNTERED SOMEONE WHO WAS NOT TACTFUL WHEN THEY SPOKE TO THEM. IT COULD HAVE MEANT THE INFLICTION OF PERMANENT SPIRITUAL DAMAGE FOR THE YOUNG BABE. THE WRONG THING SPOKEN CAN CAUSED A SPIRITUAL SETBACK FOR SOME PEOPLE, DESTROYING THEIR FAITH IN GOD.

> *Be ye therefore wise as serpents, and harmless as doves.*
>   MATTHEW 10:16

WE ARE TO BUILD UP THE LIVES OF OTHER INDIVIDUALS OF THE CHURCH AND WE ARE TO NEVER TEAR THEM DOWN. I PRAY TO GOD THAT YOU WOULD ALWAYS BEAR IN MIND THAT SOMEBODY HELPED YOU ALONG YOUR WAY INTO CHRISTIANITY.

Positive; or negative?

TO ASK THE QUESTION, "DID I SAY THAT" CAN BE POSITIVE OR NEGATIVE. WHICH DO YOU PREFER?

A. A BRIGHT BEAUTIFUL SMILE COMING BACK TO REMIND YOU OF WHAT YOU SAID, WITH JOY, BEING THAT YOU HAVE ENHANCED THE LIFE OF THAT INDIVIDUAL, KNOWING THAT HE/SHE WILL NEVER FORGET THE WORDS YOU HAVE SPOKEN INTO THEIR LIVES?

OR WOULD YOU PREFER:

B. TEARY EYES AND A DROOPING, SOUR FACE, PROJECTING HOPELESSNESS AND DESPAIR BECAUSE YOU HAVE GIVEN THEM THE WRONG ADVISE OR INFORMA-

TION WHICH LEAD THEM DOWN THE WRONG PATHWAYS OF LIFE; THIS IS A DREADFUL SCENE AND YOU WOULD BE IRRESPONSIBLE.

Honey Say It!

SOME PEOPLE ACTUALLY EXPECT OTHERS TO KNOW OF THEIR DEDICATION TO THEIR SPOUSE, WHEN IN FACT THEY HAVE NEVER MADE ANY VERBAL STATING OF THIS FACT. IF YOU WANT OTHERS TO KNOW, THEN BY ALL MEANS TELL THEM! JUST SAY IT! OTHERS MAY SPEAK-UP FOR YOU, BUT, ABSOLUTELY NO ONE CAN REPRESENT YOU, LIKE YOU!

THE DESTRUCTION OF YOUR MARRIAGE MAY BE HINGED UPON THE SIMPLE OVERSIGHT OF FAILING TO AC-KNOWLEDGE YOUR SPOUSE IN THE <u>PRESENCE</u> OF OTHER PEOPLE.

MANY MARRIED COUPLES ARE YET ENJOYING THE RO-MANTIC FLAMES OF THEIR MARITAL BLISS, FOR THE SAKE OF KNOWING HOW TO COMMUNICATE TO ONE ANOTHER VER-BALLY, WHICH MAY NOT ALWAYS BE EASY, BUT, IT IS NEVER IMPOSSIBLE.

THE HUSBAND WHO KNOWS HOW TO SPEAK TO HIS OWN WIFE, AS SWEET WORDS LIKE HONEY DRIPPING FROM HIS LIPS, POURING LIKE MELTED BUTTER, FALLING ON HER SOFTLY LIKE ROSE PEDALS, STILL CAUSING HER HEART TO FLUTTER, WILL NOT LIKELY BE THE ONE TO RECEIVE DI-VORCE PAPERS.

HE STILL KNOWS JUST WHAT WORDS WILL TINGLE HER TOES AND TAKE HER MIND BACK OFTEN TO THE DAY THEY COMMITTED TO EACH OTHER IN WEDLOCK!! THE EX-CITEMENT IS RENEWED, AND HE CAN ACTUALLY MAKE HER FEEL THAT SHE IS YET THE CINDERELLA OR THE BEAUTIFUL PRINCESS SHE ONCE WAS, ALTHOUGH SHE MAY NOW BE 20-30 POUNDS OVER WEIGHT, YET HE STILL LOVES HER VERY MUCH.

THE HUSBAND, WHOSE BELLY HAS NOW BECOME HIS

DINNER TABLE, WHILE HIS HAIRLINE HAS RECEDED LEAVING HIM MORE OF A FACE TO WASH NOW, SHOULD NOT BE MADE TO FEEL AS IF HE HAS LOST THE LOVE OF HIS SPOUSE AS A RESULT! LISTEN, IF YOU STILL LOVE YOUR SPOUSE THEN YOU FOR SURE OUGHT TO BE THE VERY ONE TO SAY SO!

JUST BECAUSE YOU SAID "<u>I DO</u>" ON THE WEDDING DAY, DID NOT MEAN THAT WAS TO BE A ONE TIME EVERLASTING VERBALIZATION IN REPRESENTATION OF YOUR MARRIAGE FROM NOW ON!

THE WEDDING DAY WAS JUST THE BEGINNING TO A VERY LONG LINE OF SAYING "<u>I DO</u>" THAT WOULD FOLLOW YOU TO THE VERY END OF YOUR LIFE. SO NOW AT THIS POINT AND TIME OF YOUR RELATIONSHIP YOU OUGHT TO BE SAYING; "I STILL DO", NOT "*I DID!*"

WHENEVER YOU LEAVE YOUR HOME TO RUN AN ERRAND, OR TO GO TO CHURCH, THE GROCERY STORE, TO VISIT A RELATIVE OR A FRIEND FOR THAT MATTER, IF YOU DESIRE YOUR SPOUSE TO ACCOMPANY YOU, OPEN YOUR MOUTH TO SAY SO!

DON'T JUST GRAB A COAT OR A HAT AND THE KNOB OF THE DOOR AND EXPECT FOR YOUR SPOUSE TO FOLLOW LIKE A LITTLE DUCKLING FOLLOWING AFTER ITS MOTHER. THIS BEHAVIOR, OF NEVER SAYING ANYTHING TO THE OTHER SPOUSE MAY WORK FOR SOME PEOPLE, BUT THAT SUCH BEHAVIOR WILL NOT BE THE WORKING ORDER FOR THE GREATER PERCENTAGE OF ALL MARRIED COUPLES.

Gesture or Talk?

HUSBAND, WHENEVER YOU DISCUSS BUSINESS MATTERS ABOUT THE HOME, OR THE RELATIONSHIP, IT IS IMPORTANT FOR YOU TO OPEN YOUR MOUTH AND VERBALLY COMMUNICATE WITH YOUR WIFE. YOU MAY NOT FEEL LIKE IT, YOU MAY NOT WANT TO TALK RIGHT NOW, BUT DON'T JUST SEND UP A CARELESS GESTURE.

WHAT YOU ARE SAYING, WITHOUT EVEN TRYING, IS I DON'T CARE, AND YOU ARE INDICATING THAT SHE CAN DO

WHATEVER SHE WANTS TO DO ABOUT THE BUSINESS OF THE HOUSE, OR THE RELATIONSHIP. "MAKE YOUR OWN DECISION; I DON'T REALLY CARE TO BE INVOLVED WITH YOU IN THE MATTER."

GESTURES SUCH AS SHRUGGING THE SHOULDERS, AND RAISING THE EYEBROWS, WAVING YOUR ARMS, AND EVEN JERKING YOUR HEAD (TO ONLY NAME A FEW), MAKE MANY UNINTENDED NEGATIVE STATEMENTS. GESTURES CAN ALSO MEAN THE SOON DEMISE OF YOUR MARRIAGE RELATIONSHIP.

SAY; "I LOVE YOU." SAY; "YES, I STILL WANT YOU." JUST BECAUSE YOU COME HOME EVERY NIGHT, CONTRARY TO YOUR OWN BELIEF, DOES NOT NECESSARILY SAY THAT YOU STILL WANT TO BE IN THE RELATIONSHIP WITH YOUR SPOUSE.

SAY; "I LIKE YOUR HAIR" IF YOU TRULY LIKE THE HAIRDO. SAY; "YOU LOOK GOOD TO ME" IF YOU BELIEVE THEY STILL LOOK GOOD TO YOU. SAY; "YES, WE'RE IN THIS LOVE TOGETHER."

SAY TO YOUR CHILDREN, "YOU CAN BE WHAT EVER YOU WANT TO BE", WHERE THERE IS A WILL, THERE IS A WAY. DON'T CRUSH, AND SHATTER THEIR DREAMS.

WHATEVER YOU WANT FROM THE LORD, ALL YOU HAVE TO DO IS <u>ASK</u>! SPEAK WHATEVER YOU WANT, IN FAITH, BELIEVING. TRUST GOD AND GET WHAT YOU WANT!

> *And all things; whatsoever ye shall ask in prayer, believing, ye shall receive.*
> ST. MATTHEWS 21:22
> *Ye lust and have not: ye kill, and desire to have, and cannot obtain: ye fight and war, yet ye have not, because ye ask not.*　JAMES 4:2

IT TAKES MORE THAN DESIRE; YOU HAVE GOT TO SAY IT IN FAITH BELIEVING WHATEVER YOU HAVE SAID!

> *Be careful for nothing; but in everything by prayer and supplication with thanksgiving let*

your request be made known unto God.

Philippians 4:6

Open Your Mouth!

Don't treat God as if you are actually doing Him a favor by allowing Him an opportunity to help you.

I will not get too deep into this subject; my point is that gestures do speak for themselves, but you need to remember that a gesture will often say what you never intended to say. Your mouth must speak!

You may have taken your spouse for granted, but don't you even think about taking God for granted. You're not as quiet as you may have pretended and the Lord knows all about it.

Don't even play with God! He knows you're the one; whether you told Him of the incident or not, who actually pushed the button to start the action at hand.

You were the one who flirted and/or made a verbally suggestive comment to trigger an excited response towards you from the another person. However, you still choose to make others believe that you don't understand the other persons' behavior toward you!

Not So Wide!

How about the arguments and the fights you seemed to have been engaged in <u>so</u> <u>frequently</u>? You may have told your friend, a family member, an officer of the law, or a judge in a court of law that you did not *do* any thing wrong, but did you even bother to tell any of them about the intentionally nasty and wrong things that you uttered from your mouth to cause the problems?

Your own mouth is the cause of everything that you are going through. Perhaps you've discovered that you possess a real evil gift of gab, you have the ability to push buttons to the point that, most people you come in contact with are shaken or even infuriated by those awfully vicious words spoken from your mouth.

Listen, it's not that everyone dislikes you, however people will tend to avoid you and other people of like character, who choose to bully their way through a conversation, being argumentatively contentious.

Such people know just the right things to say about other people to get the fight going. They are always seeking to attack the character of other people never having anything good to say.

Some telephone gossip is so hot the telephone receiver ought to melt in the hands of all parties involved in the conversation. Conversations of such, will leave you in a position of saying; "I did not say that", or rather asking yourself; "Did I say that?"

Most people will not own up to having said degrading and ungodly trash about another person, being that the participating parties, who talked, did so in secret vowing confidentiality. Isn't it amazing how such hideous comments find their way to the forefront of the information highways? 

Take notice also of how speedily such words are noised about to all parties who are interested in verbally degrading trash and garbage, and to those persons of no particular interest at all!

Just Keep Talking Wrong!

I was always taught that talk is contagious. If you keep on talking about other people long

ENOUGH, SOONER OR LATER YOU WILL FIND YOURSELF IN THE VERY SAME PREDICAMENT.

DID YOU EVER HEAR A PARENT TALK BECAUSE OF A NEIGHBOR'S, A FRIEND'S, OR EVEN A CHURCH MEMBER'S DAUGHTER BECOMES PREGNANT? THEY GENERALLY GO ON UNTIL IT HAPPENS TO THEIR OWN DAUGHTER OR UNTIL THEIR SON IMPREGNATES SOMEBODY ELSE'S DAUGHTER.

AMAZINGLY, THE DISCOVERY IS MADE, THAT IT IS THE TALKING PARENT'S OWN SON, THAT HAS INDEED IMPREGNATED THE YOUNG LADY WHO IS AT THE CENTER OF THEIR OWN NEGATIVE ATTENTION. MY!! WHAT TROUBLE OUR MOUTHS CAN GET US INTO.

THERE ARE THOSE PERSONS WHO DON'T POSSESS THE NECESSARY SKILLS TO VERBALLY TRANSMIT THAT WHICH THEY RECEIVED FROM OTHERS. NEITHER DO THEY KNOW HOW TO VERBALLY EXPRESS THEMSELVES WHEN GIVING AN ACCURATE ACCOUNT OF WHAT THEY HAVE SEEN. SOMETIMES TO LACK SUCH VERBAL SKILLS CAN BE VERY PAINFUL FOR OTHERS.

I WILL NEVER FORGET THE MONTH OF "AUGUST", IN THE YEAR' OF 1980'. I LIVED AT AN APARTMENT COMPLEX ACROSS THE STREET FROM A TACO BELL RESTAURANT, WITH A FRIEND AND HIS WIFE. A YOUNG FEMALE ACQUAINTANCE, WHOM I HAD KNOWN FOR A LONG TIME FROM THE NEIGHBORHOOD WHERE I WAS RAISED, WAS EMPLOYED THERE.

THAT SAME YOUNG LADY TOLD THE POLICE OUT OF HER OWN MOUTH, THAT I HAD ROBBED THE TACO BELL RESTAURANT AT GUNPOINT.

ON THAT PARTICULAR OCCASION, AS I WENT TO MY CAR TO LEAVE THE RESTAURANT; I REMEMBER SEEING HER AS SHE FOLLOWED ME OUTSIDE. SHE PRETENDED TO SWEEP THE SIDEWALK AS SHE TOOK NUMBER OF THE LICENSE PLATE OF MY CAR. AT THE TIME I WAS NOT AWARE THAT SHE WAS GETTING THE NUMBER OF MY LICENCE PLATE. I THOUGHT THAT SHE WAS ACTING AS STRANGE AS USUAL. SHE WAS AIWAYS RATHER WEIRD ACTING!

A POLICE DETECTIVE CONTACTED ME THROUGH MY PARENTS HOME TELEPHONE NUMBER, WHERE THE LICENCE TAGS ON MY CAR WERE STILL REGISTERED AND ASKED THAT I COME DOWN TO THE PRECINCT HEADQUARTER. HE TOOK AN INSTANT POLAROID SNAPSHOT OF ME, AND QUESTIONED ME FOR A WHILE. IT WAS LATER DETERMINED THAT I WAS NOT THE ONE THAT COMMITTED THE ROBBERY AT ALL!

THAT SAME DETECTIVE DISCOVERED THAT THERE WAS ABSOLUTELY NO WAY THAT IT COULD HAVE BEEN ME WHO ROBBED THE RESTAURANT. I TOLD THE DETECTIVE AT THE TIME OF QUESTIONING ME, THAT I KNEW EXACTLY WHO ACCUSED ME OF ROBBING THE RESTAURANT, AND I DESCRIBED HER BEHAVIOR AS SHE TOOK THE LICENCE PLATE NUMBER OF MY CAR. ALTHOUGH IT MAY HAVE BEEN ABNORMAL TO LAW ENFORCEMENT POLICIES, TO GIVE UP INFORMATION ABOUT AN INFORMANT WHO BLOWS THE WHISTLE ABOUT A POTENTIAL CRIME, THE DETECTIVE ACKNOWLEDGED TO ME THAT I WAS RIGHT ON AND EXACT ABOUT MY INFORMATION CONCERNING THE YOUNG WOMAN.

HE FORBADE ME TO CONTACT HER OR TO SAY ANYTHING TO HER IF I WERE TO COME INTO CONTACT WITH HER ANYTIME SOON, AND HE WARNED ME OF THE TROUBLE THAT I WOULD BE FACING IF I RETALIATED AGAINST HER FOR POINTING THE FINGER AT ME FALSY, ACCUSING ME OF COMMITTING A CRIME. SOUNDS TO ME AS IF HE KNEW THAT I HAD MY INFORMATION TOGETHER!

NEVERTHELESS, THAT YOUNG LADY <u>SAID</u> I WAS THE ONE!

MANY PEOPLE TODAY ARE IN THE PENITENTIARY BECAUSE SOMEBODY <u>SAID</u>; "THEY LOOKED LIKE THE ONE."

WITHOUT AN ADEQUATE ALIBI, THEY WERE UNABLE TO AVOID BEING PROSECUTED AND PENALIZED. GENERALLY PEOPLE WHO READILY POINT THE FINGER AT ANOTHER INDIVIDUAL AND SAY FOR A CERTAIN, THAT THEY ARE FOR SURE THEY HAVE IDENTIFIED THE RIGHT PERSON, ARE TOO EMBARRASSED AND OFTEN TOO UNGODLY TO ADMIT THAT

THE WRONG PERSON HAS INDEED BEEN FINGERED!

I HAVE SEEN CERTAIN PEOPLE REMINDED OF THEIR OWN DOCUMENTED TESTIMONY WHICH HAD BEEN PREVIOUSLY TRANSCRIBED BY A SKILLED PROFESSIONAL COURT REPORTER, AND THAT SAME PERSON WILL MAKE A DESPERATE ATTEMPT TO TRY AND SAY; "DID I SAY THAT", OR THEY WOULD SAY "I DID NOT SAY THAT", OR THEY MIGHT SAY THEY DID NOT REMEMBER SAYING THAT PARTICULAR THING!

Hidden Talker!!!

AT TIMES THERE MAY BE SOME ISSUES TO WHICH YOU HONESTLY DO NOT UNDERSTAND, IT IS MOST INTELLIGENT TO SIMPLY INQUIRE OF THE TEACHER OR THE PASTOR IN A MANNER OF HONESTY AND HUMILITY, TO GET AN UNDERSTANDING. YOU SHOULD JUDGE WITHIN YOURSELF AS TO WHETHER YOUR COMMENTS WILL BRING LIFE OR DEATH, OR CREATE CONFUSION IN THE SPIRIT OF THE PERSON OF WHICH THEY ARE SPOKEN?

THE EVIL INTENTIONS AND THE UNDERLYING MOTIVES IN YOUR COMMENTS, IS WHAT WILL COME BACK TO CAUSE YOU PAIN. GET A GRIP AND STOP TRYING TO FOOL OTHER PEOPLE AND EVEN YOURSELF! SOONER OR LATER YOU WILL HAVE TO FACE THE TRUE FACTS ABOUT YOURSELF, OPENLY, BEFORE YOUR PIERS.

OFTEN TIMES IT IS TOO LATE TO JUST SAY; "I DID NOT MEAN TO CAUSE A PROBLEM", "I'M SORRY!" HOWEVER, IF YOU DO NOT CONTROL YOUR OWN MOUTH, YOU WILL BE THE ONE TO HURT THE MOST AND YOU WILL BE VERY SORRY.

THERE ARE ALWAYS THOSE PERSONS WHO SECRETLY AND INTENTIONALLY LEAD FROM THE BACKGROUND AGAINST THE AGENDA OF THE ESTABLISHED LEADERSHIP IN THE CONGREGATION OF THE CHURCH. MANY PEOPLE WILL HAVE LEFT THE MINISTRY IN MOST CASES BEFORE THE UNDERCOVER CULPRIT HAD BEEN EXPOSED.

THERE ARE ALSO CONTENTIOUS PERSONS BEHIND THE SCENES WHO ARE DISAGREEABLE WITH MOST EVERY-

ONE AND WILL SEEK TO OVERTHROW THE MEANING OF EVERY SERMON AND THE TEACHING OF THE PASTOR OR ANY MINISTER OR ANY GIVEN LESSON TAUGHT BY THE LEADER OF THE SUNDAY SCHOOL CLASS, OR AN AUXILIARY.

YOU MAY BE INFLUENCED TO BELIEVE THAT NOBODY CARES ABOUT WHAT YOU HAVE TO SAY, IF SO YOU HAVE BEEN DECEIVED! MOST OF ALL, IF IT APPEARS THAT NO ONE ELSE SEEMS TO CARE ABOUT WHAT YOU HAVE TO SAY, THE FACT IS YOU SHOULD CARE!

Do You Care?????

"Who' Said It?"

> For the mouth of the Lord hath spoken it.
> ISAIAH 1:20

Statements Possess a Powerful Punch!

YOU WILL OFTEN HEAR THE QUESTION ASKED, "WHO SAID IT ANYWAY", OR RATHER WHO GAVE YOU THE AUTHORITY TO SAY WHATEVER YOU HAVE JUST SAID?

THE QUESTION OF WHO SAID IT, IS NOT TO BE ASCERTAINED AS IF THE ORAL REFERENCE HAS BEEN PLACED UPON WHO'S TALKING TO YOU FROM THE OUTSIDE, BUT IT SHOULD PLACE REFERENCE ON THE VOICE THAT IS SPEAKING FROM WITHIN YOU.

MOST PEOPLE LACK TRUE RESPECT FOR STERN INSTRUCTIVE ADMONITION. WHO ARE YOU WILLING TO OBEY?

WHEN YOU KNOW FOR A FACT THAT THE LORD SAID IT TO YOU FIRST, STAND BEHIND WHATEVER YOU HAVE SAID WITHOUT GUILT OR ANY SHAME IN THE FACE OF NEGATIVE OPPOSITION. SINCE YOU INTENDED TO SAY WHATEVER YOU HAVE SAID, DON'T TAKE IT BACK FOR FEAR THAT SOMEBODY REALLY DIDN'T LIKE WHAT YOU'D BEEN LEAD TO SAY.

49

I find then a law, that when I would do good,
evil is present with me. ROMANS 7:21

Undisclosed Danger!

A POSSIBLE EVIL INFLUENCE IS LURKING ABOUT WITHIN THE NATURE OF THE FLESH FOR AN OPPORTUNITY TO ACTUALLY RESIDE AS THE CONTROLLING AUTHORITY FOR SPEAKING OUT, ALTHOUGH IT HAS NEVER BEEN INVITED. THE PRESENT EVIL WITHIN , IS WHAT WE HAVE TO SPEAK TO.

EVIL IS NATURALLY INGRAINED INTO THE NATURE OF THE FLESH SINCE DATING BACK TO THE BEGINNING OF THE FALL OF MAN. FOR THIS REASON ALONE, CHRIST CAME TO REDEEM US BACK TO THE FATHER, SO THAT WE WOULD NOT HAVE TO LIVE SUBJECT TO THE WILL OF THE FLESH, KNOWING THAT THE GREATER WILL OF THE FLESH IS DESTRUCTION.

THE COMMON NATURE OF THE CONTENT OF EVIL SEEKS TO ALWAYS OVERTHROW AND TO DESTROY ALL RATIONALLY ELEVATED THOUGHTS OF FAITH WITHIN THE MIND, AND THE SPIRIT OF AN INDIVIDUAL. EVIL NATURALLY BRINGS US DOWN FROM OUR ONCE ELEVATED PERCEPTIONS OF FAITH IN THE LORD, TO CONDESCENDING THOUGHTS AND ACTS OF SIN RELATIVE TO THE FAITHLESS MANNER OF WHICH WE SPEAK ON A CONSISTENT BASIS.

 EVERY INDIVIDUAL BELIEVER MUST SPEAK DIRECTLY, TAKING AUTHORITY OVER THE POWER OF THE EVIL OF THE FLESH, IN THE NAME OF JESUS! ONLY THEN WILL ALL REOCCURRING PROBLEMS OF THE FLESH, BE SUFFICIENTLY DEALT WITH AND RESOLVED.

RENOUNCE THE WORKS OF THE DEVIL AND EVERYTHING ASSOCIATED WITH THE POWERS OF DARKNESS, THAT MAY BE LOOMING ABOUT YOUR ATMOSPHERE TO ESTABLISH A REMAINING RIGHT TO DOMINATE YOUR FLESH ALLOWING ALL SORTS OF EVIL FOR A POSSESSION OF YOUR SOUL!

TAKING CONTROL OF YOUR SITUATION IS VERY NEC-

ESSARY, IF YOU PLAN TO ESTABLISH YOUR OWN TRUE IDEN-
TITY, NEGATING THE POSSIBILITIES OF ANY RUMORS ABOUT
YOUR CHARACTER FROM EVER BEING POWERFUL ENOUGH
TO BLOCK THE LIGHT OF YOUR SUCCESS!

I Know Who!

Men's hearts failing them because of fear,
ST LUKE 21:26

BELOVED DO NOT BE AFRAID! NEITHER LET YOUR
HEART BE WEARY. SETUP RESISTANCE WITHIN YOUR SELF
TO BLOCK-OUT FRUSTRATION AND STRESS. FEAR HAS THE
ABILITY TO TAKE AWAY YOUR TRUE IDENTITY.

DESTROY THE PRESENCE OF FEAR, AND THE OPEN-
ING THAT FEAR USED TO ENTER INTO YOUR LIFE! PRAYER
AND FASTING WILL STRONGLY AID YOU IN COMING TO TERMS
WITH <u>*who*</u> YOU ARE, WHETHER YOU ARE PLEASED OR DIS-
PLEASED WITH YOUR FINDING.

HAVE YOU EVER REALIZED, OR HAVE YOU EVER FOUND
OUT, WHO YOU ARE?

HOW LONG ARE YOU GOING TO ALLOW SOMEONE ELSE
TO TELL YOU WHO YOU ARE?

HAVE YOU FORGOTTEN WHO YOU ARE IN JESUS?

UNLESS I TELL *you* WHO I AM, YOU DON'T KNOW WHO
I AM! JESUS HAS THE ONLY REAL ABILITY TO DEFINE WHO
YOU REALLY ARE. YOU NEED TO COME TO TERMS WITH THE
DIVINE REALITY OF JESUS IN ORDER TO COME CLOSE ENOUGH
TO HIM, FOR HIM TO TELL YOU WHO YOU REALLY ARE. YOU
WILL ACCEPT WITH JOY WHATEVER THE LORD SAYS ABOUT,
WHO YOU ARE. FAITH IN GOD WON'T FAIL YOU.

COME ON, CONFESS IT RIGHT NOW "I AM AFRAID OF
FEAR!"

YOU NEED TO BE FEARFUL OF BEING AFRAID, AS PART
OF YOUR DAILY DEMEANOR, BECAUSE FEAR WILL CAUSE A
<u>SPIRITUAL HEART ATTACK</u>, WHICH IN TURN CAN AND WILL
DEVELOP AND MATERIALIZE INTO PHYSICAL HEART PROB-

LEMS UPON THE EXTENDED ALLOWANCE OVER TIME.

> *And for me, that utterance may be given unto me, that I may open my mouth boldly, to make known the mystery of the gospel, For which I am an ambassador in bonds: that therein I may speak boldly, as I ought to speak".*
>
> EPHESIANS 6: 19-20

THE PHRASE; "I AM AN AMBASSADOR IN BONDS", BESPEAKS OF THE FACT THAT THE APOSTLE PAUL WAS AN INDEBTED REPRESENTATIVE OF CHRIST. PAUL STATES; "I AM", MEANING I KNOW WHO I AM SO LET ME TELL YOU, ALSO SUGGESTING THAT HE IS TIED AND ANCHORED TO THE LORD BY HIS OWN WILL.

BASKING IN THE PRESENCE OF THE SPIRIT OF THE LORD, PAUL, DISCOVERED THE POWER OF THE WORD OF THE LORD, REALIZING THAT IF IT TAKES GETTING INTO THE PRESENCE OF THE LORD TO DISCOVER WHO I AM, THEN IT TAKES STAYING THERE TO MAINTAIN THE STATUS OF MY FIND-INGS.

PEOPLE NEED WHAT WE HAVE TO OFFER THEM IN THE WORD OF GOD. YOU AND I ARE CHRIST'S REPRESEN-TATIVES, THEREFORE WE SHOULDN'T BE AFRAID OF THE TER-RIBLE EXPRESSIONS ON THE REJECTING FACES OF THE PEOPLE IN THE AUDIENCES WHERE WE DELIVER OUR MES-SAGE OF DELIVERANCE, FAITH, AND HOPE.

WHENEVER YOU ARE CHALLENGED OR REJECTED, IT IS ACTUALLY NOT YOURSELF BEING REJECTED, IT'S THE SPIRIT OF OUR LORD AND SAVIOR AND OUR GOD BEING REJECTED AND CHALLENGED.

> *So that we may boldly say, the Lord is my helper, and I will not fear what man shall do unto me.*　　　　HEBREW 13:6

TO ENSURE THAT PEOPLE WILL BE ABLE TO RECEIVE OF THE LORD, BE STRONG AND BE BOLD. AS LONG AS YOU'RE

SURE THE LORD IS INSTRUCTING YOU TO SAY IT, BE COM-
PLETELY CONFIDENT TO FACE ANYONE AND TO SAY WHAT-
EVER THE LORD IS REQUIRING YOU TO SAY.

IN OTHER WORDS, I SUGGEST THAT YOU BE BIG ABOUT
THE TASK PRESENTLY BEFORE YOU. TAKE ON THE CHAM-
PION MENTALITY ABOUT SPEAKING UP FOR THE LORD,
KNOWING THAT YOU ARE A CONQUEROR AND AN OVERCOMER
IN THE LORD JESUS CHRIST.

> *and calleth those things which be not as though
> they were.* ROMANS 4:17 B

A DESIRED REQUEST DOES NOT HAVE TO BE PRES-
ENTLY MANIFESTED AND VISIBLY IN EXISTENCE ALREADY
BEFORE YOU CAN SPEAK IT OUT OF YOUR MOUTH AND COM-
MAND THAT IT COME FORTH AND CLAIM IT TO BE YOURS.
SAY IT, UNTIL IT LITERALLY LEAPS BEFORE YOU. SAY IT,
TILL YOU SEE IT!

IT'S NOT ABOUT HOW FAST YOU GET RESULTS; RATHER
IT IS ABOUT KNOWING THAT THE RESULTS YOU DESIRE MUST
LEAP FORTH, RIGHT INTO YOUR POSSESSION. BELIEVE THIS!
THOSE THINGS THAT YOU DESIRE MOST FROM THE LORD,
WILL COME BECAUSE OF THE COMMAND OF FAITH, TO THE
WORD OF GOD, WHICH IS ON THE LINE AT THE TIME OF
YOUR REQUEST.

DON'T SAY IT JUST FOR THE SAKE OF PLEASING YOUR
REASONING OF FAITH IN GOD ONLY, BECAUSE IT IS THE
RELIGIOUSLY CORRECT THING TO DO. BUT, GO THE VERY
NEXT STEP AND SAY IT BECAUSE YOU ACTUALLY EXPECT MANI-
FESTATIONS AS A RESULT OF YOUR FAITH IN GOD QUICK,
FAST, AND IN A HURRY WITH EVERY FIBER OF YOUR TOTAL
BEING. DON'T BE AFRAID TO PUT YOUR FAITH AND TRUST
IN THE LORD TO THE ULTIMATE LIMIT, TESTING THE VA-
LIDITY OF THE SPOKEN WORDS OF FAITH OUT OF YOUR OWN
MOUTH.

Moses Said It!

God spoke many plagues upon the house of Pharaoh and the Egyptians. In all of the plagues to which God had spoken out of His own mouth to Moses, things began to happen upon demand.

God told Moses, to go tell Pharaoh or in other words, speak to Pharaoh. But, Moses like many people today, said; "My Lord who am I?"

Pharaoh will not hearken unto my voice. The children of Israel also will not hearken unto my voice. According to the history of Moses' upbringing, he really had a legitimate issue that naturally caused him to question whether or not he was actually the man for the job.

God; in His infinite wisdom, He already knew the concerns that Moses would have being required to return to the land of Egypt to deliver Israel, so He revealed the divine favor that had been given to Moses.

Perhaps, many hindrances to the working power of faith are in the fact that true believers have not yet come to the full knowledge of who they really are, and what it is that they have inherited as a result!

 The power of what is spoken is <u>absolutely reliant</u> upon the power that an individual possesses, and confidently exercises with authority! Jesus tells the disciples:

> *But, ye shall receive power, after that the Holy Ghost is come upon you: And you shall be witnesses unto me both in Jerusalem, and in all Judea, and in Samaria, and unto the uttermost part of the earth.*　　　Acts 1:8

In other words, because you have the power

YOU WILL SPEAK OUT OF YOUR MOUTH TO SAY SO. THE WORD *POWER*, BEING INTERPRETED MEANS <u>*ability*</u>. THIS WORD DERIVES FROM THE GREEK WORD <u>DUNAMIS</u>, WHICH IS WHERE WE GET THE ENGLISH WORD DYNAMITE. IT IS TO POSSESS POWER UNDERNEATH THE <u>*skin*</u>.

IN MUCH CLEARER TERMS, IT IS TO BE POWERFUL. NOT AS A LETTER, A DECREE, OR A LICENSE OF SOME SORT PLACED IN THE HAND THAT ENABLES A PERSON TO ACT OR TO LEGALLY PERFORM, BUT RATHER THIS POWER IS AN EN-DOWING OR A SENSE OF POURING DOWN OF POWER TO AN INDIVIDUAL, THE SAME AS THE ANOINTING.

IT IS GOD'S POWERFUL ABILITY GIVEN LITERALLY TO THE BELIEVER TO OPERATE IN THE SPIRIT REALM ACCORD-ING TO THE DIVINE WILL OF GOD. THIS, ALTHOUGH BE-ING DONE IN THE NATURAL, IS EXCLUSIVELY THE ABSOLUTE WILL AND POWER OF THE SPIRIT OF GOD ALONE.

> *If any man speak, let him speak as the oracles of God; if any man minister, let him do it as of the ability which God giveth; that God, in all things may be glorified through Jesus Christ, to whom be praise and dominion for ever and ever. Amen"!!*   I PETER 4:11

IN OTHER WORDS, WE DO SPEAK AS ORACLES OF GOD (MOUTHPIECES), BY THE DIVINE WILL OF GOD.

> *For the prophecy came not in old time by the will of man: but Holy men of God spake as they were moved by the Holy Ghost.*   II PETER 1:21

THE SCRIPTURE IS SELF-EXPLANATORY IN ITSELF. DON'T SPEAK ACCORDING TO WHAT YOU FEEL, OR BECAUSE SOMEONE PUSHED YOU TO THE BOILING POINT SO THAT YOUR EMOTIONS ARE STIRRED TO THE MAXIMUM. WE SHOULD NOT BE INFLUENCED BY FAMILY, FRIENDS, SPOUSES, OTHER MEMBERS OF THE CLERGY, MEDIA, NEWS, CURRENT EVENTS, OR EVEN POLITICS.

ALLOW GOD TO SPEAK TO YOU! SPEND TIME WITH GOD AND TRUST HIM TO TELL YOU WHAT, HOW, AND WHEN TO SAY. TO FEEL INADEQUATE WITHIN YOUR SELF AND TO BELIEVE THAT WHAT YOU FEEL IS A REALITY, AT BEST IS ONLY A HINDERANCE TO THE MOVE OF GOD AMONG THE PEOPLE THAT ARE TO RECEIVE WHAT WE HAVE BEEN GIVEN TO SHARE WITH THEM.

> *"...See, I have made thee a god to Pharaoh..."*
> EXODUS 7:1

GOD SAID TO MOSES; "LET ME TELL YOU, WHO, YOU ARE." REALIZING MOSES DIDN'T REALLY KNOW WHO HE WAS, NOR THE POWER THAT HE NOW POSSESSED, GOD ENLIGHTENED HIM. GOD IS FAITHFUL TO GIVE YOU THE REALISTIC CLARITY OF JUST WHO YOU ARE IN HIM, AND NEVER TO LEAVE YOU IN THE DARK.

IN EXODUS 11: 1; GOD REVEALS TO MOSES THAT HE WILL SEND A FINAL PLAGUE. MOSES HAS ALREADY SEEN THE INCORPORATED POWER BETWEEN GOD AND HIMSELF, BEING BOLD WITHIN AND EXTREMELY CONFIDENT WITH GOD, HE SPOKE THE FINAL PLAGUE AS WAS COMMANDED BY GOD.

> *And Moses said, thus saith the Lord, about midnight will I go out into the midst of Egypt: And all the first born in the land of Egypt shall die from the first born of Pharaoh that sitteth on his throne, even unto the first born of the maid servant that is behind the mill; and all the first born of beast, And there shall be a great cry through out all the land of Egypt, such as there was none like it, nor shall be like it any more. But against any of the children of Israel shall not a dog move his tongue, against man or beast: that ye may know how that the Lord doth put a difference between the Egyptians and Israel.* EXODUS 11:4-7

WHATEVER GOD HAS APPOINTED YOU TO SPEAK, HE WILL ALSO BRING IT TO PASS. WHENEVER I SPEAK A WORD OF PROPHECY, I ONLY SPEAK BECAUSE GOD HAS SPOKEN TO

ME ALREADY. THE LORD IS MY SOURCE, AND OF COURSE MY FRIEND, HE IS NEVER WRONG! WHATEVER GOD SAYS IS RIGHT. OPEN YOUR MOUTH, DECENTLY AND IN ORDER AND THE PROPER RESULTS WILL FOLLOW.

> *God is not a man, that he should lie; neither the son of man, that he should repent: hath he said, and shall he not do it? Or hath he spoken, and shall he not make it good? Behold, I have received commandment to bless: and he hath blessed: and I cannot reverse it.*
>
> NUMBERS 23:19-20

YOU SEE, GOD ALWAYS MEANS WHATEVER HE SAYS AND HE NEVER SPEAKS AHEAD OF HIMSELF, BECAUSE IT IS NOT POSSIBLE. GOD IS ALREADY THERE IN THE FUTURE EVEN BEFORE THE FUTURE KNOWS OF IT'S SPACE AND TIME IN EXISTENCE. GOD IS ALWAYS ACCURATE, SO JUST SAY WHATEVER HE SAID!

GOD IS TOO PERFECT TO EVER MAKE A MISTAKE OF ANY KIND, EVER! HE IS PERFECTING EVERY SECOND OF EVERY MINUTE OF THE LIVES OF EVERY CREATURE ON THE FACE OF THE ENTIRE UNIVERSE. ABSOLUTELY NOTHING WILL EVER HAVE THE POWER TO BLUR THE VISION OF GOD, OR TO CLOG THE HEARING OF HIS EARS. HE CANNOT BE POIGNANTLY HINDERED OR STOPPED BY ANYTHING OR ANYONE IN THE COSMOS!

Against Your Word?

NEVER WORRY ABOUT ANYONE SPEAKING OUT AGAINST WHAT GOD HAS SPOKEN THROUGH YOU, AS LONG AS YOU ARE SURE THAT GOD SAID IT.

I HAVE HAD SOME PASTORS TO RESIST THE MESSAGE THAT I HAD GIVEN AS IF I WERE THE DEVIL HIMSELF. THEY KNEW THAT IT WAS GOD GIVEN INFORMATION THAT WAS SPOKEN FROM MY MOUTH BY THE HOLY GHOST! NO NATURAL MAN COULD HAVE KNOWN THE THINGS SPOKEN, OTHERWISE, THROUGH THE ABILITY OF HIS OWN MIND.

Many people upon hearing a spoken prophetic word allow the enemy to snatch the word from their hearts. After a spoken word, many times very swiftly, the fruitfulness of those same words will follow.

As a personal rule of mine, I make it known that the words to which I have just spoken are from the Lord and not of myself. Direct the attention to Jesus in the very same manner always no matter how wonderfully people appear to speak of you.

Never touch God's glory, by touching what God has spoken through you, taking the credit for what was spoken as if it was spoken divinely of yourself! Your flesh does not have the ability to speak the absolute things of God, without God first! The very will of the flesh is enmity *(separation)* against God. Jesus teaches us that "Flesh and blood cannot inherit the kingdom of God".

> *Thy kingdom come. Thy will be done in earth*
> *as it is in heaven. (Jesus taught)*
>
> St Matthew 6:10

His dominion, the King's dominion, is to be to the believers here in the earth, as it is to the Father's throne in Heaven. We must receive impartation, in order to impart. Know of whom you are, in order to know what to speak and of whom it is you represent when you speak.

In doing so, you will always be sure, who said it!

4

Speak Up!!!

> That if thou shalt confess with thy mouth the lord Jesus, and shalt believe in thine heart that God hath raised him from the dead, thou shalt be saved, for with the heart man believeth unto righteousness, and with the mouth confession is made unto salvation.
>
> ROMANS 10:9-10

Acknowledge What You Believe!

CONFESS -VERBALLY ACKNOWLEDGE, TO ADMIT HAVING KNOWLEDGE OF A PARTICULAR CIRCUMSTANCE OR SITUATION. TO VERBALLY' DECLARE A BELIEF OR TO TRUTHFULLY EXPRESS DISBELIEF. IN A COURT OF LAW, ONE WHO GIVES A CONFESSION IS HEARD AS A <u>TRUTHFUL WITNESS</u>. A WITNESS MUST HAVE ACCURATE KNOWLEDGE OF A PAST EVENT, CRIME, AND DISASTERS OR BE ABLE TO GIVE CURRENT, CREDIBLE, AND UNALTERED ACCOUNTS OF PRESENT HAPPENINGS.

I; confess right now that Jesus Christ is Lord. I; believe Jesus with my total being, and I; am not ashamed!

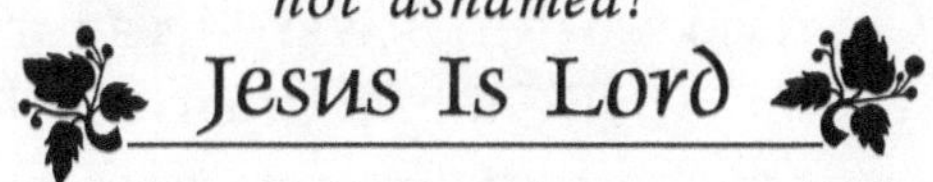

Confessing the truth is the type of thing that you just can't do right off the top of your head at the spare of the moment. To be true to the convictions of your own heart, careful evaluation to all subject matters at hand, must be given before you confess.

Confession is none discriminate to age limits and it also yields no preference to gender, in that anyone who is consciously aware of the true understanding of confessing, can do it.

People don't confess Jesus Christ as being the Son of God, because they have not believed in their hearts that He really is the Son of God. It is not hard to confess what is truly regarded as truth, in the heart. True believers readily acknowledge the reality of Jesus Christ, and the power of the word of God.

Your confession of Jesus Christ as Lord and Savior releases the power of freedom over your life from the bondage of sin and shame as long as your acknowledgments possess the necessary convictions to determine the validated truth of whatever you say you believe. Your confession must be true!

Truthful Exposure!

I am relentlessly determined to focus on the confessions of truth. My purpose is to see that people begin making wholesome confessions of power and authority. A real true born again child of God, will confess truth daily according to the word of God that will assuredly establish them. I grew up on a principle, (In the Church of God in Christ) which says; "Everything in you has got to come out!", be it good or bad.

If you are truthful, truth will proceed from

YOUR CHARACTER. WE HAVE GOT TO STOP EXPECTING THE TRUTH TO COME OUT OF THE UNTRUTHFUL!

GOD IS THE EVIDENCE OF THE TRUTH IN THE WORD, WHEREAS THE EVIDENCE REVEALS THE INFALLIBLE TRUTH AS A RESULT. OTHER FORMS OF CONFESSION ARE NOT NECESSARILY TRUE OR EVEN TRUTH FOR THAT MATTER, JUST BECAUSE THEY CAME FROM AN INDIVIDUALS MOUTH!

A FORGED CONFESSION, OR A CO-REHEARSED CONFESSION, SHOULD NOT BE ASCERTAINED AS IF TO BE BELIEVABLY A FREEWILL OR AN AT-WILL CONFESSION.

OUR REAL FOCUS HERE IS ONLY ON TRUE CONFESSION. CLOSE OBSERVATIONS MUST BE GIVEN TO THE CHARACTER OF A WITNESS TO ESTABLISH THE CREDIBILITY OF THEIR CONFESSION. WHENEVER A CONFESSION IS ACTUALLY TRUE, THE WITNESS WILL NOT MIND THE SCRUTINY OF EXAMINATION, AND WILL NOT BE AFRAID OF STEPPING UP TO THE MICROPHONE TO SPEAK UP.

THE HEARTTHROB OF CONFESSING MEN AND WOMEN ALIKE THAT PROMPTS THEM TO RELEASE THE TRUTH FROM THE INNERMOST PART OF THEMSELVES, IS GRAVELY RELIANT UPON THE AUSPICES OF THE MIND, THAT HAS TO SPEAK TO THE WILL, SO THAT THE WILL THEN COMMANDS THE MOUTH TO CONFESS.

GO AHEAD AND GIVE UP ON HIDING WHATEVER IS ON THE INSIDE OF YOU, BECAUSE THE LORD ALREADY KNOWS ABOUT THE HIDDEN THINGS OF YOUR HEART. TELL THE TRUTH! THE TRUTH IS STRONGLY INCUMBENT INCLUSIVELY UPON THE SUBSTANTIATED EVIDENCE WHICH HAS TO BE PROVEN BY AT LEAST TWO OR THREE WITNESSES, EXCEPT IN THE WORD OF GOD.

And that you put a difference between holy and unholy, and between unclean and clean.
LEVITICUS 10:10

THIS SCRIPTURE CAN ALSO BE TAKEN IN PARAPHRASE TO MEAN THAT WE SHOULD PUT A DIFFERENCE BETWEEN THE TRUTH AND THE UNTRUTHFUL. THE PRE-

SENTATION OF THE UNTRUTH IS ALWAYS SET BEFORE US TO BE ACCEPTED AS A PROPER CHOICE. LOTS OF THINGS ARE TRUE, <u>BUT NOT ALL ARE TRUTH</u>! <u>BELIEVE THIS</u>!

IT IS TRUE THAT CANCER IS DEADLY, BUT THE TRUTH IS THAT ALL CANCER PATIENTS DON'T DIE AS A RESULT OF THE CANCER THAT IS PRESENT IN THEIR BODIES. TRUE: ALL FIRES BURN, BUT NOT JUST ANY TEMPERATURE OF FIRE WILL BURN EVERY MATERIAL SUBSTANCE. NOW THIS IS THE TRUTH!

A MULTIPLICITY OF TEMPERATURES ARE REQUIRED TO BURN MANY DIVERSE MATERIALS, AND THE TRUTH IS, THERE IS EVEN A FIRE FOR THE SOUL OF MAN. THE BIBLE DECLARES THIS FACT TO BE SO. IT IS THE LAKE OF FIRE THAT BURNS WITH FIRE AND BRIMSTONE 7-X^s HOTTER THAN ANY FIRE KNOWN TO MAN.

IF YOU ARE OF GOD, THEN SO IS YOUR CONFESSION. IT IS NOT GOOD TO BE DOUBLE-MINDED, DOUBLE-TONGUED, OR CONTRADICTORY OF YOUR TRUE PURPOSED CONFESSION. TRUTHFUL PEOPLE TAKE A STAND EVEN IN THE FACE OF OPPOSITION.

They Heard It All!!

DURING A CONFESSION, THE UNDERLYING CONVICTIONS OF THE PERSON CONFESSING ARE ALSO BEING STATED WHETHER THEY KNEW IT OR NOT. EVERYONE UNDER THE SOUND OF YOUR VOICE THAT ARE ATTUNED TO THE SPIRIT OF THE LORD, WILL HEAR YOUR HEART THROB. WHENEVER WE CONFESS, IT BECOMES CLEAR, AS TO WHICH SIDE OF THE ISSUE WE ARE STANDING ON. THERE IS STILL YET MANY TRUTHFUL PEOPLE IN THIS WORLD WHO ARE NOT AFRAID TO SPEAK OUT AND CONFESS THE TRUTH.

BE TRUTHFUL, SO THAT THE DISPOSITION OF YOUR VERY OWN PRESENCE, IS HEALING, UPON YOUR ENTRANCE IN A ROOM OR IN A CROWD OF PEOPLE, LIKE THE APOSTLE PETER WHOSE SHADOW HEALED ALL THE PEOPLE THAT IT

TOUCHED. PETER'S CONFESSION OF CHRIST WAS ACCU-
RATELY TRUTHFUL, ALTHOUGH HE ONCE DENIED THE
VERY TRUTH OF HIS VERY OWN CONFESSION.

UPON THE RETURN TO HIS CONFESSION AND CON-
VICTION, ON THE DAY OF PENTECOST, PETER STOOD
BOLDLY AND DECLARED;

"This is that spoken by the Prophet Joel."

HE DEFENDED THE INTEGRITY OF THE BRETH-
REN ON THAT GLORIOUS DAY ENCOURAGING THE
GALILEANS TO BELIEVE. PETER WAS QUICK TO SPEAK UP,
AS HE; HIMSELF WAS ALREADY CONVINCED. PETER BE-
ING FILLED WITH THE HOLY GHOST, SAID;

*"These men are not drunken as you suppose, but
this is that awesome promise of God, which was
spoken of by the Prophet Joel."*

(my own paraphrasing)

PETER AND JOHN WENT UP TO THE TEMPLE TO
PRAY AT THE HOUR OF PRAYER. THEY DID NOT ACCI-
DENTLY HAPPEN BEFORE THE TEMPLE ON THEIR WAY TO
THE CITY MARKET, THEY WERE INTENTIONALLY ON THEIR
WAY TO THE HOUSE OF THE LORD TO WORSHIP.

THERE THEY WERE CONFRONTED BY A CRIPPLED MAN,
WHO WAS LAME ON HIS FEET, BEGGING ALMS AT THE GATE
OF THE TEMPLE CALLED BEAUTIFUL. AS HE ASKED FOR
WHAT HE WANTED, AS HE USUALLY WOULD DO, PETER SPOKE
UP IN THE THIRD CHAPTER OF THE BOOK OF ACTS AND
SAID;

"Silver and gold have I none, but such that I have give I thee."

PETER'S CONVICTIONS WERE IN TACT WHEN HE AGAIN
SPOKE UP AND SAID TO THE LAME MAN BEGGING AT THE
GATE,

"Look on us."

PETER WAS ACTUALLY SAYING TO THE LAME MAN, SIR,
WHATEVER IT IS THAT WE DO IN FACT HAVE TO OFFER YOU,
CERTAINLY WILL NOT BE WHATEVER YOU ARE ASKING FOR.
PETER AND JOHN, BY THE POWER OF THE HOLY GHOST,

THEY THEN IMPARTED THE VIRTUE OF THE TRUTH OF CHRIST'S HEALING POWER TO THE LAME MAN, HEALING HIS CRIPPLED ANKLES.

ON SO MANY OCCASIONS THE APOSTLE PETER OPENED HIS MOUTH TO CONFESS HIS CONVICTION IN CHRIST.

ANANIAS AND SAPPHIRA SOLD A POSSESSION OF THEIR VERY OWN AND PROMISED TO GIVE THE MONEY, EVERY CENT OF THE MONEY, TO THE CHURCH. THEY CONSPIRED TO FALSELY CONFESS A LIE BEFORE PETER, ABOUT THE AMOUNT OF MONEY TO WHICH THEY HAD RECEIVED. BEING INSPIRED BY THE HOLY GHOST, THE APOSTLE PETER SAID TO ANANIAS AND SAPPHIRA,

"Why has the Devil filled your heart to conspire
and lie to the Holy Ghost?"

RIGHT THERE ON THE SPOT PETER REBUKED THEM BOTH (***one by one on seperate occasions***), TO THE POINT THAT DEATH FELL ON THEM, IMMEDIATELY!

Ordained To Speak For Yourself!

NOW, IT IS A TRUTHFUL SAYING; "IF YOU HOLD YOUR PEACE, AND LET THE LORD FIGHT YOUR BATTLE, VICTORY BELONGS TO YOU!" THIS STATEMENT BEING TRUE IS NOT A CONTRADICTION TO WHAT I AM SAYING AT THIS PARTICULAR INFERENCE OF THIS CHAPTER.

 MANY OF THE ELDERS (WHOM MOST ARE NOW WITH THE LORD) WOULD SAY; "SILENCE IS GOLDEN, AND/OR SILENCE GIVES CONSENT." THEY WOULD SAY EITHER ONE OF THESE TWO THINGS ABOUT SILENCE UPON JUDGING THE CIRCUMSTANTIAL BALANCE OF ANY STATEMENT MADE WHICH WOULD HAVE CALLED FOR THE INTERJECTION OF SILENCE, OR FOR AN INDIVIDUAL TO SPEAK UP.

THE MERE FACT THAT AN INDIVIDUAL KEPT SILENT, COULD ACTUALLY BE MORE BENEFICIAL TO THEM THAN IF THEY WERE TO SPEAK AND ALSO VERY WISE! TO BE

QUIET WHEN BEING QUESTIONED ABOUT YOUR KNOWL-
EDGE OR INVOLVEMENT IN A SPECIFIC MATTER OR EVENT,
MEANT THAT YOUR SILENCE ANSWERED, VERY PLAINLY.

WHENEVER WE LEARN TO BE SILENT AT THE RIGHT
TIMES, OUR SILENCE IS CONSIDERED TO BE RATHER PRE-
CIOUS FOR THE BENEFIT OF OUR PROSPERITY. ONE
MIGHT ACTUALLY PROTECT THEIR OWN INTEGRITY AND
KEEP THE SALVATION OF THEIR OWN SOUL IN TACT
THROUGH SILENCE.

YET, IT IS NOT FAIR TO COMPARE THE FACT OF YOUR
SILENCE ALONE, TO JESUS HOLDING HIS PEACE.

HOLDING YOUR PEACE ON A CONSISTENT BASIS
WHILE REFUSING TO SPEAK UP DOESN'T MEAN THAT YOU
ARE ACTUALLY BEING LIKE JESUS CHRIST. WHENEVER
YOU KEEP SILENT AND HOLD YOUR PEACE WHEN YOU
OUGHT TO BE SPEAKING, IS ACTUALLY AN ERROR.

> *He was oppressed, and was afflicted, yet he*
> *opened not his mouth: He is brought as a lamb*
> *to the slaughter, and as a sheep before her shear-*
> *ers is dumb, so he openeth not his mouth.*
>
> ISAIAH 53:7

JESUS DIDN'T KEEP SILENT BECAUSE HE COULDN'T
SPEAK UP FOR FEAR THAT HE HAD ABSOLUTELY NO DE-
FENSE FOR HIMSELF. JESUS WAS ALREADY PREORDAINED
TO KEEP SILENT AND NOT TO SPEAK, AT SUCH A TIME AS
WHEN HE WOULD BE IN THE CAPTIVITY OF THE RO-
MANS AND THE JEWS.

PROPHECY HAD GONE FORTH MANY YEARS PRIOR
TO THE COMING OF THE MESSIAH, STATING THAT HE
WOULD NOT UTTER A WORD AT THE TIME OF HIS CAP-
TURE. A TRUE PROPHECY HAS GOT TO OBEY THE SPO-
KEN WORD OF THE PROPHET, ELSE IT BECOMES NULLI-
FIED AS A WORD OF PROPHECY SOLELY BECAUSE THAT
WORD COULD NOT HAVE COME BY THE WILL OF GOD
SINCE IT DID NOT COME TO PASS. THE MANIFESTATION
OF THE PROPHECY MUST TESTIFY OF THE ALTRUISM OF

THE PROPHET.

WHEN PEOPLE FEEL THAT THEY ARE IN CONTROL TO THE POINT THAT THEY ARE DOING ALL OF THE TALKING NEVER ALLOWING THE WORD OF GOD, OR THE SPIRIT OF GOD TO SPEAK TO THEM, IT IS JUST LIKE GOD TO HOLD HIS PEACE.

THE ROMANS AND THE JEWS FELT THAT THEY KNEW WHAT THEY WERE DOING WHEN THEY TOOK JESUS HOSTAGE AND DECLARED HIM A BLASTPHEMER, INSTEAD OF RECOGNIZING HIM AS THE SAVIOR! GOD NEVER SENT ANGELS WITH A MESSAGE TO THE ROMANS PRIOR TO CRUCIFYING THE SAVIOR. THE THUNDER DID NOT ROAR, LIGHTENING DID NOT FLASH, NEITHER DID ANY PROPHETS, OR THE APOSTLES SPEAK UP TO DEFEND THE LORD, ALL BECAUSE OF GOD! GOD REMAINED SILENT!

Without Even Asking!

MOST PEOPLE SPEAK UP QUITE SWIFTLY TO SPREAD THE LATEST GOSSIP, EVEN MORE SWIFTLY THAN THEY WOULD EVER OPEN THEIR MOUTHS TO SPEAK UP FOR THE LORD. PEOPLE DON'T MIND GIVING A PIECE OF THEIR MIND WHEN THEY HAVE BEEN OFFENDED AND THEIR FEELINGS HAVE BEEN HURT!

PEOPLE DON'T MIND SPEAKING UP AS LONG AS IT IS FOR THE BENEFIT OF THEM SELVES. THEY JUST REFUSE TO OPEN THEIR MOUTHS FOR THE LORD, EVEN UNDER PRESSURE.

EVEN SAVED PEOPLE WILL VERBALLY TEAR YOUR HEAD OFF IF THEY FEEL THAT YOU HAVE WRONGED THEIR FAMILY MEMBERS, EVEN BEFORE THEY GET THE COMPLETE STORY AND ALL THE EVIDENCE OF WHAT ACTUALLY TOOK PLACE.

MEMBERS OF THE CHURCH WHO ARE NOT EVEN A PART OF THE BOARD OF DIRECTORS IN THE MINISTRY WILL OFFER THEIR OPINION ON HOW THEY FEEL THAT THINGS OUGHT TO BE GOING AROUND THE CHURCH,

WHETHER YOU ASK THEM OR NOT.

PEOPLE SPEAK UP EVEN WHEN THEY HAVE NOT BEEN ASKED TO DO SO; IT'S WHEN THEY HAVE BEEN CALLED UPON TO SPEAK THAT THEY SEEM TO HAVE A PROBLEM. THEY JUST FEEL THEY HAVE THE RIGHT TO HAVE THEIR SAY, THOUGH OUT OF ORDER, BECAUSE THEY PAY A TITHE AND GIVE AN OFFERING.

ACTS 25TH - 27TH CHAPTER, APOSTLE PAUL WAS ORDAINED OF GOD AND PERMITTED TO SPEAK BY THE AUTHORITY OF HEROD AGRIPPA. PAUL WAS IMPRISONED AND SENTENCED TO DIE, BECAUSE AT ONETIME HE WAS AGAINST CHRIST AND ALL OF HIS FOLLOWING BELIEVERS.

PAUL (WHO WAS THEN CALLED SAUL) HAD GIVEN THE VERBAL CONSENT FOR MANY OF THE EARLIER FOLLOWERS OF CHRIST TO BE PUT TO DEATH, OTHERS HE CONSENTED TO BE PERSECUTED, AND OTHERS WERE SENT INTO EXILE. PAUL HAD A SERIOUS VENDETTA AGAINST THE CHURCH OF OUR LORD JESUS CHRIST, UNTIL ONE DAY ON THE DAMASCUS ROAD AT HIGH NOON, WHEN THE LORD APPEARED BEFORE HIM.

HIS ENCOUNTER WITH THE LORD DRAMATICALLY CHANGED HIS LIFE. GOD, KNOWING THAT SAUL WOULD NEVER BE THE SAME AGAIN, ALSO CHANGED HIS NAME.

THE NAME "SAUL OF TARSUS", WOULD NOT HAVE SET VERY WELL AS A CITIZEN OF ROME. SAUL WAS A JEWISH NAME AND HE WAS NOW COMMISSIONED OF THE LORD TO PREACH TO THE GENTILES, THEREFORE GOD DROPPED THE S AND ADDED THE LETTER P TO CALL HIS NAME PAUL. CERTAINLY MAKING AN ACCEPTABLE PLATFORM TO THE GENTILES AND FOR THE ROMANS. GOD WAS PREPARING PAUL TO SPEAK UP.

MANY PEOPLE HAVE A DESIRE FOR THEIR NAMES TO BE CHANGED TO REVEREND, EVANGELIST, APOSTLE, PROPHET, PROPHETESS, AND MORE FREQUENTLY TO PASTOR! GOD IS NOT CHANGING NAMES JUST FOR THE GLAM-

OUR AND THE POPULARITY THAT COMES WITH THE MINISTRY. THERE IS A PARTICULAR ENDOWMENT OF THE HOLY GHOST INGRAINED INTO EACH OF THESE GOD GIVEN TITLES.

THEREFORE, IF THE LORD DOES NOT GIVE YOU THE TITLE, YOU SHOULD NOT EVER BE FOUND WEARING THE TITLE, BECAUSE YOU CERTAINLY WILL NOT BEAR THE ANOINTING. IN SUCH A CASE YOU ARE NOT AN AMBASSADOR OF THE LORD, YOU HAVE ACTUALLY BECOME AN IMPOSTURE AGAINST THE LORD, OR RATHER A DESIRING *FAKE!*

COMMUNITY ACTIVISM AND POLITICS ARE CONFLICTING AGENDAS TO THE ACTUAL PURPOSE OF THE MINISTRY OF THE CHURCH. IT'S A SHAME BEFORE THE LORD, THAT TOO MANY PREACHERS ARE MORE WILLING TO BE A VOICE IN THE COMMUNITY BECAUSE IT MAKES THEM LOOK GOOD PUBLICLY, BUT THEY WILL NOT EVEN SPEAK UP AGAINST SIN ACROSS THE PULPITS TO THE PEOPLE IN ATTENDANCE DURING THE WORSHIP SERVICES OF THEIR OWN CHURCHES.

YOU MAY HAVE A DRIVE TO SPEAK UP AND TO SPEAK OUT ON ISSUES, AND RIGHTFULLY SO, AS YOU HAVE BEEN CALLED TO TALK WITHOUT FEAR AND WITHOUT PREJUDICE. IT IS ONLY OBVIOUS THAT YOU MAY HAVE LEAPED FROM THE STARTING BLOCKS WITH THE WRONG AGENDA ON YOUR MIND.

 IN PAUL'S CAPTIVITY, HE IS EXAMINED BY FESTUS, THE NEW CAESARIAN GOVERNOR. FESTUS SPOKE UP IN PAUL'S DEFENSE, HE SAID;

"I have found this man nothing worthy of death."

MANY DEVOUT JEWS OF THE COMMUNITY NEVER DEVELOPED RESPECT FOR PAUL'S CONVERSION, THEY ONLY SAW HIM AS A TRADER. MEN OF COMMON CARNALITY, PURPOSEFULLY REFUSE TO ACKNOWLEDGE THAT THEY SEE A REAL TRUE CHANGE IN YOUR LIFE, ALTHOUGH THEY ARE AWARE THAT YOU HAVE EMBRACED THE FIN-

ISHED WORK OF THE CROSS OF CHRIST JESUS.

I WROTE A SONG THAT SAYS; "YOU CAN'T TELL IT, LIKE I CAN!" KING AGRIPPA AFTER HEARING FESTUS ON PAUL'S BEHALF, READILY TURNS TO PAUL AND GIVES HIM THE CONSENT TO SPEAK FOR HIMSELF, PAUL ACCEPTS THE INVITATION.

PAUL TELLS OF HIS LIFE, BOTH BEFORE AND AFTER HAVING MET CHRIST ON THE ROAD TO DAMASCUS. HE TELLS OF THE CONVICTIONS THAT HAVE BEEN IMPREGNATED AND DEEPLY IMBEDDED INTO HIS SPIRIT. HAVING BEEN COMMISSIONED TO PREACH TO THE GENTILES, PAUL SPEAKS ASSUREDLY, TO THE POINT THAT, FESTUS INTERRUPTS PAUL AND DECLARES TO HIM;

"Much learning has made thee mad."

PAUL'S CONVICTIONS AT THIS POINT ARE SO GREAT, HE NEVER STOPS TALKING EVEN AFTER HAVING BEEN DECLARED A MAD MAN, HE CONTINUES TO SPEAK OF HIS RELATIONSHIP WITH CHRIST. PAUL, REPLIES TO FESTUS;

"I'm not a mad man"

PAUL SPEAKS UP WITH GREAT CONVICTION OF THE HEART, SO MUCH SO, THAT AGRIPPA ABRUPTLY INTERRUPTED PAUL'S SPEECH AGAIN AND SAID,

"Paul almost thou hast persuaded me to be a Christian."

WOULDN'T IT BE AWESOME THAT WHENEVER WE SPOKE UP FOR THE LORD, BECAUSE OF OUR DEEP INNERMOST BELIEFS, AND CONVICTIONS TO PERSUADE PEOPLE TO BECOME BLOOD WASHED CHRISTIANS, THEY RESPOND IN AWE OF EXCITEMENT TO THE TRUTH ABOUT OUR LORD AND CONFESS THAT YOU HAVE TOTALLY PERSUADED THEM TO BECOME CHRISTIANS. THIS IS OUR PURPOSE AS MOUTHPIECES OF THE LORD!

WE SHOULD NOT SPEAK UP TO THE SINNER, ONLY BECAUSE THEY TEND TO AGGRAVATE US, OR THE DRUNKARD BECAUSE HE BEGS, OR EVEN TO THE GAYS AND PROSTITUTES BECAUSE THEY ARE DETESTABLE IN OUR SIGHT. WE HAVE TO REMEMBER, THAT IT IS NOT ABOUT US, BUT

RATHER IT'S ALL ABOUT THE LOVE OF JESUS CHRIST!

> *And whatsoever you do in word or deed, do all*
> *in the name of the Lord Jesus, giving thanks to*
> *God and the father by him.*   COLOSSIANS 3:17
> *Let not then your good be evil spoken of.*
>   ROMANS 14:16

So You Meant Well!

GOOD INTENTIONS JUST WILL NOT DO! IT IS IMPERATIVE THAT WHENEVER YOU SPEAK, YOU SAY ONLY WHAT YOU MEAN AND MEAN WHAT YOU SAY. BE STRAIGHT AND FORWARD SPEAKING THE TRUTH IN LOVE, NO MATTER WHAT IT IS, BECAUSE PEOPLE NEED WHAT GOD HAS GIVEN YOU TO SAY.

NOW, YOU MAY BE <u>LABELED</u> AS MEAN, UNLOVING, UNKIND, IMPATIENT, INTOLERABLE, AND EVEN UNCARING OF OTHERS FEELINGS BECAUSE YOU SPEAK THE TRUTH, BUT BECAUSE YOU DO LOVE AND CARE, YOU ARE OBLIGATED TO SHARE THE TRUTH AT ALL TIMES. THE PROTECTION OF PEOPLE'S FEELINGS SHOULD NOT BE A DEFINING FACTOR RELATIVE TO WHATEVER YOU DO, OR DO NOT SAY. THE SAME PRINCIPLE APPLIES TO THE MESSAGE OF THE GOSPEL, OPEN YOUR MOUTH!

Make It Plain!!!

PEOPLE DEVELOP SEVERE PHYSICAL COMPLICATIONS IN THEIR BODIES BECAUSE THEY KEEP AN ABUNDANCE OF DETRIMENTAL THINGS BOTTLED-UP ON THE INSIDE WHICH SHOULD HAVE BEEN VERBALLY OUSTED AND RELEASED OUT OF THEIR MOUTHS.

DOCTOR'S OFFICES ARE FILLED TO THE CAPACITY ON A DAILY BASIS BECAUSE SO MANY PEOPLE WILL NOT RELEASE THE MANY DEGRADING AND DEADLY FAMILY SECRETS FESTERING ON THE INSIDE OF THEMSELVES.

THE WILLINGNESS TO SPEAK UP, RELEASES THE PRESSURE OF UNNECESSARY TENSION AND EMOTIONAL

BUILDUPS DEEPLY EMBEDDED INSIDE THAT HAS THE ABILITY TO CAUSE A MAJOR BREAK DOWN IN THE BODY OF THAT INDIVIDUAL.

UNSPOKEN WORDS WHICH SHOULD HAVE BEEN RELEASED, WILL CONTINUE TO BE A DEBILITATING FACTOR IN THE PSYCHOLOGICAL DESTRUCTION AND MENTAL BREAKDOWN, POSSIBLY CAUSING MANY SERIOUS RESIDUAL PROBLEMS OF THE MIND AND MENTAL HEALTH.

PEOPLE WHO WILL NOT SPEAK-UP, OFTEN BLAME GOD FOR THE OUTCOME OF THEIR LIVES WHEN IN FACT THEY HAD THE ABILITIES TO MAKE THE NECESSARY CHANGES TO PREVENT THE RESIDUAL HEARTACHES AND PAINS THAT ARE FESTERING ON THE INSIDE OF THEMSELVES NOW!

SAY SOMETHING AND STOP CRYING ABOUT PEOPLE RUNNING OVER YOU, EVEN IF THEY SEEM TO BE UNMOVED BY WHATEVER YOU HAVE TO SAY. AT THE VERY LEAST, THEY WILL KNOW THAT YOU STRONGLY OPPOSE THEIR ACTIONS TOWARDS YOU AND THAT YOU INTEND FOR THOSE SAME ACTIONS TO CEASE IMMEDIATELY!

WHY WAIT ON SOMEONE ELSE TO SAY SOMETHING ON YOUR BEHALF? THAT SOMEONE YOU MAY BE WAITING ON, MAY NEVER SPEAK UP FOR YOU, BECAUSE THEY COULD NOT FEEL WITHIN THEMSELVES WHAT YOU FEEL RIGHT NOW, AND THEY MAY NEVER BE ABLE TO RELATE TO WHATEVER YOU MAY HAVE FELT IN TIMES PAST! THE PERPETRATING OFFENDER INTENTIONALLY COMMITTED THOSE ACTIONS AGAINST YOU, IN THE MOST NEGATIVE POSSIBLE INTENT.

SOME PEOPLE WOULD RATHER LIVE WITH STOMACH ULCERS AND CANCER IN THEIR BELLIES AS RESULT OF STRESSING THEIR DIGESTIVE SYSTEMS, BECAUSE OF NERVOUSNESS IN THEIR SYSTEM THEY TEND TO LOSE THEIR APPETITES. THEY WANT OTHERS TO SAY THAT THEY HAVE ALWAYS HAD A PLEASANT SPIRIT ABOUT THEMSELVES, EVEN WHENEVER IT WAS ABSOLUTELY OBVIOUS THAT THEY WERE BEING SEVERELY MISTREATED.

SOME SAY THAT THEY COULD NEVER SAY ANYTHING TO THE PEOPLE WHO BROUGHT ABOUT THE INFLICTION OF PAIN UPON THEM BECAUSE THEY DID NOT FEEL THAT IT WOULD BE VERY CHRIST-LIKE TO STAND UP IN DEFENSE OF THEMSELVES.

PERHAPS YOU CARRY SUCH FEELINGS BEING IGNORANT OF THE DAMAGE THAT YOU ARE DOING TO YOUR OWNSELF! NOT EVEN MEDICAL PROFESSIONALS HAVE THE ABILITY TO KNOW, THAT, WHATEVER THEY MIGHT BE DOING TO YOU IS CAUSING YOU PAIN EVEN AFTER THE NECESSARY PRECAUTIONS HAVE BEEN TAKEN TO PREVENT PAIN, UNLESS YOU SAY SOMETHING REGARDING THE PAIN.

NOW DON'T BECOME CONFUSED AS IF I AM SUGGESTING TO YOU THAT YOU OUGHT TO BEGIN TO START MAKING UNWARRANTED TROUBLE, SEEING THAT YOU WILL HAVE DEVELOPED A SPIRIT OF CONTENTIOUSNESS (ARGUMENTATIVE). I WOULD NEVER ENCOURAGE ANYONE TO BECOME ARGUMENTATIVE IN THEIR DAILY CHRISTIAN DEMEANOR, POSTURING THEMSELVES ON THE DEFENSIVE.

IT WOULD BE VERY WISE AND BENEFICIAL FOR YOU NOT TO ALLOW YOURSELF TO BECOME ILL BECAUSE OF YOUR ALLOWED EMOTIONAL DISTRESS, WITH WHICH YOU DO HAVE THE POWER TO ALLEVIATE AND TO RID YOURSELF OF THE ANGUISH.

IT DOESN'T MAKE MUCH SINCE TO ME THAT ANYONE WOULD KEEP AN ELEMENT OF DANGER ON THE INSIDE OF THEMSELVES; WHICH HAS THE POWER PACKED EQUIVALENCE OF A PRESET TIME BOMB, THAT HAS BEEN SET TO GO OFF IN THE FORM OF CANCER OR IN THE FORM OF A MASSIVE HEART ATTACK OR A STROKE, OR TO PERHAPS HAVE AN ANEURYSM TO BURST AND TO KILL THEM, <u>GRAVE YARD DEAD</u>!

OPEN UP YOUR MOUTH AND SAY SOMETHING, YOU HAVE GOT TO TALK TO SOMEBODY. THERE IS SOMEBODY WHO WILL LISTEN TO YOU AND NEVER EVER REVEAL YOUR PRIVATE DISCUSSION OF THE SERIOUS MATTERS YOU HAVE

KEPT OVER AN EXTENDED PERIOD OF TIME. THERE ARE SO MANY PEOPLE DEAD TODAY OF WHOM PERHAPS MIGHT HAVE STILL BEEN ALIVE, HAD THEY DISCOVERED THE RELEASE FOR THE DEADLY INFORMATION INSIDE OF THEMSELVES.

Don't Bet On Waiting!

TRYING TO WAIT UNTIL CERTAIN PEOPLE DIE, BEFORE YOU ALLOW CERTAIN VERY SERIOUS ISSUES TO BE REVEALED, MAY NOT NECESSARILY BE THE SOLUTION TO THE SITUATIONS OF YOUR LIFE, BEING THAT THE OTHER PERSON/PERSONS MAY OUTLIVE YOU!

IF PROTECTING SOMEONE ELSE BY KEEPING THE SECRET OF THEIR OUTRAGEOUS BEHAVIOR, OR ACTIONS THAT COULD CAUSE THE OTHER PERSON TO BE PUT AWAY IN JAIL FOR A LONG TIME, CAUSES THE DESTRUCTION OF YOURSELF INWARDLY, PERHAPS YOU OUGHT TO RETHINK THE MATTER OF THE SECRET.

THE GREATEST THING YOU CAN DO, IF IN FACT THERE IS NO ONE ON THE FACE OF THE EARTH YOU FEEL YOU COULD TALK TO, IS TO GO DOWN ON YOUR KNEES AND RELEASE EVERYTHING IN PRAYER TO THE LORD! HE WILL HEAR YOUR PRAYER AND HE WILL NEVER EVER LET YOU DOWN.

PERHAPS YOU ARE IN DISTRESS OR IN NEED OF SOMEONE TO PRAY FOR YOU OR TO PRAY WITH YOU; NO ONE WILL EVER KNOW OF YOUR NEED IF YOU DO NOT OPEN YOUR MOUTH AND SAY SOMETHING. SPEAK UP!! I LIKE TO TELL THE PEOPLE OF THE CHURCH THAT I AM SPIRITUAL, BUT NOT TELEPATHIC, YET I AM VERY PRACTICAL!

YOU SHOULDN'T WAIT ON SOMEONE ELSE TO SPIRITUALLY GAZE INTO YOUR LIFE TO SEE YOUR NEEDS. YOU DON'T NEED A DIVINE REVELATION OF THE THINGS THAT YOU ALREADY KNOW! YOU SHOULD SPEAK UP AND SAY SOMETHING REQUESTING PRAYER AND PRAY TO SEE THE NECES-

SARY CHANGE.

I HAVE WITNESSED A SICK PERSON OF THE CHURCH BECOME VERY DISENCHANTED WITH OTHER MEMBERS OF THAT SAME LOCAL CHURCH BODY, BECAUSE THEY DID NOT RECEIVE A VISIT OR A PHONE CALL FROM THAT INDIVIDUAL, WHOM THE SICK INDIVIDUAL DESIRED SPECIAL VISITATION FROM THEM TO OFFER PRAYERS FOR THEIR CONDITION.

THEY DID NOT EVEN PICK UP THE TELEPHONE OR HAVE SOMEONE ELSE TO PICKUP THE TELEPHONE AND CONTACT THOSE INDIVIDUALS OF WHICH THEY FELT WOULD GET A PRAYER THROUGH TO GOD FOR THEM. THE PEOPLE OF GOD OF WHOM ARE CALLED TO BE THE INTERCESSORS FOR THE BODY OF CHRIST, NEED AT TIMES TO KNOW WHAT TO INTERCEDE FOR, THEREFORE IT IS YOUR PLACE TO TELL THEM WHATEVER THE NEED IS IN YOUR LIFE.

STOP FORCING YOUR FRIENDS TO PLAY THE ROLE OF THE ALL KNOWING CHRIST, BY PLACING THEM IN SITUATIONS WHERE THEY HAVE TO ATTEMPT TO FIGURE OUT YOUR AREAS OF NEED. IF YOU HAVE TO GIVE A PROPHET THE INFORMATION THAT THEY NEED FOR THE PURPOSE OF SPEAKING TO YOU ACCURATELY AT A TIME WHEN A WORD OF PROPHECY IS BEING GIVEN, YOU SHOULD KNOW THAT INDIVIDUAL IS PROBABLY NOT ANOINTED AS A PROPHET OF GOD! THEY SHOULD ALREADY KNOW AND NOT HAVE TO GUESS OR ENQUIRE!

THE QUICKEST WAY TO GET WHATEVER YOU DESIRE IS TO KNOW WHAT YOU WANT FIRST OF ALL, OPEN YOUR MOUTH AND MAKE A SPECIFIC REQUEST FOR THAT EXACT THING, TO THE PEOPLE THAT YOU WOULD LIKE TO AGREE WITH YOU IN PRAYER.

PART OF SPEAKING UP, IS GOING AHEAD IN PRAYER FOR YOUR FELLOW CHURCH MEMBERS, ASKING THE LORD TO BLESS THEM AS WELL AND TO MEET THEIR NEEDS. PRAY FOR ONE ANOTHER!

One can put a thousand demons to flight, but two can put ten thousand demons to flight or maybe even more on the very powerful strength of agreement; however the other person or persons have got to know that you are having trouble with demons to which you are attempting to rid yourself of.

Ask; The Door Is Always Open!

Too many people who are truly saved, are afraid of being criticized for asking for help whenever they needed it. While it may be true that some people will in fact make light of your area of need, the real focus is that if you never open your mouth and ask for whatever you need or want, you will never get it!

You need to speak up, someone will help you, as the Lord has already ordained it to be so. Ask for water whenever you get thirsty, just as you have to ask for food whenever you are indeed hungry and cannot get these things for yourself.

Imagine the outcome of walking into a fast food establishment, and upon approaching the front counter, where food orders are placed, you only stood there looking and staring at the menu, never ever saying anything to place an order. If you did not ask for anything, you most definitely will receive nothing, not even the service of the awaiting employees there to assist you. The response to your being there certainly would not be favorable for you.

If you never ask for a ride, you will definitely have to walk wherever you go. If it is money you need, you have got to say something to someone,

AND IF THE FIRST PERSON CANNOT OR WILL NOT ASSIST YOUR NEED THEN JUST ASK ANOTHER PERSON TO HELP YOU.

No matter how bad a man may desire to marry a woman, the key is that he will definitely have to ask for her hand in marriage.

If you need a job, get up off of the couch and go look for it and whenever you find the job, ask to apply for the position. The job will not fall into your lap, on the couch, in front of the television!

How great is your desire to be saved, or to walk closer to God? Don't procrastinate in speaking up whenever you are in need of a service, of prayer, a hand out, or just simply the one needing to say the right thing to the right people to release yourself of the pressure within.

Ask! *Ask!!* *Ask!!!*

Do it right,

BUT,

<u>*Speak - Up!!*</u>

5

Word up

Pathetic; Apathy

> When I say unto the wicked, thou shalt surely die; and thou givest him not warning, nor speakest to warn the wicked from his wicked way, to save his life; the same wicked man shall die in his iniquity; but his blood will I require at thine hand.
>
> EZEKIEL 3:18

You Just Won't Say Anything at All!

THERE IS A SERIOUS PROBLEM AMONG THE RELIGIOUS COMMUNITIES WORLDWIDE, WHICH HAS GROWN TO FESTER IN THE HOME, SPREADING TO JOBS, TO FACULTY AND STUDENT BODIES ON THE SCHOOL CAMPUS, AND EVEN TO THE CAMPUS OF MANY CHURCHES. THIS PROBLEM HAS ESCALATED TO A PROGRESSIVE RAGE.

CAPITAL HILL DICTATES LAWS AND IDEAS AS MANDATES TO THE NATION'S HEADS OF SOCIETY. THE HEADS DICTATE IN A TRICKLING DOWN EFFECT TO THE INDIVIDUAL HOMES, AND SINGULARLY TO THE LIVES OF EVERY INDIVIDUAL. THIS REGULATING DOWNPOUR HAS AFFECTED THE ONCE DISCIPLINED WELFARE OF THE CHURCH COMMUNITY AT LARGE.

THE CHURCH HAS ALWAYS FOUGHT VIGOROUSLY, CHALLENGING THE PHILOSOPHICAL METHODOLOGIES OF THE WORLD AND THE UNGODLY RULES OF SOCIETAL ENGAGEMENT. THE CHURCH HAS HELD ON TO ITS BIBLICAL AFFIXATION IN LIGHT OF PUBLIC VIEW FOR CENTURIES. IN SOME INSTANCES, THE CHURCH IS IN NEED OF RETURNING TO ITS STANDING POSITION OF FAITH IN GOD AND IT'S ERECT POSTURE IN RIGHTEOUSNESS AND CONTINUE TO EMBRACE THE WRITTEN WORD OF GOD.

DON'T EVEN ALLOW THE IDEA IN YOUR MIND, THAT THE WAYS OF THE WORLD ARE GETTING STRONGER, WHILE THE PRESENCE OF THE CHURCH MAY BE DWINDLING AWAY TO OBSCURITY. AS GOD IS ETERNAL, THE CHURCH IS ALSO ETERNAL IN CHRIST FOREVER! AMEN!

PEOPLE, AT A MORE RAPID PACE, MAY BE REJECTING THE CHURCH AS A WAY OF GOVERNING THEIR LIFESTYLES, BUT THE CHURCH WILL NOT LEAVE THE PRESENCE OF THIS WORLD UNTIL GOD TAKES THE CHURCH OUT OF THE WORLD, BY WAY OF THE RAPTURE!

Too Slow To Speak!

THE VISIBLE CHURCH AS A WHOLE IS NOT AS TENACIOUS AS IT ONCE WAS, BECAUSE TOO MANY MOUTHS ARE UNRESTRAINED AND OUT OF CONTROL, TALKING ALL OF THE TIME! THE MOUTHS THAT ARE SPEAKING, ARE NOT SPEAKING THE WORD OF TRUTH ACCORDING TO GOD'S HOLY ORDINANCE.

WE ARE SUBTLY EXPERIENCING THE DEVASTATING REOCCURRENCE OF THE SERPENT AND EVE, IN THE GARDEN OF EDEN. JUST AS THE SERPENT BEGUILED EVE IN THE GARDEN, THE PRESENT EVIL OF SOCIETY HAS HAD A BEGUILING EFFECT ON THE CHURCH.

EVE; THE FIRST WOMAN OF CREATION AND MOTHER OF ALL PEOPLE OF THE EARTH, WAS THE WIFE OF ADAM. THE CHURCH, IS THE BRIDE OF CHRIST AND THE MOTHER AND NURTURER OF ALL THE CHILDREN OF GOD, BEGOT-

TEN OF THE SECOND ADAM, JESUS CHRIST OF NAZARETH.

THE DEPICTION OF THE SLITHERING SERPENT WOULD DEFINITELY BE SYMBOLIC TO SYSTEMIC SOCIETY ITSELF, WITH ALL OF IT'S LYING SUBTLETIES, DECEPTIVELY TWISTING THE MINDS OF IT'S OWN MEMBERS WHICH MUST LIVE WITHIN THE MANDATED SOCIAL CONFINES.

ON AN IMPORTANT NOTE; THE EFFECTIVENESS OF THE PRINCIPLE ART OF BEGUILING A PERSON, AN ORGANISM, OR EVEN AN ORGANIZATION IS NOT TO BE THOUGHT OF AS BEING AN INSTANTANEOUS OVERTAKING POWER, THAT CAN HAPPEN AT ANY MOMENT.

HOMES ARE BROKEN BEYOND REPAIR, AS A RESULT OF THE EXTREME MISGUIDED IDEALISM ABOUT MARRIAGE, AND OFTEN THE VAST MISUNDERSTANDINGS THAT HAVE CAUSED THE EXISTING MARITAL BREAKDOWNS OF WHICH ARE THE BREEDING GROUNDS FOR DIVORCE.

MANY HOMES ARE INITIALLY BUILT ON THE BROKEN FOUNDATIONS OF SINGLE PARENT HOUSEHOLDS, WHICH ARE INCOMPLETE AND LACKING THE FULL MEASURE OF GOD'S GRACEFUL IDEALISM FOR THE HOME. GOD'S IDEA OF THE FAMILY ACCORDING TO THE WORD OF GOD, WAS NEVER TO BE RELATIVE TO HAVING ONLY ONE PARENT IN THE HOME.

EVEN THE MARRIAGE VOWS ARE SEALED WITH THE PHRASE, "UNTIL DEATH DO US PART!" IN OTHER WORDS, THE SAME TWO ADULTS WHO ENTERED INTO THE MARRIAGE COVENANT, SHOULD ALWAYS REMAIN THERE UNTIL IF AND WHEN DEATH WILL HAVE CLAIMED ONE OF THE PARTNERS IN THE RELATIONSHIP, UNLESS GOD RETURNS TO RAPTURE THE CHURCH BEFORE THE UNION COULD EVER BE BROKEN BY DEATH.

SOCIETY HAS COME OUT IN THE OPEN TO ENCOURAGE THE AVAILABILITY OF THE DIVORCE COURTS, AS MEANS OF A SOLUTION TO A BROKEN MARRIAGE RATHER THAN TO TAKE IMMEASURABLY EFFECTIVE EFFORTS TO AID AND TO COUNSEL FOR THE PURPOSE OF RESTORING

THE MARRIAGE.

SOCIETY HAS ALSO COME OUT OF THE CLOSET TO UPHOLD ISSUES IN TOTAL OPPOSITION TO MARRIAGE THAT ARE AGAINST THE BIBLE. HOWEVER, THE COMPLETE BREAK DOWN OF OUR ONCE HIGHLY REGARDED BIBLICAL MORAL STANDARDS, ARE NOT SOLELY TO BE BLAMED ON SOCIETY.

THE REAL SOCIETAL PROBLEM, IS NOT THE INCURABLE, HABITUAL LIFE STYLES OF THE CAN'T HELP ITS; IT IS CLEARLY <u>SIN</u>!

THE CHURCH IS NOT SPEAKING OUT AGAINST THE AGENDA OF SATAN'S KINGDOM, PREVENTING THE INCREASE IN STRENGTH AMONG THE PEOPLE OF THE LORD, AS IT USED TO. WE AS A NATION HAVE DEVELOPED THE SORRY ATTITUDE OF TELLING PEOPLE TO JUST LIVE THEIR OWN LIVES, AND TO LET OTHERS LIVE THEIR OWN LIVES THE WAY THEY CHOOSE, BE IT RIGHT OR WRONG!

IT'S ALL RIGHT, AS LONG AS IT'S NOT BOTHERING ME; "TO EACH HIS OWN", IS OFTEN THE RESPONSE. WE HAVE BECOME SOMEWHAT "<u>PAGANISTIC</u>", IN OUR VIEWS ABOUT LIFE AND OUR RELATIONSHIP TO THE CHURCH.

 SATAN SEDUCES THE YOUTH, WHILE MOST EVERYONE SAYS ABSOLUTELY NOTHING ABOUT IT OR SHOW ANY CONCERN FOR THE DOWNWARD SPIRAL OF THE YOUNG PEOPLE OF THE COMMUNITY. NOT MANY PEOPLE CHOOSE TO REACH OUT AFTER THE YOUTH, WHOSE LIVES CLEARLY DEPICT SERIOUS TROUBLE, AND A POSSIBLE SHORT LIFE SPAN.

BECAUSE WE DO NOT ALL HOLD RESPECT FOR THE SAME FAMILY VALUES NOWADAYS, PARENTS CANNOT ALWAYS BE HELPED WITH THEIR CHILDREN .

THE PEOPLE OF THIS TWISTED SOCIETY WERE IN A HURRY TO SEE THE MORALS OF YESTERDAY BE GONE OUT OF THE WINDOW TO FLY AWAY SOMEWHERE TO NEVER-NEVER-LAND. A FEW YEARS AGO, MAYBE A DECADE OR TWO, EVERYBODY WAS TALKING ABOUT THE "NEW WAVE",

AND NOW WE FREQUENTLY HEAR OF THE "NEW AGE." I LIKE TO SAY;" <u>NEW WAVE</u>, "SAME WATER." <u>NEW AGE</u>, "SAME GOD!"

SOCIETY WOULD HAVE YOU TO BELIEVE THAT GOD DOES NOT POSSESS THE SAME POWER AND CONTROL OVER THE CHURCH THAT HE ONCE HAD IN THE EARTH, AND THAT PERHAPS HE DOES NOT EVEN REALLY EXIST.

THIS IDEA IS FOOLISHNESS! DO NOT EVER ALLOW YOURSELF TO BELIEVE THAT GOD DOES NOT CARE ANYMORE, OR THAT SINCE EVERYTHING ELSE HAS CHANGED; ANYTHING AND EVERYTHING GOES, AND GOD IS OK WITH IT.

SOME WILL SAY THAT NOBODY HAS TO TELL ANYONE WHAT TO DO. WHY DO WE NEED A LEADER ANYWAY? WHO SAYS, THAT WE HAVE TO GO TO CHURCH JUST TO BE SAVED? I CAN TEACH MYSELF HOW TO LIVE THE WAY I THINK THAT GOD WANTS ME TO LIVE ON MY OWN, THOSE CHRISTIANS ARE NOT REAL ANYWAY. IT'S ALL A WAIST OF TIME. THIS ATTITUDE IS WHAT I CALL "*<u>Pathetic Apathy</u>*."

(DEFINITION: PATHETIC - *arousing pity, pitiful*)

This know also, that in the last days perilous times shall come For men shall be lovers of their own selves, covetous, boasters, proud, blasphemers, disobedient to parents, unthankful, unholy, Without natural affection, trucebreakers, false accusers, incontinent, fierce, despisers of those that are good, Traitors, heady high minded, lovers of pleasures more than lovers of God; Having a form of godliness, but denying the power there of: from such turn away
II TIMOTHY 3:1-5

THE BIBLE STATES THAT THESE TERRIBLE TIMES IN WHICH WE NOW LIVE WOULD DEFINITELY COME. THE WORD OF GOD IS IMMUTABLE, MEANING THAT WHATEVER GOD HAS ALREADY SAID IN HIS WORD IS TRUTH

AND CAN NEVER CHANGE. PEOPLE LOOK AROUND, THESE TIMES ARE REALLY HERE!

AS WE EMBRACE THE HORRIFIC DAYS AHEAD, IT IS PARAMOUNT THAT WE DO NOT EMBRACE THE SINFULNESS OF THE PEOPLE, WHILE WE EMBRACE THE SINNERS. WE MUST LEARN TO SEPARATE THE BABY FROM THE BATH WATER, AND THROW OUT THE DIRTY BATH WATER, WHILE PROTECTING THE BABY FROM ALSO BEING THROWN OUT.

Don't Embrace the Sin!

WHENEVER I SAY; "EMBRACE THE SINNER AND NOT THE SIN"; I'M SIMPLY SAYING; "TAKE IN THE PERSON, BUT THROW OUT THE VISE." "LOVE THE INDIVIDUAL, WHILE AT THE SAME TIME, HATE THE WRONG THINGS THEY DO."

AS GOD HAS EMBRACED US WITH HIS GRACE, LOVE, AND TRUTH; HAVEN DELIVERED US FROM THE VERY BONDAGE OF SIN, WE OUGHT TO EMBRACE THE SINNER WHO REALLY DESIRE A CHANGE IN THEIR LIVES. THEY NEED SOMEONE OF THE LIVING BODY OF CHRIST TO LOVE THEM ENOUGH TO DIRECT THEM INTO THE KNOWLEDGE OF THE RIGHT KIND OF A CHANGE.

PEOPLE CHANGE EVERYDAY, BUT THEY CONTINUE TO MAKE THE WRONG KIND OF CHANGES. FOR AN INSTANCE, THEY LEAVE ONE WRONG RELATIONSHIP, ONLY TO GET INTO THE NEXT WRONG RELATIONSHIP, AND SO ON. PEOPLE MOVE FROM HOUSE TO HOUSE, AND FROM JOB TO JOB, AND EVEN MORE FREQUENTLY, FROM CHURCH TO CHURCH, AND/OR FROM RELIGION TO RELIGION, AND THE BEAT GOES ON.

IT'S A BAD THING TO BE HEADED FOR A DITCH THAT YOU MAY NOT REALLY BE AWARE OF, WHEN THERE IS SOMEONE ELSE WHO SEES THE DITCH AHEAD OF YOU, BUT THEY GIVE YOU NO WARNING AT ALL.

THE PEOPLE THAT WE ARE TO SPEAK TO MIGHT BE DRIVEN BY THE OBVIOUS NEED OF LEANING ON ANOTHER

INDIVIDUAL, WHEREAS THEY JUST NEED FOR SOMEONE ELSE TO SOUND THE ALARM TO MAKE AN AWARENESS OF THE DANGER AHEAD. WHETHER THEY ARE SAVED, OR YET LIVING IN SIN, THEY ARE TRULY CO-DEPENDANT.

YOU MAY BE ABLE TO IDENTIFY WITH THEIR STRUGGLES. YOU MAY SAY; "I'VE BEEN THERE, AND I'VE DONE THAT", IT REALLY DOES NOT EVEN MATTER. YOU ARE STILL RESPONSIBLE TO OPEN YOUR MOUTH AND TO SAY THE RIGHT THING, THAT WILL PREVENT THEM FROM REMAINING IN THE SAME CONDITION.

WHATEVER YOU HAVE COME TO KNOW THROUGH THE TRUTH OF GOD'S WORD, YOU SHOULD BE WILLING TO SPEAK THE SAME, REGARDING IT AS THE TRUTH. DON'T TELL A SINNER; "YOU ARE ALL RIGHT JUST AS YOU ARE".

THE AVERAGE PERSON WANTS PITY, THEY DO NOT WANT TO CHANGE! YOU EVER HEAR THE SAYING; "WELL NOBODY'S PERFECT?" THIS STATEMENT IS SAYING; "HEY, HAVE PITY ON ME FOR MY OBNOXIOUS STATE, I'M NOT THE ONLY ONE WHO HAS EVER BEEN OBNOXIOUS."

THIS PERSON IS OVERLOOKING THE FACT OF BE-ING IDENTIFIED WITH EVERY OBNOXIOUS PERSON AND THE SINFULLY WICKED THINGS THAT THEY WILL DO ON ANY SCALE. THAT INDIVIDUAL IS ACTUALLY SAYING, SUB-LIMINALLY, THAT; "EVERYBODY I'M REFERRING TO, IN-CLUDING MYSELF, ARE ALL OBNOXIOUS, SO LEAVE US ALONE!"

WHAT IS EVEN MORE PATHETIC, IS WHEN PEOPLE KNOW THAT THERE ARE OTHERS WITH LIKE STRUGGLES, THEY SEEM TO FEEL THAT THEY FIT IN SOMEWHERE. YOU GET THE FEELING THAT THEY BELIEVE; "SOMEONE RE-ALLY KNOWS WHAT I'M GOING THROUGH, SO THERE, I DON'T!!! HAVE TO CHANGE."

No Matter What You Say, You Change!!

WE CHANGE GRADUALLY EVERYDAY, EVOLVING INTO THE ETERNAL PERSONS OF OUR *chosen* ETERNAL

DESTINIES. WE GET BETTER OR WE GET WORSE. WE BECOME MORE LIKE THE WORLD OR MORE LIKE GOD. WE CHANGE VOLUNTARILY AND INVOLUNTARILY.

NOT ONLY WILL OUR BODIES GET OLDER, BUT WE WILL ALSO DEVELOP TIMELY SIGNS OF AGING, SUCH AS THE LOSS OF PIGMENTATION IN OUR HAIR AND THE GRACEFULNESS OF OUR YOUTHFUL BREAKDOWN, WHICH WILL EVENTUALLY BE WORN ON THE VERY PRESENCE OF OUR COUNTENANCE.

BEING SET IN THE WAYS OF OUR OWN CHOOSING, WE BECOME MIRROR EXAMPLES OF OUR OWN PERSONAL BELIEF SYSTEMS. TO CHANGE OR NOT TO CHANGE IS REALLY THE QUESTION OF THE FACTS STATED PREVIOUSLY.

> *Can the Ethiopian change his skin, or the leop-*
> *ard his spot? Then may ye also do good; that*
> *are accustomed to do evil.* JEREMIAH 13:23

THE QUESTION AFTER ALL IS NOT CAN YOU CHANGE, BUT RATHER IT IS, DO YOU REALLY HAVE A DESIRE TO CHANGE? CAN YOU SEE YOURSELF MIRRORED AS YOU REALLY AND TRULY ARE?

MUCH TIME IS GENERALLY SPENT IN OBSERVANCE OF THE OTHER PERSON'S LIFE-STYLE, WHEN IT IS ACTUALLY YOUR OWN LIFE-STYLE THAT BEARS THE NEED OF THE REAL SCRUTINY OF EXAMINATION. IT IS VERY EASY TO ALWAYS SEE THE WRONG IN THE LIFE OF SOMEONE ELSE.

JESUS TAUGHT:

> *Thou hypocrite, first cast out the beam out of*
> *thine own eye; and then thou shalt see clearly to*
> *cast out the mote out of thy brothers eye.*
> ST. MATTHEW 7:5

DON'T BE SO CRAZY AS TO BELIEVE THAT YOU ARE ACTUALLY BETTER OFF THAN ANYONE ELSE, BEING THAT THE TWO OR MAYBE EVEN MORE OF YOU ARE ALL IN THE EXACT SAME STATE!

THAT'S PATHETIC!

WHILE THERE ARE ACTUALLY SOME PEOPLE WHO ARE BETTER AT LIVING UNGODLY THAN OTHERS, IT IS REALLY PATHETIC TO GO AROUND ADVERTISING THEIR LOWER LEVEL OF UNGODLY LIVING EVERYWHERE THEY WENT, WOULDN'T YOU THINK SO?

YOU WOULD ACTUALLY BE IN A PITIFULLY SUNKEN STATE OF MIND TO BEHAVE YOURSELF IN SUCH A MANNER, AS TO PROJECT YOURSELF AS THE VERY BEST SINNER AROUND.

Gay, What-cha Say??

HOMOSEXUALITY AND LESBIANISM, IS NOW AND WILL ALWAYS BE AGAINST THE CREATIVE DESIGN PLAN OF GOD FOR THE MATING OF MALE AND FEMALE COUPLES, AND FOR THE PRODUCTIVE FAMILY STRUCTURE.

THE BIBLE CLEARLY GIVES STATEMENTS OF GOD'S REJECTION OF SUCH LIFE-STYLES, BEGINNING WITH GENESIS, CHAPTER 19, THE CITIES OF SODOM AND GOMORRAH WERE BURNED TO ASHES, BECAUSE OF THE WICKEDNESS, ALONG WITH OTHER SURROUNDING CITIES.

MY PERSONAL VIEWPOINT IS THAT THE THOUGHT OF SAME SEX UNIONS IS IMMORALLY DISGUSTING. THIS IS THE MOST BACKWARDS LIFE-STYLES EVER HEARD OF. OF EVERY KIND, GOD CREATED A MALE FOR A FEMALE, A GIVER AND A RECEIVER, OR RATHER TWO OPPOSITES TO BE LOVERS.

THE IDEA OF MATING TWO OF THE SAME KIND IN GENDER, TWO MALES, OR TWO FEMALES, IS DETESTABLE AND SERIOUSLY PURPOSELESS. THIS IDEA IS STRAIGHT OUT OF THE PIT OF HELL! THIS IS THE DEVIL'S ATTEMPT TO COMPLETELY DESTROY THE NATURAL REPRODUCTION OF MANKIND IN THE EARTH ACCORDING TO THE DIVINE PLAN OF GOD.

Since Satan could not stop the natural reproduction of mankind in the earth, he chose the alternative of corrupting mankind; many have bought into the idea line, sink, and hook!

No two males or two females, together sexually, can ever at anytime bring forth offspring! God gave the man for the seed and the woman or the female to be the incubator of the seed, for child bearing; this is ultimately the divine plan of God for sexual relationships, it is to replenish the earth and to multiply.

Let Me Break It Down!

Whenever a man and a woman come together in marriage, usually there is only the two of them, unless there are already children to be added to the union.

After a few years and sometimes immediately, children are born to the union. This is where the multiplication plan of God begins for the two. The families of the bride and the groom each gained another family member upon the uniting in marriage of this couple.

The children born to the union become grandchildren, nieces, and nephews, and eventually later on they themselves are to one day become parents, uncles, aunts, and grandparents. The cycle goes on and on unless the devil's advocate and agenda of homosexuality and lesbianism successfully interrupts this natural process of life.

This gay life-style exterminates the plan of God for a man or a woman who allow themselves to participate in such behavioral patterns of living, destroying the possibility of a family that would bring more life to the earth. You see there is more to having a relationship with a person than saying that; "if It feels good, go for it, because it must be right."

The gay life-styles, by the way is not God's fault. That statement is the lie told by many of the participants of the gay life-style and it is frequently given as an explanation to their own pathetic situation. The real truth is that the responsibility and fault lies solely upon the gay persons themselves!!

It is not God who puts thrill-seeking ideas about perverted sexual fantasies with the same sex in the mind of an individual, to which generally takes place long before the initial act occurs. The heartfelt consciousness of mankind will bring about a very strong since of conviction of wrong doings of all types, relative to their teachings and upbringing.

It's up to you to respond to the word of God, to make the right decision about not doing the wrong thing. Whenever you know that you are about to do the wrong thing or even go the wrong way, stop and get a grip on yourself. Take responsibility for your actions. Reward yourself and feel good about your decision to do right.

Too Late I'm Labeled!!!

Before going totally and completely into the gay life style, the individual culprits are generally prejudged by their mannerisms and their compromising demeanor, and soon labeled accordingly.

This causes the hardening of the heart towards God, and the inability to hear and to receive the ever unchanging message of the gospel. Such labeling desensitizes the seriousness

IN THE HEART DISABLING THE NEED TO KNOW THE AC-
TUAL TRUTH ABOUT AN INDIVIDUAL'S SPIRITUAL CONDI-
TION, BUT THEIR SPIRITS BELONG SOLELY TO THE TRUTH
OF GOD'S WORD, IF THEY WILL ALLOW IT TO BE SO.

LABELS LIKE, "PUNK, SISSY, FAGGOT, BULL-DAGGER,
BUTCH, LES-BEAU, AND DIKE" TO ONLY NAME A FEW, ARE
SOME OF THE NEGATIVE LABELS THAT ARE GIVEN TO GAY
PEOPLE, BY THE PEOPLE OF THE SOCIETY.

OF COURSE THE BIBLE HAS IT'S OWN SET OF LA-
BELS, FOR WHICH I MIGHT FIND MYSELF GIVING MUCH
ATTENTION TO, IF I WERE YOU, SUCH AS, "ABOMINATION"
(LEVITICUS 18) "DEFILEMENT" (GENESIS 19) "WICKED-
NESS" (ROMANS 1) "BURNED IN THEIR LUST"; "LASCIVI-
OUS" (GALATIANS 5) "UNCLEANNESS" AND (II TIMOTHY
3) "UNHOLY", "LOVERS OF THEIR OWN SELVES", "WITH-
OUT NATURAL AFFECTION". BUT I CORINTHIANS 6: 9
LABELS THEM AS BEING "EFFEMINATE", PERTAINING TO
PERSONS WHO ARE GUILTY OF ADDICTIONS TO SINS OF
THE FLESH, "(VINES BIBLE DICTIONARY)."

IF YOU BELIEVE THAT IT IS ACTUALLY TOO LATE
FOR YOU BECAUSE OF THE LABELING THAT HAS BEEN LAID
UPON YOU BY THE PEOPLE OF YOUR DAILY SURROUND-
INGS WHO SEE YOU ON A FREQUENT BASIS, YOU HAD BET-
TER TAKE A CLOSE LOOK AT WHAT THE BIBLE SAYS ABOUT
YOUR SUGGESTIVE BEHAVIOR.

FRIEND, THE GAY LIFE IS AGAINST THE ORIGINAL
IDEA OF THE LIFE THAT GOD INITIALLY GAVE YOU, AND
GOD DOES NOT JUST CLOSE HIS EYES AND LOOK IN THE
OPPOSITE DIRECTION AWAY FROM YOUR ALTERNATIVE
LIFE-STYLE, AS MANY PEOPLE DO HERE IN THIS PRESENT
LIFE. PERHAPS YOU HAD BETTER LET JESUS BE THE *ALTER*
OF YOUR ALTERNATIVE LIFE-STYLE!

YOU WOULD BE SURPRISED TO KNOW THAT SOME
PEOPLE ACTUALLY THINK THAT YOU OUGHT TO BE DEAD,
SO ARE YOU GOING TO JUST GO AHEAD AND DIE?

IT IS NEVER TOO LATE FOR GOD TO DELIVER YOU

AND TO PUT YOU BACK ON TRACK, WHILE VINDICATING YOU OF ALL OF THE ACCUSATIONS, AND THE NEGATIVE STATEMENTS MADE IN REFERENCE TO YOURSELF. YOU MAY NOT WANT TO BELIEVE THAT YOU ARE OFF TRACK, BUT YOU ARE! <u>SERIOUSLY</u>!

IF YOU REALLY BELIEVE THAT THE GAY LIFE IS A WAY OF LIFE, YOU ARE MORE PATHETIC THAN YOUR BELIEF! GAY, IS A VERY SINFULLY SELFISH WAY TO LIVE, AND SINFULNESS IS NOT LIFE, IT IS DEATH! SO, YOU ARE NOT LIVING, YOU ARE DEAD EVERY STEP OF THE WAY THROUGH THE GAY AGENDA AND LIFE-STYLE, BOTH NATURALLY AND SPIRITUALLY.

ALL OF THE TIME THAT IS SPENT MEANDERING THROUGH THE CONFUSION OF THE GAY LIFE-STYLE, YOU ARE DESTROYING YOUR SOUL AND SENDING YOURSELF TO HELL ETERNALLY, BECAUSE YOU HAVE CHANGED THE NATURAL USE OF YOUR BODY. (ROMANS 1:) NOW THE CHOICE IS YOURS?

EVEN MORE PATHETIC TO ME ARE THE PRESENTLY PRACTICING GAYS IN THE CLERGY AND IN THE CHURCH, WHO ACTUALLY BELIEVE THAT THEY MIGHT BE SOMEHOW SECRETLY BLOOD-WASHED IN THE BLOOD OF JESUS, AND EXCUSED FROM THE PUNISHMENT OF THEIR SINS (WHILE THEY ARE YET ACTIVELY HOMOSEXUALLY INVOLVED), AS LONG AS THEY STAY WITH THE LOCAL CHURCH SOMEWHERE.

TO BELIEVE THAT GOD WILL MAKE SOME KIND OF EXCUSE FOR YOU JUST BECAUSE YOU COME TO THE GATHERING OF THE CHURCH ON A REGULAR BASIS, IS CRAZY! JESUS WAS HUNG UP ON THE CROSS FOR ALL OF YOUR HANG-UPS, AND THE INDWELLING POWER OF THE HOLY GHOST WILL GIVE YOU THE POWER TO OVERCOME YOUR HOMOSEXUALLY PERVERTED WAYS, THROUGH DELIVERANCE. I CALL YOU TO SURRENDER! IN THE NAME OF JESUS! <u>*NOW*</u>!!!

WE ARE MORE THAN CONQUERORS THROUGH JESUS

CHRIST OUR LORD, THEREFORE, YOU SHOULD KNOW THAT YOU HAVE BEEN GIVEN THE POWER TO CONQUER THE GIANT OF YOUR OWN FLESH, AND YOUR OWN WILL. IT IS NOT WISE TO STAY ON THE LOSING SIDE, KNOWING THAT JESUS HAS DECLARED US THE WINNERS, SO COME ON WITH THE WINNERS. AS LONG AS YOU LIVE, YOU HAVE THE OPPORTUNITY TO CHANGE.

MY RESEARCH ON THIS SUBJECT IS FROM THE *King James* BIBLE!!!!!

Apathy

WE SHOULD ALL KNOW THAT SIN, AS RELATING TO ONES OWN BODY, IS NOT THE ONLY SIN. BY FAR, *SEX*!!!, IS NOT THE ONLY SIN!!!!!!

> *"All unrighteousness is sin: etc..."* I JOHN 5:17

YES, THE WORLD IS FULL OF SIN, THEREFORE YOUR ATTITUDE MAY BE; "WHY BOTHER." IT IS EXTREMELY IMPERATIVE TO BOTHER, BECAUSE SIN PAYS WAGES.

> **For the wages of sin is death; but the gift of God**
> **is eternal life through Jesus Christ our Lord.**
> ROMANS 6:23

SIN DOES NOT WRITE ANY BOUNCING CHECKS. WHATEVER THE PRICE, IT WILL BE PAID. JUST BECAUSE THE DEED WAS DONE IN THE DARK WHERE NOBODY SAW YOU, DON'T BE FOOLED INTO THINKING THAT YOU MAY HAVE ACTUALLY GOTTEN AWAY WITH WHATEVER YOU DID, THE LORD SAW YOU.

HE PAID ATTENTION, AND I'LL GUARANTEE YOU, THAT HE TRIED TO PREVENT YOU FROM DOING THE EVIL DEED. WHATEVER THE CLASSIFICATION, SIN OF COMMISSION OR SIN OF OMISSION, SIN IS SIN! THERE ARE SINS OF THE FLESH, AND THERE ARE SINS OF THE SPIRIT. SINS OF THE FLESH ARE THE WORKS OF THE FLESH, IN OTHER WORDS, THE THINGS WE ACTUALLY DO IN OUR

BODIES TO CAUSE US TO BECOME <u>IMMORALLY UNCLEAN</u>.

> *Now the works of the flesh are manifest; which are these; adultery, fornication, uncleanness, lasciviousness, Idolatry, witchcraft, hatred, variance, emulations, wrath, strife, seditions, heresies, envyings, murders, drunkenness, revellings, and such like of the which I tell you before, as I have also told you in time past, that they which do such things shall not inherit the kingdom of God.*   GALATIANS 5:19-21

JESUS TAUGHT US TO PRAY; "THY KINGDOM COME IN EARTH, AS IT IS IN HEAVEN." SIN HAS THE ABILITY TO SHUT US OUT OF THE PRESENT KINGDOM OF THE LORD, RIGHT HERE, RIGHT NOW ON EARTH. I CAN'T IMAGINE LIVING OUTSIDE OF THE KINGDOM OF GOD WHERE THE PRESENCE OF THE LORD CAN'T BE FOUND.

SIN WILL <u>ROB</u> YOU OF YOUR PEACE, YOUR DIGNITY, YOUR SELF WORTH, YOUR SELF-ESTEEM, AND THE RIGHT TO APPROACH THE THRONE OF GRACE WITH BOLDNESS!

IT IS A HURTFUL THING TO LOSE BECAUSE OF SIN. IT IS ALSO POSSIBLE TO LOSE EVERYTHING IN LIFE FOR ANY NUMBER OF REASONS AS A RESULT OF SIN.

DON'T GET RELIGIOUS ON ME! I AM REFERRING TO "UN-REPENTED SINS", "UNCONFESSED SINS", AND DEFINITELY "UN-RENOUNCED SINS." HAVE YOU REPENTED OF ALL OF YOUR SINS BEFORE THE LORD!

THE PROBLEMATIC BINDING FORCE OF SIN IS THE ATTACHED PLEASURE OF SELFISHNESS. IT IS FOUNDED UPON THE ATTITUDE OF SAYING; "I WANTED TO, AND I ENJOYED IT", DISREGARDING WHETHER OR NOT IT WAS AGAINST GOD; "I WANTED TO REALIZE SOMETHING FOR ME, SO I DID IT!"

YOU CANNOT EVEN SPELL <u>S I N</u> WITHOUT THE LETTER I IN THE MIDDLE. SO IT IS MY OPINION THAT WHEN WE SAY I DO WHATEVER I PLEASE; WE ARE NOT ONLY

BEING GROWN AND EXERCISING THE FREEDOM OF OUR OWN CHOICE, WE ARE ACTUALLY COMMITTING SIN!!

YOUR SINS WILL ALWAYS AFFECT MORE THAN JUST YOU. SUFFERING IS REALLY PAINFUL WHEN IT IS BROUGHT ABOUT BY SOMEONE ELSE'S WRONGDOING.

> *Having therefore these promises, dearly beloved, let us cleanse ourselves from all filthiness of the flesh and of the spirit, perfecting holiness in the fear of God.* II CORINTHIANS 7:1

Please Don't Say It!!

GO AHEAD AND CLEAN UP YOUR ACT! GO BACK INTO THAT CLOSET, AND CHANGE THE NEGATIVE IDEAS, WHICH YOU MAY HAVE BELIEVED ABOUT YOURSELF, BEFORE YOU COME OUT TO THE PUBLIC AND BEGIN TO BLURT OUT THOSE DEADLY AND SINFUL THINGS OF THE FLESH THAT ARE SEEKING PERMANENT ATTACHMENT TO YOU.

THERE HAS ALWAYS BEEN A REASON FOR THE THINGS IN THE CLOSET, TO BE THERE AND TO STAY THERE. THOSE TERRIBLE THINGS SHOULD NEVER BE BROUGHT OUT!

SOME THINGS THAT YOU HAVE THOUGHT ABOUT DOING OR EVEN SAYING, NO ONE SHOULD EVER HAVE KNOWN THAT YOU HAD THOUGHT ABOUT THOSE THINGS. YOUR STRUGGLES SHOULD HAVE NEVER BEEN PUT ON OPEN DISPLAY.

RUN THE LOOSE DEMON BACK INTO THE CLOSET AND CRUCIFY HIM THERE, IN THE NAME OF JESUS! WHATEVER THE NAME OF THE VICE THAT MAY INDEED BE A PLAGUE IN YOUR LIFE, IT IS TRULY TELLING A LIE ON YOU. THAT IS <u>NOT</u> REALLY WHO YOU ARE!

YOU MAY HAVE ACCEPTED THE PACKAGE, BUT IT'S NOT REAL. DOESN'T MATTER WHAT YOU FEEL IN YOUR BODY, ALTHOUGH YOU MAY BE TOO WEAK TO FIGHT BACK AGAINST THE UNGODLY FEELINGS OR JUST SIMPLY UNIN-

TERESTED IN CHANGE, IT IS REALLY NOT YOU. SO STOP TRYING TO CONVINCE YOURSELF THAT YOU ARE SOMEONE AGAINST WHOEVER GOD SAYS THAT YOU ARE IN THE WORD OF GOD!

He's Almost Happy!

(APATHY - LACK OF INTEREST OR DESIRE OF ACTIVITY)

SIN RUNS RAMPANT IN AND THROUGHOUT THE SOCIALLY EGOTISTICAL BROTHERHOOD OF THE CHURCH. SINFULNESS AS A WAY OF LIVING IS ON THE UPRISE, WHILE CHURCHMEN LACK THE INTEREST TO EXCITE CHANGE.

PEOPLE FEEL MORE COMFORTABLE SHACKING, STEALING, COMMITTING MURDER AND ADULTERY, MANUFACTURING LIES ABOUT OTHER PEOPLE, DIGGING DITCHES AND SO ON, BOTH IN AND ON THE OUTSIDE OF THE CHURCH.

SUCH SINFUL PARTICIPATION USE TO ONLY BE THE WAY OF THE UNGODLY WHO LIVED IN COMPLETE AGREEMENT WITH WORLDLY VIEWS, BUT SOMEHOW SUCH BEHAVIORAL PATTERNS HAVE COMFORTABLY FOUND A WAY TO OPENLY FIT IN AMONG THE PEOPLE OF THE CHURCH.

THESE PERSONS WERE ALWAYS AMONG THE PEOPLE OF THE CHURCH, JUST NOT SO FREQUENTLY VISIBLE IN AUTHORITY AND INVOLVED WITH THE BUSINESS OF THE CHURCH, AND PARTICIPATING IN CHURCH ACTIVITIES, AS IF THEY WERE TRULY BLOOD-WASHED BELIEVERS IN CHRIST JESUS.

THE CHURCH OFFICIALS HAVE JUMPED THE GUN IN ALLOWING THE PARTICIPATION OF THESE NONE CONFESSING UNBELIEVERS, WHO REFUSE TO SEE THE NEED FOR REPENTANCE IN THEIR OWN LIVES, LACKING THE TRUE DELIVERANCE THEY NEED TO SERIOUSLY REPRESENT CHRIST.

THESE DECEIVED PEOPLE HAVE BEEN ALLOWED TO TAKE PART IN THE ADMINISTRATION OF THE MOST SACRED AND MOST HOLY WORSHIP SERVICE OF THE MOST

HIGH, GOD.

> *Now the spirit speaketh expressly, that in the latter times some shall depart from the faith, giving heed to seducing spirits, and doctrines of "Devil's; Speaking lies in hypocrisy; having their conscience seared with a hot iron,*
>
> I TIMOTHY 4:1-2

Stone Cold Situation!

PEOPLE SEEM TO HAVE NO CONSCIOUSNESS OF THEIR WRONGDOING, THEY DO NOT EVEN CARE ABOUT THE IMAGES THEY ARE PROJECTING AS CHURCH MEMBERS OR MORE FREQUENTLY SO-CALLED "CHRISTIANS", WHILE FELLOW CHURCH MEMBERS ARE PUTTING NO PRESSURE ON THEM TO BE ACCOUNTABLE FOR THEIR SINFUL ACTIONS.

WRONG IS CALLED RIGHT, AND RIGHTEOUSNESS IS NOW LOOKED UPON AS OLD FASHIONED AND IN THE WAY, AND THE PEOPLE OF RIGHTEOUSNESS ARE PEERED AS PERSONS WHO REFUSE TO ACCEPT MODERN CHANGE.

HOLY GHOST FILLED PEOPLE, WHO HAVE THE AUTHORITY, AND ARE EQUIPPED WITH THE POWER OF THE SPIRITUAL WEAPONS OF WARFARE THAT ARE FOUND IN THE WORD OF GOD, FULL AND COMPLETELY ARMORED, KNOWING THAT THE LORD IS ON THEIR SIDE; THESE SAME PERSONS ARE TOO OFTEN OPERATING IN <u>APATHY</u>.

APATHY, UNLIKE THE PATHETIC FALLACY, BEING MOSTLY AN ATTITUDE OF THE MIND, <u>IS A SPIRIT</u>! APATHY IS MUCH MORE DANGEROUS, IN THAT, IT IS MORE EASILY INTERMINGLED TO WALK HAND AND HAND, WITH THE SPIRIT OF RELIGION. YOU CAN ACTUALLY BE IN A PATHETIC STATE AND NOT KNOW IT. EVERYONE AROUND YOU CAN BE PATHETIC, GOING DOWN POVERTY LANE AND IT SEEMS OK., BECAUSE EVERYONE IS GOING THE SAME WAY.

But, to be apathetic, means that you do see the problem, and you do have the ability to excite change, but rather you are uninterested by choice, for whatever the reason. You can do, but will not do anything! Your determination is nothing other than to keep silent on purpose; it's no accident or oversight, you see it, but will not respond.

Perhaps you feel that you're minding your own business? Well, allowing someone to get into trouble or to complete a fall, is "Apathy!" Apathy is wrong!

An apathetic attitude is one in the same of saying; "Every tub has got to sit on it's own bottom." "I've got mine and you have got to get yours." "Do whatever I did to change; you just need to experience that old time religion." "Read your own bible for yourself and don't ever ask me any questions, burn some midnight oil!" "You'll feel better when you get your own."

In some religious circles people are taught to see but don't respond to whatever they see and to hear but never listen, because it is not any of their own business. Just leave it alone! Let the Lord take care of it. He will handle it when He gets ready. The truth is that God was ready to handle the situation whenever He allowed you to see or to hear and to know first hand of the present situation.

Scared Silent!

As a young boy at the age of about eleven years, I used to hear the Pentecostal churches singing a song that said; "GOD DON'T WANT NO COWARD SOLDIERS", now it appears that cowards are the pastors of many of the churches.

Cowards, is what ought to come to your mind whenever pastors won't uphold righteousness.

Weak, jelly backed, spineless, powerless, voiceless, so-called "representatives of Christ" are all over the place. They are afraid of stirring up the comfortably seated devil in the local church or of making waves, unless it means bringing the devil *into* the life of another member of the clergy or of the body of Christ, by the way of a scandalous attack, because an individual may not be going along with any of the undercover activities that are against God.

> *Cry aloud, spare not, lift up thy voice like a trumpet, and shew my people their transgressions, and the house of Jacob their sins.* Isaiah 58:1

Don't be a weak, sorry, silent representative of the truth that you believe. Whenever you have found truth in the word of God that has permeated your spirit, you are responsible to speak the truth out of your mouth, and I don't mean for you to get a robe and start preaching.

I don't mean draw a crowd and begin teaching, but speak to that someone on your job, the neighbor across the street, the store clerk, the mechanic, the postman, the paper-man, the landscaper, the children in the neighborhood, somewhere, somebody needs to know the truth, even if you believe that they already know!

Speak the word of truth in love, anyway, because they may not know the truth as you may have at first believed.

Say It Right!

Saying the right thing, but saying it in the wrong way can be damaging to the individual you

ARE SPEAKING TO. THERE IS NO NEED IN TALKING, IF THERE IS NO DESIRE OF LOVE WITHIN YOU TO BE RECEIVED. UNLESS PEOPLE RECEIVE YOUR MESSAGE, THERE CAN BE NO CHANGE.

NEVER SUGARCOAT THE TRUTH! DON'T WATER DOWN THE TRUTH! BE CAREFUL NOT TO ALTER THE TERMINOLOGY OF THE TRUTH, SO MUCH SO, THAT THE MESSAGE IS MISUNDERSTOOD. ALWAYS BE SURE TO REMEMBER THAT THE MESSAGE SHOULD ALWAYS BE PLAIN.

WHILE WE HOLD DIFFERENT POSITIONS BECAUSE WE MAY HAVE DIFFERENT ABILITIES AND FUNCTIONS AND ALTOGETHER A DIFFERENT PURPOSE, WE MUST NEVER FORGET THAT WE ARE ALL ON THE SAME TEAM.

WE MAY ALL BE UNIQUE, BUT WE ALL HANDLE THE SAME, INFALLIBLE, IMMUTABLE WORD OF GOD. GOD WILL NEVER CHANGE, SO DON'T YOU EVER CHANGE HIS MESSAGE.

Get the Picture!

ASK YOURSELF THIS QUESTION; "DO I REALLY LOVE GOD?" IF YOUR ANSWER IS YES, THEN YOU DO HAVE A SINCE OF CARING, ABOUT YOURSELF. IT IS GOD'S DIRECT INTENTIONS THAT YOU CARE FOR YOURSELF AS WELL AS OTHERS.

HAVE YOU EVER STOPPED TO THINK JUST HOW BIG GOD REALLY IS? GOD IS GREATER THAN EVEN THE GREATEST IMAGINATION. HE IS THE GOD WHO CREATED GREATNESS! HAVE YOU LET HIM INTO YOUR HEART TO BE YOUR SAVIOR?

WELL, IF SO, THEN AFTER ALL, YOU MUST CERTAINLY HAVE A GREAT BIG HEART, NOW THAT GOD IS IN IT. HAVE YOU EVER NOTICED THAT EVERY TRACEABLE ATTRIBUTE OF THE ACTIVE CHARACTER OF GOD STEMS FROM HIS LOVE?

PEOPLE WILL CHANGE WHENEVER THEY TRULY KNOW HOW TO GO ABOUT MAKING THE NECESSARY

CHANGES THAT ARE NEEDED IN THEIR OWN LIVES. THEY DON'T ALWAYS KNOW THAT THEY NEED TO CHANGE, BELIEVE IT OR NOT!

OFTEN TIMES PEOPLE NEED AN EXPLANATION FROM WITHOUT, ON THE OUTSIDE OF THEIR OWN INNER CIRCLE, AND A STRONG SINCE OF DIRECTION AND MOTIVATION.

MORE THAN ANYTHING, THEY NEED TO BE COACHED INTO DOING RIGHT AND TAUGHT HOW TO ENTER INTO A CHANGE. WE NEED NOT ALWAYS, TO GIVE A HUNGRY MAN A MEAL JUST TO GET RID OF HIM, RATHER WE NEED TO TEACH HIM THE CHANGE OF PROVIDING FOR HIMSELF AND IN TURN HE WON'T BE HUNGRY. THIS, MY FRIEND, WILL TAKE EFFECT OVER A PROCESS OF TIME.

DO YOU REMEMBER WHEN THE LORD ASKED THE APOSTLE PETER;

"Do you love me?"

THE LORD ASKED THIS QUESTION OF PETER THREE TIMES. PETER BEING CONCERNED THE THIRD TIME SAID;

"Lord you know I love you."

THE LORD RESPONDED,

"Feed the sheep."

THE LORD DID NOT INQUIRE OF PETER'S LOVE BECAUSE HE WAS NOT SURE, BUT RATHER HE INQUIRED IN ORDER TO GIVE PETER AN OPPORTUNITY TO EXAMINE HIS INNERMOST LOVE FOR CHRIST AND TO KNOW OF THE SORT OF LOVE HE ACTUALLY HAD.

WHENEVER THE LORD SAID TO PETER; "FEED THE SHEEP", WHAT I HEAR HIM SAYING IS; "PETER SHOW ME YOUR LOVE, LOVE MY PEOPLE IN ACTION! GIVE WARNING AND SATISFY THE LONGING OF THEIR HEARTS BY MY EXAMPLES OF LOVE AND MY INFALLIBLE WORD."

STAND UP AND BE COUNTED. IF YOU'RE ON THE LORD'S SIDE, THEN SAY SO! LET THE REDEEMED OF THE LORD SAY SO. ONLY THE BORN AGAIN, BLOOD WASHED, AND THE REDEEMED OF THE LORD, HAVE THE VOICE TO

MAKE THE REAL DIFFERENCE ANYWAY. OPEN YOUR MOUTH AND SAY SOMETHING.

They See It!

THE POLICE WILL NOT ALLOW BROKEN LAWS, WITHOUT GIVING CITATIONS. UTILITY COMPANIES, WILL NOT ALLOW UNPAID UTILITIES WITHOUT INTERRUPTIONS. NEWS REPORTERS WILL NOT ALLOW DAILY OCCURRENCES TO TAKE PLACE WITHOUT REPORTING THEM. MAJOR SECURITY ENTITIES ARE READY AND WELL TRAINED AT THEIR POST, ARMED FOR ACTION, AND DO RESPOND WHEN NECESSARY.

WHENEVER A SILENT ALARM GOES OFF DURING A BREAK-IN OR ROBBERY, IT DOES NOT GO UNNOTICED. ALTHOUGH THE BURGLARS THEMSELVES MAY NOT HEAR THE ALARM, THAT DOESN'T MEAN THE ALARM DID NOT SOUND OFF. THE RIGHT PERSONS HEARD THE ALARM AND RESPONDED ACCORDINGLY TO IT. MANY TIMES THE PERPETRATORS WERE APPREHENDED AT THE VERY SCENE OF THE CRIME WITHIN MINUTES.

HOW MUCH MORE SHOULD BLOOD WASHED BELIEVERS BE ON THE ALERT, WILLING AND READY TO RESPOND TO A NECESSARY CAUSE? REPENT RIGHT NOW OF PATHETIC, APATHY. DON'T CONTINUE TO ALLOW PEOPLE TO TAKE SHORT CUTS THROUGH THE CHURCH WHILE ON THEIR WAY TO HELL!! APATHY WON'T GO UNNOTICED BY GOD.

DO YOU REALLY BELONG TO A REAL POWERFUL HOLY GHOST FILLED CHURCH, OR IS IT JUST A SOCIAL CLUB? CLUB SOCIETIES OF SOCIAL GATHERINGS, ARE FOR COMFORTABLY ESCAPING TO RELAXATION AWAY FROM AN INDIVIDUAL'S DAILY AFFAIRS. THE ESCAPING INDIVIDUALS ARE USUALLY IN RETREAT TO SITUATIONS OF INTOXICATED EASE. DON'T WORRY, JUST SIT BACK AND RELAX!

THE CHURCH IS THE HOUSE OF GOD, THE HOUSE OF TRUTH, THE HOUSE OF REFUGE, AND NOT THE "HOUSE OF <u>REFUSE</u>" AS SOME PEOPLE DESPERATELY BELIEVE.

THE TRUTH WILL MAKE YOU VERY UNCOMFORT-

ABLE AT TIMES, THIS IS A GOOD THING, LIKE IT OR NOT PEOPLE, BUT WE NEED THE TRUTH THAT IS FOUND IN THE CHURCH!

> *"And ye shall know the truth, and the truth shall make you free".*   ST. JOHN 8 :32

PEOPLE CAN'T LIBERATE THEMSELVES; AS IT TAKES THE LIBERATING POWER OF GOD'S WORD AND THE ANOINTING OF THE VERY TRUTH OF THE HOLY GHOST TO DELIVER YOU AND TO KEEP YOU IN A LIBERATED STATE. THE POWER OF THE TRUTH THAT IT TOOK TO MAKE YOU FREE AND TO SET YOU OUT BEFORE YOUR PEERS FREE FROM YOUR BONDAGE, IS THE POINT OF MY REFERENCE.

AGAIN I PLEAD WITH YOU, OPEN YOUR MOUTH AND SAY SOMETHING!!

Don't be Pathetically, disgracefully Apathetic!!!

From The Heart*

> But those things which proceed out of the mouth come forth from the heart; and they defile the man. For out of the mouth proceed evil thoughts, murders, adulteries, fornication, thefts, false witness, blasphemers." St. MATTHEW 15:18-19

Now Where Did That Come From?

It is forever bewildering how people will say anything they choose and follow-up saying; "I didn't mean to say that." People, who have no control or consciousness of speaking, are said to be mentally incompetent or crazy.

The controlling power of speech is actually deeply embedded within your own heart, corrupting your mind and commanding your mouth to say the wrong thing.

What you say, can and will, be held against you when you least expect it. Your spoken words will not soon be forgotten.

I intend for you to know your own heart by

YOUR SPEECH, MORE ASSUREDLY.

<u>WHAT YOU SAY, IS WHO YOU ARE</u>! THE WAY YOU TALK, ON A CONSISTENT BASIS, TELLS A GRAPHIC STORY IN DEPICTION OF JUST WHO YOU REALLY ARE!

*My Heart**

A SIGN WORN ON THE BACK OF AN INDIVIDUAL WILL NOT REVEAL THEIR TRUE CHRISTIAN STATUS, OR TO INQUIRE WHETHER AN INDIVIDUAL LOVES THE LORD; THEIR ANSWER TO YOU DOESN'T PROVE THEIR AUTHENTICITY. CERTAIN CHARACTERISTICAL ATTRIBUTES, WILL ALLOW AN INDIVIDUAL'S MATURITY LEVEL TO BE OPENLY DISPLAYED TO BE SCRUTINIZED.

WHEN WE CONSISTENTLY HEAR THE NAME OF THE LORD AND THE WORD OF GOD LEAPING OUT OF THE MOUTH OF AN INDIVIDUAL, WE CAN ONLY HOPE AND BELIEVE THAT THEY ARE TRUE BELIEVERS IN THEIR HEART.

ADMIRATION FOR CHRIST IS ALWAYS ON THEIR LIPS. IT SEEMS CHRIST CAN BE FOUND SOMEWHERE IN ALMOST EVERY CONVERSATION TO WHICH THEY ARE ENGAGED, LEAVING US TO BELIEVE THAT THE CONVERSATION AND THE ADMIRATION FLOW FROM DEEP DOWN WITHIN THE INDIVIDUAL.

YOUR HEART WILL EXPOSE WHATEVER IS TRULY DEEP DOWN ON THE INSIDE OF YOU, PUSHING YOUR PERSONAL CONVICTIONS OUT OF YOUR MOUTH, ESPECIALLY WHENEVER YOU'RE UNDER PRESSURE. YOUR TRUE HEART SPEAKS UP AND SPEAKS OUT IN A CRISIS. CRISES WILL SHOW YOU YOUR OWN HEART AND GIVE YOU THE OPPORTUNITY TO RID YOURSELF OF THE UNNECESSARY THINGS THAT YOU MAY HAVE STORED IN THE CLOSET CHAMBER OF YOUR HEART.

DON'T STRUGGLE WITH THROWING OUT THE EXCESS BAGGAGE THAT IS OF NO REAL ESSENCE TO YOU, JUST GO AHEAD AND GET RID OF IT.

YOU CAN DEFINITELY ALWAYS KNOW WHAT IS IN YOUR OWN HEART AND YOU WILL SURELY KNOW BEFORE ANYONE

ELSE DOES.

I HAVE HEARD REFERENCES TO SAYINGS, SUCH AS; "MY HEART DECEIVED ME." I'M NOT SURE JUST HOW THIS COULD POSSIBLY BE TRUE, BUT I AM OF THE PERSONAL OPINION, THAT ONE COULD NOT HAVE BEEN REALLY FOLLOWING THEIR HEART.

THEY MAY HAVE BEEN FOLLOWING A FEELING OR AN EMOTION WHICH MAY HAVE LED THEM TO THE DECEPTIVE REASONING THAT IS WAS THEIR HEART.

JUST IN CASE YOU HAVE NOTICED THAT YOUR HEART IS UGLY IN NATURE, CAUSING A VERY UGLY PRESENTATION OF YOUR PERSONAL DEMEANOR, YOU SHOULD MAKE AN EFFORT TO RECTIFY THE SITUATION, BEFORE YOU LOSE THE FAVOR OF BOTH MAN AND GOD.

THERE IS A REMEDY FOR WHAT YOU FIND IN YOUR HEART, WHEN YOU ARE TRULY SEEKING A SOLUTION TO FREE THE PREVIOUSLY TAKEN DARK PLACES IN YOUR HEART, FOR THE LOVE OF GOD. PRAYING IN FAITH ON A CONSISTENT BASIS AND FASTING TO BRING ABOUT THE NECESSARY DISCIPLINE WILL ENABLE GOD TO CHANGE YOUR HEART!

MANY THEOLOGIANS HAVE ARGUED AND DO STILL ARGUE RELATIVE TO THE TRUE DEFINITION OF EXACTLY WHAT THE SPIRITUAL HEART OF MAN IS? FOR CERTAIN IT IS NOT THE VASCULAR MUSCULAR ORGAN IN THE CENTER OF YOUR BODY, THAT PUMPS THE BLOOD THROUGHOUT THE BODY FROM HEAD TO TOE.

RATHER, IT IS THE TOTAL PERSONALITY, OR THE SUPER CONSCIOUSNESS OF MAN AT THE CORE OF THE CENTER OF THE SOUL. THE HEART, I'D LIKE TO SAY, IS THE HOUSE OF THE MIND AND THE HOME OF THE SPIRIT, THE BODY IS THE HOME OF THE SOUL HERE IN THE EARTH.

Know The Difference

THE HEART IS NOT THE MIND AND NEITHER IS THE MIND THE HEART. THE *mind* - IS AN INFORMATION THOROUGHFARE WHERE THOUGHTS TRAVEL TO AND FROM DESTINATIONS, THE SAME AS WOULD BE THE STREET OUT IN

FRONT OF YOUR HOUSE WHERE YOU LIVE.

MANY CARS PASS BY YOUR HOME ON A CONSISTENT BASIS, EVEN IF YOU LIVE IN A CUL-DE-SAC. YOU DO NOT ACTUALLY PHYSICALLY LIVE ON THAT STREET, UNLESS YOU ARE HOMELESS. SO ALLOW ME TO SAY, THE STREET WHERE THE HOUSE IS LOCATED, IS THE SAME AS WOULD BE LIKE YOUR MIND.

YOU DON'T LIVE INSIDE OF YOUR MIND, RATHER YOUR MIND LIVES ON THE INSIDE OF YOU. ELSE WHERE WOULD THE CONTROL OF YOUR MIND BE? GOD HAS PLACED ALL RATIONALLY THINKING HUMAN BEINGS IN THE POSITION OF BEING ABLE TO LOOK AT THEIR OWN MIND DEFINITIVELY AND COMPREHENSIVELY.

IF YOU WERE LIVING ON THE INSIDE OF YOUR MIND, THE POSITIONS WOULD BE TURNED INSIDE OUT. YOUR MIND WOULD BE LOOKING AT YOU ON A CONSISTENT BASIS. YOU CONTROL YOUR OWN MIND; YOUR MIND SHOULD NEVER BE CONTROLLING YOU! IN SUCH A CASE; YOU'VE LOST IT!

THE HOUSE THAT YOU LIVE IN DOES NOT RESIDE INSIDE OF YOUR HOME, BUT RATHER THE HOME IS ESTAB-LISHED INSIDE OF THE HOUSE. THIS IS THE VERY REASON THAT YOU COULD LOSE A HOUSE, OR SELL THE HOUSE AND PURCHASE ANOTHER HOUSE AND CALL IT YOUR HOME AND PEACEFULLY LIVE IN THE HOUSE.

WHENEVER YOU LEAVE THE HOUSE OF YOUR EARTHEN TABERNACLE, YOUR MIND WILL TRAVEL WITH YOU TO REIGN IN ETERNITY. DON'T PLAN ON LEAVING YOUR MIND BEHIND, AS IF YOU ARE CHANGING THE ADDRESS OF THE MIND THAT YOU PLANNED TO LIVE IN.

THE MIND OF CHRIST, MUST BE ALLOWED TO INFIL-TRATE THE PRESENT MIND THAT YOU ALREADY HAVE.

WHEN WE LOSE OUR MINDS FOR CHRIST OR GIVE UP THE WILL TO THINK THE WAY THAT WE CHOOSE, WE DO NOT BECOME MENTALLY INCOMPETENT OR DERANGED, WE SIMPLY ALLOW THE GOVERNING SYSTEM IN THE WORD OF GOD TO ENCOURAGE US TO BE CONTROLLED BY THE SPIRIT

OF THE LORD, ENABLING THE POWER OF THE HOLY GHOST TO BE MANIFESTED IN OUR CHOSEN SCHEME OF ACTIONS.

THE STREET IS A DEFINITE PATH TO GET TO YOUR HOUSE, EVEN AS THE MIND IS A DIRECT WAY TO GET TO YOUR HEART. IF YOU WERE EXPECTING A VISITOR TO COME TO YOUR HOUSE, YOU WOULD NOT GIVE THEM THE _wrong street address,_ UNLESS YOU DID NOT INTEND FOR THEM TO ACTUALLY GET TO YOUR HOUSE.

SO, AS A RESULT OF TRULY EXPECTING THEIR ARRIVAL, THOROUGH DIRECTIONS ARE GIVEN DIRECTLY TO YOUR STREET AND RIGHT UP TO THE FRONT DOOR OF YOUR HOME.

IN THE RUN OF A SINGLE DAY, MANY AUTOMOBILES, DELIVERY TRUCKS, AND MOVING VEHICLES DRIVE DOWN YOUR STREET, RIGHT PAST YOUR HOUSE. HOWEVER, ALL OF THE VEHICLES THAT ARE PASSING, DO NOT EVEN STOP AT YOUR HOUSE ADDRESS, BEING THAT YOUR HOME IS NOT EVEN THEIR INTENDED DESTINATION.

WHENEVER A VEHICLE DOES STOP AT YOUR HOUSE, IT IS YOUR DECISION WHETHER OR NOT YOU WILL EVEN ANSWER THE DOOR TO ALLOW A VISITOR TO ENTER YOUR HOME. UPON ENTERING YOUR HOME IT IS YET UP TO YOU WHETHER YOU WILL ALLOW THE VISITOR TO STAY AND VISIT FOR AN EXTENDED PERIOD OF TIME.

LIKEWISE, MANY THOUGHTS PASS THROUGH YOUR MIND DURING THE RUN OF THE DAY. HOWEVER, ALL THOUGHTS ARE NOT YOUR OWN, MEANING; THE THOUGHTS DIDN'T ORIGINATE FROM YOUR OWN WILLFUL DESIRE TO THINK ON THOSE THINGS. AFTER CLOSE EXAMINATION YOU WILL DISCOVER THAT THOSE SELF SAME THOUGHTS WERE NOT EVEN INTENDED FOR YOU, NOT AS A CHILD OF GOD!

NEVERTHELESS, ONLY THE THOUGHTS OF YOUR CHOOSING, ARE ALLOWED TO ENTER INTO THE DOORS OF YOUR OWN HEART TO STAY THERE, NO MATTER OF THE ORIGIN. UPON REALIZING THAT YOU HAVE ALLOWED CERTAIN THOUGHTS TO ENTER INTO YOUR OWN THOUGHT PROCESS, IT IS UP TO YOU TO RID YOURSELF OF THE ILL NATURED

AND IMPROPER CONDESCENDING THOUGHTS OF SIN.

THOUGHTS ARE OFTEN LIKE *burglars* AND *thieves*, THEY HAVE AN ATTENDANCE TO BREAK INTO THE THOUGHT PROCESS, SEEKING TO FIND ITS WAY INTO YOUR HEART DESIRING TO STEAL YOUR GOODS.

THERE MUST BE A GUARD ON DUTY AT ALL TIMES TO KEEP ALL INTRUDERS OUT. WHEN WAS THE LAST TIME YOU PUT A CHECK AT THE DOORWAY OF YOUR HEART?

FOR SOME, IT'S BEEN ABSOLUTELY TOO LONG AND FOR MANY OTHERS THE ANSWER WOULD DEFINITELY BE NEVER!

A FEW YEARS AGO THE YOUNG PEOPLE USED TO SAY; "YOU HAD BETTER CHECK YOURSELF, BEFORE YOU WRECK YOURSELF."

MANY PEOPLE HAVE PHYSICAL HEART PROBLEMS, BUT THERE ARE MANY OTHERS BY THE SCORES, WHO ACTUALLY HAVE SPIRITUAL HEART PROBLEMS RIGHT AT THE CENTER OF THEIR SOUL!

MANY PEOPLE OF THE BIBLE HAD A SPIRITUAL HEART PROBLEM, THE ONE WHO REMAINS FRESH ON MY MIND IS THE *shepherd boy* HIMSELF, KING DAVID. DAVID HAD A SPIRITUALLY SICKENING, HEART PROBLEM. DAVID ASKED GOD:

> *Create in me a clean heart, O God; and renew*
> *a right spirit within me.* PSALMS #51:10

BE HONEST WITH YOURSELF AND NEVER ALLOW YOURSELF TO THINK THAT YOU CAN FOOL GOD! IF YOU HAVE DISCOVERED YOU HAVE SPIRITUAL HEART TROUBLE, IT IS NOT ALRIGHT TO DO ABSOLUTELY NOTHING ABOUT WHAT YOU HAVE FOUND.

WHENEVER AN INDIVIDUAL NOTICES A PHYSICAL HEART PROBLEM, THEY DON'T HESITATE TO TAKE THEIR HEART PROBLEM TO THE DOCTOR, FOR GREAT FEAR OF DYING. IT IS EVEN MORE SERIOUS THAN DEATH ITSELF, TO HAVE A SPIRITUAL HEART CONDITION, KNOWING THAT WE

HAVE A SPIRITUAL DOCTOR IN THE PERSON OF JESUS CHRIST AND DO ABSOLUTELY NOTHING ABOUT THE CONDITIONS OF THE HEART.

> *The heart is deceitful above all things, and desperately wicked: who can know it?*
>
> JEREMIAH 17:9

WHEN GOD SAYS; "WHO CAN KNOW IT", HE IS REFERRING TO OTHERS ON THE OUTSIDE, LOOKING IN. YOU SHOULD KNOW YOUR OWN HEART; YOU CAN KNOW IT. DON'T MAKE EXCUSES FOR YOUR HEART, BECAUSE GOD ALREADY KNOWS.

> *I the Lord search the heart. I try the reins, even to give every man according to his ways, and according to the fruit of his doings.*
>
> JEREMIAH 17:10
>
> *If I regard iniquity in my heart, the Lord will not hear me; But verily God hath heard me; he hath attended to the voice of my prayer. Blessed be God, which hath not turned away my prayer, nor his mercy from me.* PSALMS # 66:18-20

Seriously Connected!

WHENEVER THE MOUTH OF AN INDIVIDUAL REALLY PRAYS, THEIR HEART PRAYS EVEN MORE SO THAN THE MOUTH. NO MATTER WHAT THE MOUTH IS SAYING, IT'S THE HEART THAT ACTUALLY GET GOD'S ATTENTION, TO MOVE HIM, IN RESPONSE TO OUR PRAYERS.

GOD SEARCHES THE HEART FIRST AND DEALS WITH OUR PRAYERS ACCORDINGLY. REMEMBER THE LORD WILL HAVE NO DEALINGS WITH COVERED UP WICKEDNESS, UNGODLINESS, AND NON-CONFESSED SINS IN THE HEART OF THE PERSON PRAYING.

HAVING NO DESIRE TO RID ONESELF OF SIN OR TO CHANGE THE HEART, WILL HINDER THE RESPONSE OF GOD. THE LORD DELIGHTS IN ANSWERING OUR PRAYERS, BUT THE LORD IS NOT FATTENING FROGS FOR SNAKES! IT JUST

DOESN'T MAKE SENSE FOR THE LORD TO BLESS US ONLY TO INCREASE THE KINGDOM OF SATAN.

WHAT IS YOUR REASON FOR PRAYING? HOW DO YOU STAND BEFORE GOD? JUST WHEN YOU THINK YOU'RE ENCLOSED AND UNDERCOVER, GOD SEES YOU.

"Stop Talking"

TOO MANY PEOPLE IN THE CHURCH ARE JUST LIKE THE NEW TESTAMENT PHARISEES AND THE JEWS, WHICH JESUS REBUKED, SIMPLY BECAUSE THEY WERE ALWAYS TALKING; THEY WOULD NEVER SHUT UP! THIS SORT OF MAKES YOU WONDER, WHO WERE THEY TRYING TO CONVINCE?

WHENEVER YOU RUN OUT OF HONEST THINGS TO SAY, JUST STOP TALKING. YOUR MOUTH IS A *doorway* OR A *gate,* THAT MUST BE CAREFULLY GUARDED, 24-7! SPIRITS OF ALL EVIL ORIGINS CAN BOTH COME IN AND GO OUT OF YOUR SPIRIT THROUGH YOUR MOUTH. OUT, IS WHERE YOU WANT THEM FOR SURE, BUT BE CAREFUL NOT TO ALLOW A WAY FOR THEM TO GET BACK INTO YOUR SPIRIT, BECAUSE OF YOUR MOUTH.

THE MOUTH CAN START A FIRE BURNING AND EVEN <u>ESCALATE</u> FIGHTS AND WARS. FAMILY FEUDS ARE BEGUN OVER HARSH WORDS SPOKEN! BE CAREFUL OF WHAT YOU SAY AND WHO YOU SAY IT TO, EVEN WHEN IT IS THE TRUTH.

FREQUENTLY SPEAKING OUT-OF-TURN, CAUSES PROBLEMS OF ALL SORTS. THE PROBLEM OF TALKING TOO MUCH USUALLY STEM FROM THE CHILDHOOD. THE FORMER GENERATIONS BELIEVED THAT CHILDREN WERE TO BE SEEN AND NOT HEARD. AS YOUNG CHILDREN, WE SHOULD HAVE BEEN TAUGHT THE PRINCIPLES OF COMMUNICATING DURING OUR EARLY CHILDHOOD DEVELOPMENT.

THE PARENTAL GUARDIANS AND DOMESTIC OVERSEERS SHOULD HAVE INSTILLED THE VALUES OF RESPECT, DURING A CONVERSATION, WITHIN US AS CHILDREN. AS AWESOME AS PETER FINALLY EMERGED TO BE, THERE WERE TIMES WHEN CHRIST REBUKED HIM FOR TALKING TOO

MUCH. ON THE MOUNTAIN OF TRANSFIGURATION, GOD, HIMSELF SPOKE OUT OF THE GLORY CLOUD AND SAID TO PETER;

This is my beloved son, hear ye him.

YOU EVER TEACH A SUNDAY SCHOOL CLASS OR CONDUCT A WORKSHOP SESSION AND REALLY COULDN'T GET THE POINT OVER BECAUSE SOMEONE ELSE WAS ALWAYS INTERRUPTING? HAVE YOU EVER BEEN IN A MEETING AND THE MATTERS AT HAND WERE NEVER DISCUSSED, BECAUSE SOMEONE JUST HAD TO HAVE THEIR SAY ABOUT UNRELATED ISSUES TO THE SUBJECT AT HAND?

I HAVE BEEN IN CHURCHES WHERE CERTAIN PEOPLE TALK RIGHT OUT IN THE MIDST OF THE SERVICE! IT'S A MATTER OF THE HEART WHEN THE MOUTH WON'T STOP TALKING. MANY PEOPLE DON'T KNOW THAT THE PROBLEM IS THEIR HEART AND NOT ONLY THEIR MOUTH.

There Goes That Heart!

I BELIEVE THAT ENLIGHTENING THE MIND, CONCERNING THE CONNECTION OF THE HEART AND THE MOUTH, IS EDUCATIONAL AND INFORMING; BUT LET'S EXPAND UPON THE SPIRITUAL ASPECT OF THE TOPIC, EVEN MORE IN DEPTH.

PEOPLE MAKE VOWS, BUT THEY ARE NOT TRULY DOING SO FROM THE HEART. I DON'T THINK WE REALLY UNDERSTAND THE SERIOUSNESS OF MAKING A VOW. THANK GOD FOR HIS GRACE AND FOR HIS MERCY, THAT HAS BEEN GIVEN IN SPITE OF OUR HAPHAZARDNESS.

DURING THE OLD TESTAMENT TIMES OF THE BIBLE, BREAKING VOWS WERE VERY DETRIMENTAL TO THE WELFARE OF AN INDIVIDUAL.

THERE WERE ACTUALLY TIMES WHEN ONES OWN LIFE DEPENDED UPON WHETHER OR NOT THEY WOULD HONOR THEIR VOWS. THEY RISKED LOSING THEIR POSSESSIONS, DEPENDING UPON THE VOWS MADE. A PROMISE IS JUST WHAT IT SAYS, IT IS A PROMISE AND THAT IS A THING OF THE MOUTH.

Now, a vow is a covenant and that is a thing of the heart. I was taught by many of the elders, pastors, and of course, my parents; "Your word is your bond." What you say out of your mouth ought to mean something.

God knows that I have made many efforts to live by this policy. My wife married me because, whatever I told her I would do; I did and I still do keep my word today. It means much to know that your word is dependable. However, I have heard people say from time to time; "That promises are made to be broken!"

Vows are made with the understanding that they are to be kept. Promises are made between people, with the intentions of being kept, however, the power to keep such promises is often hinged on another source other than the promissory.

The covenant vow is made between man and God, to which, the power is ingrained into the vow from the beginning, even before the covenant has been entered into!

Do you remember how that a man would give the woman the he proposed to marry a promise ring? The promise ring would not have the binding effect on the woman wearing it, as much as her wedding band would have on her, as soon as she was to be married.

The power of the promise was to set up the possibilities for permanently uniting the two in a ceremony to marry. Although many people now days seem to believe that promising to marry is enough, the promise to marry does not even bear the same weight as the marriage vows, in a court of law.

The promise ring would be worn for any period of time leading up to the day of the actual wedding where the two would enter into a much

MORE SERIOUS AND BINDING SET OF MARIAGE VOWS.

THE JESTATION PERIOD OF WEARING THE PROMISE RING, ALLOWED FOR AN OPPORTUNITY FOR EITHER PARTY TO CHANGE THEIR MINDS BEFORE ENTERING INTO CITING THE VOWS BEFORE GOD AND THEIR WITNESSES WHO MIGHT ATTEND THEIR WEDDING.

BACK IN THE DAYS OF WEARING THE PROMISE RINGS, DIVORSE WAS NOT HEARD OF AS OFTEN AS IT IS TODAY WHEREAS PEOPLE JUMP RIGHT TO THE WEDDING IN A HURRY FOR THE PURPOSE OF LEGALIZING THEIR BEDROOM ACTIVITIES!

LEGALIZED SEX DOES NOT MAKE A MARRIAGE IN THE SIGHT OF GOD. MARRIAGE IS SO MUCH MORE THAN THAT! ONLY WHEN THE VOWS ARE CITED IN THE FEAR OF GOD WITH THE INTENTIONS OF KEEPING THE VOWS, WILL THE PURPOSE FOR THE UNITING OF THE TWO INDIVIDUALS IN MARRIAGE EVEN BE REALISED.

THE WORD VOW- ACCORDING TO VINES BIBLE DICTIONARY DERIVES FROM TWO HEBREW WORDS, WHICH ARE DISTINCT IN MEANING.

> *1. Nadar'-* TO MAKE A PROMISE TO ANOTHER, WITH SANCTIONS FOR NOT COMPLETING THE PROMISE- (OR WITH PENALTIES). THIS MEANING WOULD BE EQUIVALENT TO A REVOLVING CREDIT ACCOUNT, WHERE A PROMISE IS MADE TO MAKE A PAYMENT ON A CERTAIN DATE, FOR AN INSTANCE TO THE LIKES OF A CREDIT CARD, A CAR PAYMENT OR EVEN A HOUSE NOTE. BEING IN DEFAULT OF MEETING THE PAYMENT DATE, THERE COULD BE, AND IN MOST CASES THERE WILL BE LATE CHARGES AND PENALTIES. EVEN FURTHER DEFAULT HAS RESULTING ACTIONS SUCH AS THE REPOSSESSION OF THE PROPERTY.

ON YOUR PART, YOU'VE LOST AND YOU'VE BEEN HUMILIATED, A JUDGMENT HAS BEEN ENTERED AGAINST YOU

ADVISING ANYONE INTERESTED IN ENTERING INTO A PROM-ISSORY CONTRACT WITH YOU, THAT PERHAPS THEY SHOULD NOT TRUST YOU TO KEEP YOUR WORD. REMEMBER WHEN YOU SIGN ON THE DOTTED LINE, YOUR SIGNATURE WOULD ONLY BE IN REPRESENTATION OF YOUR WORD.

ALSO, THIS DEFINITION COULD BE IN REFERENCE TO OBLIGATING ONES SELF TO PERFORM A PARTICULAR TASK, OR TO BE AT A PARTICULAR PLACE AT A CERTAIN TIME.

OF COURSE THE PROMISES ARE ALL MADE BETWEEN PEOPLE. IT DOESN'T TAKE A ROCKET SCIENTIST TO FIGURE OUT THAT PEOPLE WHO SAY, BUT DON'T DO WHAT THEY SAY, ARE LIARS. IF YOU DON'T MEAN IT, DON'T SAY IT.

THERE ARE SITUATIONS THAT WILL ARISE THAT WILL HINDER A PERSON FROM KEEPING THEIR WORD. THESE ARE THE TIMES WHEN IT IS A PERSON'S OWN RESPONSIBIL-ITY TO SAY SOMETHING ABOUT GETTING THE DEBT PAID AND MAINTAINING THE RESPECT OF THEIR WORD. DON'T DODGE, DUCK, OR HIDE, DISAPPEARING FOR A LONG PE-RIOD OF TIME, ALLOWING THE ULTIMATE DISGRACE TO YOUR NAME AND YOUR WORD.

EACH TIME YOUR BEHAVIOR IS AS SUCH, YOU PUT ANOTHER NAIL IN THE COFFIN OF YOUR CHARACTER. IN THE SIGHT OF MANY PEOPLE YOU'RE A DEAD ISSUE. GOD CAN GIVE YOUR NAME A RESURRECTION IF YOU BRING YOUR DEADLY LYING HEART AND TONGUE TO HIM AND REPENT. WHETHER YOU INTENDED TO OR NOT, YOU LIED. THAT'S RIGHT, FACE IT YOU'RE NOT INNOCENT, YOU LIED.

I HAVE HAD SITUATIONS TO REND THE VALIDITY FROM MY WORD. ALTHOUGH I COULD NOT HELP THE SITUATION, OR PREVENT IT FROM HAPPENING, I FELT POWERLESS AND ASHAMED.

PEOPLE WHO KNOW ME WILL TELL YOU THAT I DIDN'T RUN FROM THEM KNOWING THAT I OWED THEM MONEY. THEY DID NOT CARE TO HEAR THAT I COULD NOT MEET THE PROMISE OF MY OBLIGATION, BUT I TOLD THEM ANY-WAY. PEOPLE WILL NOT ALWAYS WANT TO ACCEPT YOUR

112

REASON OF EXPLANATION, BUT WHEN THEY DON'T, IT IS YOUR OBLIGATION TO DO WHAT IS ACTUALLY RIGHT.

AS LONG AS YOU ARE REAL AND HONEST FROM YOUR HEART, GOD WILL GIVE YOU GRACE AND FAVOR WITH THE VERY PEOPLE THAT MATTER THE MOST. WHENEVER MY WORD COULD NOT BE HONORED BASED ON WHATEVER I MIGHT HAVE TOLD ANOTHER INDIVIDUAL, I WAS ABLE TO PAY THE DEBT THE VERY NEXT DAY OR AT LEAST SOON AFTERWARDS.

REMEMBER THAT IF YOU OWE A DEBT, IT IS YOUR OBLIGATION TO REPAY THE DEBT. PAY IT BACK! AS SOON AS YOU ARE ABLE TO REPAY THE DEBT, GET IT DONE QUICKLY, SO THAT YOU WILL BE ABLE TO GO ON FORWARD.

PEOPLE WILL OFTEN JUDGE YOUR WORD HARSHLY, PRE-ALLEGEDLY THEY SEEM TO ALWAYS ASSUME THAT YOU ARE NOT BEING TRUTHFUL WITH THEM CONCERNING YOUR FINANCIAL STATUS. THIS IS VERY STRESSFUL, BUT DON'T QUIT BEING TRUTHFUL AND REACHING FOR THE DAY TO REPAY THEM WHAT YOU OWE. CONTINUE TO BE HONORABLE OF YOUR WORD. KEEP ON STRIVING TO DO WHAT YOU HAVE SAID THAT YOU WOULD DO, THE LORD WILL HELP YOU.

AFTER YOU HAVE DONE WHAT YOU HAVE SAID, AT LEAST PEOPLE WILL KNOW THAT YOUR INTEGRITY IS IN TACT, EVEN IF THEY DON'T RESPECT THE FACT THAT YOU CAME THROUGH. TO SAY; "WELL THEY DON'T BELIEVE ME ANYWAY AND THEY REALLY DON'T NEED THE MONEY BACK, BECAUSE THEY WILL NEVER MISS IT", IS NO REASON TO DISHONOR YOUR OWN WORD.

DON'T DREAD BEING FINANCIALLY DEPLETED FOR A LITTLE WHILE, WHENEVER YOU HAVE PAID BACK A LOAN. BE GLAD YOU WERE ABLE TO PAY BACK THE LOAN. PEOPLE DREAD PAYING DEBTS BACK! THE REAL DREAD SHOULD BE, NOT BEING ABLE TO PAY, I'VE BEEN THERE!

THANK GOD, NOW "I'M" FREE.

DON'T EVER MAKE YOUR CHILDREN PROMISES THAT

YOU DON'T INTEND TO KEEP, THEY WILL NOT FORGET. WHENEVER TRUST IS DAMAGED OR LOST BETWEEN A CHILD AND THE PARENT, IT IS ALMOST IMPOSSIBLE TO EVER RE-GAIN THE TRUST. WHATEVER YOU ARE, WHATEVER YOU PUT IN THEM, THEY BECOME JUST AS YOU ARE.

IF YOUR WAY IS WRONG, YOUR CHILD MAY BE BLINDED TO THE POINT THAT THEY WON'T REALLY BE ABLE TO SEE YOU AS WRONG AS YOU VERY WELL MAY BE. ALWAYS BE MINDFUL OF THE FACT THAT YOU ARE SHAPING THE FUTUR-ISTIC MATTERS OF THE HEARTS OF YOUR CHILDREN.

2. _Neder_-VOTIVE OFFERING (VOTIVE - ACCORD-ING TO THE WORLD BOOK DICTIONARY MEANS PROMISED BY VOW). THERE ARE TWO BASIC FORMS, THE CONDITIONAL, AND THE UNCON-DITIONAL. THE UNCONDITIONAL IS AN OATH WHERE SOMEONE BINDS THEMSELVES WITHOUT EXPECTING ANYTHING IN RETURN. THE CON-DITIONAL VOW GENERALLY HAD A PRECEDING CLAUSE, BEFORE THE OATH, GIVING THE CON-DITIONS, WHICH HAD TO COME TO PASS BEFORE THE VOW BECAME VALID.

When thou vowest a vow unto God, defer not to pay it; for he hath no pleasure in fools: pay that which thou hast vowed. Better is it that thou shouldest not vow, than that thou shouldest vow and not pay.

ECCLESIASTES 5:4-5

 THIS PARTICULAR FORM OF VOW IS DEFINITELY NOT LOOKED UPON IN THIS DISPENSATION OF GRACE AS SERI-OUSLY AS THEY USED TO BE LOOKED UPON, BUT EVERYDAY THERE ARE VOWS YET BEING MADE.

THE PROBLEM HERE STEMS FROM GOD'S GRACE BE-ING TAKEN FOR GRANTED IN THAT PEOPLE FEEL THEY HAVE THE RIGHT TO CHANGE THEIR MIND AT THE DROP OF A HAT AND NEVER SUFFER ANY PENALTY OR LOSS FOR SUCH INSTA-BILITY.

YOU NEED TO BE CAUTIOUS OF THE VOW THAT YOU

ARE ENTERING TO KEEP IT WITH ALL DILIGENCE, AS IGNO-
RANCE IS NO EXCUSE FOR BREAKING THE LAWS OF GOD.
DON'T MAKE A VOW JUST TO BE SEEN FOR A FOOLISH GES-
TURE, YOUR HEART SHOULD CERTAINLY BE INVOLVED. VOWS
ARE NOT JUST VERBAL UTTERANCES, THEY ARE WILLFUL
CHAINS AND CONSENTING FETTERS OF THE HEART TO BIND
US TO OUR OWN WORD WITH A JOYFUL ATTITUDE.

Between You and God!

VOWS ARE BINDING CONTRACTS BETWEEN *God* AND
man, LIKE AS UNTO A MARRIAGE. I WOULD SUSPECT THAT
THE AVERAGE PERSON, AT LEAST KNEW THAT MARRIAGE IS A
VOW! DON'T SAY; "I DO" UNTIL YOU MEAN IT.

ALTHOUGH MEN AND WOMEN GET MARRIED AND LIVE
TOGETHER AS HUSBAND AND WIFE, THE VOW BETWEEN THE
TWO WAS ENTERED INTO BY GOD AND THE MAN, GOD AND
THE WOMAN, BY GOD AND THE TWO OF THEM, AND LASTLY
TO EACH OF THE TWO BEING ESPOUSED TO ONE ANOTHER.

NO MATTER HOW THE WORLD SEES IT, MARRIAGE IS
A GOD CONTRACT. GOD WILL ALWAYS HAVE THE FINAL SAY
ON THE SUBJECT OF MARRIAGE. MANY PERSONS HAVE BRO-
KEN THEIR COVENANT WITH GOD, SIMPLY BECAUSE, THEY
WERE NEVER AWARE OF THE FACTUAL MEANING OF A VOW,
DUE TO THE SERIOUSNESS CONCERNING THE BOND. UPON
THE ACT OF SEPARATING IN THE DIVORCE COURT, THE TWO
PEOPLE MAY HAVE BEEN DIVIDED BEFORE THE LAWFUL
COUNSEL OF MAN, BUT PERHAPS NEVER BEFORE GOD.

ACCEPTING THE HIGH CALLING OF GOD, IS A BIND-
ING CONTRACT BETWEEN GOD AND MAN TO WHICH WE
SAY; "YES LORD!, I'LL DO YOUR WILL", AND IT'S FOR LIFE.
THE TASK ITSELF MAY BE TEDIOUS AT TIMES, WHEREAS YOU
MAY FEEL LIKE THROWING IN THE TOWEL, HOWEVER MY
SUGGESTION TO YOU IS TO HAVE A STRONG SINCE OF, <u>STICK-
TO-IT'VE- NESS</u>.

SOME PEOPLE HAVE FELT THAT THE BEST THING TO
DO WAS TO THROW UP BOTH HANDS AND GIVE UP ON THE

TASK SIMPLY BECAUSE IT DID NOT APPEAR TO BE WORKING. ALTHOUGH YOU MAY HAVE DISCOVERED THAT PEOPLE IN GENERAL WILL NOT ALWAYS WORK WITH YOUR PROGRAM, ESPECIALLY CONCERNING THE MINISTRY, DON'T EVER GIVE UP!

YOUR TRUST IN GOD SHOULD BE STRONG ENOUGH TO OUT WAIT AND TO EVEN OUT WEIGH, THE OPPOSITION, BEING THAT GOD IS ON YOUR SIDE! THAT'S RIGHT YOU HAVE BEEN ORDAINED BY THE LORD TO DO WHATEVER IT IS THAT YOU ARE DOING, AND HERE'S WHY YOU SHOULD NEVER EVER QUIT!

> *And Jesus said unto him, no man, having put*
> *his hand to the plow, and looking back, is not*
> *fit for the kingdom of God.* ST. LUKE 9:62

THAT'S RIGHT, YOU AND I ARE IN FOR LIFE AND SHOULD BE IN IT TO WIN IT! YOU CANNOT JUST QUIT AT YOUR OWN CONVENIENCE, BECAUSE YOU ARE BOUND AND BONDED TO THE WORK OF THE LORD, EVEN WHEN YOU MAKE MISTAKES, AND FOR SOME REASON OR ANOTHER YOU MAY BE STILL STRUGGLING WITH YOUR OWN FLESH.

THE LORD HAS PUT A CHARGE TO YOU, SO RECEIVE IT WHOLE HEARTED SO THAT SPEAKING FORTH THE WORD OF GOD WILL NOT BE JUST A MOUTH OR A HEAD THING, BECAUSE YOU HAVE THE KNOWLEDGE.

THE MOUTH AND THE HEART MUST JOIN TOGETHER AND AGREE TO DYNAMICALLY EXPLODE IN THE SPIRIT REALM, BREAKING UP THE FALLOW GROUND IN THE HEARTS OF PEOPLE. THE SPIRIT OF GOD SHOULD COME LEAPING FORTH OUT OF YOUR MOUTH TO SET AN APPROVAL ON THE SPOKEN WORD AND BRING DELIVERANCE, HEALING, AND SALVATION.

LET'S LOOK AGAIN AT ANANIAS AND SAPPHIRA, PETER SAID;

> *Why have you allowed the Devil to fill your*
> *heart to lie to the Holy Ghost?*

ANANIAS DIDN'T SEEM TO REALIZE THAT WHEN HE

AND HIS WIFE AGREED TO SELL THEIR OWN POSSESSION, THEY ENTERED INTO A VOW WITH GOD. HOWEVER, PETER SAID TO THEM; "THE DEVIL HAS FILLED YOUR *heart!*" THE MEANING OF THE WORD FILLED IN THIS PARTICULAR CONTEXT, MEANS THAT THE DEVIL HAD CONTROLLED THEIR *hearts* TO CAUSE THEM TO LIE TO THE HOLY GHOST.

BE ADVISED ABOUT SPEAKING UP TOO QUICKLY TO SAY, I WILL. THE LORD HEARD YOU SPEAK UP VOLUNTARILY KNOWING WHETHER OR NOT YOU INTENDED TO CARRY OUT THE WORD OF YOUR VOW. PETER SAID TO ANANIAS;

"You did not lie to "man", but, to God!!"

DON'T BE AFRAID TO GO AHEAD AND MAKE GOD A VOW, AND KEEP THE VOW THAT YOU MAKE. FULFILL THE COMMITMENT AND THE CONDITIONS OF YOUR VOW.

YOUR RELATIONSHIP WITH GOD WILL INCREASE TO A POINT OF TRUST. I KNOW THAT GOD CAN BE TRUSTED, BUT CAN GOD TRUST YOU? WOULD THE LORD TESTIFY THAT HE COULD TRUST YOU?

> *Be not rash with thy mouth, and let not thine heart, be hasty to utter anything before God; for God is in heaven, and thou upon earth; therefore let thy words be few.*
>
> ECCLESIASTES 5:2

GOD KNOWS YOUR HEART. WHEN PRAISES GO UP, LET THEM COME UP FROM A TRUE HEART. WHEN YOU SING A SONG, OR STAND ON THE FLOOR TO USHER, DO IT WITH A PURE HEART. DON'T SPEAK THE WORD OF TRUTH ONLY TO SAY; *"There I said it"*, OR TO GET A PAT ON THE BACK.

> *Thy word have I hidden in mine heart, that I might not sin against thee.* PSALMS #119:11

IN ORDER TO APPEAL TO THE SIN PRESENT IN THE LIVES OF PEOPLE IN ATTENDANCE AT THE TIME OF SPEAKING, THE WORD OF GOD MUST BE IMMANENTLY FLOWING FROM THE FOUNTAIN OF OUR HEARTS. AN ABILITY TO HOLD ONTO THE ATTENTION SPANS OF THE PEOPLE WILL NOT

BRING CHANGE.

WHEN THE PEOPLE IN ATTENDANCE WILL DESIRE FOR YOU TO APPEAL TO THEIR PARTY SIDE, OR GIVE THEM A RECREATIONAL SHOWCASE AT THE MOST NONE PLAYFUL TIMES OF STANDING TO DECLARE THE GOSPEL OF GOD. GUARD YOUR HEART! DISREGARD THEIR ANTICS, AND THE PRESSURE FOR ENTERTAINMENT.

LISTEN TO THE APOSTLE PAUL

> *And my speech and my preaching was not with enticing words of mans wisdom, but demonstration of the spirit and power.*   I CORINTHIANS 2:4

THE APOSTLE PAUL GUARDED THE VERY FRONT DOOR OF HIS HEART!

People Guard Your Heart!!!

In Spoken Confidence*

> And God said, let there be light and there was ...
> GENESIS 1:3, A
>
> Jesus, said unto him, it is written...
> ST. MATTHEW 4:7, A

"You've Got To Know!"

MANY BELIEVERS ARE LIVING BENEATH THEIR PRIVILEGES, AS A RESULT OF NOT YET HAVEN DISCOVERED THE TREASURE IN THEIR OWN EARTHEN VESSELS. YOU CAN'T ALWAYS BE SURE THAT THOSE WHO SAY THAT THEY ARE TRUE BELIEVERS; ARE REALLY CONVINCED WITHIN THEMSELVES THAT THEY TRULY BELIEVE?

WHAT IS PROJECTED WHENEVER THEY SPEAK AS A CHILD OF THE MOST HIGH GOD, APPEAR TO BE MUCH LESS THAN CONFIDENCE. THOUGH WE ALL HAVE BEEN GIVEN THE ABILITY TO SPEAK AS A BONUS, JUST FOR COMING TO THE EARTH, IT SEEMS; WE ARE MORE EXCELLENTLY BLESSED WITH THE FATHERS MANNER OF SPEAKING FORTH

THE MOMENT WE ARE TRANSFORMED INTO THE IMAGE OF GOD'S DEAR SONS.

YOU MAY HAVE NEVER EVEN HEARD OF SUCH A PREEXISTING ENDOWMENT ON THE INSIDE OF YOU, BUT THIS IS REAL, THERE IS A REAL TREASURE HIDDEN WITHIN THE SPIRIT OF EVERY INDIVIDUAL. MANY PEOPLE WHO ARE LIVING, ON WHAT I WILL CALL, "THE WRONG SIDE OF THE TRUTH", HAVE DISCOVERED THIS TREASURE AND HAVE ATTEMPTED TO TAKE ADVANTAGE OF IT, THOUGH UNSUCCESSFUL!

THE MOST BENEFICIAL PART OF BEING SAVED, IS BEING TAUGHT THE LIVING BENEFITS AS A BELIEVER THAT ARE UPON YOU NOW SINCE YOU HAVE BEEN SAVED! ACCEPTING CHRIST IS ONLY THE INITIAL STEP TO BECOMING WHO GOD HAS ORDAINED YOU TO BE, BEFORE THE FOUNDATION OF THE WORLD.

NOW THAT YOU HAVE COME INTO THE REALITY OF THE TRUTH ABOUT CHRIST, YOU SHOULD HAVE AN EVEN GREATER DESIRE TO KNOW EVERYTHING THERE IS TO KNOW ABOUT THE KINGDOM OF THE LORD AND WHAT IT MEANS TO ACTUALLY BE A PART OF IT.

MANY HAVE NOT FULLY BELIEVED THE TRUTH OF THE GOSPEL AND THEY STILL STRUGGLE WITH THE ACTUALITY OF THEIR OWN SALVATION. THEY HAVE PROBLEMS EMBRACING THEIR CHANGE, SO THEY ARE AT A DISADVANTAGE TO STAND BEHIND ANYTHING THEY SAY THAT THEY BELIEVE.

RELATIVE TO CHRISTIANITY, THE SAID BELIEVERS ARE OFTEN WIELDING DULL AND SOMETIMES THE BROKEN BLADES OF THEIR SWORDS, WHICH IS THE LACK OF CONFIDENCE OR RATHER THE TOTAL ABSENCE OF CONFIDENCE ALL TOGETHER IN THE WRITTEN WORD OF GOD.

EVERY BELIEVER OUGHT TO KNOW THE BIBLE FOR THEMSELVES FROM COVER TO COVER, BEING SHARP ON BOTH SIDES OF THEIR BIBLICAL BLADES.

WE AS CHRISTIANS OFTEN LACK THE KNOWLEDGE

OF THE INHERITED CONFIDENCE THAT MANY WILL RE-CEIVE, WHEN FAILING TO BE TAUGHT! THEY MEANDER IN AND THROUGHOUT THE CHURCH AND IN THE SOCI-ETY, BEING BIBLICALLY ILLITERATE!

DULLNESS OF HEARING THE WORD OF GOD, AS IT RELATES TO LACKING INTEREST IN BEING TAUGHT THE WAYS OF GODLY LIVING, HAS CAUSED A GRAVE DEFICIENCY IN ANY POSSIBILITY OF SPIRITUALLY UNDERSTANDING A TRUE RELATIONSHIP BETWEEN GOD, WHO IS A SPIRIT AND THE NATURAL REALISTIC EXISTENCE OF MANKIND, FOR WHICH SUCH HINDRANCES CANNOT BUILD CONFI-DENCE!

MANY PEOPLE LEAP AT EVERY OPPORTUNITY TO EXERCISE THE RIGHT TO CHOOSE, BUT THEY FAIL TO TAKE ADVANTAGE OF THE RIGHT TO BELIEVE IN THE CHOICES THAT THEY HAVE MADE.

PEOPLE LACK THE ASSURANCE TO CONFIDE IN AN ABILITY TO LIVE IN A SOCIETY THAT TOTALLY DISALLOWS THE GENERAL AND PUBLIC TEACHINGS OF THE BIBLE AS A MANDATE FOR CLEAN LIVING, SAME AS WHAT IS SEEN DAILY IN AN ISLAMIC OR EVEN A JEWISH BELIEVING SO-CIETY.

THE UNGODLY PEOPLE OF THE WORLD ACTUALLY LAUGH AT THE PEOPLE OF THE CHURCH, WHENEVER IT COMES TO CONFIDENTLY KNOWING THAT THEY BELIEVE, WITHOUT A DOUBT, THAT JESUS IS THE SON OF GOD AND THAT HIS BLOOD HAS WASHED US FROM OUR SINS. THE WORLD HAS DISCOVERED THAT MOST PEOPLE OF THE CHURCH REALLY DON'T BELIEVE IN THEIR CONFESSIONS. 

WHAT WE SAY OUT OF MOUTHS HAS SO MUCH POWER, WHENEVER WE HAVE SPOKEN WHAT WE BELIEVE, BECAUSE WE SPEAK IT WITH THE ULTIMATE CONFIDENCE OF GOD WHO GAVE US THE ABILITY TO SPEAK LIKE HIM.

PEOPLE MAKE A LOT OF STATEMENTS AND DECLA-RATIONS DURING A WORSHIP SERVICE, BUT THEY THEM-SELVES NEVER SEEM TO RETURN TO THOSE THINGS SPO-

KEN OUT OF THEIR MOUTHS, DURING A CRISIS OUTSIDE OF THE FELLOWSHIP OF THE WORSHIPERS.

LET ME ASK YOU; WOULDN'T YOU RETURN TO A STATEMENT THAT YOU HAD MADE, KNOWING THAT YOU COULD RELY ON THE TRUTH IN THAT STATEMENT? DO YOU HAVE CONFIDENCE IN THE WORDS THAT YOU SPEAK?

WHAT KIND OF RESULTS DO YOU GET FROM THE SPOKEN WORDS OF YOUR MOUTH? CAN YOU SAY FOR CERTAIN, THAT YOU SPOKE TO SEE THE MANIFESTED RESULT OF WHATEVER YOU SPOKE OUT OF YOUR MOUTH, BECAUSE YOU BELIEVE IN THE WORD OF GOD, WITHOUT A DOUBT?

Always Believe In You!

THROUGHOUT THE EXPLORATION OF THE SCRIPTURES, WE KNOW THERE IS IMMEDIATE ACTION, IN RESPONSE, TO THE COMMAND OF GOD. WHENEVER GOD SAID; "LET THERE BE", WHATEVER HE COMMANDED CAME INTO EXISTENCE IMMEDIATELY AND IT YET REMAINS IN EXISTENCE TO THIS VERY DAY, AS IT ALWAYS WILL BE.

HAVE YOU REALIZED THE TOTAL ABSENCE TO ANY KIND OF A STRUGGLE OR RESISTANCE TO THE REQUEST OR TO THE COMMAND OF GOD?

GOD'S SPOKEN WORD IS SO ASSURED, THAT MANIFESTATIONS OF HIS SPOKEN WORDS CAME INTO EXISTENCE AND IMMEDIATELY BECAME PERMANENTLY AFFIXED AND IMMOVABLY DETERMINED TO REMAIN AS IT'S ORIGINAL CREATIVE REALIZATION.

IN OTHER WORDS, THE WORLD AND EVERYTHING THAT HAS BEEN PLACED UPON THE FACE OF THE EARTH ARE ONLY THE MANIFESTED RESULTS OF GOD'S OWN AWESOMELY <u>SPOKEN</u> THOUGHTS!!

WHATEVER GOD THOUGHT, HE SPOKE AND BECAUSE GOD SPOKE WHATEVER HE THOUGHT, EVERYTHING THAT WAS NOT, IMMEDIATELY BECAME AND BEGAN TO EXIST IN THIS COSMOS THAT WE NOW REFER TO

AS OUR WORLD.

Nothing Just Happened

TOO MANY PEOPLE HAVE TAKEN OFF WITH THE THEORY OF EVOLUTION, AS IF THERE WAS NO CREATIVE DESIGN AT WORK DURING THE CREATION OF THE WORLD. JUST LOOK AT YOURSELF IN THE MIRROR AND TAKE A LOOK OUT OF THE WINDOW AT THE WORLD AROUND YOU AND TELL ME THAT YOU HONESTLY BELIEVE THAT YOU ACTUALLY HAPPENED INTO EXISTENCE, WITHOUT ANY TYPE OF A SUPERNATURAL DESIGN IN MIND FOR THE SPECIFICATION OF THE MAKEUP OF YOUR TYPICAL BE-ING!

HAD NOT THERE BEEN ANY CREATIVE DESIGN AT WORK, EVERYONE WOULD PROBABLY LOOK EXACTLY ALIKE. THERE WOULD NOT HAVE BEEN DIVERSITIES OF PEOPLE OR SPECIFIC HAIR COLORS, TEXTURES, SKIN COLORS, PEOPLE'S HEIGHT, THEIR WEIGHT, OR EVEN THE SHAPE OF THEIR OWN INDIVIDUAL PHYSIQUE.

AGAIN I REPEAT, GOD SAID IT AND IT WAS SO!!!

THE AWESOME ABILITY TO SPEAK OUT INTO THE ATMOSPHERE, AND TO CALL THINGS INTO EXISTENCE, IS TO BE KNOWN AND UNDERSTOOD AS "EXOUSIA (EKS-ZOO-SEE-UH)", WHICH IS-**THE ABSOLUTE, AND UNRESTRICTED POWER OF GOD.**

GOD NEVER EXPECTED ANY RESISTANCE, NOR DOES HE EVER EXPECT A CHANGE OR ANY TYPE OF A REVERSAL TO ANYTHING HE HAS EVER SPOKEN. WHATEVER HE SAID OUT OF HIS MOUTH BACK THEN, IT STILL IS TODAY. THAT'S POWER! JESUS KNEW THAT THE WRITTEN WORD IS ETERNALLY AFFIXED. THEREFORE HE SAID WITH UN-IMAGINABLE CONFIDENCE; "IT IS WRITTEN."

In the beginning was the word, and the word was with God, and the word was God. The same was in the beginning with God. All things were made by him: and without him was not anything made

*that was made. In him was life; and the life was
the light of men. And the light shinneth in darkness and the darkness comprehended it not.*

St. John 1:1-5

Jesus knew the power of the pronounced declaration of the written word of God, because he "<u>is</u>" the prophetic manifestation of the spoken word of God, who came in the flesh. Knowing who He is, had great bearing and unrelenting power on whatever He said. There is no mistake or insecurity involved, whenever Jesus speaks. Action is the immediately result of Jesus speaking! Action is the command no matter what He speaks; It Is So!

Being insecure, because we don't know who we are, prevents us from knowing what to expect in terms of a manifestation. But, I can assure you, that whenever you know who you are and are sure of the things we desire, doubting nothing when you speak, we will experience power in action.

*God Is Sure

We serve an awesome God who is most confident in Himself! There is no searching of His understanding, because God does not ever need to search for anything. God already knows everything there is to know and all things are at His disposal. He knows more about forgetting, than you and I will ever know about learning and remembering whatever we have learned.

God cannot help being who He is, He has absolutely no choice in the matter at all, because there is absolutely no one else that He could ever be, other than God! God is so great at being who

124

HE IS, BECAUSE THERE IS NO ONE ELSE IN THE ENTIRE EXISTENCE OF THE UNIVERSAL COSMOS WHO COULD EVER BE WHO HE IS.

THERE IS NOT ANOTHER NOWHERE OR ANOTHER EVERYWHERE ALL OF THE TIME PLACE TO CALL ETERNITY POWERFUL ENOUGH TO PRODUCE ANOTHER MASTERFUL COSMO-CENTRIC, EVERLASTING SPIRIT TO CALL IT GOD!

OUR GOD; KNOWS THE BEGINNING TO THE END, BUT EVEN MORE EXCELLENTLY, HE KNOWS THE FINAL STOPPING POINT OF EVERY END, BACK UP, TO THE VERY STARTING POINT OF ALL BEGINNINGS. HE IS AN EVER UNCHANGING GOD, IN ALL MANNER OF HIS BEING. GOD, AND EVERYTHING ABOUT HIM, EVERYTHING HE SAID, AND EVERYTHING HE HAS DONE, IS <u>IMMUTABLE</u>- MEANING NOT CAPABLE OF EVER CHANGING OR SUBJECT TO BEING CHANGED AT ANYTIME!

IN CHAPTER ONE, WE DISCUSSED THE BIBLICAL FACT THAT GOD MADE MAN'S MOUTH, THEREFORE, **I AM MORE LIKE GOD THAN I THOUGHT**, BEING MADE LIKE AS UNTO HIS OWN LIKENESS AND IN HIS OWN IMAGE! THIS PRECIOUS GIFT OF SPEAKING IS CERTAINLY MORE THAN MEETS THE HEARING OF ALL LISTENING EARS.

Hear Him!

EVERYBODY CAN HEAR GOD SPEAK INDIVIDUALLY, IF THEY ARE WILLING TO TUNE IN TO HIM THROUGH PRAYER. THERE USE TO BE A TELEVISION ADVERTISE- MENT ON THE BROADCASTING NETWORK, THAT USED TO SAY; "WHEN E. F. HUTTON SPEAKS, <u>EVERYBODY LISTENS</u>." 

HEARING DOES NOT LIE SOLELY AND COMPLETELY WITHIN THE WORKING ORDER OF THE HEARING CANAL IN THE EARS OF THE HEARER. A DEAF MUTE CAN HEAR THE LORD SPEAKING TO THEM, EVEN IF IT IS THEIR DEAF- NESS THAT GOD HAS TO SPEAK TO INITIALLY.

RELATIVE TO THE DIVINE ORDER OF GOD; THE MOUTH HAS GOT TO BE MORE POWERFUL THAN THE EAR.

FAITH COMETH BY HEARING ACCORDING TO HEBREWS 10:, BUT THE WORD OF GOD HAS GOT TO SOUND OUT OF THE MOUTHS OF THE CHOSEN PEOPLE OF GOD BEFORE AND EAR CAN HEAR.

THERE ARE MULTIPLE HINDRANCES AND A MULTIPLICITY OF REASONS WHY PEOPLE DO NOT ALWAYS HEAR WHAT IS SPOKEN, RIGHT IN THE GENERAL VICINITY OF THEIR OWN HEARING RANGE. MANY PEOPLE DON'T HEAR SPIRITUAL THINGS BECAUSE THE CAN'T!

ATMOSPHERIC, SPIRITUALLY ILL-FATED CONDITIONS, JUST ABOVE OUR HEADS IN THE SPIRIT REALM, PRODUCE MAJOR DISTURBANCES IN AREAS OF OUR SENSITIVITY, WHICH STEAL OUR ATTENTIVENESS AND SEVERELY DAMAGE OUR ABILITY TO HEAR. WE AS PEOPLE, HAVE OFTEN LEARNED THE BEHAVIOR OF FAILING TO PAY ATTENTION TO WHAT IS BEING SAID, NO MATTER WHO IS SPEAKING.

THE FOREMOST AND THE UTTERMOST HINDRANCE TO HEARING, IS TO LACK A DESIRE TO HEAR. THE POWER UNLEASHED BY SUCH FORWARD REJECTION AND EVEN OUTRIGHT REFUSAL, IS IMMEASURABLE. WE ARE LOOKING AT THE DANGER OF REFUSAL, WITHOUT EXAMINATION TO WHAT IS BEING REFUSED.

CAREFUL CONSIDERATION IS EXTREMELY NECESSARY IN REFERENCE TO HEARING THE VOICE OF GOD, BECAUSE HE HAS THE ANSWERS AND THE SOLUTIONS TO EVERY PROBLEM, THE SUM TOTAL TO EVERY EQUATION, HE KNOWS THE ENTIRE BREAKDOWN TO ALL CHEMICAL COMPOSITIONS, HE KNOWS THE DEPTHS AND TEMPERATURE OF HELL AND HE KNOWS THE HEIGHT AND EXACT LOCATION OF HEAVEN. WHAT'S MORE IMPORTANT IS THE FACT THAT GOD KNOWS WHETHER OR NOT YOU'LL BE THERE IN HEAVEN OR IN HELL.

I KNOW THAT I HAVE LEFT OFF LIGHT-YEARS OF THINGS, TO WHICH GOD KNOWS. MY MIND IS ONLY *finite,* AS IS YOURS, WHENEVER IT RELATES TO THE KNOWL-

EDGE OF GOD'S TOTAL EXISTENCE. THERE IS ONLY SO MUCH OF THE KNOWLEDGE OF AN <u>INFINITE</u> GOD, THAT I CAN OBTAIN! OUR MINDS STOP AT A CERTAIN POINT, WHILE GOD'S EXISTENCE CONTINUES ON IN THE NEVER-ENDING REIGN OF ETERNITY!

MOST PEOPLE ALLOW MANY DIVERSE FORMS OF FEAR TO HINDER THEM FROM HEARING THE VOICE OF THE ALMIGHTY GOD. SOME PEOPLE, BECOME ANXIOUSLY HYPERACTIVE, WHICH IS A VERY SERIOUS FORM OF FEAR, TO HINDER THEM FROM HEARING. THEY JUST CONTINU-OUSLY MOVE AHEAD OF GOD'S DIRECTION AND INSTRUC-TION, ANXIOUSLY ANTICIPATING THE NEXT MOVE! THEY CAN'T WAIT!

CAN I TELL YOU, THAT WAITING IS NOT PATIENCE, AND PATIENCE IN ITSELF IS NOT WAITING! WAITING IS WAITING! IT IS LONGING FROM ONE TIME TO ANOTHER, FROM ONE EVENT TO ANOTHER, OR RATHER EVEN EXIST-ING FROM ONE PERIOD INTO THE NEXT, ETC. BUT, PA-TIENCE IS THE MANNER IN WHICH WE CONDUCT OUR-SELVES WHILE WE WAIT. YOU CAN WAIT IMPATIENTLY!

I COULD GO ON TO CONTINUE NAMING THE DIF-FERENT HINDRANCES, NAME BY NAME, BUT I WILL RE-SOLVE IN SAYING THAT ALL OF THE WORKS OF THE FLESH, THAT ARE AGAINST GOD, CAN HINDER YOU FROM HEAR-ING THE VOICE OF GOD.

MOST IMPORTANTLY, THE LACK OR RATHER THE ABSENCE OF FAITH AT THE TIME AND POINT OF HEAR-ING, WILL MOST SEVERELY HOLD BACK THE ABILITY TO HEAR GOD. AN ATTEMPT TO LISTEN WITH YOUR NATU-RAL SENSE OF HEARING CAN HINDER YOUR ABILITY TO HEAR GOD, AS THERE IS NOTHING NATURAL ABOUT GOD SPEAKING AT ALL, GOD IS A SPIRIT! 

YOU CAN BE IN THE MIDST OF A NUCLEAR EXPLO-SION AND HEAR THE VOICE OF GOD. GOD SPEAKS IN A WAY THAT NO ONE ELSE, POSSIBLY CAN SPEAK! ONLY GOD CAN SPEAK TO THE INNER-MAN, AS HE IS THE ONLY

ONE WHO KNOWS WHERE THE SPIRIT-MAN IS AND HOW TO SPEAK TO HIM. HAVE YOU HEARD HIM SPEAK TO YOUR HEART LATELY?

God Speaks By His Spirit!

THE SPIRIT OF GOD CAN SPEAK STRAIGHT THROUGH A STONY HEART AND PRICK THE VERY SOUL OF MAN.

THE SPOKEN WORD OF GOD IS SO POWERFUL THAT EVEN THE DEAD CAN HEAR HIM SPEAK, UNDER THE MANY TONS OF EARTH AND TOMBSTONES. I MEAN LITERALLY, DEAD MEN AND WOMEN CAN AND WILL HEAR THE VOICE OF GOD RIGHT NOW, IF HE CHOOSES TO SPEAK TO THEM AND ALLOW THEM TO HEAR HIS VOICE.

DO YOU REMEMBER LAZARUS (ST. JOHN, 11TH CHAPTER)? FOR EXACTLY FOUR DAYS, BEING DEAD IN HIS GRAVE ALREADY, LAZARUS HEARD THE VOICE OF THE SON OF GOD CALLING HIM FROM THE GRAVE.

PETER, IN THE BOOK OF THE ACTS, RAISED A DEAD WOMAN CALLED TABITHA, WHOSE ACTUAL NAME WAS DORCUS, FROM THE DEAD.

JESUS STOPPED A FUNERAL AND TOUCH THE COFFIN OF A DEAD YOUNG BOY AND THE LAD WAS RAISED INSTANTLY. THE FUNERAL WAS TURNED OUT IMMEDIATELY AND THE MOURNING OF THE PEOPLE WAS TURNED INTO LAUGHTER AND REJOICING, THERE WAS A RESURRECTION ON THE SPOT AND A REAL CELEBRATION.

OF COURSE WE OFTEN CELEBRATE WITH TEARS OF JOY SOMETIMES DURING THE HOME-GOING SERVICES OF OUR DEARLY DEPARTED BORN AGAIN LOVED ONES, ALTHOUGH WE ARE SADDENED BY THEIR DEPARTURE IN DEATH, IMAGINE CELEBRATING THEIR RESURRECTION FROM THE DEAD! <u>GLORY</u>! <u>HALLELUJAH</u>!

WHENEVER JESUS SPEAKS, THE <u>SPIRITUALLY</u> DEAD WHO ARE NOT YET BORN-AGAIN AND WASHED IN THE BLOOD OF JESUS, AND THE NATURALLY DEAD PEOPLE

WHO'S LIFELESS GROUNDED BODIES HAVE YIELDED ALL VITAL SIGNS OF LIFE, LIVE, BOTH NATURALLY AND SPIRITUALLY.

LET'S GO BACK TO THE OLD TESTAMENT FOR A MOMENT, TO A TIME WHEN GOD COMMANDED THE PROPHET EZEKIEL TO SPEAK TO THE DEAD, DRIED OUT AND SCATTERED BONES OF A ONCE GREAT ARMY. THE SCATTERED FRAMES REMAINED ON THE BATTLEFIELD, WHERE THEY HAD ALL GIVEN UP THE GHOST IN DEATH, DURING WAR.

THIS PLACE WE WILL ALWAYS REMEMBER AS THE VALLEY OF DRY BONES. THE LORD GOD COMMANDED THE PROPHET EZEKIEL SAYING; *"Son of man, can these bones live?"* GOD NEVER ASK QUESTIONS, TO WHICH HE DOES NOT HAVE THE ANSWER. LISTEN CAREFULLY TO THE CONVERSATION:

> *Ezekiel: I answered, O Lord God,*
> *though knowest.*
> *Lord God: Prophesy upon these bones,*
> *and say unto them, O ye dry bones, hear*
> *the word of the Lord. Thus saith the*
> *Lord God upon these bones. Behold I*
> *will cause breath to enter into you, and*
> *ye shall live.*

GOD BREATHES THE BREATH OF LIFE INTO THESE DRY BONES, WHERE THERE IS NOT EVEN LUNGS YET TO RECEIVE THE BREATH. IN OTHER WORDS, IT HAPPENED BEFORE ANYONE COULD VISIBLY FOCUS UPON THE MIRACULOUS WORK OF GOD!

THIS POWER IS UNSPEAKABLE TO THE SPIRITUALLY ILLITERATE AND TO THE UNFAITHFUL; THERE ARE NO WORDS TO DESCRIBE SUCH DISPLAY OF POWER OTHER THAN TO SAY; <u>GOD IS</u>! WHY NOT OBEY HIS COMMAND?

> *Lord God: And I will lay sinews upon*
> *you, and will bring up flesh upon you,*
> *and cover you with skin, and put breath*

within you, and ye shall live; and ye shall know that I am the Lord.

GOD SPOKE LIFE TO THESE DRIED OUT SCATTERED BONES. BUT GOD, IN HIS INFINITE WISDOM, BEING THE MAKER AND CREATOR OF MANKIND, SPOKE SECONDARILY TO THE PROPHET EZEKIEL, IN ESSENCE TO MAINTAIN, PROTECT, AND TO SUSTAIN THIS SECOND CHANCE, BREATH OF LIFE. WHEN GOD SPEAKS, HE SPEAKS SURE AND COMPLETE. HE WILL NEVER ALLOW YOU OR MYSELF TO HALF-DO ANYTHING.

DON'T EVER GO RUNNING OFF WITH A HALF MESSAGE, BECAUSE OF EXCITEMENT. SEEK THE LORD GOD, TO KNOW THAT YOU HAVE THE COMPLETE MESSAGE, IN AN EFFORT THAT HIS PURPOSE WILL BE FULFILLED. THE PROPHET EZEKIEL DID NOT HAVE TO ADD OR TAKE ANYTHING AWAY FROM THE WORD OF THE LORD, AS HE STATED; "LORD GOD YOU ONLY KNOW; ALWAYS (MY PARAPHRASING)", YES THE LORD DOES KNOW.

Ezekiel: So I prophesied as I was commanded; and, as I prophesied, there was a noise, and behold a shaking, and the bones came together, bone to his bone. And, when I beheld, lo the sinews and the flesh came up upon them, and the skin covered them above: But there was no breath in them. Then said he unto me;

Lord God: Prophesy unto the wind, prophesy son of man, and say to the wind, thus saith the Lord God; come from the four winds, O breath, and breathe upon these slain, that they may live.

Ezekiel: So I prophesied as he commanded me, and the breath came into them, and they lived, and stood upon

their feet, an exceeding great army.

Just Like He Said!

Always follow God until the task is completed. Don't stop now that you've said whatever you wanted to say, if God hadn't given you the command to say, your say is null and void anyway. Don't knight yourself the King of your own ministry, as if you called yourself to the ministry. The news report, to which you are delivering should only be the gospel of God!

Not only did the bones live, but they stood upon their feet with life and strength in them, to go on their way through life. They were able to once again find their way in life, to the point of production. When the prophet arrived at the scene there were scattered bones everywhere he looked. But when he left they were a clothed army equipped for battle once again as a result of the spoken word.

God knows what he is telling you, especially whenever it doesn't make since to you.

As He has spoken mysteries in past times, He still speaks mysteries to His people, who will listen in these present times. You, may not understand the mystery, but keep on speaking as He speaks. Don't deviate! The person or persons, to whom you are speaking to, most likely will understand clearly and vividly the mysterious words to which you are speaking for sure. You must understand that God is still God, and very much so!

The blessing itself only comes upon your act of obedience. God, is the mystery of mysteries Himself, there is nothing hidden from Him, but there are many unimaginable things still hid-

 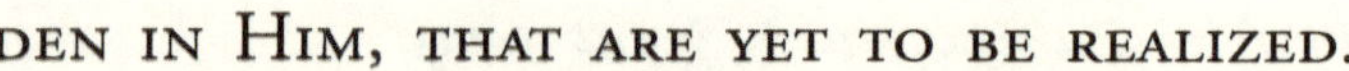

DEN IN HIM, THAT ARE YET TO BE REALIZED.

IF WE, UNDERSTOOD EVERY LITTLE DETAIL THERE IS TO KNOW ABOUT THE TOTAL CONSISTENCY IN THE MAKEUP OF THE PERSONALITY OF GOD, HE WOULDN'T BE GOD! BUT! HE IS GOD!

GOD KNOWS THOSE OF US WHO LIVE, HE KNOWS EVERYONE IN THE GRAVE ALREADY AND HE KNOWS ALL OF THOSE PERSONS WHO ARE YET TO BE BORN.

> *For as many as are led by the spirit of God, they*
> *are the sons of God.* ROMANS 8:14

AS WE ARE LED BY THE SPIRIT, WE BECOME THE SONS OF GOD, THAT'S RIGHT, EVEN THOUGH YOU MAY BE A WOMAN. IN OTHER WORDS, YOU AND I HAVE BEEN ACCEPTED AND RECEIVED OF GOD. HE'S OUR FATHER! HERE, YOU SEE ANOTHER MYSTERY UNFOLD.

TO BE CALLED A SON OF GOD, HAS ABSOLUTELY NOTHING TO DO WITH YOUR GENDER. HOWEVER, IT HAS EVERYTHING TO DO WITH BEING ABLE TO GIVE CHRIST TO THE MASSES OF THE PEOPLE OF THE EARTH, BY WAY OF PENETRATING THE CENTER CORE OF THE HEART OF EVERY INDIVIDUAL THAT WILL RECEIVE FROM US. UNLESS YOU BECOME A SON, YOU WILL NEVER BE QUALIFIED TO TRULY GIVE CHRIST.

PERHAPS IF YOU AND I WERE TO BEGIN TO TALK GENDER, WE WOULD BOTH ARRIVE AT THE POINT OF UN-DERSTANDING THAT EVERY MALE HAS BEEN CREATED TO  GIVE, BY MEANS OF ERECT PENETRATION THROUGH THE AID OF THEIR REPRODUCTIVE ORGANS.

THE SPIRIT AND THE NATURAL ARE PARALLEL IN TRUTH, IN THAT WE MUST TAKE AN ERECT POSTURE IN OUR FAITH IN GOD AND RIGHTEOUS LIVING, IN AN EF-FORT TO PENETRATE THE HEARTS OF MANKIND ALL OVER THE FACE OF THE EARTH, BECOMING REPRODUCTIVE IN THE SPIRIT.

SO NOW, LIKE FATHER LIKE SON, (THIS IS AWE-

SOME), WE SPEAK AS HE HAS SPOKEN AND IT WORKS.

DON'T GO OFF THE DEEP END, IN YOUR UNDER-STANDING. NEITHER, CAN YOU OR MYSELF SPEAK A WORLD INTO EXISTENCE AND NEITHER CAN YOU OR MY-SELF SPEAK TO ABSOLUTELY NOTHING AND CREATE SOME-THING. THERE ARE SPEAKING LIMITATIONS ESTABLISHED ACCORDING TO THE WORD OF GOD.

THE ACTUALITY OF OUR GIFT IS AS SUCH: WE HAVE WHAT IS TO BE UNDERSTOOD AS THE CREATIVE RELEASE, IN OUR SPOKEN WORDS. THE WORLD HAS ALREADY BEEN CREATED. THERE IS NO NEED TO TRY AND DO ALL OVER AGAIN WHAT GOD HAS DONE.

THE ANOINTED PURPOSE FOR SPEAKING FORTH IS TO EXPERIENCE THE CREATIVE RELEASE IN THE SPIRIT REALM SO THAT THE THINGS THAT ARE ALREADY GIVEN TO US IN THE SPIRIT CAN BE MANIFESTED IN THE REALM OF THE NATURAL. THAT'S JUST LIKE GOD!

GOD HAS ALREADY PROVIDED FOR US BY HIS GRACE, EVEN THOUGH WE MAY NOT KNOW THAT THOSE THINGS HAVE BEEN DEPOSITED INTO THE REALM OF OUR ABILITY TO RECEIVE FROM THE LORD, WE HAVE THE DI-VINE PRECEDENCE THROUGH FAITH IN THE SON OF GOD TO COMMAND THE MANIFESTED EVIDENCE OF THINGS TO LITERALLY COME LEAPING INTO OUR OWN PRESENCE AND IF WE CONTINUE TO BELIEVE AND NEVER DOUBT, THEY WILL SOON APPEAR.

YOU SEE, WE CAN EVEN DICTATE TO THE OUTCOME OF OUR DESTINIES. WE HAVE POWER OVER THE OUT-COME, IN OTHER WORDS, WE MUST ONLY BELIEVE AND SPEAK THE WORD OF GOD. TAKE AUTHORITY OVER THE PRESENT CIRCUMSTANCES, RIGHT IN THE MIDDLE OF THE SITUATIONS.

> *For verily (truly) I say unto you, if ye have faith*
> *as a grain of mustardseed, ye shall say unto this*
> *mountain remove hence to yonder place; and it*
> *shall be removed; and nothing shall be impos-*

sible unto you.　　　　　St. Matthew 17:20

In The Word Of God*

There are many scripture references that are relative to speaking faith-filled words, to which Jesus instructed, like this scripture reference. I'm here, thank God; to let you know this principle really works. You won't experience the awesome direct power of command through speaking faithfully, until you go ahead and open your mouth and speak!

Now understand, that these words must be positively faith filled words of *faithful reality*. The power of God won't manifest in fictitious circumstances.

For whatsoever is not of faith is sin.

Romans 14:23 C

See, unless you speak according to faith, you speak in error. At the most unsuspecting times you may be speaking sinfully, because of the continual lack of faith. God can do anything, but fail and He can heal anything, but doubt and unbelief.

Don't question the wisdom and judgment of God or ever allow yourself to second guess Him. We have been taught for years to be very sure that we have heard from God or rather to be sure that it is God.

This teaching has proven to be one of the greatest hindrances in the lives of many believers and an opportunity for most people to learn to waist an extreme amount of precious time concerning the things of the Lord.

How can we as creatures check the actual validity of the true character of our creator who made us?

GOD IS RIGHT THE FIRST TIME HE SPEAKS, AND HE NEVER SPEAKS IN ERROR, NEITHER DOES GOD EVER SPEAK AHEAD OF HIMSELF AT ANYTIME. SINCE TIME BEGAN, NEVER DID GOD EVER SAY SOMETHING AND COME BACK LATER AND SAY; "I MADE A MISTAKE, I DIDN'T MEAN THAT, I MEANT TO SAY SOMETHING ELSE." HE'S TOO PERFECT TO MAKE A MISTAKE! BELIEVE THAT!

YOU DON'T NEED TO WAIST TIME BEING RELUCTANT TO RECEIVE THE LORD; GOING OVER IN YOUR MIND AND MAKING SURE THAT IT'S GOD SPEAKING, BECAUSE ABSOLUTELY NO ONE ELSE SPEAKS LIKE GOD! THE DEVIL CAN DUPLICATE OR RATHER EVEN EMULATE MOST THINGS, BUT NEVER THE VOICE OF GOD! GOD GAVE SATAN THE VOICE HE HAS, AND DON'T YOU EVER FORGET THIS FACT!

YOU NEED ONLY TO BE SURE TO RECEIVE GOD, WHENEVER HE SPEAKS TO YOU AND GET IN A HURRY. ACCEPT WHAT HE TELLS YOU. GO WHEREVER HE SENDS YOU. DO WHATEVER HE TELLS YOU. SEE WHAT HE SHOWS YOU. HEAR WHATEVER HE SAYS AND SPEAK WHATEVER HE HAS SPOKEN.

> *He that hath an ear, let him hear what the spirit*
> *saith unto the church.*
> REVELATION 2:7,11,17,29, 3:6,13 & 22

SEE, YOU HAVE GOT TO FIRST AND FOREMOST HAVE AN EAR OR RATHER HAVE A GODLY DESIRE TO HEAR THE LORD GOD.

> *But as many as received him, to them gave he*
> *power to become the sons of God, even to them*
> *that believe on his name.* ST. JOHN 1:12

KNOW HIM AND SPEAK AS HE HAS SPOKEN, WITH POWER, AUTHORITY, AND EXPECTATION, WHICH WILL BRING YOUR DESIRABLE RESULTS. WE HAVE THIS ACCESS THROUGH JESUS CHRIST OUR LORD.

What Faith Is!

WHENEVER WE SPEAK WORDS OF FAITH, WHICH IS SPIRITUAL, IT HAS TO BE DONE WITH SPIRITUAL INTENTIONS, WHICH WILL ENABLE US TO OBTAIN SPIRITUAL RESULTS WITH NATURAL MANIFESTATIONS. OFTEN THE FOCUS IS NOT EVEN ON WHAT FAITH ACTUALLY IS, WE ARE USUALLY PREOCCUPIED TO THE POINT OF DISCOVERING WHAT FAITH CAN DO!

JESUS TAUGHT US THAT; IF WE HAD AS LITTLE AS THE FAITH OF A GRAIN OF MUSTARD SEED, THAT WE COULD ACTUALLY DO GREAT BIG THINGS! HOWEVER, OUR REAL PROBLEMS ARE NOT WITH THE ACQUISITION OF THE <u>TINY GRAIN</u> OF FAITH ITSELF, AS SO MANY CHRISTIANS SEEM TO READILY RECEIVE AND PERMANENTLY HOLD ONTO AS THEIR ONLY POSSESSION OF FAITH.

IT IS HOWEVER, THE FACT THAT WE FAIL TO KNOW WHAT IS ACTUALLY INGRAINED INTO THE TINY <u>GRAIN</u> AND TO CONFIDENTLY EMBRACE IT!!!

NATURALLY SPEAKING, WE MUST NEVER FORGET THE FACT, THAT WITHIN THE TINY LITTLE MUSTARD SEED, IS A GREAT BIG MUSTARD TREE, THAT IS TO DEVELOP OVER A PROCESS OF TIME. THE GREAT BIG MEGATON TREE, WAS ALREADY IMPUTED INTO THE TINY LITTLE ALMOST, INVISIBLE SEED.

 SO YOU SEE, IT IS NOT THE FACT THAT YOU CAN ACTUALLY DO SUPERNATURALLY POWERFUL THINGS; BUT, FAITH ALL BY ITSELF IS ACTUALLY SUPERNATURALLY POWERFUL BEFORE IT EVER EVEN FALLS TO THE EXCLUSIVE POSSESSION OF EVERY INDIVIDUAL BELIEVER.

ONCE THAT FAITH IS ACTUALLY IN YOUR HANDS, IT IS JUST WAITING TO EXPLODE INTO THE EXISTENCE OF THE MANY EXPECTED THINGS, WHEN IT IS APPLIED TO THE WORD OF GOD.

DON'T BE HINDERED BY WHAT YOU SEE IN THE NATURAL. FAITH TRANSCENDS ALL NATURAL BOUNDARIES,

WHENEVER IT HAS BEEN ACTIVATED BY TOTAL BELIEF AND TRUST IN GOD.

WHATEVER IS PRESENTLY BEFORE US, RIGHT NOW, DOES NOT NECESSARILY HAVE THE POWER TO DICTATE THE EXISTENCE OF WHATEVER WILL ALWAYS BE IN OUR FUTURE, IT HAS NO BEARING ON WHAT WILL BE IN RESPECT OF YOUR FAITH. YOU MUST SPEAK TO WHATEVER IT IS THAT YOU ACTUALLY EXPECT AND DESIRE ACCORDINGLY TO THE WILL OF GOD.

BEFORE WE TRULY SPEAK LIKE THE FATHER, WE MUST KNOW FIRSTLY, THAT GOD SPEAKS IN REFERENCE TO THE COMPLETENESS OR THE FINISHED PRODUCT OF A THING! GOD SPEAKS ALL OF THE WAY TO THE END OF THE THING!

See It Like God!

ALTHOUGH GOD SEES YOU RIGHT WHERE YOU ARE, THE REAL FOCUS OF HIS INVESTED INTEREST IS CENTERED UPON WHERE YOU HAVE BEEN PREDESTINED TO BE! EVEN THOUGH YOU OR SOMEONE ELSE THAT YOU MAY KNOW ARE ON A FAILING DECLINE AT THIS POINT OF YOUR LIFE, GOD DOES NOT SEE A FAILURE, RATHER HE SEES THE SUCCESSFUL INDIVIDUAL THAT HE HAS SENT TO THIS WORLD, FOR A PURPOSE THAT MAY IN FACT BE BEYOND YOUR COMPREHENSIVE SCOPE OF REASONING, MOMENTARILY.

HOW MANY TIMES HAVE YOU EVER HEARD THE WORDS; *"Who would have ever thought that you would have turned out the way you did?"*

THOSE INDIVIDUALS NEVER KNEW WHO YOU WERE PREDESTINED TO BECOME JUST SHORTLY, THEY WERE ONLY ABLE TO SEE YOU IN THE REALM OF RIGHT NOW, OR MOST LIKELY THEY WERE STUCK ON THE STUPIDITY OF YOUR PAST.

THE PERSON THAT IS SICK TODAY MAY VERY WELL

BE THE VERY DOCTOR OF TOMORROW! MANY, HABITUAL CRIMINALS, HAVE GONE ON TO BECOME LAW ENFORCEMENT OFFICERS AND MAJOR CRIMINAL DEFENDERS, AFTER HAVEN LIVED THE LIVES OF REAL LOSERS!!!

THE PICTURE IS ACTUALLY MUCH LARGER, IN TERMS OF THE SCOPE OF VISIBILITY ALLOWED BY THE AVERAGE INDIVIDUAL. THEY ARE RELUCTANT TO LOOK AND TO SEE BEYOND THEMSELVES. SO, FROM NOW ON, YOU SHOULD BEGIN RESPONDING TO THOSE SELF SAME TYPES OF STATEMENTS BY SAYING;

"Who would have ever thought that I <u>wouldn't have turned out this way</u>, God commanded me to turn out this way!"

ONLY WHEN, WE FAIL TO SPEAK TO WHATEVER IS PRESENTLY BEFORE US, CAN THOSE MOUNTAIN-LIKE THINGS THAT ARE INDEED STANDING IN OUR WAY, CONTINUE TO REMAIN AS THEY ARE.

BEGIN SPEAKING RIGHT NOW, SAY; 'I HAVE POWER IN JESUS NAME, AND I WILL SEE CHANGE NOW!"

COMMAND THE DEAD ISSUES OF YOUR LIFE THAT ARE NOT RELATIVE TO ANY SIN OR SINFUL PRACTICES; THAT ARE TRULY IN NEED OF BEING RESURRECTED, TO STAND UP AND LIVE! SPEAK AND EXPECT THE COMMANDED RESULTS IMMEDIATELY!

TELL THE TRESPASSING ENEMY TO BACK OFF AND EXPECT HIM TO DO JUST THAT! DON'T BE AFRAID AND DON'T TAKE DOWN. GO FORWARD AND DON'T YOU EVER BE FOUND BACKING UP!

In Spoken Confidence, I am the righteousness of Christ!

Say It Like The Father!!!

Anointed To Preach!!!

> But what saith it? The word is nigh thee, even in thy mouth, And in thy heart: that word of faith, which we preach. ROMANS 10:8
>
> The spirit of the Lord God is upon me; because the Lord hath anointed me to preach good tidings unto the meek; he hath sent me to bind up the brokenhearted, to proclaim liberty to the captives, and the opening of the prisons to them that are bound; To proclaim to the acceptable year of the Lord, and the day of vengeance of our God; to comfort all that mourn; To appoint unto them that mourn in Zion, to give unto them beauty for ashes, the oil of joy for mourning, the garment of praise for the spirit of heaviness; that they might be called trees of righteousness, the planting of the Lord, that he might be glorified. ISAIAH 61:1-3
>
> The spirit of the Lord is upon me, because he hath anointed me to preach the gospel to the poor; he hath sent me to heal the brokenhearted, to preach deliverance to the captives, and recovering of sight to the blind, to set at liberty them that are bruised, to preach the acceptable year of the Lord
>
> ST. LUKE 4:18-19

Say It Anyway! By The Anointing

THE VALIDATED ESTABLISHMENT OF AN ANOINTED ENDOWMENT, FOR THE PURPOSE OF PREACHING THE GOSPEL, IS TOTALLY RELIANT UPON THE FACT THAT AN INDIVIDUAL HAS BEEN DIVINELY CALLED TO PREACH.

OTHERS MAY IN FACT BE IMPRESSED TO OPERATE IN THE MINISTRY OF REACHING, BUT THERE IS A VERY DISTINCT DIFFERENCE BETWEEN THE TWO SCENARIOS OF PREACHING AND REACHING, ALTHOUGH WE MUST BE DETERMINED TO REACH WHEN WE PREACH.

YOU CANNOT BE CALLED FOR ANY OTHER PURPOSE, AND HAVE AN ANOINTING FOR PREACHING ON YOUR LIFE. GOD ANOINTS WHOMEVER HE CALLS AND ONLY WHATEVER HE CALLS ACCORDING TO HIS OWN PURPOSE.

Did He Call You???

IF THE LORD DID NOT CALL AND PREDESTINATE YOU BEFORE THE FOUNDATION OF THE WORLD, BEFORE YOU WERE FORMED IN THE BELLY OF YOUR MOTHER, YOU HAVE NOT BEEN CALLED OF GOD. [EPHESIANS 1:]

THE ANOINTING EMPOWERS YOUR ABILITY TO OPERATE WITHIN THE CONFINES OF THE CALL ITSELF, BUT THE ACTUAL CALL INITIATES THE GIVEN AUTHORITY FOR YOU TO STAND AS A PREACHER OF THE MOST HIGH, GOD BEFORE THE PEOPLE.

THE CALL TO PREACH THE GOSPEL, FIRSTLY, WILL NOT COME BY WAY OF A SECOND HAND INFORMANT! SOMEONE ELSE MAY IN FACT GIVE A CONFIRMATION OF THE FACT THAT YOU HAD ALREADY HEARD THE LORD CALLING YOU TO PREACH.

JUST BECAUSE HANDS WERE LAID UPON YOUR HEAD AND YOU WERE TOLD TO GO OUT AND TO PREACH THE GOSPEL, DID NOT MEAN THAT THE HAND OF THE LORD WAS ALSO UPON YOU INSTRUCTING YOU TO DO THE SAME.

There Is A Purpose!

THE ANOINTING IS FOR THE PURPOSE OF LEADING PEOPLE TO THE DECISION TO MAKE CHRIST THEIR SAVIOR AND THEIR LORD.

IF PREACHING IS NOT WHAT GOD WANTS IT TO BE, IT'S NOT PREACHING AT ALL.

TO ALLOW A BLUNDER IN THE PULPIT IS TO DANGEROUSLY TAMPER WITH THE FAITH OF INDIVIDUALS WHO ARE DEPENDING ON THE PREACHED WORD TO MAKE IT THROUGH THEIR DAILY LIVES.

> *How then shall they call on him whom they have not believed? And how shall they believe in him of whom they have not heard? And how shall they hear without a preacher? And how shall they preach, except they be sent? As it is written, how beautiful are the feet of them that preach the gospel of peace, and bring glad tidings of good things! So then faith cometh by hearing, and hearing by the word of God*
>
> ROMANS 10:14-15,17

LONG BEFORE YOU REALIZED IT, OR BEFORE ANYONE ELSE HEARD THAT YOU HAD DISCOVERED THE CALL UPON YOUR LIFE, YOU WERE ALREADY CALLED.

NOT THAT SOMEONE HAS TO VALIDATE THE CALL ON YOUR LIFE, BEFORE YOU WILL ACTUALLY BE QUALIFIED TO PREACH, BUT OTHERS KNOW THE MISTAKES THAT COME WITH PREACHING THAT CAN HELP YOU AND ENHANCE THE ABILITY THAT HAS INDEED BEEN PLACED ON YOUR LIFE.

Instructed; To Instruct, Taught; To Teach

THERE IS NOT A SINGLE INSTRUCTOR IN A LEARNING INSTITUTION OR A TEACHER IN A CLASSROOM, THAT HAS NOT BEEN INSTRUCTED OR TAUGHT, BEFORE THEY WERE QUALIFIED TO INSTRUCT OR TO TEACH ANYONE ELSE!

WHAT COULD YOU TEACH ANYONE, WHEN YOU'VE NEVER HAD ANY BIBLICAL TEACHING OR INSTRUCTIVE DE-

POSIT POURED INTO YOUR LIFE BY ANY CAPABLE BIBLE IN-STRUCTORS? WHAT COULD YOU PREACH, WITHOUT KNOW-ING THE WORD OF GOD?

PREACHING IS NOT ABOUT YOUR HEAD KNOWLEDGE OF THE WRITTEN WORD OF GOD ALONE, IT'S ABOUT YOUR RELATIONSHIP AND YOUR EXPERIENCE WITH GOD WHO CALLED YOU! GOD CAN'T USE YOU WITHOUT AN EXPERI-ENCE.

CAN YOU ACTUALLY LEAD WHERE YOU HAVE NEVER BEEN AND SUCCESSFULLY REACH THE INTENDED DESTINA-TION; IN SPITE OF THE HINDRANCES, STUMBLING BLOCKS, BENDS AND THE CURVES?

FOLLOWING THE SIGNS ON THE ROAD SIDE WOULD BE IMPOSSIBLE, IF NO ONE EVER TOLD YOU HOW TO FOL-LOW THE MEANING OF THE SIGNS.

What Are You Preaching?

PREACHING IS ALL ABOUT OBEDIENCE TO THE CALL OF GOD, TO RECEIVE AN ENDOWMENT FOR THE PURPOSE OF SENDING THE MESSAGE OF THE GOSPEL, RIGHT TO THE HEARTS OF THE LISTENER.

MANY PREACHERS HAVE ALLOWED THEMSELVES TO BECOME DESPONDENT, BECAUSE PEOPLE WHO SHOULD BE RESPONSIVE TO THEIR MESSAGE, SHOWED NO PARTICULAR INTEREST AT ALL.

THE POWER OF THE GOSPEL IS UNEQUIVOCALLY IM-MEASURABLY ABUNDANT IN ITS ENTIRETY, ALTHOUGH PEOPLE WILL RESPOND POSITIVELY OR NEGATIVELY TO PREACHING.

IN EFFORT FOR THE INGRAINED FACTS OF THE TRUTH OF CHRIST TO PRODUCE THE EXTREME LIFE CHANGING EF-FECTS, THE GOSPEL MUST BE PREACHED.

SOMEONE HAS GOT TO STAND IN THE GAP, TO DE-CLARE THE MESSAGE OF HOPE. BUT, IT CANNOT BE JUST ANYONE WHO DECIDES TO SAY A WORD TO EVERYONE THEY COME IN CONTACT WITH, ON THEIR OWN.

GOD WOULD NOT GO THROUGH ANY SELECTIVE PRO-

CESS TO APPOINT CERTAIN PERSONS TO CARRY THE WORD OF GOD, IF JUST ANYBODY COULD PREACH THE GOSPEL! THE PROPHET ISAIAH SAID;

"the spirit of the Lord is upon me."

ISAIAH KNEW THAT THE HAND OF THE LORD WAS UPON HIMSELF, BUT HE ALSO RECOGNIZED THE PURPOSE. ISAIAH SAID;

"for he hath anointed me to preach the gospel."

ARE WE SO DIFFERENT IN THIS LATTER GENERATION THAT WE NO LONGER NEED THE ANOINTING? DON'T BE FOOLISH OR LIGHT HEARTED CONCERNING THIS MATTER. YOU NEED AN ANOINTING TO PREACH THE GOSPEL!

"You need an unction, to function!"

GOD'S ENABLING GRACE, GIVES CONSENT FOR OUR LIVES TO BE EMPOWERED BY THE ANOINTING OF THE HOLY GHOST! JESUS CHRIST, REITERATED THE WORDS OF PROPHET ISAIAH IN THE BOOK OF ST. LUKE 4:18-19.

Note CAREFULLY: HE DID NOT SAY; THE THEOLOGI-CAL *Logistical* SEMINARIES OF THE BIBLE IS INSIDE OF ME FOR IT HAS TAUGHT ME HOW TO PREACH!

HE MADE A VERY DISTINCT REFERENCE TO THE SPIRIT OF THE LORD, BEING UPON HIMSELF. WE DO NEED THE LEARNING VERY DESPERATELY, BUT WE ALSO NEED THE BURNING TO PURIFY THE KNOWLEDGE THAT WE HAVE AC-QUIRED.

Note: JESUS CHRIST IS THE ANOINTING; SO WE OUR-SELVES, AS PREACHERS NEED A RELATIONSHIP WITH JESUS ALSO!

THE ANOINTING, IS ANOTHER WORLD OF KNOWL-EDGE ALTOGETHER BY IT'S SELF. PERHAPS MY REFERENCE IN DEFINITION MIGHT HELP YOUR UNDERSTANDING, IF YOU WERE TO SEE THE ANOINTING, JUST LIKE SO;

{AN-OINT-ING, -THE SPIRITUAL CONSISTENCY OF THE HIGHEST POWERFUL ENDOWMENT OF GOD'S TRUE HOLINESS EMPOWER-ING NATURAL MEN AND WOMEN ALIKE TO FLOW AT THE ALARM-ING RATE OF HIS AWESOME GODLINESS IN LOVE. IT IS FIRSTLY AN INTERNAL SPIRITUAL ENDOWMENT, THAT IS PLACED ON THE

INSIDE OF AN INDIVIDUAL BY THE HAND OF THE LORD; BY WHICH THE "ANOINTED" INDIVIDUAL WILL THEN BE ABLE TO REACH ALL THE WAY TO THE INSIDES OF OTHER NEEDING PERSONS, BY THE WILL OF THE SAME GOD WHO ANOINTED THEM!!!}

Is there no <u>balm</u> in Gilead; is there no physician there? Why then is not the health of the daughter of my people recovered?

JEREMIAH 8 :22

BALM- IS AN ANCIENT SALVE USED FOR MANY MEDICAL NEEDS. THIS "BALM", WOULD BE RUBBED ON THE SURFACE OF THE SKIN, TAKEN INTERNALLY, OR SOMETIMES USED FOR EMBALMING THE DEAD. (IT MAY BE PERCEIVED BOTH NATURALLY AND SPIRITUALLY, AS A MEDICINE FOR THE BODY OR FOR THE SIN SICK SOUL.)

MOST PEOPLE HAVE NEVER ASSOCIATED THE ANOINTING TO THE LIKENESS OF <u>AN</u> <u>OINTMENT</u>. OINTMENTS ARE USED TO SOOTHE OR TO HEAL, BEING MOSTLY TOPICAL SOLUTIONS SUCH AS CREAMS, LOTIONS, OILS, OR LIQUIDS CONTAINING MEDICINES.

CRACKING OR BREAKING SKIN CAN BE HEALED, SOOTHED AND SOFTENED SIMULTANEOUSLY UNDER THE CARE OF THE VERY SAME OINTMENT. HOWEVER, THERE IS A DIFFERENT OINTMENT TO FILL THE CARE OF EVERY NEED.

BY A VERY SIMILAR PRINCIPLE, MANY NEEDS ARE MET, WHILE PREACHING OF THE GOSPEL. THERE ARE LIKEWISE, DIVERSITIES OF ANOINTINGS AS PERTAINING TO THE SPIRITUAL GIFTS IMPARTED BY THE SELFSAME SPIRIT OF GOD FOR EVERY INDIVIDUAL, AS THERE IS NO TWO PEOPLE ALIKE.

AN OINTMENT IS APPLIED TO THE OUTER LAYER SKIN SURFACE; HOWEVER, THE ANOINTING GOES INTO THE LIFE OF AN INDIVIDUAL BY THE HOLY GHOST. THE OIL OF GOD AND THE WINE OF GOD IS POURED OUT BY HIS OWN HAND.

THE OIL REPRESENTS THAT FLOW OF THE SPIRIT OF GOD. IT DOESN'T FLOW UPWARDS, IT FLOWS DOWNWARDS FROM THE ANOINTED INDIVIDUAL TO THE RECEIVING PERSONS UNDER THE SOUND OF THEIR VOICES.

THE WINE REPRESENTS THE SURE MATURATION AND THE SATURATED ABILITY TO PRODUCE WHAT IS NEEDED AND

DESIRED FROM THE LORD.

GOD HAS ENTRUSTED MANY THINGS TO MANKIND BEGINNING AT THE GARDEN OF EDEN, UP UNTIL THIS PRESENT POINT AND TIME. HOWEVER, THE OIL OF GOD AND THE WINE, GOD WILL NOT ENTRUST THE DISTRIBUTIVE CARE TO ANY MAN ON THE FACE OF THE EARTH.

ANYONE AND EVERYONE IS CAPABLE OF PLACING AN OINTMENT OF SOME SORT UPON THE SKIN SURFACE OF AN INDIVIDUAL, HOWEVER, ONLY GOD CAN ANOINT.

SAMUEL, THE HIGH PRIEST OF GOD IS GIVEN THE TASK TO ANOINT TWO VERY DISTINCT INDIVIDUALS TO BE THE KING OVER ALL THE TRIBES OF ISRAEL AND JUDAH.

ANOINT MEANS TO POUR; SAMUEL POURED THE OIL OF THE ANOINTING OIL ON THE HEADS OF KINGS SAUL AND DAVID. AS SAMUEL POURED THE OIL ON EACH OF THEM, GOD POURED THE ANOINTING INTO EACH OF THEM.

You Don't Own The Anointing!

I HAVE ENCOUNTERED PEOPLE WHO PROJECT THEMSELVES AS IF THEY HAVE A <u>MONOPOLY</u> ON THE ANOINTING OF GOD. PERHAPS YOU HAVE ALSO ENCOUNTERED SUCH PEOPLE! IF THEY TRULY HAVE AN ANOINTING WORKING ON THE INSIDE OF THEMSELVES, THE LORD ANOINTED THAT INDIVIDUAL! ABSOLUTELY NO ONE HAS THE POWER TO ANOINT THEMSELVES.

NO ONE ON THE FACE OF THE EARTH HAS THE GIVEN ABILITY TO INFLUENCE GOD, AS PERTAINING TO WHETHER OR NOT ANOTHER INDIVIDUAL SHOULD OR SHOULDN'T BE ANOINTED!

ONLY GOD HAS THE ABILITY TO KNOW WHEREVER AND WHATEVER AN INDIVIDUAL IS PREVIOUSLY ORDAINED TO BE LATER ON IN THAT INDIVIDUAL'S LIFE.

> *And of the angels he saith, who maketh his angels spirits, and his ministers a flame of fire.*
>
> HEBREWS 1:7
>
> *For our God is a consuming fire*
>
> HEBREWS 12:29

Burning Within!

THE FIRE OF THE CALL TO PREACH IS AS A ROLLING FLOWING RIVER OF FIRE IN THE BOSOMS OF THE CHOSEN VESSELS OF THE LORD, THAT ESTABLISHES THE URGENCY TO MOTIVATE YOU. THE PROPHET JEREMIAH SAID; *"the word of God was like fire shut up in his bones."*

THE ONLY RELIEF FOR BIBLE-BURN OR RATHER THE WORD-OF-GOD BURNING ON THE INSIDE OF YOUR BELLY, IS TO OPEN YOUR MOUTH AND LET THE WORD COME OUT!

PREACHER, CATCH ON FIRE AND BURN WITH THE HOLY GHOST! DON'T BE A WATERED DOWN RELIGIOUS FIRE FIGHTER READY TO EXTINGUISH EVERY FIRE OF THE HOLY GHOST THAT YOU WERE NOT RESPONSIBLE FOR STARTING.

THE FIRE OF THE HOLY GHOST WILL PURIFY AND JUSTIFY ALL WHO WILL SURRENDER AND ALLOW THE FIRE TO BURN WITHIN THEM! FIRE IN ITSELF HAS GOT A REAL SENSE OF ATTRACTIVENESS THAT WILL GRASP THE ATTENTION OF ONLOOKERS.

WHATEVER YOU HAVE ACQUIRED THROUGH INDEPENDENT OR INSTITUTIONAL STUDYING THE WORD OF GOD, RELEASE THE FIRE OF THE HOLY GHOST UPON IT, EVEN IF OTHER PREACHERS TAUGHT YOU.

I AM NOT AGAINST PREACHERS GOING ON TO FURTHER STUDIES OF THE WORD OF GOD AT A THEOLOGICAL SEMINARY, I ONLY PRAY THAT THEY WOULD REFRAIN FROM LEAVING OUT THE MAIN INGREDIENT NECESSARY FOR THE POWER OF PREACHING THE GOSPEL!

THE INDWELLING POWER OF THE HOLY GHOST IS THE MAIN INGREDIENT.

THE PROPHET ISAIAH STATES, AND AGAIN I QUOTE,

"he hath anointed me to preach the gospel."

Allow The Anointing To Show-Up*

ONLY THE ANOINTED, CAN REACH AND TOUCH THE SOULS OF MAN. FAR TOO MANY PREACHERS ARE ENTERTAINING, LIKE MOVIE STARS, STAND-UP COMICS, MUSI-

CIANS, ACTORS, AND ON STAGE-PERFORMERS OF PLAYS. THEY CONDUCT THEMSELVES IN PULPIT PERFORMANCES SIMILAR TO VOCAL AND INSTRUMENTAL MUSICAL ENTERTAINERS, BOTH ON STAGE AND IN MUSIC VIDEOS.

THE PREACHED WORD HAS TO BE JUST SO ENTERTAINING, IN ORDER TO KEEP THE PEOPLE OF THE LOCAL CHURCH FROM NODDING OFF TO SLEEP OR SIMPLY WALKING OUT OF THE SERVICE.

MOST PREACHERS HAVE A GREAT DESIRE TO BECOME EXPOSITORY; THE WORDS EXPO (SHOW), _expose_, AND/OR EXPOSITION ARE ALL FOUND IN THE ONE WORD. THE PREFIX EX- MEANS OUT. THEREFORE WE ALSO SEE THE WORD EXPOSIT-WHICH IS OUT PUT OR TO PUT OUT. UNLIKE THE WORD DEPOSIT, WHICH IN TURN MEANS TO PUT IN OR TO LEAVE IT THERE.

PREACHERS ARE TAUGHT TO BE ON OPEN DISPLAY IN THE MIDST OF THEIR SERMONIC DELIVERY. THEY DEVELOP THE ART OF ENGAGING THEMSELVES INTO ARGUMENTATIVE TYPE DISCUSSIONS ALL BY THEMSELVES, DURING A SERMON.

OFTEN THEY ARE TALKING TO AN AUDIENCE THAT IS NOT EVEN INTELLECTUALLY PRESENT, TO DIGEST THE VERNACULAR OF THEIR DIALOGUE. THERE ARE A LOT OF PEOPLE WHO STUDY THE BIBLE ONLY FOR THE SAKE OF ARGUING THE ISSUES OF THE BIBLE. AN ARGUMENT IS ALL THEY DESIRE AS IT RELATES TO A BIBLICAL DISCUSSION.

EXPOSITORY PREACHERS BECOME MASTER STORYTELLERS. THEY CAN RAISE THE ENAMEL ON THE TEETH OF PERSONS IN ATTENDANCE AT THE TIME OF A PARTICULAR SERMON, *(figuratively speaking)*. THEY CAN HOLD THE ATTENTION OF MOST ANYONE WHO WILL LISTEN TO WHAT THEY HAVE TO SAY.

THEY HAVE MASTERED THE ART OF LEAVING AN INDELIBLE IMPRESSION OF THEMSELVES, RATHER THAN LEAVING VERY CLEAR AND UNFORGETTABLE REVELATORY EXPLANATIONS FROM THE WORD OF GOD THAT WILL FOREVER CHANGE THE LIVES OF PEOPLE.

WE SHOULDN'T ONLY BE INTOXICATED WITH MASTERING THE EXEGETICAL OR ISOGESICAL ART OF GETTING EVERY POSSIBLE ANGLE OF UNDERSTANDING OUT OF THE WORD OF GOD, BUT WE SHOULD DESPERATELY SEEK EVERY OPENING IN THE LIVES OF PEOPLE TO PUT THE WORD OF GOD INTO THEIR HEARTS AND MINDS.

SUCH MASTERFUL SPEAKING ARTISTRY, CAN DILUTE AND COMPROMISE THE MEANING OF THE MESSAGE, DURING THE ENTERTAINING FIASCO.

ENCOURAGE YOURSELVES TO BECOME <u>DEPOSITORY</u>, INSTEAD OF ONLY BECOMING A MASTER <u>EXPOSITORY</u> PREACHER!

PURPOSEFUL PREACHING ALSO SERVES TO INSTRUCT, TO INFORM, TO ILLUMINATE, TO EQUIP, TO EMPOWER, AND TO ANNIHILATE THE DEVASTATING HOLD OF SIN'S MOST AWFUL GRIP.

*Preaching Is Very Serious**

PEOPLE HAVE BEEN BRUISED BATTERED AND SCARRED. THEY SEEK HEALING, DELIVERANCE, AND HELP FOR THEIR HURTING PITIFUL SOULS, SOLUTIONS FOR THEIR BUSTED AND BROKEN LIVES, AND A FIX FOR THE DYSFUNCTION OF THEIR FAMILIES.

WHEN WE BARE-DOWN AND STUDY THE WORD OF GOD, FAST AND PRAY, WE FIND THE ANSWERS THAT MAY HAVE BEEN HIDDEN, EVEN FROM US. LEANING TO YOUR OWN UNDERSTANDING, YOU DON'T ALWAYS HAVE THE ANSWERS OR SOLUTIONS THAT PEOPLE ARE SEEKING SO DESPERATELY.

DON'T USE THE PLATFORM OF PREACHING AS ONLY A MEANS OF FINANCIAL GAIN AND POPULARITY. PREACHING IS TO BE EMBODIED WITH THE NECESSARY DIRECTIVES TO DISCOVER OUR MOST REAL AND TRUE CONNECTION WITH OUR CALLING AND THE GOD WHO CALLED US!

The Lord is not slack concerning his promise, as some men count slackness; but is longsuffering to us-ward, not willing that any

> *should perish, but that all should come to re-*
> *pentance.*   II PETER 3:9
> *For I know the thoughts that I think toward*
> *you, thoughts of peace, and not evil, to give you*
> *an expected end.*   JEREMIAH 29:11
> *For God so loved the world, that he gave his*
> *only begotten Son, that whosoever believeth*
> *in him should not perish, but have everlasting*
> *life.*   ST. JOHN 3:16

WE ARE NOT CALLED TO CONTINUE TO CONDEMN PEOPLE, BECAUSE MANKIND WAS ALREADY CONDEMNED DUE TO THE SINFUL NATURE OF THE FLESH AND UNBELIEF.

Your Help Cometh!

THE ANOINTING TO THE PREACHER IS AS THE POWER CHORD IS TO APPLIANCES AND LAMPS; EVEN AS A STRONG BATTERY IS TO AN AUTOMOBILE. IT IS THE CONNECTION TO THE POWER SOURCE TO GET YOU STARTED, THAT ALSO SERVES IN THE SAME CAPACITY AS THE GENERATOR AND/OR ALTERNATOR TO KEEP YOU UP AND RUNNING.

THE ANOINTING WON'T JUST DROP YOU LIKE AN AIRPLANE CRASHING DOWN TO THE EARTH, FROM THE HIGH ALTITUDES OF THE SKY WRECKED AND TOTALLY FINISHED, WHENEVER THE ASSIGNED TASK HAS BEEN COMPLETED.

THE ANOINTING ALSO SERVES AS THE LANDING GEAR, WHICH WILL ABSOLUTELY NEVER MALFUNCTION, IT WILL LET YOU DOWN EASY.

THE ANOINTING IS OUR NAVIGATIONAL SYSTEM TO ENABLE US TO TRAVEL THROUGH THE ADMINISTRATIVE GUIDANCE OF ALL GODLY IMPUTATIONS DURING OUR TIMES OF STANDING IN THE GAP.

WHENEVER WE REALIZE THAT WE ARE NOT OUR OWN, WE WILL BECOME MOST EFFECTIVE IN OUR ASSIGNED TASK AND WE WILL SEE THE GLORY OF GOD MOVING THROUGH OUR MINISTRIES. WE BELONG TO GOD! HE CHOSE ME, I DID NOT CHOOSE HIM AND NEITHER DID YOU!

> *Ye have not chosen me, but I have chosen you,*

> *and ordained you, that ye should go and bring*
> *forth fruit, and that your fruit should remain:*
> *that whatsoever you ask of the father in my*
> *name, he may give it you.*   ST. JOHN 15:16

GOD KNOWS THE TRYING THINGS THAT YOU AND I HAVE BEEN THROUGH, JUST TO GET TO WHERE WE ARE PRESENTLY. THROUGH THE BAPTISM OF TRIALS AND TRIBULATIONS AND THE HARDSHIP THAT OFTEN COMES WITH BEING DEDICATED TO JESUS, THE PRICE WAS PAID FOR THE ANOINTING ON OUR LIVES. THE ANOINTING IS NOT CHEAP AND IT CERTAINLY IS NOT FOR FREE!

BEAR IN MIND, THAT TO LOSE THE ANOINTING OR EVEN TO FORSAKE SUCH A POWERFUL ENDOWMENT, IS TO GIVE UP ON EVERYTHING THAT ESTABLISHES THE VALIDITY OF YOUR MINISTRY. I HAVE BEEN ENDOWED WITH THE POWER OF THE HOLY GHOST.

It's Not About Me!

WHENEVER I STAND TO DECLARE THE WORD OF GOD, I STAND IN THE SURE CONFIDENCE OF THE POWER AND DEMONSTRATION OF THE HOLY GHOST WITH CONVICTION POWER. I'VE GOT THE WORD DOWN IN MY BELLY, IN THE UTTERMOST PART OF MY BEING, WHICH IS THE VERY DRIVING MOTOR MECHANISM THAT ENABLES ME TO BELIEVE IN THE PERFECTED POWER OF THE GOSPEL!

I'M NOT AFRAID OF THE GOSPEL AND NEITHER WILL I FORSAKE THE ANOINTING OF GOD! WHATEVER, I AM GIVEN TO SAY, I CAN AND WILL SAY, BECAUSE OF THE ANOINTING. WE MUST NEVER BE AFRAID OF DELIVERING THE MESSAGE OF HOPE.

> *Be not afraid of their faces: for I am with thee*
> *to deliver thee, saith the Lord. Thou therefore*
> *gird up thy loins, and arise, and speak unto*
> *them all that I command thee: Be not dismayed*
> *at their faces, lest I confound thee before them.*
>
>   JEREMIAH 1:8,17

ABSOLUTELY NO ONE CAN SAY THE THINGS THAT GOD HAS COMMISSIONED YOU TO SAY. YOU ARE UNIQUE TO THE

WILL AND THE PURPOSE OF GOD.

NO ONE ELSE CAN PREACH THE WORD OF GOD, IN THE MANNER TO WHICH GOD HAS GIVEN YOU. OTHERS, FOR CERTAIN, MAY PREACH AS WELL AS YOU DO OR MAYBE EVEN BETTER THAN YOU, BUT THEY WILL DO SO IN THEIR OWN PERSONALIZED MANNER.

THE MIND, TO WHICH YOU HAVE BEEN GIVEN, DOES NOT THINK EXACTLY LIKE THE MIND OF ANYONE ELSE. WHENEVER YOU WILL HAVE GONE FORTH AS AN ORIGINAL PREACHING THE GOSPEL, YOUR OWN SIGNATURE WILL HAVE BEEN ENGRAVED AND DEEPLY INGRAINED INTO THE MINISTRY TO WHICH YOU HAVE BEEN ENDOWED.

No Competition*

NEVER, EVER WORRY ABOUT ANYBODY ELSE'S STYLE OF PREACHING. PREACHING STYLES ONLY SERVE THE PURPOSE FOR A DISTINCTION IN THE PERSONAL IDENTIFICATION OF INDIVIDUALITY.

OTHERS MAY BE MORE THEOLOGICALLY ASTUTE THAN YOURSELF, HOWEVER, SUCH LEARNING DOES NOT CONSTITUTE THE FACT THAT THE LESSER OF THE TWO OR MORE OF YOU, AS IT PERTAINS TO THE DIFFERENT LEVELS OF THEOLOGICAL INFORMATION, HAVE AN INABILITY TO SPREAD THE MESSAGE OF THE GOSPEL.

*BE CAREFUL OF FEELING THAT YOU HAVE ATTAINED THE HIGHEST POSSIBLE LEVEL OF LEARNING, HAVING TOO MUCH KNOWLEDGE FOR THE BETTER GOOD OF PREACHING OF THE GOSPEL.

> *Brethren, I count not myself to have apprehended: but this one thing I do, forgetting those things which are behind, and reaching forth unto those things which are before I press toward the mark for the prize of the high calling of God in Christ Jesus.* PHILIPPIANS 3:13-14

ONE OF THE GREATEST THINGS THAT ANY PREACHER SHOULD LEARN TO DO, IS TO FORGET THE THINGS THAT WERE LEFT BEHIND IN THEIR PAST THAT WOULD HINDER

THEIR ABILITY TO PREACH THE GOSPEL. OTHERWISE, YOU MAY FIND YOURSELF BEING STUCK IN THE SLIME OF YOUR PAST FAILURES, FEELING INADEQUATE TO FOLLOW THE LEADING OF THE LORD TO MINISTER TO THE PEOPLE OF GOD.

PERHAPS YOU NEED TO VIEW FORGETTING IN THE SENCE OF EMPTYING OUT YOUR MENTAL STORAGE OF THE FAILURES AND THE SINS AND THE MISTAKES OF YOUR PAST, SO THAT YOU WILL BE ABLE TO ACQUIRE THE THINGS OF GOD AND BECOME VERY EFFECTIVE TO DELIVER THE MESSAGE OF THE GOSPEL.

ONCE YOU HAVE DONE THE NECESSARY THINGS TO PLEASE THE LORD, AND HAVE BEGUN TO FLOW IN THE ANOINTING, BE VERY CAREFUL NOT TO ALLOW PEOPLE TO PUMP YOUR HEAD AND CAUSE YOU TO FEEL AS IF YOU HAVE ARRIVED. YOU'RE THE BOMB!

PAUL'S STATEMENT IS INDICATIVE OF SAYING; I DON'T KNOW IT ALL, I HAVE NOT LEARNED EVERYTHING THAT I WILL EVER NEED TO KNOW FOR THE SAKE OF PREACHING THE GOSPEL TO THIS DYING WORLD. I HAVE NOT ARRIVED AND I'M NOT THE ONE! NO MATTER HOW HIGH I MAY APPEAR TO BE TO YOU, I HAVE NOT MADE IT TO WHERE MY GOD IS TAKING ME BY HIS SPIRIT, I'M NOT FINISHED.

I WILL GET WHERE GOD HAS DESIGNATED AND PREORDAINED MY LIFE TO BE IN HIS WILL IN DUE TIME, AND IN DUE SEASON, ACCORDING TO HIS PURPOSE FOR ME.

⋆ *You May Know Too Much!*

HAVEN STUDIED AND OBTAINED TO THE POINT OF EXCELLENCE, BEING ELOQUENT OF SPEECH AND WELL ACCOMPLISHED IN STAGE PRESENCE, DOES NOT ILLUSTRATE THAT YOU HAVE FOUND YOUR EXACT PLACE IN GOD.

NEITHER, DOES IT SHOW THAT YOU HAVE PLEASED THE LORD TO THE POINT THAT HE HAS PLACED YOU WHEREVER YOU ARE STANDING PRESENTLY IN THE MINISTRY WHICH MAY BE THE THEOLOGICAL MINDSET OF MANY.

LEARNING IS ALWAYS A GOOD THING, BUT PEOPLE ARE NOT ALWAYS CAPABLE OF HANDLING THE ABUNDANCE OF

KNOWLEDGE TO WHICH THEY HAVE ACQUIRED THROUGH EDUCATIONAL STUDIES.

It's not good to be gullible of knowledge alone. A vast majority of the attending crowd may actually be mesmerized over your ability to acquire and to retain knowledge at such high volumes, but don't get carried away.

Your instructor had also been a student first. Someone else knew already, before even your instructors thought about finding out.

Study, by all means and pay attention to the knowledge that you have acquired, to first apply it to your own life. Pride will suggest that the knowledge that you have acquired is for everyone else, because you are beyond the need!

This is a big lie that should never be allowed into your thought process. If the message that you bring to the people is good enough for them, then it must have been good enough for you first.

Careful examination through the word of God will always play a very important role in knowing the truth of that which you have learned.

What is your response when people inquire of the message you have just delivered through preaching? I suggest that you be on your "Ps and Qs", and be about your most extreme whit's.

There will be people who will want to know how much you really believe in the message that you are delivering to the church. I really do love the word of God, don't you; listen to what the word has to say for an answer:

> *Let your speech be always with grace, seasoned*
> *with salt, that ye may know how ye ought to*
> *answer every man.* Colossians 4:6
> *But sanctify the Lord God in your hearts: and*
> *be ready always to give an answer to every man*
> *that asketh you a reason of the hope that is in*

you with meekness and fear.   I PETER 3:15

YOU CAN ACTUALLY KNOW TOO MUCH OF THE WRONG THING, WHETHER BY THE EXAMPLES OF OTHER'S WRONG DOINGS OR BY ALLOWING THE WRONG LITERATURE TO GET INTO YOUR HANDS, WHICH MAY BE FILTERING THROUGH YOUR MESSAGE.

IT IS DANGEROUS TO PREACH ANOTHER MAN'S CONVICTIONS, AS IT IS NOT ALWAYS CLEARLY DETERMINED, HOW OTHERS CONVICTIONS WERE DEVELOPED.

Come Up High!

TO PREACH THE WRONG THING WITH NO DESIRE TO CORRECT THE MATTER, WILL CAUSE SERIOUS SPIRITUAL REPERCUSSIONS!   WE MUST BE WATCHFUL THAT THE <u>UPS</u> ARE NEVER LOST TO THE <u>DOWNS</u>.

IF YOU ARE GOING TO STAY ON THE TOP, YOU ARE GOING TO HAVE TO THINK UP, BECAUSE LOW DOWN UNGODLY THINKING, WILL CAUSE YOU TO BECOME GROUNDED, WHICH WILL IN TURN LEAVE YOU AT A LOSS FOR HAVING SOMETHING UPLIFTING TO SAY.

ON-THE-TOP THINKING IS YOUR RESPONSIBILITY ALONE.   IN EFFECT, THAT YOUR MESSAGE WILL BE UPLIFTING.   IT IS ALSO IMPORTANT THAT YOU HOLD HIGH REGARDS FOR THE PEOPLE OF THE CHURCH BODY, LOCALLY, AS WELL AS OTHERS THAT ARE ABROAD.

> *And be not conformed to this world: but be ye transformed by the renewing of your mind, that ye may prove what is that good, and acceptable, and perfect, will of God. For I say, through the grace given unto me, to every man that is among you, not <u>to think</u> of himself more highly than he ought to think; but to think soberly, according as God has dealt to every man a measure of faith.*   ROMANS 12:2-3

WHY WOULD YOU EVEN PREACH TO PEOPLE IF THEY ARE SO INCAPABLE OF RECEIVING THE MESSAGE THAT YOU ARE BRINGING? THE PROBLEM IS NOT THE PEOPLE, IT IS YOU!

Able? Stay Humble!

YOUR ABILITY TO SPEAK THE TRUTH OF THE GOSPEL WITH NON-PROHIBITED POWER COMES FROM THE MEASURE OF FAITH IN WHICH YOU HAVE BEEN ENDOWED. YOU MIGHT WANT TO CONSIDER THE FACT THAT THE ONLY REASON THAT YOU ARE EXTEMPORANEOUSLY EXHAUSTIVE IS BECAUSE OF THE RIGHT NOW AVAILABILITY OF THE PRESENCE OF GOD.

YOU MAY BE A QUICK THINKER WITH A VERY SHARP INTELLECT AND A SMOOTH TONGUE THAT RIDE ON THE VELVETY RESONANCE IN THE CAPTIVATING TONE OF YOUR VOICE THAT IS ABLE TO ARREST AN AUDIENCE THE MOMENT YOU OPEN YOUR MOUTH. BUT, DON'T EVER FORGET THE FACT THAT YOUR VOICE CAME FROM GOD.

GOD'S PEOPLE WILL BE SAVED AND DELIVERED BY HIS WORD EVEN IF YOU PREACH AND LOSE YOUR SOUL! BE A HEARER AND A DOER OF YOUR OWN MESSAGES!

Preacher Be Bold!

DON'T, HOLD BACK OR LIGHTEN UP ON THE MESSAGE OF HOPE, SIMPLY BECAUSE PEOPLE DON'T SEEM TO BE GOING ALONG WITH YOU. THE TRUTH IS TO NEVER BE SO WASHED OUT, THAT IT'S TRUE ESSENCE FADES LIKE THE COLORS OF IMPROPERLY LAUNDERED CLOTHES!

MANY SCIENTIST, SCHOLARS AND THEOLOGIANS VIEW THE BIBLE AS NOTHING MORE THAN A RELIGIOUS TEXTBOOK ON HISTORICAL THEMES AND EVENTS THAT GOD OR A GODLIKE ENTITY, OR POSSIBLY EVEN NATURE MIGHT HAVE BEEN RESPONSIBLE FOR.

THEY SEEM TO BELIEVE THAT THEY HAVE DISCOVERED, THAT GOD AND THE SUPERNATURAL WORKINGS IN SCRIPTURES OF THE BIBLE, CAN NO LONGER BE FOUND ANYWHERE IN EXISTENCE IN THESE PRESENT TIMES.

IN OTHER WORDS, EVERYTHING THAT GOD IS GOING TO DO, HE HAS ALREADY DONE, SO THEY BELIEVE. GOD MAY HAVE DONE IT BEFORE, BUT MY QUESTION TO YOU IS,

HAS HE DONE IT FOR YOU YET?

LIKEWISE, THEY SAY THAT GOD HAS SAID EVERYTHING THAT HE IS EVER GOING TO SAY. HE HAS ABSOLUTELY NO REASON TO SPEAK TO MANKIND PERSON-TO-PERSON EVER AGAIN.

SADLY, BUT MANY WHO ATTEND CHRISTIAN CHURCHES THINK OF SUCH CARNAL FINDINGS AS TRUTH. TO THOSE THAT BELIEVE THAT GOD HAS DISSIPATED OR DISINTEGRATED, GOD IS ALIVE AND WELL, AND HE IS ALIVE IN ME AND HE OUGHT TO BE ALIVE IN YOU! GOD IS STILL SAVING THE LOST; HE'S NOT FINISHED YET!

> *The fool has said in his heart, there is no God.*
> *They are corrupt, they have done abominable*
> *works, there is none that doeth good.*
>
> PSALMS #14:1

THE DIFFERENCE BETWEEN THE NOW FOOL AND THE FOOL BACK THEN, IS THE STATEMENT; "THERE IS NO GOD." THE NOW FOOL OF THESE MORE MODERN GENERATIONS HAS SAID THAT THE GOD OF THE BIBLE IS NO **MORE**! ALL HAVE MISSED OUT ON THE REAL TRUTH AND THE PRESENT REALITY OF GOD.

RELIGIOUSLY INFLUENCED PEOPLE OF THE CHURCHES OF TODAY MAY NEVER VERBALIZE THAT THEY ARE CONSIDERING THE THEORY THAT THERE IS NO GOD; HOWEVER, THEY ARE OFTEN WILLING TO ACKNOWLEDGE THAT THEY DIDN'T BELIEVE THAT GOD WAS WORKING ON THE BEHALF OF THEMSELVES OR ANY OTHER PERSON FOR THAT MATTER!

OFTEN THE MOVE OF THE SPIRIT CONCERNING HEALING AND MIRACULOUS CIRCUMSTANCES IS DISCOUNTED AS PHENOMINAL AND ACREDITED TOWARDS THE USE OF MEDICINE, AND IN SOME CASE WHERE THE POWER OF GOD HAD MOVED IN THE MIDST OF THE PEOPLE OF GOD, EDUCATION HAS BEEN REARED AS THE RULING FACTOR INVOLVED IN BRINGING THE DESIRED EXPERIENCES OF LIVING INTO FRUITION. PEOPLE BELIEVE IN MAGIC AND ALL THAT IS NATURALLY ACQUIRED; THEY DON'T ALWAYS EMBRACE THE POWER OF THE HOLY GHOST.

PEOPLE MAY NOT ALWAYS AGREE WITH WHAT YOU SAY, JUST AS ELIHU DID NOT AGREE WITH JOB. HE HAD NO REVELATION CONCERNING JOB'S SITUATION, THEREFORE IT IS MY OWN OPINION AND MY CONVICTION THAT HE SHOULD HAVE NEVER DOUBTED JOB.

> *For I am full of matter, the spirit within me <u>constraineth</u> me.* JOB 32:18

WHEN WAS THE LAST TIME YOU FELT HARD PRESSED TO SAY THE RIGHT THING TO ANOTHER BROTHER OR SISTER IN THE BODY OF CHRIST, BECAUSE YOU FELT CONVICTED OF THE SPIRIT WITHIN YOU, BEING MOVED BY THE ANOINTING? THE ANOINTING DESTROYS THE YOKE OF BONDAGE.

> *and it shall come to pass in that day, that his burden shall be taken away from of thy shoulder, and his yoke from off thy neck, and the yoke shall be destroyed because of the anointing.* ISAIAH 10:27

YOKES MUST BE DESTROYED BEYOND REPAIR! ANYTHING BROKEN CAN BE MENDED OR SIMPLY PUT BACK TOGETHER. WHENEVER DELIVERANCE COMES, IT IS IMMUTABLE AND IT REMAINS IN TACT. TRUE DELIVERANCE WILL HOLD TIGHT UNDER ALL CIRCUMSTANCES. DELIVERANCE, TO WHICH CAN BE UNDONE IS NOT TRUE DELIVERANCE.

NEVER PREACH TO SEE THE YOKE OF BONDAGE, ONLY BROKEN, OVER THE LIFE OF AN INDIVIDUAL. PREACH TO SEE THE YOKES LITERALLY DESTROYED!

GO AHEAD AND PREACH UNTIL CHANGE HAS BEEN EXCITED IN THE LIVES OF YOUR LISTENING AUDIENCE, WHETHER IN THE LOCAL CONGREGATION OF WHICH YOU ARE THE PASTOR OR IN THE PULPIT WHERE YOU HAVE BEEN INVITED.

SOME PASTORS MAY NOT APPRECIATE A VERY STRONG MESSAGE FROM THE PULPIT, BUT DON'T STOP, BECAUSE THAT PASTOR MAY BE THE VERY ONE IN NEED OF THAT PARTICULAR MESSAGE.

Don't Taint Your Witness!*

KNOWING THAT YOU ARE SPIRIT LED AND SPIRITU-ALLY CONTROLLED DURING THE DELIVERY OF YOUR MESSAGE AND AFTER THE SERVICE HAS ENDED, IS WHAT MATTERS.

THERE ARE MANY THINGS THAT WE SHOULD NOT BE PARTAKERS OF AND MANY PLACES WHERE WE SHOULD NEVER BE FOUND, ALTHOUGH WE WOULD BE INNOCENT IN TERMS OF OUR VISITATION.

BEING DELIVERED OF ALCOHOLISM, WHEREAS MOST PEOPLE KNOW THAT YOU WILL NOT EVEN TAKE A DRINK OF ALCOHOL AT A SOCIABLE GATHERING IS NO REASON THAT YOU SHOULD BE COMFORTABLE HANGING AROUND THE LIQUOR STORE AND CLUB SETTINGS. STAY AWAY!

THERE IS JUST NO REASON TO HANG OUT IN DRUG INFESTED DOPE HOUSES AND NIGHTCLUBS JUST TO SAY THAT YOU WERE WITNESSING.

A WITNESS HAS GOT TO SEE SOMETHING; SO WHAT DO YOU SEE IN THOSE FORBIDDEN PLACES THAT ENABLES YOU TO BE A MORE POWERFUL WITNESS FOR THE LORD?

AND WHAT ABOUT THE WITNESS THAT YOU ENTERED INTO THOSE PLACES WITH, DID IT HAVE ANY LASTING AFFECT ON THE PEOPLE IN THERE? DID YOUR WITNESS OF THE LORD REMAIN THERE WITH THOSE UNSAVED PEOPLE TO THE POINT THAT THEY HAVE CHANGED THEIR MINDS ABOUT BEING THERE ALSO?

WHENEVER THE DRUG ADDICT OR THE DRUG DEALER BEGIN TO SEEK THE LORD FOR DELIVERANCE, THE LORD WILL ALLOW THEM TO <u>FIND YOU</u>, WHEREVER YOU MIGHT BE. THAT IS IF HE INTENDS TO USE YOU!

THE LIGHT BULB THAT APPEARS TO BE ILLUMINATING THE ENTIRE ROOM IS ACTUALLY PULLING POWER FROM THE POWER SOURCE IN ORDER TO GIVE LIGHT, AS IT IS TOTALLY INCAPABLE OF ILLUMINATING ITSELF.

WHENEVER THE SWITCH HAS BEEN TURNED OFF, ALL

OF THE POWER THAT HAD BEEN PREVIOUSLY RUNNING THROUGH THE ILLUMINATED LIGHT BULB, IS ALL GONE, LEAVING THE LIGHT BULB TO APPEAR DARKENED, WITHOUT ANY LIGHT, UNTIL THE SWITCH HAS BEEN TURNED ON ONCE AGAIN.

THE ANOINTED PREACHERS WHO DRAINS THEMSELVES THROUGH DELIVERING THE MESSAGE OF THE GOSPEL, ARE NOT DOING THEMSELVES A DISSERVICE BY DOING SO. THEY ARE ACTUALLY CONDUCTING THEMSELVES IN THE MANNER THAT HAS BEEN CONDUCIVE FOR MEETING THE NEEDS OF ALL OF THE OCCUPANTS IN THE ROOM, JUST LIKE THE LIGHT BULB.

THE MOMENT THE ANOINTING HAS BEEN SWITCHED OFF, THE PREACHER IS ACTUALLY FINISHED, LIKE THE LIGHT BULB THAT IS NOW DULL WITH NO POWER RUNNING THROUGH IT.

JUST AS THE LIGHT BULBS ARE OF DIVERSE WATTAGES, AND DIFFERENT SHADES OF LIGHT; REMEMBER THAT THE ANOINTING IS LIKEWISE DIVERSE IN STRENGTH AND FLOW RELATIVE TO THE PURPOSE OF THE ANOINTED INDIVIDUAL.

> *For we dare not make ourselves of the number, or compare ourselves with some that commend themselves; but they measuring themselves by themselves, and comparing themselves among themselves, are not wise. But we will not boast of things without our measure, but according to the rule which God hath distributed to us, a measure to reach unto you. For we stretch not ourselves beyond our measure, as though we reached not unto you: for we are come as far as to you also in preaching the gospel of Christ: Not boasting of things without our measure, that is, of others men's labours; but having hope, when your faith is increased, that we shall be enlarged by you according to our rule abundantly, To preach the gospel in the regions beyond you, and not to boast in another Mans things made ready to our hand.* II CORINTHIANS 10:12-16

WHILE OTHERS APPEAR TO BE MORE ANOINTED THAN YOU, IT IS SIMPLY BECAUSE GOD HAS EVIDENTLY PLACED A

GREATER PURPOSE UPON THE LIFE OF THE OTHER INDI-VIDUAL. DO WHAT YOU HAVE BEEN CALLED UPON TO DO AND YOU WILL FIND THAT YOU HAVE ENOUGH OF THE ANOINTING TO COMPLETE THE TASK TO WHICH YOU HAVE BEEN ASSIGNED.

WE SHOULD NEVER COMPETE FOR THE NUMBER OF SOULS THAT ANY PARTICULAR PREACHER CAN REACH, OVER ANOTHER PREACHER. THERE IS ENOUGH <u>LOST</u> SOULS IN THE WORLD TO KEEP EVERY SINGLE ANOINTED PREACHER GOING FORTH IN THE GOSPEL UNTIL JESUS CHRIST RETURNS TO RAPTURE THE CHURCH OUT OF THE WORLD.

More OF THE ANOINTING AND AN EVEN GREATER TASK COULD POSSIBLY BE TOO MUCH FOR YOU, TO WHICH GOD ALREADY KNOWS!

WHENEVER THE ANOINTING FLOWS FROM YOUR PER-SONAL BEING, PEOPLE AROUND YOU, FROM ALL WALKS OF LIFE, WILL KNOW IT! THEY MAY NOT KNOW EXACTLY WHAT TO CALL IT, BUT THEY WILL KNOW THAT IT IS THE SUPER-NATURAL POWER OF GOD WORKING WITHIN YOU.

Open Your Mouth!

THE ANOINTING DOES NOT OPERATE UNDER THE POWERFUL HINDRANCES OF SILENCE AND FEARFUL RE-STRAINTS! EARS ARE FOR HEARING, BUT AN EAR CANNOT HEAR A MESSAGE THAT HAS NEVER BEEN SPOKEN.

SO, EVEN AS YOU ARE ANOINTED TO PREACH, YOU ARE EVEN MORE ANOINTED TO SAY WITH EXCELLENCE! WHEN THE WEIGHT OF THE WORLD IS UPON YOUR SHOUL-DERS, YOU STILL HAVE THE POWER TO SAY IT ANYWAY!

SOMEBODY WILL HEAR YOU JUST IN TIME TO RECEIVE CHRIST INTO THEIR OWN HEART! THE WORDS SPOKEN OUT OF YOUR MOUTH, SHOULD NOT JUST BE BABBLING, HUFFING, PUFFING AND ENTICING WORDS OF MEN'S WISDOM, FOR THE BENEFIT OF KEEPING EVERYONE HAPPY, WITH YOU.

THERE WILL BE THOSE TIMES WHEN YOU MAY FEEL THAT YOU HAVE SPOKEN A VERY UNIQUE MESSAGE, ONLY TO DISCOVER THAT GOD HAD GIVEN THE SAME MESSAGE TO

OTHER MINISTERS ACROSS THE LAND. MANY OTHERS WILL HAVE PREACHED THE SAME MESSAGE ON THE VERY SAME DAY THAT YOU DID.

IT'S VERY EASY TO GET OFF THE TRACK THINKING THAT YOU HAVE TO BE THE ONE TO DELIVER BRAND NEW REVELATIONS AND FIRST TIME INFORMATION, TO WHICH NO ONE HAS EVER HEARD OF BEFORE.

* Who's Number one???

PRIDE DICTATES THAT YOU MUST BE NUMBER _1_; OUT IN THE FRONT OF EVERYONE ELSE OR AT LEAST THAT YOU KEEP UP AND STAY WITH THE TREND OF EVERYONE ELSE IN THE MINISTRY. GOD IS NOT PRODUCING CLONES AND DU-PLICATES.

GOD IS RAISING-UP PEOPLE IN THE MINISTRY WHO KEEP GOD FIRST AND DON'T PAY TOO MUCH ATTENTION IF OTHERS SEEM TO BE AHEAD OF THEM IN THE MINISTRY.

WHEN THE HOLY GHOST WILL INSTRUCT YOU TO FORSAKE YOUR THEOLOGICAL STUDIES AND PULPIT EDICTS IN EFFORT TO MEET THE NEEDS OF SOME PERSON OR MAYBE EVEN MANY OF THE PEOPLE PRESENT BEFORE YOU, ARE YOU SUBMITTED TO THE POINT THAT YOU WILL OBEY? IT IS AL-WAYS BETTER TO KNOW THAT YOU ARE ABIDING IN THE VINE!

IN ORDER TO TRULY BE SAVED, THE CONTROLLING SPIRIT OF THE FLESH MUST DIE, IN AN EFFORT FOR THE SPIRIT OF THE LORD TO LIVE ON THE INSIDE OF YOU!

THERE WILL BE NO PREACHING AFTER DEATH, AC-CORDING TO THE WORD OF GOD EVERY CHANCE FOR SAL-VATION WILL HAVE ALREADY BEEN EXHAUSTED. THE BODY OF THE DEARLY DEPARTED, WILL NOT EVEN BE COMMITTED TO THE GRAVE WITHOUT THE PREACHER HAVING THE LAST AND FINAL WORD.

GRIEF STRICKEN PEOPLE, MOST TIMES, WILL SEEK THE ANOINTED COUNSELING OF THE PREACHER.

DON'T ALLOW PEOPLE TO DEMEAN YOUR MINISTRY IN THE GOSPEL. DON'T ENGAGE YOURSELF IN A VERBAL ARGUMENT OR A FISTICUFFS, BUT DON'T BE MADE TO FEEL

AS LOW AS SOME PEOPLE WILL TRY TO BRING YOU EMO-
TIONALLY. HOLD YOUR HEAD HIGH AND BE MINDFUL THAT
YOU REPRESENT THE MOST-HIGH, GOD!

What shall we then say to these things? If God
be for us, who can be against us?

ROMANS: 8 :31

YOU ARE ALWAYS BETTER OFF WHEN THE WRONG
PEOPLE WHO ARE NOT BENEFICIAL FOR THE ANOINTING ON
YOUR LIFE, SEPARATE THEMSELVES FROM YOU.

PEOPLE MAY ACT AS IF THERE IS A MAJOR PROBLEM
WITH YOU AS A PERSON, WHEN IN FACT, THE REAL PROB-
LEM IS WITH THEMSELVES. AS PASTOR OF THE CHURCH
YOU WOULD BE ASTONISHED TO DISCOVER THAT EVERYONE
UNDER THE LEADERSHIP OF YOUR MINISTRY, IS NOT FOL-
LOWING YOUR LEAD.

Don't Forget Who You Are*

BE MINDFUL TO WALK <u>CIRCUMSPECTLY</u>, WHICH IS TO
WALK IN RESPECT OF THE AGREEMENT TO THE ANOINTING
THAT IS ON YOUR LIFE. YOU DO NOT PROTECT THE ANOINT-
ING NECESSARILY, BECAUSE THE ANOINTING IS NEVER IN
ANY KIND OF DANGER OF BEING DESTROYED BY ANYONE OR
ANYTHING. THE ANOINTING PROTECTS YOU!

THE ANOINTING IS GREATER AND MORE POWERFUL
THAN ANYTHING OR ANYONE, THAT WILL EVER COME
AGAINST THE ANOINTING, FOR THAT MATTER! THE ANOINT-
ING IS YOUR GREAT SHIELD IN THE TIME OF BATTLE.

DON'T CHEAT THE INVESTMENT OF GOD BY REFUS-
ING TO BELIEVE IN YOURSELF AS THE MOUTHPIECE OF GOD.
IF OTHERS ARE TRULY TO BELIEVE IN YOU, YOU MUST SEE
YOURSELF THROUGH THE WORD OF GOD AND ACCEPT WHAT
YOU SEE.

BE CONFIDENT AND PREACH UNTIL THE PILLARS OF
HELL ARE SHAKEN. PREACH UNTIL HEAVEN HAS A REASON
TO REJOICE. PREACH UNTIL LIFE LITERALLY WALKS INTO A
DEAD CHURCH AND BRINGS THE DEATH OF THAT MINISTRY

TO A SWIFT DEMISE.

PREACH UNTIL THE "SHE-KI'-NAH GLORY" FILLS THE ROOM, CAUSING EVERY BELIEVER TO REVERENCE AND ACKNOWLEDGE THE PRESENCE OF GOD.

PREACH UNTIL THE LIGHT OF CHRIST DISPELS THE DARKNESS OF SIN AND DISPLACES THE WILL OF SATAN!

PREACH UNTIL DEMONS RESIGN THEIR ASSIGNED POST, WITHOUT THE USUAL RESISTANCE!

Know Who Jesus is; Also!

JESUS IS THE WORD OF GOD MANIFESTED IN THE FLESH, SEEN OF MEN AND OF ANGELS. JESUS IS THE <u>PRE-VISUALIZATION</u> OF ALL PROPHETIC UTTERANCES, THROUGHOUT ALL OF THE AGES, IN WHICH HE MANIFESTED THE TRUTH OF EVERY PROPHECY THAT SPOKE OF HIS COMING TO THE EARTH.

JOHN THE BAPTIST PROPHESIED THAT JESUS WAS INDEED COMING AND THAT HE WAS EVEN MIGHTIER THAN JOHN. HE CONTINUED TO PROPHESY, UNTIL ONE DAY HE SAID; "HERE HE IS!"

THERE IS, AND THERE HAS ALWAYS BEEN, A LIVING SOUL IN MAN FROM THE BEGINNING! JESUS CHRIST, IN CONTRAST TO THE BODY OF EVERY OTHER HUMAN BEING; IN HIS BODY, WAS <u>GOD</u>!

JESUS IS WHAT IS REFERRED TO AS A DICHOTOMY, WHICH MEANS THAT HE WAS EQUALLY DIVIDED INTO TWO DISTINCT PARTS, MAN AND GOD. JESUS IS THE ONLY REAL TRUE GOD-MAN EVER TO WALK THE FACE OF THE EARTH. ALL OTHERS HAVE BEEN GODLY MEN AND WOMEN. JESUS WAS NEVER SUBJECT TO OBEY HIS FLESH, RATHER HIS FLESH WAS SUBJECT TO GOD ON THE INSIDE AND DID OBEY, ALWAYS!

MANKIND IS REFERRED TO AS A TRICHOTOMY, WHICH MEANS, THE BODY, THE SOUL, AND THE SPIRIT. WE MUST TRULY BE EMPOWERED BY JESUS IN AN EFFECT TO NEVER BE SUBJECT TO THE FLESH, BUT THAT THE FLESH WILL BE SUB-

JECT ALLOWING THE INDWELLING POWER OF THE HOLY
GHOST ON THE INSIDE OF US TO BE IN CONTROL.

Final Note To The Anointed :

Don't ever touch the influence of the other Anointed people of God with the words of your mouths, touching them in any way that will bring shame and will not bring glory to the name of Christ, even if you feel that you have a reasonable right.

There is enough power in the life of a preacher that may be living in a backslidden state, to send you straight to hell for touching their name, their person, or even their families.

Leave their character, their influence, and their ministries, alone! You will not be excused because you are anointed.

Now You Ought To Believe This!!

The 'devil Heard You!*

> And the devil that deceived them was cast into the lake of fire and brimstone, where the beast and the false prophet are, and shall be tormented day and night forever and ever. REVELATION 20:10

"He Didn't Know!"

NEVER ENGAGE YOURSELF MENTALLY, EMOTIONALLY OR EVEN SPIRITUALLY IN ANY TYPE OF A CASUAL CONVERSATION WITH THE DEVIL, NOT EVEN AS A SILENT LISTENER. YOU CANNOT TALK TO THE DEVIL, PERSON TO PERSON, OR FACE TO FACE ON THE STRENGTH OF YOUR OWN WILL AND INTELLECT AND WIN OUT OVER HIM IN ANY TYPE OF A DEBATE.

YOU MIGHT SAY AT YOUR AGE NOW, THAT YOU KNOW EVERY TRICK IN THE BOOK AND YOU CAN'T BE FOOLED; BECAUSE YOU'VE PLAYED THE GAMES AND CALL A SPADE A SPADE AND DIDN'T TAKE ANY WOODEN NICKELS! <u>F.Y.I.</u>! THE DEVIL <u>IS</u> THE STRATEGIC MANIPULATION OF THE GAMES THAT YOU'VE LEARNED TO PLAY SO SKILLFULLY OVER THE YEARS!

The devil IS; every trick in the book and yes of course you need to be informed that the devil IS definitely the influence of the street knowledge that you may seem to be so well versed at displaying.

We all have human vulnerabilities from the beginning of the existence of sin, which Satan will target in effort to exploit. The name Satan means-"Accuser of the brethern";

Satan consistently seeks to expose everything unrighteous in us, to prove to us how unlike God we are. Which in turn, his ultimate intent is to convince us that we need not to even bother trying to communicate with God being sinners, because we don't deserve the blessings of the Lord! He's a Liar!

The blessings of the Lord are for the people of the Lord! That's you and me! Us! We who are the forgiven, blood washed, spirit filled believers, are the people of the Lord that trust, lean, and depend on Him to bless us. So if God don't give the blessings to you and to me, there would be no one to receive them!

When Satan comes in a little closer to exploit those found areas of weakness, most people make the mistake of acknowledging his devilish entrance with great fear and worry, instead of resisting him, in the name of Jesus.

People actually spend more time talking about whatever the devil is doing to them, rather than testifying of the victory in Christ Jesus over the devil. Give God the praise continually for all that He has done!

No Fairytale!

The devil is not all-powerful! The devil has a

GREAT IMAGINATION AND BIG IDEAS THAT CANNOT BECOME A REALITY WITHOUT A WARM BODY LIKE YOURS TO CARRY OUT HIS DEVILISH PLANS!

GOD IS THE AWESOME CREATOR; THE DEVIL IS A CREATED BEING WHO ONLY HAS THE POWER TO IMITATE THE THINGS CREATED. HE CAN'T DUPLICATE THOSE THINGS THAT HAVE BEEN CREATED. HE CAN LOOK LIKE IT, VISUALIZE IT, AND EVEN CAREFULLY EXAMINE IT UP CLOSE, BUT HE CAN'T EVER BECOME LIKE THE CREATED PHYSICAL FORMS OF MAN.

BEFORE THE FOUNDATION OF THE WORLD CHRIST MADE PLANS TO BECOME FLESH, LIKE THE CREATED MAN, TO REDEEM THEM BACK TO GOD, DELIVERING MAN FROM THE FALLEN STATE OF SIN, SINCE THE FALL IN THE GARDEN.

OVER THE YEARS SINCE THE GARDEN INCIDENT, BLOOD SACRIFICES WERE OFFERED UP BEFORE THE LORD TO ATONE FOR THE SEPARATION OF MAN FROM HIS CREATOR, AS A RESULT OF SIN, TO BRING US BACK INTO THE FELLOWSHIP OF BEING AT-ONE WITH GOD.

AS TIME PROGRESSED ONWARDS, THE BLOOD SACRIFICES OFFERED UP FOR SINS, WOULD NO LONGER SUFFICE THE ATONEMENT, AS REQUIREMENT OF THE FATHER. THE SACRIFICES SOON FAILED AS A RESULT OF CONTAMINATED BLOOD FOR A NUMBER OF REASONS.

OTHER SECTS AND CULTS HAD BEGUN TO OFFER UP ANIMAL SACRIFICES TO OTHER GODS AND EVEN TO SATAN, FOR A PURPOSE OF WHICH I AM NOT AGREEABLE TO. A ONE OF A KIND, HUMAN SACRIFICE, BEARING UNCONTAMINABLE BLOOD THAT SATAN COULD NOT DUPLICATE OR CONTAMINATE, WAS NEEDED TO SEAL THE DEAL WITH GOD ON THE BEHALF OF MANKIND. JESUS CHRIST CAME TO THE EARTH FOR A PERFECT SACRIFICE, AND HE FINISHED THE DEAL OF ATONEMENT. (AT-ONE-MENT)

THE SACRIFICES BECAME WEAKENED AND UNACCEPTABLE IN THAT A LESSER PERCENTAGE OF THE ANIMALS WERE BEING BORN WITHOUT SPOT OR BLEMISH, ALSO BEING INFECTED WITH DISEASES FROM THE POINT OF BIRTH PRO-

DUCING CONTAMINATED BLOOD.

THROUGH IMPURITY OF THE BLOOD, THE FLESH HAD ALSO BECOME CONTAMINATED. THROUGH THE SPOILING OF FOOD STUFFS, INSECT BITES AND ACQUIRED DISEASES IN THE LIVESTOCK SPREAD FROM AND TO OTHER ANIMALS INFECTING THEM. SICKNESS AND DISEASE PREVENTED THEM FROM BEING OFFERED AS SACRIFICES. ONLY A PERFECT SACRIFICE COULD PLEASE GOD!

WHENEVER AN ANIMAL IS ATTACKED BY A LION OR A TIGER, A CROCIDILE OR SOME OTHER PREDATOR, AND IS NOT SUCCESSFULLY KILLED AND CONSUMED, THEY ARE OFTEN SERIOUSLY INFECTED WITH GERMS AND OTHER DEADLY BACTERIA THAT IS SPREAD THROUGHOUT THE ENTIRE BODY OF THE ANIMALS OF PREY THROUGH THE SALIVA OF THE ATTACKING PREDATOR.

THE SALIVA IN THE MOUTHS OF THOSE PREDATORS CARRY ANY NUMBER OF HIGHLY CONTAGIOUS BACTERIA AND DISEASES THAT ARE AS DEADLY AS THEIR VICIOUS ATTACKS. AS A RESULT, WHENEVER AN ANIMAL SUFFERS AN ATTACK, DEATH MAY VERY WELL BE AS LIKELY RESULTING FROM INFECTION, IF NOT IMMEDIATELY RESULTING FROM THE DEATH OF THE ATTACK.

OTHER DISEASES MAY EVEN BE AIRBORNE AND EVEN HIGHLY CONTAGIOUS THROUGH PHYSICAL CONTACT. THE ANIMALS OF TODAY HAVE TO BE PERIODICALLY VACCINATED, TO PREVENT THE SPREAD OF DEADLY DISEASE. MOST ANIMALS LIVE WITH DEADLY DISEASES IN THEIR BODIES DAILY, THAT WOULD KILL A HUMAN UPON BEING CONTAMINATED WITH THE DISEASE, AFTER ONLY A SHORT PERIOD.

JESUS BEING INCARNATE TO THE EXACT IMAGE OF THE CREATED MAN, CAME IN A PREPARED BODY TO REDEEM US BACK TO GOD THE FATHER! THAT'S RIGHT, HE DUPLICATED THE CREATION OF MAN A SECOND TIME! SATAN WAS AND STILL IS TO THIS DAY, CONSISTENTLY GNAWING AT THE SOULS OF MAN, PULLING THEM DEEPER INTO THE PIT STAINED WITH SIN, DRAGGING THEIR HOPELESS SOULS CLOSER TO

THE ETERNAL FLAMES OF THE LAKE OF FIRE.

THE LAW HAD FAILED US, IN THAT IT WAS WEAK THROUGH THE FLESH OF ANIMAL SACRIFICES AND WAS INCAPABLE OF KEEPING US IN RIGHT STANDINGS WITH GOD. ALTHOUGH THE STATE OF MAN WAS BAD, IT IS GETTING EVEN WORSE BY THE MOMENT.

"Mighty Jesus! Wow!"

JESUS BEING WHO HE IS, REMAINED WHO HE WAS AND SIMULTANEOUSLY HE BECAME WHO WE ARE. HE WAS CRUCIFIED, BURIED IN THE GRAVE AND GOD RAISED HIM FROM THE DEAD; NOW THIS IS SOME KIND OF POWER.

NO MATTER WHAT THE DEVIL DOES, HE CAN'T DUPLICATE THIS POWER!

THERE IS NOTHING IMITATION AT ALL ABOUT JESUS, WHO IS ALIVE FOR EVERMORE. HE DIED ONCE ON THE CROSS OF CALVARY AND HE WILL NEVER EVER DIE AGAIN. BUT SATAN, ON THE OTHER HAND, WILL DIE ACCORDING TO REVELATION 20: 10.

SATAN IS NOT THE OPPOSITE-EQUAL OF JESUS; AS A MATTER OF THAT FACT ABSOLUTELY NO ONE IS THE OPPOSITE-EQUAL OF CHRIST. ALL THAT ARE *equal* TO JESUS CHRIST ARE WITH HIM IN THE GODHEAD, AND THERE IS NEVER OPPOSITION AT ANYTIME, BEING THEY ALL ARE ONE; FATHER, SON, AND THE HOLY GHOST!

NOW SATAN IS IN OPPOSITION TO CHRIST, BUT HE IS NOT EQUAL TO JESUS AT ALL. HE DOES NOT EVEN HAVE THE POWER OF CREATION AND HE IS NOT EVEN ETERNAL IN HIS REIGN AS AN ADVERSARY TO THE KINGDOM OF GOD, AS THAT WAS NOT THE CREATED PURPOSE OF HIS EXISTENCE.

HE IS DOOMED WITH AN IRREVOCABLE, IRREVERSIBLE DEATH SENTENCE ON HIS HEAD. MAYBE YOU DIDN'T KNOW IT, BUT THE DEVIL IS COMPLETELY DEFEATED. ON THE CROSS OF CALVARY, JESUS FINISHED THE BATTLE AGAINST SATAN. THE DEVIL HAS BEEN REBUKED ALREADY AND WE DO NOT READ OR HEAR OF ANYWHERE IN THE WORD

OF GOD, THAT THIS ACTION HAS EVER BEEN OVERTURNED OR REVERSED.

THE LORD IS NOT GOING TO REBUKE HIM AGAIN, HE HAS BEEN REBUKED ALREADY AND THAT'S FINAL. GOD THE FATHER, REBUKED HIM IN HEAVEN, BEFORE THE THRONE OF GOD AND CAST HIM OUT ETERNALLY FROM THE PRESENCE OF HIS GLORY IN HEAVEN.

JESUS, TOTALLY DEFEATED SATAN IN THE EARTH, ON THE CROSS OF CALVARY. DON'T WAIST TIME WITH THE DEVIL, CAST HIM OUT AND PUT HIM IN HIS PLACE. TELL HIM WHERE TO GO QUICKLY, SPEAKING IN AUTHORITY BY THE POWER OF THE NAME OF JESUS CHRIST. SATAN; IS! NOT! TO! BE! FEARED!!!! HE'S NOT THE BIG BAD "KING OF THE JUNGLE."

> *Be sober, be vigilant; because your adversary the devil, as a roaring lion, walketh about, seeking whom he may devour.* I PETER 5:8

He Is A Deceiver!

THE DEVIL DOES NOT EVEN POSSESS THE CHARACTISTICAL PHYSICAL ATTRIBUTES IN THE MAKEUP OF THE LION, HE JUST ROARS LOUD AND FIERCE LIKE HIM, JUST ENOUGH TO INSIGHT FEAR UPON ANY FEARFUL PEOPLE. IN OTHER WORDS, THE DEVIL CANNOT EVEN SCARE YOU UNLESS YOU ARE SCARY! DON'T BE AFRAID, HE DOES NOT EVEN HAVE ANY CLAWS OR TEETH.

THE PURPOSE OF THE LION'S ROAR IS TO SEEK OUT THE WEAKER, MORE VULNERABLE PREY THAT WILL PUT UP THE LEAST FIGHT. ONE OF WHICH WILL ALMOST WILLFULLY LIE DOWN AND DIE BECAUSE OF THE LION'S VICIOUS ATTACK.

LION'S ALSO HAVE SOME WEAKNESSES, WHICH CAN BE VULNERABLY EXPLOITED IN A FIERCE BATTLE. SO, EVEN IN THEIR OWN LUNGING ATTACK AGAINST A PREY, LION'S ARE YET CAUTIOUS NEVER KNOWING WHERE RESISTANCE IS GOING TO COME FROM. LION'S KNOW THAT THERE IS A

POSSIBLE CHANCE OF A FIGHT, SO THEY ROAR TO EXCITE THE MAJORITY, IN EFFORT TO DISCOVER WHERE THE WEAKER ONES ARE, SO THAT THERE WILL NOT BE MUCH RESISTANCE TO THEIR ATTACK.

INSTINCT TELLS THE MORE AGILE MEMBERS OF THE HEARD TO FLEE FOR THEIR LIVES. THE WEAKER ONES, WHO GET CAUGHT RUNNING BEHIND OR EVEN SLEEPING, ARE ALMOST ALWAYS TAKEN FOR A KILL.

THE DEVIL MAKES A LOT OF NOISE, TO OVERTAKE YOU WITH FEAR, BECAUSE HE KNOWS THAT YOU HAVE BEEN ENLIGHTENED OF THE FACT OF YOUR AUTHORITY OVER HIM AS A BELIEVER. HE KNOWS WHEN YOU'RE AWARE OF HIS INABILITY, THROUGH THE WORD OF GOD.

HE CREATES MAJOR DISTURBANCES, INSIGHTS RIOTS, SPARKS BIG FIGHTS, ETC.; BUT YOU ACTUALLY HAVE TO GIVE IN TO THE WILL AND TO THE AGENDA OF THE DEVIL, IN ORDER FOR HIM TO TAKE CONTROL OVER YOU AND WIN.

THE DEVIL DOES NOT HAVE THE PHYSICAL ABILITY TO KNOW WHEN HE HAS GOTTEN YOU. HE KNOWS THAT HE HAS HIT YOU, BUT HE DOES NOT HAVE THE SENSIBILITY TO KNOW THAT YOU'RE EVEN HURT! YOU HAVE TO TELL HIM!

HE WILL GIVE YOU AN IDEA, BUT HE WILL NOT KNOW THAT YOU THOUGHT ABOUT IT, UNTIL YOU ACT UPON THE THOUGHT OR SAY SOMETHING. DON'T BE FOOLED INTO THINKING THAT THE DEVIL IS A MIND READER, BECAUSE HE'S NOT!

THE DEVIL WILL GIVE YOU SYMPTOMS OF SICKNESS, BUT HE WILL NOT KNOW THAT YOU HAVE ACCEPTED THE SICKNESS UNTIL YOU CONFESS IT OR EVEN BEGIN TO REACH FOR THE MEDICINE BOTTLES. THE DEVIL MAY KNOCK YOU DOWN, BUT HE WON'T KNOW THAT YOU CAN'T GET UP, UNLESS YOU CHOOSE TO LIE THERE ON THE GROUND.

YOU NEED TO ALSO KNOW THAT THE LORD CAN KEEP YOU FROM EVER GETTING INTO ANY SITUATIONS OF TROUBLE WITH THE DEVIL. JUST <u>TRUST</u> IN THE LORD JESUS. FAITH

IN JESUS MEANS THAT YOU BELIEVE HIM, BUT, WHENEVER YOU TRUST IN HIM, IT MEANS THAT YOU'RE GOING TO LET HIM DO IT FOR YOU. STOP BEING AFRAID AND JUST LET JESUS DO IT FOR YOU.

Do Allow Jesus!

INSTEAD OF MOANING AND GROANING, MURMURING AND COMPLAINING OVER ALL OF YOUR PROBLEMS, YOU SHOULD OPEN YOUR MOUTH TO THE POSITIVE FORCEFUL-NESS OF THE FAITH THAT IS WITHIN YOU AND PRAISE GOD! GIVE HIM THE GLORY! IN THE PRESENCE OF PRAISE, FIRSTLY AND FOREMOST, YOU WILL FIND THE VERY PRESENCE OF CHRIST. PAINFUL, LINGERING OF ALL SORTS, WILL RELENT ITS ANTAGONIZING EXISTENCE IN THE PRESENCE OF PRAISE.

THE JOY OF THE LORD LEAPS FORTH THROUGH GIV-ING PRAISE TO THE LORD. THE LORD INHABITS THE PRAISES OF HIS PEOPLE, WHICH MEANS THAT HE CHOOSES TO DWELL IN THE PRAISES OF HIS PEOPLE. TO DWELL IS TO RESIDE OR TO LIVE. THE VERY NEXT TIME THAT YOU BEGIN TO PRAISE THE LORD, LOOK FOR HIM IN THE MIDST OF YOUR PRAISE. OPEN THE DOOR TO YOUR HEART AND LET JESUS IN.

THE LORD IS A MIGHTY BATTLE-AX IN THE TIME OF A BATTLE, SO WHENEVER YOU'RE IN A BATTLE WITH SATAN, GO AHEAD AND PRAISE JESUS.

YOU MAY BE IN THE TENTH ROUND OF A TEN-ROUND FIGHT WITH THE DEVIL, WITH JUST TEN SECONDS LEFT TILL THE BELL SOUNDS TO END THE FIGHT; IT'S NOT TOO LATE TO LET JESUS IN, IT IS JUST THE RIGHT TIME; LET HIM IN!

NEXT TIME, GO AHEAD AND TAG JESUS, AT THE INI-TIAL SOUND OF THE VERY FIRST BELL OF THE FIRST ROUND. AT THE OPENING OF THE FIGHT, JESUS IS WAITING TO EN-TER THE FIGHT TO WIN THE BATTLE FOR YOU.

YOUR JOY IS AT STAKE, WHENEVER YOU PROCRASTI-NATE IN CALLING ON THE LORD, I HOPE YOU UNDERSTAND THIS? CALL ON THE LORD WITH THE RIGHT MOTIVATIONS

IN FAITH, HOPE, AND TRUST, BECAUSE IF YOU CALL ON HIM OUT OF HOPELESSNESS AND DESPAIR, YOU WILL HAVE TO WAIT UNTIL YOU GET YOUR HOPES UP AND YOUR FAITH IN TACT!

DO YOU REMEMBER CALLING THE BANK TO INQUIRE OF YOUR ACCOUNT AND A TELEPHONE REPRESENTATIVE OR A RECORDING TOLD YOU THAT THE COMPUTERS ARE DOWN; "WE ARE UNABLE TO ACCESS THAT INFORMATION FOR YOU?" WHEN THE COMPUTERS ARE DOWN, YOU CANNOT TAP INTO THE TERMINAL SOURCE OF THE SYSTEM YOU ARE SEARCHING, BECAUSE OF PREVENTIVE HINDRANCES. YOU HAVE TO WAIT UNTIL THE COMPUTERS ARE BACK UP.

WHEN YOU ALLOW YOURSELF TO WALLOW AND SULK OVER YOUR SITUATION, AND DO NOT PRAISE THE LORD, THE SITUATIONS WILL REMAIN AS THEY ARE, MUCH LONGER THAN THEY WERE REALLY SUPPOSED TO.

> *"Lift up your heads, O ye gates; and be ye lift up*
> *ye ever-lasting doors; and the King of Glory shall*
> *come in. Who is the King of Glory? The Lord*
> *strong and mighty, the Lord mighty in battle.*
> PSALMS # 24:7-8

YOU AND I ARE THE HEADS OF THE GATES AND THE GATES OF THE HEADS. WE ARE THE ENTRY-WAYS TO THE PRESENCE OF THE LORD, IN THIS PRESENT ATMOSPHERE BEFORE ALL MEN EVERYWHERE. WHENEVER AND WHEREVER THE LORD COMES IN, HE'S COMING IN THROUGH HIS PEOPLE. WE HAVE ACCESS TO HIM, SIMPLY BECAUSE, HE HAS BEEN ALLOWED ACCESS TO US, BY US.

JESUS IS NOT LIKE US, WHENEVER WE LET HIM IN, HE COMES IN. WHEN WE FINALLY OPEN THE DOOR, HE WILL NOT JUST SAY; "TOO LATE!! I DON'T WANT TO COME IN NOW. I'VE BEEN OUT HERE KNOCKING ALL OF THIS TIME; IT TOOK YOU TOO LONG TO OPEN THE DOOR."

> *Draw nigh to God, and he will draw nigh to you:*
> JAMES 4:8 [Aj]

THERE ARE TIMES WHEN SATAN IS NOT SOLELY THE

BLAME FOR WHAT WE ARE GOING THROUGH. BUT, WHEN YOU BEGIN PLASTERING HIS NAME ALL OVER YOUR SITUATION, HE TAKES ADVANTAGE OF THE OPPORTUNITY TO ACTUALLY GET INTO YOUR AFFAIRS AND EXERCISE HIS DEVILISH CONTROL OVER THEM.

I HAVE BEEN FALSELY ACCUSED! IN THOSE SITUATIONS, I HAD TO JUST BEAR IT OUT AND CONTINUE ON LIVING MY LIFE, UNTIL I HAD BEEN EXONERATED OR EVEN VINDICATED AND EVEN IN THE LIGHT OF THE FACT THAT THE TRUTH OF SOME SITUATIONS HAVE NOT YET COME OUT IN THE OPEN, I CHOOSE TO KEEP ON PRAISING THE LORD, ANYWAY!

THE DEVIL, ON THE OTHER HAND, WILL NOT SEEK VINDICATION OR EXONERATION! AND BE ADVISED OF THE FACT THAT HE WILL NEVER, BECAUSE HE CAN NEVER, PRAISE THE LORD. SATAN'S GREATEST DELIGHT IS IN YOUR TOTAL DESTRUCTION AS IT RELATES TO PRAISING AND WORSHIPPING THE LORD.

EVEN IF YOU ARE HELPING HIM TO HURT YOU BY THE WAY OF YOUR OWN SINFUL PARTICIPATION, AND YOU TRUTHFULLY KNOW THAT YOU ARE PARTIALLY THE BLAME FOR YOUR SITUATION, YOU STILL CAN NEVER CONVERSE WITH THE DEVIL AND WIN, ALTHOUGH YOU MIGHT HAVE THOUGHT THAT HE WAS YOUR PARTNER IN THE UNFAVORABLE ACTS THAT YOUR ARE FRUSTRATED OVER.

YOU CANNOT CONVINCE SATAN TO CHANGE HIS MIND ABOUT CAUSING YOU TROUBLE. HIS OPINION OF EVERY BELIEVER OF JESUS CHRIST IS DAMNABLY FIXED. NO NEED IN TRYING TO CALL A TRUCE WITH THE DEVIL, BECAUSE HE WILL NOT COME TO THAT KIND OF A TRUTHFUL, HONEST AGREEMENT WITH YOU!

THE LORD IS DOING MORE FOR YOU RIGHT NOW, THAN THE DEVIL CAN EVER DO TO YOU IN A LIFETIME!

The 'devil's Not Interested!

THE DEVIL'S DESTRUCTION IS ETERNALLY FIXED AND

SOON TO COME. IT'S THE LORD'S DOING, SINCE FROM THE BEGINNING OF TIME. THE DEVIL'S SITUATION CAN'T BE CHANGED, NO MATTER HOW PEOPLE ARE MADE TO FEEL ABOUT IT.

GOD LISTENS TO US, HE IS ATTUNED TO OUR INDIVIDUAL CRIES, AS WELL AS THE OUTCRIES OF THE COUNTRY AS A WHOLE. IT WOULD BE DAMAGING TO THE RELATIONSHIP BETWEEN MAN AND THE GOD WHO CREATED HIM, IF MAN WERE CAPABLE OF SPEAKING TO GOD ON THE DEVIL'S BEHALF, SO THAT GOD MIGHT RECONSIDER THE PUNISHMENT THAT HAS ALREADY BEEN PRONOUNCED ON THE DEVIL.

THE DEVIL MAY HAVE YOU GOING AROUND IN CIRCLES, BUT DON'T TELL HIM! IF YOU FEEL THAT HE MAY DRAW BLOOD FROM YOU, BECAUSE OF HIS VICIOUS THREATS TOWARDS YOUR LIFE, JUST PLEAD THE ALREADY DRAWN-OUT, SHED BLOOD OF JESUS INSTEAD. THE BLOOD OF JESUS IS CERTAINLY NOT WHAT HE IS EXPECTING FROM YOU! DON'T CRY AND STOP THROWING THOSE TANTRUMS.

THOUGH IT MAY APPEAR THAT YOU ARE LOSING THE BATTLE AGAINST THE DEVIL, DON'T GIVE IN. THE DEVIL MAY HAVE YOUR FINANCES SQUEEZED IN A VICE, BUT DON'T LET HIM KNOW IT, BY RENEGING ON YOUR FINANCIAL OBLIGATIONS TO THE CHURCH! YOU COULD NEVER PAY YOU WAY OUT OF THE TROUBLE THAT YOU ARE HAVING, BUT, BE ADVISED THAT YOU CAN GIVE YOUR WAY OUT! KEEP GIVING TO THE LORD!

YOUR CHILDREN MAY APPEAR TO BE TROUBLE PRONE, BUT DO NOT ACCEPT TROUBLE, BY GETTING INVOLVED, FROM A TROUBLE MAKING PERSPECTIVE. KEEP ON SPEAKING JESUS, TO THE SPIRITS OF YOUR CHILDREN!

THE WAY OF THE WORLD BELONGS TO SATAN'S AGENDA. THE DEVIL MAY WREAK HAVOC ON YOUR JOB, BUT DON'T QUIT THE JOB, WALK IN THE VICTORY OF JESUS.

WHENEVER I HEAR A PERSON CONFESS TO BEING VICTORIOUS, I WANT TO KNOW, WHERE IS YOUR BATTLE SCARS?

You can't run and hide behind the bushes, under a rock, or even behind the name of someone else's reputation. The name of your church, or church organization will not help you either.

Whoever your parents were, or whomever they weren't, won't help you. Weak fearful wimps, who are afraid of the devil, will never win. How do you suppose that you will ever really know that you are truly a champion and a victor, if you never face your opposition in battle, head on, and go on to conquer your enemy?

A hymn writer once wrote;

"I must tell Jesus, all of my trials, I cannot
bear these burdens alone, in my distresses he
kindly will help me, Jesus will help me and
Jesus alone."

You're not alone, you don't have to make a lot of threats to Satan, as pertaining to what the Lord is going to do, just praise Jesus and watch the Lord move.

Refrain from giving the devil inside information about your situations. The sooner believers become aware of this great truth, more believers are going to be victorious.

Fighting From the Air

 Now that you're aware that you are a winner, I'm going to share an imparted mystery from the Holy Ghost. Past failed religious teachings and insufficient studies, have taught believers to spend too much time in the presence of the devil. We spend time rebuking and binding the devil, mainly because we want to be spiritual and very powerful.

The power of the Lord is at work on the inside of us, but, we make the mistake of telling the

DEVIL THAT WE HAVE POWER, RATHER THAN RELYING ON THE POWER ON THE INSIDE OF US TO PARALYZE THE PRESENT INTRUSION OF THE ENEMY.

TOO MUCH TIME SPENT TALKING TO THE DEVIL IS EQUIVALENT TO FIGHTING A GROUND WAR IN THE INFANTRY DIVISION OF THE MILITARY. SOMETIMES, COMING DANGEROUSLY FACE TO FACE WITH ENEMY OPPOSITION, WHEREAS, DEATH IS OBVIOUSLY INEVITABLE.

SATAN IS NOT AFRAID OF WHO YOU ARE AND HE DOESN'T LIKE YOU! BUT; SATAN DOES FEAR THE POWERFUL PRESENCE OF GOD ON THE INSIDE OF YOU, THAT ACTUALLY MAKES US WHO WE ARE. IF HE CAUSES YOU TO FORGET FOR A MOMENT THAT GOD IS ON THE INSIDE OF YOU, IT IS ENOUGH TO ENTER INTO YOUR SITUATION TO DEFEAT YOU.

GET THE WARFARE UP OFF OF THE GROUND WHERE THE ENEMY HAS GOT YOU SUBDUED, FIGHTING YOU IN YOUR MIND, FOR THE RIGHT TO DOMINANTLY EXERCISE CONTROL OVER YOU. *Psalms #24: 7 & 8, says;* "LIFT UP YOUR HEAD", WHICH MEANS TO LOOK UP TO THE LORD AND SEEK HIS GUIDANCE AND INSTRUCTION AND WALK IN THE POWER THAT GOD HAS GIVEN TO YOU.

WHEN BULLETS ARE FLYING OUT ON THE BATTLE FIELD, ONE CARELESS MOVE CAN BE FATAL. SO WATCH WHERE YOU WALK WHILE YOU MAKE AN ATTEMPT TO APPROACH THE ENEMY, BECAUSE THERE ARE SPIRITUAL LAND MINES, TO WHICH MAY CAUSE YOUR NEXT STEP TO BECOME WRONGFULLY FATAL TO THE PURPOSE OF GOD ON YOUR LIFE.

IN OTHER WORDS, GET YOUR EYES OFF OF THE PROBLEM AND SET THEM ABOVE ON THE LORD. TO LIFT YOUR HEAD IS ALSO TO REVERENCE THE LORD AND TO ACKNOWLEDGE OUR GOD IN THE NAME OF JESUS. PRAISING GOD WILL LIFT YOUR SPIRIT TO HIS SPIRIT.

THE SUCCESS OF THE GULF WAR, "**OPERATION DESSERT STORM**", WAS HIGHLY ATTRIBUTED TO THE FIERCE AIR STRIKES. THE ENEMY WAS DEFEATED BEFORE THEY EVEN

KNEW WHAT HIT THEM. BOMBS WERE BURSTING EVERY-
WHERE! SCUD MISSILES WERE SHOT DOWN IN MIDAIR, BY
THE AID OF AMERICA'S PATRIOT MISSILES, STRONGLY DIS-
ABLING THE ENEMIES MISSILES FROM REALLY CAUSING ANY
MAJOR DESTRUCTION, FOR WHICH THEY WERE CAPABLE.

WE ALSO HAVE VERY QUICK AND POWERFULLY EX-
PLOSIVE ARSENAL IN THE SPIRIT, THAT ARE MUCH MORE
POWERFUL THAN THE DEVIL'S DEVISES. WE TOO MUST FIGHT
OUR ENEMY, FROM THE AIR. SATAN IS THE PRINCE OF THE
AIR, AND THE RULER OF THE DARKNESS.

SATAN, OFTEN COWARDLY, FIGHTS US FROM THE
PLACE OF HIS HEAVENLY DISLODGE IN THE AIR, HITTING US
FROM THE DARKENED ELEVATED POSITIONS OF HIS OWN UN-
GODLY INFLUENCE AND POWER, WHEREAS, IF WE ARE LACK-
ING THE POWER OF THE HOLY GHOST IN OUR LIVES, WE
COULD NEVER SEE HIS ORIGIN OF ATTACKS AGAINST US.

DARKNESS, FIRSTLY DOES NOT NECESSARILY HAVE TO
MEAN THE OBSCURITY OF ILLUMINATION, IT MAY OFTEN
MEAN UNREVEALED KNOWLEDGE, AND THE HIDDEN DETAILS
ABOUT THE HAPPENSTANCES OF AN INDIVIDUALS LIFE.

THEREFORE, THOSE OF US WHO ARE KNOWLEDGE-
ABLE OF THE POWER OF PRAISE AND WORSHIP, AND ARE
WILLFUL TO GET INVOLVED AT EVERY OPPORTUNITY TO
EXCERCISE OUR PRIVILEDGE TO TOUCH GOD IN PRAISE AND
WORSHIP, WE APPLAUD OUR POSITIONS IN GOD TO DEFEAT
THE ENEMY THROUGH OUR ARTICLES OF PRAISING AND
WORSHIPPING.

CLAPPING OUR HANDS: SIGNIFIES THAT WE RECOG-
NIZE THE VICTORY AND ACCEPT THE POWER THAT WE HAVE
OVER SATAN, BY DOING SO WE CONFUSE THE DEVIL. CLAP-
PING OUR HANDS ALSO APPLAUDS THE ENTRANCE OF JESUS,
TO THE POINT THAT, WE ALLOW HIS MOVE TO TAKE OVER
THE BATTLE AND CARRY US ON, TO WIN THE WAR.

NOW: AS WE GO FORTH CLAPPING OUR HANDS, LET'S
DROP THE FIRST BOMB. HIT HIM HARD, SAY; "THANK YOU
JESUS!" THOUGH IT IS VERBALLY ARTICULATED OUT OF OUR

MOUTHS, THIS WEAPON IS TO BE CONSIDERABLY RECEIVED AS; *"Mind Arsenal."*

"THANK", IS AN OLD ENGLISH WORD THAT WAS FIRST SPELLED "THANC", SHORT FOR "THANCIEN"; WHICH MEANS TO BE THOUGHT WORTHY OF OR RATHER TO THINK ABOUT IN A GRACIOUS MANNER. I BELIEVE THAT IF YOU DO NOT "THINK" GOD, YOU WILL NOT "THANK" GOD!

HERE IS THE POWER OF THINKING GOD, CONSISTENTLY. THE MIND IS THE BATTLEGROUND, THE DEVIL IS TRYING TO TAKE THE CONTROL OF YOUR THOUGHT-LIFE. AS LONG AS YOU CAN THINK JESUS, YOU WILL FIND THAT SATAN DOES NOT HAVE THE POWER TO CONQUER YOU. YOU WILL FIND THE ENEMY TO BE STRONGLY DISORIENTED, NOW THAT YOU HAVE BECOME TRULY THANKFUL TO GOD.

SECONDLY, LET'S DROP THE NEXT BOMB ON THE ENEMY BY SAYING; "I PRAISE YOU JESUS!" MY FRIEND, PRAISE IS ALSO *"Body Armour"*, *Isaiah 61: 3 "THE GARMENT OF PRAISE."*

THE ARMOUR OF GOD, TO WHICH PAUL ADMONISHES THE PEOPLE OF THE BODY OF CHRIST TO TAKE ON, ARE ACTUALLY AREAS OF PRAISE AND WORSHIP THAT WE SHOULD FIND OURSELVES CONSISTENTLY EXPLORING AS BELIEVERS. *Ephesians 6: 13-17*

AS WE LOOK THROUGH THE SCRIPTURES, WE SEE WAS IS REFERRED TO AS A LISTING OF THE DIFFERENT PARTS OF THE ARMOUR IN A PARTICULAR ORDER. HOWEVER, THE THINGS LISTED ARE INSTRUCTIONS FOR ACQUIRING THE STRONG COVERING TO SUSTAIN US AS EVENTUAL WORSHIPPERS.

A. *LOINS GIRT ABOUT WITH TRUTH* : *the position of praise, whereas we are intimately balanced upon the power of the truth of Jesus Christ, as we engage ourselves to praise the Lord.*

B. *BREASTPLATE OF RIGHTEOUSNESS* : *the effectual change of our hearts that binds us to the heart of God. Here is the place of which we discover deep assurance of the truth; in the God of our praise.*

C. *FEET SHOD WITH THE PREPARATION OF THE GOSPEL OF PEACE* : *the place of which we are made conformable in the newness of life in Christ; praising God without wrath or doubting, knowing that all has been settled, relative to our old walk of life. We praise Go knowing that the power of the gospel has truly changed our lives. He saved our soul! We now have peace with God! All is well!*

D. *SHIELD OF FAITH* : *the area in which we arrive at knowing we can trust God for whatever we need from Him, and we praise God for everything that we have become in Him. Nothing will be able to knock us back from our place of praise in Him, and neither will our hearts ever be pierced through with with any weapon of the enemy, to stop us from giving God the praise.*

E. *HELMET OF SALVATION* : *herein is where we know that our praise and worship is true because we have been transformed by the renewing of our minds, and we know for sure that our redeemer liveth. Jesus is alive and well! We know that we've been washed in the blood of the Lamb.*

F. *SWORD OF THE SPIRIT; WHICH IS THE WORD OF GOD* : *in this place we are totally involved, weilding the cutting blades of the double edged sword of the word, establishing our rites as a worshipper to all the host of heaven, and our reasonable rights to praise and to worship the Lord in the congregation of the righteous; which is the body of Christ at large.*

OUR COMPLETE FOCUS IS GOD; NOT ON WHATEVER THE ENEMY IS TRYING TO DO. THE ENEMY KNOWS WHO'S FIGHTING YOUR BATTLES. LOOK AT HIM THROUGH YOUR SPIRITUAL EYES AND YOU WILL SEE THAT HE IS ON THE RUN. HE'S TRYING TO ESCAPE, NOW THAT HIS WEAPONS HAVE BEEN DISABLED THROUGH GENUINE PRAISE TO GOD.

GO AHEAD AND TAKE HIM OUT NOW! HIT HIM WITH A MEGATON BOMB. HERE GOES! SAY; *"HALLELUJAH; TO GOD BE THE GLORY!" "Spiritual Aero-dynamics" Flight Equipment for the Spirit-man!*

THE ENEMY IS NO LONGER OUT OF REACH OR EVEN ABLE FLEE, RUNNING FROM ANY POSSIBLE RETALLIATION TO WHATEVER HE HAS DONE TO US. HE'S A MASTER AT *"HIT*

AND RUN!" HE LOVES TO THROW HIS PUNCH AND THEN TO HIDE HIS HAND, LEAPING UP INTO THE INVISIBLE REALM IN THE HIDDEN ATMOSPHERES, JUST ABOVE OUR HEADS IN THE NATURAL REALMS OF THE HEAVENLIES.

THIS IS THE HIGHEST PRAISE THAT YOU COULD EVER OFFER UP AT ANYTIME AND IT IS EVEN HIGHER THAN THE INTENSIVELY ELEVATED FIERCE BATTLE WITH THE DEVIL! THIS WEAPON OF PRAISE REACHES ALL THE WAY UP INTO THE HIDDING PLACE OF THE ENEMY, BLASTING HIM RIGHT OUT OF OUR ATMOSPHERE. NOW BEGIN TO PRAY IN THE SPIRIT, AND BLESS GOD IN THE HOLY GHOST, OUT OF YOUR MOUTH!

Did You Finish Him Off?

DANCE IN THE DEVIL'S ASHES NOW THAT HE IS FINISHED! HERE'S WHAT JUST TOOK PLACE.

WHENEVER THE PRAISES WENT UP BEFORE THE LORD WITH THE SPIRIT OF PRAISE IN THE HOLY GHOST, THE LORD TOOK OVER THE BATTLE RIGHT OUT IN MIDAIR, ALLOWING YOU TO MOVE ASIDE, WHILE STILL UP IN THE MIDDLE OF THE HIGH PRAISE IN THE PRESENCE OF HIS GLORY, AS HE DEFEATED THE ENEMY FOR YOU IN MID-AIR!

WHILE YOU WERE YET PRAISING THE LORD, YOU WERE BEING DECLARED THE WINNER OF THE BATTLE! EVERYTHING OUT OF PLACE, BEGAN TO MOVE BACK INTO PLACE.

NOW THAT YOU KNOW WHAT TO DO, DON'T TELL THE DEVIL, JUST GO AHEAD AND DO WHAT YOU KNOW TO DO!!!

THE LORD WILL IMPREGNATE YOUR SPIRIT WITH VARIOUS VISIONS, DREAMS, AND GOALS FOR THE MINISTRY. HE WILL ALSO REVEAL MYSTERIES OF THINGS PRESENT AND OF THINGS TO COME, RIGHT BEFORE YOUR VERY EYES, THAT HAVE BEEN HIDDEN IN THE PAGES OF YOUR BIBLE FOR YEARS.

SOME PEOPLE ACTUALLY BELIEVE THAT THERE ARE NO NEW REVELATIONS AND THAT WHATEVER GOD WILL TELL ONE, HE WILL TELL ANOTHER. GOD WILL TELL THOSE THAT LIVE CLOSEST TO HIM, SOME THINGS THAT HE WILL NOT

BE ABLE TO TELL OTHERS.

IF THE MILITARY CAN WITHHOLD EXCLUSIVELY, CLASSIFIED INFORMATION FROM THE AVERAGE INDIVIDUALS OF THE COUNTRY, CERTIFYING THAT MOST PEOPLE ARE NOT CAPABLE OF HANDLING SUCH SERIOUS INFORMATION, THEN WHAT ABOUT GOD?

GOD HAS THE RIGHT TO WITHHOLD INFORMATION TOO IMPORTANT TO BE MISHANDLED BY THE WICKED, OR TO BE HAPHAZARDLY DIVULGED, OR UNTIMELY RELEASED IN THE PRESENCE OF THE ENEMY?

IT IS THE WILL OF GOD THAT ALL PEOPLE WOULD COME TO KNOW HIM IN THE FULLNESS OF HIS POWER. YET HIS DIVINE PURPOSE AND PLAN FOR EVERY INDIVIDUAL WILL VARY. ACCORDING TO THE SOVEREIGN WILL OF GOD, HE WILL GIVE GOOD GIFTS AND WEAPONS OF WARFARE AGAINST THE ENEMY, TO ALL WHO BELIEVE ON HIS NAME.

Can You Keep A Secret?

THERE ARE MANY PEOPLE ENDOWED WITH SPECIAL GIFTS, FOR THE PURPOSE OF THE HIGHER CALLING OF GOD. THEY HAVE BECOME MORE EXCELLENT IN THE USAGE OF THEIR SPIRITUALLY ENHANCED BIBLICAL KNOWLEDGE AND ARE MORE SUCCESSFUL AT USING THEIR SPIRITUAL GIFTS FOR THE LORD.

LOTS OF PEOPLE ARE GREAT DREAMERS; OTHERS, GOD HAS GIVEN MIND-BLOWING VISIONS. ALL OF THIS IS VERY GOOD, HOWEVER, THERE IS A SERIOUS PROBLEM IN THE HOUSEHOLD OF FAITH, PEOPLE NEVER GIVE THE LORD A CHANCE TO MATURE THEM BEFORE THEY GO BLABBING THE THING, IN THE PRESENCE OF THE DEVIL.

EVERYONE, WITH WHOM YOU SHARE THE JOY OF YOUR EXCITEMENT, IS NOT REALLY AS EXCITED ABOUT YOU AS THEY MAY PRETEND. THEY WOULD RATHER KEEP YOU DOWN! AT LEAST, IF YOU DO GET UP TO PROGRESS IN LIFE, THEY WOULD DEFINITELY WANT TO ENSURE THAT YOU NEVER EXCEED THEIR PROGRESS.

They would prefer that you remain underneath the control of their own thumb. Some people actually allow the influence of the devil to dictate their success, and in turn, those same persons are influenced to throw a wrench in yours.

Be gravely aware of certain people who are really able to help you as you climb to success, but will not help; when out of the blue they begin to inquire of your efforts to succeed.

Upon knowing where you are, they will do absolutely nothing to encourage you or to lift the pressures that come along with working towards your accomplishments. If there is money you need, they do not give it to you, or they don't give you enough to really fit the need.

They never even speak a word on your behalf to other people of any status who could help you, neither do they open any doors for you.

Of course, I am only talking about the people who have the ability to do all of the above. These are the people, who are probably hindering your success from behind the scenes.

Tricky People!*

Witches and warlocks are everywhere you look nowadays. Daily, according to the devil's agenda, they comfortably operate in the demonic realms, and simultaneously they are comfortably hidden within the local membership of many of the churches.

From the top of the choir stand, to the pulpits, out within the pews, and to the back door, so you will always have to be aware of just who it is that you are talking to.

The religious spirit, to which the average churchgoer is guilty of possessing and are not even

SEEKING THE IN-FILLING OF THE HOLY GHOST, THAT SELF SAME RELIGIOUS SPIRIT WORKS HAND AND HAND WITH ALL OF THE DARK SPIRITUAL WORKS OF WITCHCRAFT AND VOO-DOO; ETC.

PEOPLE ARE CHANTING DEMONIC CHANTS WITHOUT ANY FEAR AT ALL, AS A MEANS OF THEIR SPIRITUAL FULFILL-MENT. THIS BEHAVIOR IS ON THE UPRISING. PEOPLE IN ONLY A RELIGIOUS ATMOSPHERE, ARE NOT REALLY PRAYING FOR YOU IN THE NAME OF JESUS, AS MUCH AS THEY WILL PREY ON YOU TO DETER YOUR SUCCESS IN THE LORD, IF THEY CAN.

THEY WILL GRIN, HUG YOU, AND KISS YOUR FACE AND EVEN BUY EXPENSIVE GIFTS FOR YOU, WHILE IT IS NOT AT ALL EVEN REAL, IT'S ALL FAKE. THE CHURCH IS THE ONE PLACE YOU WOULD NOT THINK THAT THERE WOULD BE SO MUCH JEALOUSY, OR SUCH AS TO THE LIKENESS OF THE PRE-VIOUSLY MENTIONED BEHAVIOR, BUT IT'S THERE.

IF IT APPEARS THAT YOU ARE BECOMING MORE POPU-LAR WITH THE PEOPLE OR EVEN GAINING MORE INFLUENCE WITH CHURCH MEMBERS, SOME PEOPLE, EVEN SOME PAS-TORS, WILL SET YOU UP FOR PUBLIC FAILURE TO DESTROY YOUR INFLUENCE TO THOSE WHO MAY BE WELL WISHERS AND HAVE COME TO LOVE YOU VERY MUCH.

WHENEVER YOU ARE FALSELY ACCUSED AND THE PAS-TORAL CLERGY OR OTHER PERSONS WITHIN THE MINISTE-RIAL LEADERSHIP IN CHARGE WILL NOT GIVE YOU A PROPER HEARING, KNOW THIS, THE DEVIL IS BEHIND IT ALL FOR SURE, EVEN IF THEY ARE NOT AWARE OF THE FACT THEM-SELVES!

IF DOING THE WORK OF THE MINISTRY HAS BROUGHT ON THE ATTACK, BY ALL MEANS DON'T STOP DOING THAT WHICH PLEASES THE LORD, HELP IS ON THE WAY. WHAT-EVER TROUBLE THE MINISTRY GETS YOU INTO, STAYING WITH THE MINISTRY WILL ALSO GET YOU OUT. JUST BE SURE THAT YOU ARE NOT TALKING TOO MUCH TO THE WRONG PEOPLE, ABOUT YOUR MINISTRY.

And that ye study to be quiet, and to do your own business, and to work with your own hand, as we commanded you;　I THESSALONIANS 4:11

Did You Know They Weren't Real?

SOME PEOPLE NEED TO TELL SOMEBODY, ANYBODY, OR TO SHOW THEM THE WORK THEY ARE DOING FOR GOD. SOMEONE ELSE WILL EVENTUALLY STEP IN AND TAKE THE CREDIT FOR ALL OF YOUR HARD WORK AND RECEIVE THE RECOGNITION, AS IF IT WAS REALLY ALL OF THEIR IDEA, SIMPLY BECAUSE YOU HAVE GIVEN THEM ALL OF THE INSIDE INFORMATION.

YOU NEED TO KNOW WHEN YOU ARE ONLY BEING PROBED FOR INFORMATION. PEOPLE WILL PRETEND TO KNOW WHAT IS GOING ON WITH YOU, WHEN IN ACTUALITY THEY DO NOT KNOW A THING AND THEY PROBABLY DIDN'T EVEN CARE OR HAVE A CLUE. GENERALLY, PEOPLE WHO ARE ALWAYS IN YOUR FACE, DOING A LOT OF UNRESTRAINED TALKING, ARE NOT HONEST. THEY HAVE HIDDEN AGENDAS WITH YOUR PERSONAL BUSINESS ATTACHED TO IT.

YOU STAND A CHANCE OF BEING MANIPULATED UNDER THE FALSE PRETENSES THAT OTHERS ARE REALLY GENUINELY INTERESTED IN YOUR MOTIVATIONS AND YOUR DREAMS, AS IF THEY WERE THEIR OWN.

BE CAUTIOUS AND DON'T GO THROUGH LIFE BELIEVING THAT EVERYBODY IS WITH YOU. LISTEN TO SILAS AS HE TELLS OF HIS EXPERIENCE WITH THIS SELFSAME TYPE OF PERSON. PAUL DID NOT ALLOW HIMSELF TO BE TAKEN IN BY THE FLATTERING WORDS FALLING OFF OF THE LIPS OF THIS YOUNG WOMAN.

And it came to pass, as we went to prayer, a certain damsel possessed with a spirit of divination met us, which brought her masters much gain by sooth saying: The same followed Paul and us, and cried saying, these, men are servants of the most high God, which shew unto us the way of salvation. And this did she many days. But Paul, be-

*ing grieved turned and said to the spirit, I com-
mand thee in the name of Jesus Christ to come
out of her. And he came out the same hour.*

ACTS 16:17-18

THANK GOD, FOR SPIRITUAL DISCERNMENT. THE PEOPLE OF GOD, OUGHT TO KNOW THE EVIL PRESENCE OF THE DEVIL, NO MATTER WHAT'S COMING OUT OF THE MOUTH OF THE PEOPLE DOING THE TALKING.

STOP GRINNING AND BLUSHING LIKE A CHESHIRE CAT, WHEN THE DEVIL FLIRTS WITH YOU AND FLATTERS YOU WITH HIS LIPS, EVEN IF YOU ENJOY WHAT'S BEING SAID ABOUT YOU. DON'T GIVE INDICATIONS THAT YOU HAVE BEEN TAKEN IN. BE PRAYERFUL AND STAY ON GUARD.

IT WOULD BE TO YOUR ADVANTAGE IF YOU WOULD LEARN WHEN TO BEGIN CELEBRATING AND TO REALIZE THAT EVERYONE IS NOT INVITED TO THE PARTY OF YOUR CELEBRATION.

ALWAYS TELL THE DEVIL, WHENEVER HE DECIDES TO SHOW UP UNANNOUNCED, THAT HE'S NOT INVITED TO PARTY WITH YOU. JUST BE SURE THAT YOU DIDN'T TELL HIM WHAT WAS GOING TO TAKE PLACE WITH YOU AHEAD OF TIME.

✳ *Turn Away From That devil!*

JUST A REMINDER: WHENEVER YOU GET ANGRY, IT'S NOT THE DEVIL'S BUSINESS. WORK QUICKLY TO GET RID OF THE ANGER. WHEN YOUR EMOTIONS FLARE, WHATEVER THAT MIGHT BE, DON'T DISCUSS IT WITH THE DEVIL OR EVEN IN THE DEVIL'S PRESENCE.

DON'T EVER ALLOW YOURSELF, EVER AGAIN, TO BE SO OVER TAKEN TO THE POINT THAT YOU CANNOT PRAISE GOD. EVEN IF YOU DO NOT FEEL LIKE IT, GO AHEAD AND PRAISE GOD. WHENEVER YOU DON'T FEEL IT, GOD DOES. KEEP ON PRAISING GOD. YOU WILL FEEL HIS PRESENCE VERY SOON.

THE DEVIL IS NOT OMNIPRESENT, MEANING THAT HE'S NOT EVERYWHERE AT THE SAME TIME, LIKE GOD. BUT, IF YOU SENSE HIS PRESENCE, BEGIN TO PRAISE GOD. HE

CAN'T STAND IN THE PRESENCE OF GOD. HE WILL GET OUT, IN A HURRY, WHENEVER GOD COMES IN.

Submit yourselves therefore to God, resist the devil, and he will flee from you.   JAMES 4:7

GIVING YOURSELF TO PRAYER AND PRAISE, ON A DAILY BASIS, BUCKLING UNDER THE WEIGHT OF FREQUENT AND SOMETIMES PERIODICALLY FASTING TO INSURE THE NECESSARY DISCIPLINE TO OBEY AND TO FOLLOW THE WORD OF GOD TO THE LETTER, IS THE ONLY WAY TO REALLY KNOW THAT YOU HAVE SUBMITTED YOURSELF TO THE LORD.

LET GOD KNOW, NO MATTER WHAT COMES OR GOES, THAT YOU ARE STAYING WITH HIM ON THE WINNING SIDE. SUCH A BEHAVIORAL STATUS WILL DEFINITELY KEEP THE DEVIL ON THE RUN.

THE DEVIL WILL TELL YOU A LITTLE GOOD, IN ORDER TO TELL YOU A WHOLE LOT OF BAD THINGS, SIMPLY BECAUSE YOU WILL LISTEN! THE DEVIL WILL TELL YOU ENOUGH TRUTH TO GET YOUR ATTENTION, ONLY TO SUCK YOU IN LIKE A VACUUM. HE WILL ALSO TRY TO USE ANY NEGATIVE TRUTH ABOUT YOU, AGAINST YOU, TO DISCOURAGE YOU IF HE CAN. BUT DON'T LISTEN TO HIM!

IF THE PSYCHICS REALLY KNEW THE NEXT LOTTERY NUMBERS TO COME UP, DO YOU REALLY THINK THEY WOULD TELL YOU AND SKIP AN OPPORTUNITY TO BE FILTHY RICH?

THEY WON'T TELL YOU OF THE DETRIMENT, OR THE NEGATIVE DOWNFALLS, OR THE PAIN AND SUFFERING INVOLVED WITH WINNING THE MONEY, OR WHAT YOU WILL HAVE TO GIVE UP, IN ORDER TO OBTAIN THE PROMISE OF THEIR PSYCHIC FORETELLING.

PSYCHICS, ARE DEMONICALLY INFLUENCED AND THEY LACK THE POWER TO KNOW ABOUT YOU, WITHOUT YOUR CONFIRMATORY HELP. THEY HAVE TO FEEL YOUR VIBRATIONS; PICK UP YOUR VIBES. THEY PLAY WORD GAMES WITH YOU. WHENEVER THEY COME ACROSS SOMETHING TRUE ABOUT YOU, THEY ARE JUST AS AMAZED AS YOU ARE.

YOU MAY NOT HAVE CONSIDERED THAT WHENEVER

YOU SIT AND DIVULGE YOUR GUT WRENCHED FEELING BEFORE THESE DIVERSE SPIRIT IDIOMS, IT IS THE DEVIL SITTING ON THE OTHER SIDE LISTENING TO YOUR EVERYTHING, TAKING ACCOUNT AND TYING A BIGGER KNOT IN THE SPIRITUAL NOOSE AROUND YOUR NECK.

Flirting With Death!

NECROMANCY AND SEANCES, ARE NOT JUST COMMUNICATION WITH THE DEAD, AS MUCH AS IT IS DEATH ITSELF! SUCH EXTREME PRACTICES WITH THE DARK SIDE, WILL CERTAINLY ENSURE ETERNAL DAMNATION AND SPIRITUAL DEATH.

MAKE UP IN YOUR MIND NOT TO BE DECEIVED BY THE LIES OF THAT OLD WICKED ENEMY. HE WAS IN HEAVEN ONCE, IN THE EXCELLENCY OF THE GLORY OF THE LORD, AND WAS NOT PERMITTED TO STAY! KNOWING THAT YOUR DESTINY IS HEAVEN, SATAN SHOULD NEVER EXERCISE ANY INFLUENCE OVER YOU, FOR ANY PURPOSE.

THE DECEIVER HIMSELF, WILL WANT YOU TO BELIEVE THAT HE HAS BEEN LIED ON, BUT DON'T BELIEVE IT. EVIL INFLUENCES AND CONTROL ARE NOT MAN-MADE. UNGODLY LURES OF PERVERTED LUST ARE NOT NATURAL CHARACTERISTICS OF THE CURIOSITY OF MANKIND. JESUS SAID THAT; *"Satan is a murderer and a liar from the beginning and the father of every lie."* ST. JOHN 8 : 44

He! Is! Not! Your!! Friend!!!

THE BIBLE TELLS US; YOU HAVE TO FIRST DESIRE TO BE A FRIEND BEFORE YOU RECEIVE A FRIEND. AN ENEMY DOES NOT READILY RECEIVE FRIENDS OF THEIR KNOWN OPPOSITION. HATRED IS TOO POWERFUL, TO ALLOW ANYONE TO EVER FOCUS ON BEING LOVED.

I DON'T SEE SATAN BEING CAPABLE OF BEING A FRIEND. GOD SAID; "LET US MAKE MAN", AT THAT POINT

SATAN KNEW THAT HE WAS ETERNALLY REPLACED AS A WORSHIPPER AND TOTALLY OUSTED FROM THE GLORIOUS PRESENCE OF THE LORD.

TO BEFRIEND MANKIND IS ONLY A COVER UP AND A GREATER SCHEME TO ANNIHILATE HIS REPLACEMENTS. SINCE SATAN CAN NO LONGER WORSHIP GOD, HE DOESN'T WANT ANYONE ELSE TO WORSHIP GOD EITHER; SO GO AHEAD AND WORSHIP GOD AND GIVE

The Lord the praise,

Hallelujah!!!

Quit Lying*

⋯❖⋯

> *Thou shalt not bear false witness against thy neigh-*
> *bor.*   EXODUS 20:16
> *Lie not one to another, seeing that ye have put off*
> *the old man with his deeds*   COLOSSIANS 3:9

Shame On You!!!

LYING CAN BE DATED AS FAR BACK AS EVEN BEFORE TIME CAME INTO EXISTENCE. IT IS SHUNNED AND REJECTED AS AN ACCEPTABLE POLICY FOR HANDLING DAILY AFFAIRS BY THE MORE INTELLECTUALLY HONEST PEOPLE OF THE WORLD.

PEOPLE CAN LIE THEIR WAY OUT OF MOST ANYTHING, EXCEPT FOR THE ETERNAL JUDGMENT OF HELL! EACH TIME YOU SUCCEED AT TELLING ANOTHER LIE AN ETERNAL DEATH SENTENCE IS BEING BROUGHT UPON YOUR SOUL .

GOD STILL HATES LYING, ALTHOUGH LIARS MAY FEEL THAT IT IS NEW, IT'S ACTUALLY ANCIENT.

LIAR - AN INDIVIDUAL' WHO TELLS LIES, OR PERJURES THEMSELVES ON A CONSISTENT BASIS. ONE WHO SPREADS THE UNTRUTH IN-

TENTIONALLY AND PASSES IT OFF AS TRUTH
BY WAY OF SPEAKING, SINGING, OR IN THEIR
LIFE STYLES! (PARAPHRASING BY W.T.)

NO MATTER HOW DEEP THE TRUTH IS BURIED UN-
DERNEATH LIES, IT ALWAYS FIND ITS WAY BACK TO THE
SURFACE, WITHOUT THE PERMISSION OF THE LIAR. <u>GOD
IS NO LIAR</u>! TRUE SPIRIT FILLED BELIEVERS, CANNOT
STAND A LIAR EITHER, BECAUSE THE HOLY GHOST IS
GOD; GOD IS TRUTH!

THE DECEITFUL ART OF LYING IN COMPARRISON TO
THE WILLFUL ACT OF TELLING THE TRUTH, DRASTICALLY
UNVAILS THE DIVERSELY CONTRASTING DIFFERENCE BE-
TWEEN TRUE SAINTS AND SINNERS!

I HAVE ALWAYS WONDERED WHY PEOPLE SIMPLY WON'T
TELL THE TRUTH! IT'S REALLY HEART BREAKING TO KNOW
THAT PEOPLE DON'T FIND AS MUCH FULFILLMENT IN THE
TRUTH, AS MUCH AS THEY ENJOY PERSONALLY ASSOCIATING
WITH LIES. I HAVE OBSERVED THE RUSH THAT LIARS AP-
PEAR TO DISPLAY WHEN THEY HAVE AN INDIVIDUAL DRAWN
IN TO WHAT'S SUPPOSED TO BE A TRUE STORY.

"It's A Lie!"

PEOPLE SOMETIMES MAKE FALSE, UNTRUE CONFES-
SIONS AND BRING FALSE ACCUSATIONS ABOUT OTHER
PEOPLE UNINTENTIONALLY, SIMPLY BECAUSE THEY DON'T
RESEARCH THE INFORMATION THEY ARE TRANSMITTING
TO OTHERS. MORE FREQUENTLY THOUGH, INTENTIONAL
LIES ARE TOLD DISREGARDING THE KNOWN TRUTH!

THERE IS NOTHING MORE EMBARRASSING AND DE-
FLATING TO YOUR EGO THAN TO KNOW THAT A CONVER-
SATION, WHICH LEFT YOU WITH FEELINGS OF EUPHORIA,
ALMOST AS IF STARS WERE ENCIRCLING YOUR HEAD, HAS
BEEN FOUND TO BE NOTHING MORE THAN AN OVER-
BLOWN LIE! MOST LIARS HARDLY EVER CONFESS THE
FACT THAT THEY HAVE LIED TO YOU!

LOTS AND LOTS OF PEOPLE STILL HOLD SORE MEMO-

RIES OF PAST LIES, THAT WERE TOLD TO THEM OR SPREAD THROUGHOUT THE COMMUNITY ABOUT THEM.

CONFESS ALL OF YOUR DEEPLY INWARD HURTS TO CHRIST AND ALLOW HEALING TO BE RELEASED UPON YOUR LIFE. RELEASE THE HURT AND FREE YOURSELF FORM THE PAIN AND FORGIVE THOSE PEOPLE FOR THEIR WILLFUL ATROCIOUS ACTS OF LYING.

YOU EVER SEE ARTIFICIAL FRUIT THAT LOOKED SO LUSCIOUS, LOOKED LIKE YOU COULD SINK YOUR TEETH INTO IT, ONLY TO FIND OUT THAT THE FRUIT TO WHICH YOU WERE SERIOUSLY TEMPTED TO PARTAKE OF, WAS MADE OF PLASTIC, WAX, OR WOOD MATERIALS; THEY WERE ONLY FAKE?

SO IT IS WITH FALSE INFORMATION, THAT CAN NEVER BE TRUE OR REAL! YOU SHOULD NEVER ALLOW YOURSELF TO BECOME TOO DEEPLY ENGROSSED WITH IT. DON'T CONTINUE TO HOLD ON TO A FACT THAT HAS BEEN PROVEN TO BE WRONG, GIVING IT THE BENEFIT OF THE DOUBT HOPING FOR THE TRUTH.

They Don't Care!*

PEOPLE SEEK TO JUSTIFY THEIR WRONG EVEN WHEN THEY HAVE BEEN CAUGHT RIGHT IN THE MIDDLE OF THE LIE THEY ARE TELLING! IT DOESN'T SEEM TO MATTER TO WHOM, WHERE, WHEN, OR EVEN HOW OFTEN THEY PRACTICE THIS YET DEVILISH ART.

WHILE THEY DO NOT MIND LYING, THEY DO NOT ON THE OTHER HAND, LIKE BEING LIED TO! LIARS SEEK TO TAKE ACTION AGAINST OTHER LIARS! ISN'T THAT AMAZING!

YOU WOULD THINK THAT LIARS UNDERSTOOD AND ACCEPTED ALL LIES. THE PROBLEM IS THAT THEY HAVE LIED FOR SO LONG THAT THEY HAVE UNINTENTIONALLY CONVINCED THEMSELVES THAT THEY ARE TRUTHFUL, OR AT LEAST THAT THEY HAVE A GOOD REASON FOR LYING. THEY HAVE EXCUSED THEMSELVES OF THE GUILT OF BE-

ING A LIAR, WHILE THEY INTEND TO HOLD OTHERS AC-
COUNTABLE FOR BEING JUST LIKE THEY ARE.

NO MATTER HOW SWIFT AND SLY YOU MAY BE AT
DODGING AND GETTING AWAY FROM THE DIRECT FACE
OFF WITH THE TRUTH, LYING WILL CATCH UP TO YOU .
JUST AROUND THE VERY NEXT CORNER MAY IN FACT BE
THE UNEXPECTED APPOINTMENT WITH YOUR JUDGMENT!

TO TELL LIES AND TO SING LIES, IS USUALLY AL-
WAYS PROJECTED TOWARDS THE ATTENTION OF OTHERS.
HOWEVER, TO LIVE A LIE, STRONGLY SUGGEST THAT YOU
HAVE LIED TO YOURSELF, TO THE POINT, THAT YOU ARE
CONVINCED THAT OTHERS SHOULD ALSO BELIEVE YOUR
LIES. LYING IS TOO SERIOUS TO BE FOOLING WITH ACCI-
DENTALLY OR WITH DIRECT INTENTIONS!

"What Reason Do You Have?"

INCREDIBLY, MAJOR EXCUSES ARE GIVEN FOR TELL-
ING TERRIBLE LIES. THE EXPLANATIONS GIVEN ARE ONLY A
CONTINUATION AND AN EXTENDED ATTEMPT TO DELIVER
MORE DECEITFULNESS THROUGH A LYING EFFORT TO COVER
UP ALL OF THE PREVIOUS LIES.

ALTHOUGH YOU MAY HAVE SEARCHED WITHIN YOUR-
SELF FOR A TRUE ANSWER FOR THE REASONS THAT YOU LIE,
OTHERS ARE ALSO LEFT TO WONDER HOW IT IS THAT YOU
HAVE THE NERVE TO LIE RIGHT DOWN THE THROAT OF AN-
OTHER INDIVIDUAL? ALLOW ME TO EXPLAIN IT LIKE THIS!

YOU'RE CONSISTENTLY DRIVEN AND SEDUCED BY A
LYING SPIRIT, WHICH YOU DID NOT RESIST OR EVEN PRAY
TO RESIST. YOU WERE SO SURE THAT YOU COULD GET AWAY
WITH IT AND THAT NO ONE WOULD PROBABLY EVER FIND
OUT THE REAL TRUTH OF YOUR FABRICATION.

YOU MIGHT HAVE LIED TO PROVE A POINT TO SOME-
ONE YOU WERE SEEKING TO IMPRESS, WHILE THEY WERE
NOT EVEN IMPRESSED.

SOME PEOPLE HOLD ON TO THE SECRET OF LIES
FOR MANY YEARS. THEY EVENTUALLY FORGET THAT THEY

TOLD THE LIES AND THE REASON THEY AGREED TO NEVER REVEAL THE FACT THAT THEY LIED. IF YOU HAVE NOT REPENTED OF THE LIES THAT YOU HAVE TOLD, YOU ARE STILL GUILTY.

THE GUILT FOR BEING A LIAR WON'T JUST DISSIPATE WITH TIME AND DON'T TELL YOURSELF THAT THE PERSONS YOU HAVE LIED ON WILL BE ALRIGHT AND THAT THEY WILL SOON GET OVER IT.

SUPPOSE SOMEONE DIED FOR THE LIE YOU TOLD, ALTHOUGH THE DAMAGE THAT HAS BEEN DONE CANNOT BE UNDONE AND CONFESSING THAT YOU HAVE LIED TO PEOPLE WILL NOT BRING BACK THEIR LOVED ONES, YOU STILL NEED TO CONFESS THE TRUTH! GOING OUT TO THEIR GRAVE SIGHT IS CERTAINLY NOT THE ANSWER, YOU NEED TO TALK TO THE LORD AND REPENT TO HIM!

CONFESSION WILL NOT GIVE BACK THE YEARS THAT A PERSON MIGHT HAVE SPENT BEHIND PRISON BARS, BUT YOU STILL NEED TO ADMIT THAT YOU LIED! PEOPLE THAT WERE SERIOUSLY AFFECTED BY THE LIES YOU TOLD COULD NEVER RECEIVE YOUR ADMISSION OF GUILT WHEN YOU REPENT FOR LYING, BECAUSE THEY ARE NOW SLEEPING IN THEIR GRAVES.

LYING BURNS THE BRIDGES OF HEALTHY ACCEPTABLE RELATIONSHIPS, TO WHICH CAN NEVER BE REPAIRED, REPLACED, OR EVEN REBUILT FOR THAT MATTER. PEOPLE SHUN YOU WHEN THEY KNOW THAT YOU LIE! THEY SEE YOU COMING AND TURN AND GO THE OTHER WAY, AVOIDING YOU.

*Spiritual Damage**

WHENEVER WE SPEAK, OUR OWN SPIRITS HEAR US FIRSTLY; AND WHATEVER THE MOUTH SPEAKS IS THEN TAKEN IN AND RECEIVED FOR A DEPOSIT INTO OUR SPIRITS. THIS CAN BE VERY HARMFUL TO OUR WELL BEING, SO WE SHOULD BE EXTREMELY CAUTIOUS ABOUT WHAT WE ALLOW TO ENTER INTO OUR SPIRITS FROM OUR OWN MOUTHS. YOU EVER

HEAR THE SAYING; "YOU ARE WHAT YOU EAT?"

LYING, IS BOTH A NATURAL THING, AND A SPIRITUAL THING. BEING THAT IT IS USUALLY GEARED TOWARDS OUR DAILY LIVES IN THE NATURAL, THE GREATER PENALTY IS FELT IN THE SPIRIT OF ONES OWN EXISTENCE!

WE EVENTUALLY BECOME LIARS IF WE WILLINGLY TAKE IN LIES, WHETHER THE LIES COME FROM OUR MOUTHS OR FROM THE MOUTHS OF OTHERS.

> *A wicked doer giveth heed to false lips; [and] a*
> *liar giveth ear to a naughty tongue.* PROVERBS 17:4

TELLING LIES IS NOT JUST SOMETHING YOU MAY HAVE GROWN ACCUSTOMED TO DOING. YOU MIGHT SAY; "WHAT'S THE BIG DEAL, EVERYBODY DOES IT, I MEAN, TELL A LIE EVERY NOW AND THEN?" LISTEN CAREFULLY TO THE SCRIPTURE;

> *Know ye not, that to whom ye yield yourselves*
> *servants to obey, his servants ye are to whom ye*
> *obey; whether of sin unto death, or of obedience*
> *unto righteous.* ROMANS 6:16

LYING REQUIRES THAT YOU OBEY THE DEVIL, WHETHER YOU KNEW IT OR NOT. THE DEVIL WON'T TELL YOU THAT WHEN YOU OBEY HIM, YOU BECOME MORE AND MORE LIKE HIM, EVEN TO THE POINT OF BECOMING IDENTIFIABLY RECOGNIZED AS ONE OF HIS CHILDREN.

FOR AN EXAMPLE, YOU MIGHT SAY; "LYING REALLY WORKS, WOW! I GOT OUT OF THAT!" YOU MIGHT EVEN WANT TO SAY TO ANOTHER INDIVIDUAL TO WHICH YOU ARE SEEKING TO IMPRESS, WITH YOUR GREAT ABILITY TO LIE YOUR WAY THROUGH LIFE WITHOUT EVER HAVING TO COME OUT OF YOUR POCKET; "HUH, STICK WITH ME AND YOU WILL NEVER HAVE TO PAY FOR ANYTHING, WATCH THIS!" THE PERSON YOU LIED TO MAY NEVER FORGET IT.

IN THE COURTROOM YOU MIGHT SAY; "YES YOUR HONOR, I SOLEMNLY SWEAR TO TELL THE TRUTH!" *NOT!*

Liar!

You don't become a *tenth degree black belt liar* over night. By the time you get to this point, you've had the problem a long time. Lying is gradually progressive, the more you lie the better you become. No one ever taught a little child to lie, every time they got caught in a lie, they worked even harder towards not being caught the very next time.

As a matter of fact, telling the truth is what we have had to teach and consistently work to enforce because they insisted on telling a lie to avoid being punished. Lying came natural. Lying is the work of the flesh, which is enmity (separation) from God. You may be in denial, but God knows the real truth and the origin of your problem.

> *Ye are of your father the Devil, and the lust of your father ye will do. He was a murderer from the beginning, and abode not in the truth, because there is no truth in him. When he speaketh a lie, he speaketh of his own; for he is a liar, and the father of it.* St. John 8 :44

Anyone that is of God abides in the truth of God's written word. Their word means something. They can generally be trusted under most circumstances. People of God intend to show themselves trustworthy and truthful, knowing that they must reflect the very image of God.

Persecution will come to those persons that will live godly in this world. They are often disliked by liars and dishonest people. The people of God will not forfeit the favorableness of their good names for the sake of even a small white lie.

No need of trying to continue the fiasco of lying, Jesus has clearly stated exactly who you

 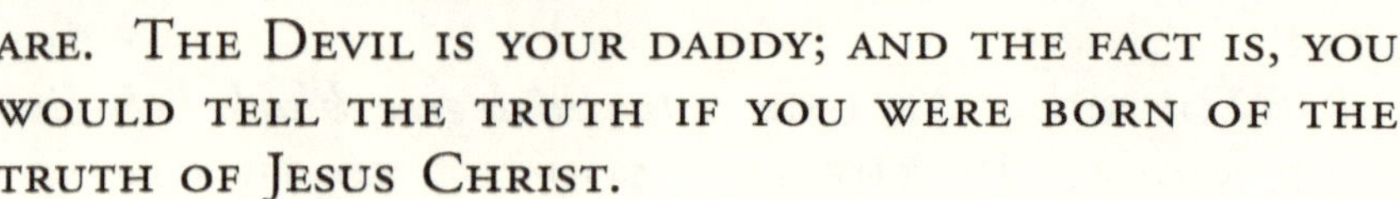

ARE. THE DEVIL IS YOUR DADDY; AND THE FACT IS, YOU WOULD TELL THE TRUTH IF YOU WERE BORN OF THE TRUTH OF JESUS CHRIST.

People Know Who You Are!

NOW THAT YOUR NAME IS ESTABLISHED WITH THE ASSOCIATION OF BEING A LIAR, NO ONE REALLY EXPECTS YOU TO STOP LYING. UNLESS YOU ARE BORN AGAIN AND WASHED THROUGH THE WORD OF GOD AND THE PRECIOUS SHED BLOOD OF JESUS, YOU WILL ALWAYS HAVE A PROBLEM COMING TO TERMS WITH THE EVIL INSIDE OF YOU.

YOUR PROBLEM HAS A TENDENCY TO DRIVE YOU TO LOOK AT THE CALLER I.D. AND REFUSE TO PICKUP THE TELEPHONE RECEIVER, WHENEVER THE TELEPHONE RINGS. YOU LOOK OUT OF THE PEEPHOLE AND REFUSE TO OPEN THE DOOR WHENEVER A VISITOR COMES TO YOUR HOME BECAUSE YOU FEAR HAVING TO FACE THE LIES THAT YOU'VE BEEN TELLING.

PEOPLE DON'T CALL YOU WHEN THEY NEED SOMEONE THEY CAN TRUST, YOUR REPUTATION PRECEDES YOU. NEITHER, WILL THEY CONSIDER YOU WHEN THEY GIVE GIFTS, BECAUSE THEY FEEL THAT YOU ARE SO UNWORTHY.

JESUS IS NOT MAKING INTERCESSION FOR LIARS AND YOU NEED HIM, UNLESS YOU HAVE BEEN LIED TO ABOUT YOUR NEED FOR CHRIST ALSO!

I pray for them: I pray not for the world, but for them which thou hast given me; for they are thine.
ST. JOHN 1 7:9

YOU HAD BETTER EXAMINE YOURSELF WHENEVER YOU SAY; "I AM YOURS LORD, EVERYTHING I AM AND EVERYTHING THAT I AM NOT." NO LIAR; AND YES THAT INCLUDES YOU IF YOU ARE A LIAR, BELONGS TO GOD.

YOU MAY DANCE BEHIND THE PEW OR IN THE AISLE WITH OTHERS AS THEY DANCE IN THE SPIRIT. YOU MAY BE

THE PASTOR, OR THE FIRST LADY OF THE CHURCH, CHURCH MOTHER, DEACON, AUXILIARY MEMBER, TRUSTEE, CHOIR MEMBER, DIRECTOR OF THE CHOIR, MINISTER OF MUSIC, USHER, ANNOUNCEMENT CLERK, OR EVEN THE CHURCH SECRETARY, IT DOESN'T MATTER, IF YOU'RE A LIAR, YOU ARE NONE OF HIS.

EXAMINE YOURSELF! NO NEED IN TRYING TO FOOL EVERYBODY THROUGH CROCODILE TEARS AND LOUD WHALING. GET THAT LYING SPIRIT OUT OF YOU!

THE DEVIL HAS MANAGED TO DESENSITIZE YOU AND TO GET A VERY STRONG, POWERFUL GRIP ON YOUR SOUL. BE WILLING TO CONFESS YOUR SIN PROBLEM TO THE LORD AND REPENT. YOU ARE NO LONGER INNOCENT OF BEING UNAWARE THAT LYING IS A SIN.

HOW MANY STORMS HAVE YOU CAUSED IN YOUR LIFE OR IN THE LIVES OF OTHERS, BECAUSE OF LYING AND DISHONESTY?

A LYING TONGUE IS LIKE A SHORT FUSE OR STEM; DESIGNED TO IGNITE EXPLOSIVE DYNAMITE TNT OR THE DETONATOR TO IGNITE C-4! A LYING TONGUE CAN ALSO BE COMPARED TO THE EXECUTIONER'S SWITCH OF THE ELECTRIC CHAIR OR THE LEVER RELEASING LETHAL TOXIC POISON, FLOWING INTRAVENOUSLY IN THE DEATH CHAMBER.

LYING IS LIKE AN AVALANCHE OR A LANDSLIDE, ONCE IN MOTION, THERE IS NO STOPPING THE ACTION UNTIL IT HAS RUN IT'S DESTRUCTIVE COURSE TO THE BITTER END.

"Lies Hurt!"

LIARS WILL HAVE HURT THEMSELVES THE MOST BY THE TIME THEY REALIZES THEIR ACTUAL STATE OF *being*, MUCH PAIN AND HEARTACHE HAS BEEN CAUSED.

SATAN AND HIS HOST OF DEMONS ARE MORE COMFORTABLE NOW THAT YOU ARE IN AGREEMENT WITH THEM. DEMON SPIRITS ARE ASSIGNED TO HOLD YOU IN A LYING STATE. YOU ARE NO THREAT TO THE WORKS OF

DARKNESS, WHICH THE PEOPLE OF GOD ARE CONSISTENTLY WARRING AGAINST. MAYBE YOU DID NOT REALIZE THAT YOU WERE A TEAM PLAYER ON THE LOSING SIDE, BUT YOU ARE!

EVERY TIME YOU LIE AND SUCCEED IN DECEPTION, YOU HAVE SCORED ANOTHER POINT FOR THE DEVIL. NO MATTER HOW MANY POINTS YOU SCORE, YOUR TEAM HAS ALREADY LOST. SATAN HAS THE BIG "L"(LOSER) ON HIS FOREHEAD!

LIARS ARE MIXED IN EVERYWHERE, THEY ARE PEOPLE OF PHENOMENAL TALENTS AND SKILLS; USUALLY THEY ARE OFTEN THOROUGHLY EDUCATED AND VERY STUDIOUS WITH HIGH I.Qs. THEY ARE FOUND AMONG THE VERY RICH IN FINANCIAL WEALTH; THEY ARE PERSONS OF GREAT INFLUENCE IN THE SOCIETY, AND HAVE BECOME WELL-TRUSTED BECAUSE THEY ARE GREAT SPEAKERS THAT KNOW HOW TO TALK.

THEY ARE SO SMART THAT FROM THE TIME THEY SET THEIR FOCUS UPON CERTAIN INDIVIDUALS, THEY KNOW THOSE INDIVIDUALS CANNOT BE LIED TO, HOWEVER THE LYING SPIRIT ON THE INSIDE OF THEMSELVES WON'T ALLOW THEIR OWN INTELLIGENCE TO INSTRUCT THEM *not* TO LIE.

LUCIFER LIED; HE SAID THAT HE WOULD EXALT HIS THRONE AS HIGH OR EVEN HIGHER THAN GOD'S THRONE. WELL, THE REST IS HISTORY, BECAUSE, WE NOW KNOW WHAT BECAME OF THAT LYING DECLARATION FROM THE MOUTH OF LUCIFER, NOW THE INFAMOUS SATAN.

SATAN HAS BEEN ETERNALLY DECLARED, TERMINALLY GUILTY. EVERYONE WHO FOLLOWS HIM IS ALSO GUILTY BY ASSOCIATION. TO SAY THAT THERE IS A LITTLE DEVIL IN EVERYBODY, EVEN THOUGH AN INDIVIDUAL HAS BEEN WASHED IN THE BLOOD OF JESUS, IS ALSO A MAJOR UNDERMINING DECEPTION FROM THE PIT OF HELL!

WHEN JESUS STEPS IN, SATAN HAS TO FLEE. REMEMBER, A LIAR WILL NOT TARRY IN THE LORD'S SIGHT. THE

Devil cannot stay.

Don't play in the dark by telling lies. To you it may have been just a little white lie, maybe too small for anyone to be concerned with. A lie is a lie and it doesn't matter whether it is intentional or not. It is, what it is!

> *Be not deceived: evil communications corrupt good manners*   I Corinthians 15:33 b
> *Let no corrupt communication proceed out of thy mouth, but that which is good to the use of edifying, that it may administer grace unto the hearers.*   Ephesians 4:29

As we converse with others, it is imperative that we establish truth among ourselves. Truth is the strength of powerful up-building communication.

In the beginning, Satan brought doom, simply because he lied. A third part of Heaven was also corrupted, they lost their most beautiful rights to worship.

Guess what, you do not have to lose yours!!!

Quit Lying!!

GOD's Ears; Your Mouth!

> Be careful for nothing; but in everything by prayer and supplication with thanksgiving let your request be made known unto God. **PHILIPPIANS 4:6**
> PRAY WITHOUT CEASING.
> **II THESSALONIANS 5:17**
> And he spake a parable unto them to this end, that men ought always to pray, and not faint;
> **LUKE 18:1**

By All Means Possible, Pray!!!!!

MANY TESTIFY THAT THEY HAVE BEEN SAVED AND DELIVERED, BUT THE POWER OF PRAYER IS YET OBSCURE, AS WELL AS UNDISCOVERED WITHIN THEIR LIVES. GOD SO EX-PLICATIVELY DEFINED THE POWER AND THE PURPOSE OF PRAYER, OFTEN IN THE WORD OF GOD.

THE UNBELIEVER WHO FEELS UNWORTHY TO ASK GOD FOR ANYTHING AND THE UNBELIEVING BELIEVER WHO DOUBTS THE POWER OF THEIR OWN PRAYER; BOTH NEED TO DISCOVER THAT REAL MISSING ELEMENT IN ESSENCE TO

PRAYER, WHICH IS THE POWERFUL AND MOST REALISTIC ENGAGEMENT OF PRAYER.

MANY PEOPLE FEEL THAT THEY LACK A COMPLETE UNDERSTANDING OF PRAYER. THEY DON'T UNDERSTAND WHO REALLY IS WORTHY OF TALKING TO GOD. IF WE ARE ABLE TO ENGAGE IN A PRAYERFUL DIALOGUE WITH GOD, WHERE SHOULD SUCH AN AWESOME ACTIVITY TAKE PLACE AND HOW DO WE EVEN BEGIN TO PRAY?

PEOPLE QUESTION, WHO IS REALLY LISTENING ON THE OTHER END OF PRAYER WHENEVER THEY DO PRAY AND THE AMOUNT OF TIME THEY HAVE TO COMPLETE THEIR PRAYER? IT IS NOT ABOUT HOW LONG YOU PRAY OR WHERE YOU ARE WHENEVER YOU PRAY, JUST GO AHEAD AND PRAY!

SO MUCH TIME IS SPENT QUESTIONING, THAT PEOPLE NEVER ACTUALLY GET TO THE POINT OF PRAY-ING. PRAYER IS THE TYPE OF THING YOU CANNOT BOTH DO AND DOUBT, AT THE SAME TIME. DOUBTING AND QUESTIONING PRAYER WILL DEFINITELY PARALYZE THE POWER OF PRAYER AND NULLIFY ANY POSSIBILITY FOR THE REQUESTED RESPONSE.

*Unsuccessful Praying**

FAILURE TO EMBRACE GOD OF THE HOLY BIBLE, THROUGH JESUS CHRIST, DELETES THE POSSIBILITY OF ANY REALISTIC RESPONSE TO PRAYER.

UNBELIEF IS THE MOST ACCURATE AND POWERFUL DESTRUCTION OF A PRAYERFUL DIALOGUE. SOME BELIEVE THAT PRAYER IS ONLY ACTING UPON THE ENGAGEMENT OF THE UTTERANCE OF REPETITIOUS WORDS. OTHERS BELIEVE, THAT IN REPETITIVE REQUEST, THE ARM OF THE LORD WILL HAVE BEEN TWISTED IN THEIR FAVOR.

GOD CAN'T BE FORCED TO GIVE YOU AN ANSWER TO YOUR PRAYER, BEFORE THE DESIGNATED TIME OF HIS IN-TENDED RESPONSE. ALTHOUGH WE PRAY IN FAITH BELIEV-ING, FAITH ALONE REQUIRES PATIENCE. SOME REFUSE THE IDEA OF PRAYER, FOR REASON OF THE FACT THAT THEY

DON'T LIKE TO WAIT! WAITING IS NOT ALWAYS THE CASE!

THE HAND OF THE LORD IS THE ONLY SUCCESSFUL MEANS OF FITTING THE NEED. IT IS NEVER NECESSARY TO GO OUT ON YOUR OWN, WITHOUT THE LORD.

SOME CHOOSE OTHER WAYS OUTSIDE OF THE WILL OF GOD TO GET WHAT THEY WANT. OTHER WAYS MAY INDEED BE QUICK IN TERMS OF ALLOWING PEOPLE TO GET WHAT THEY WANT, BUT THE OTHER WAYS ALSO HAVE CONSEQUENCES.

HAS THE LORD DONE SOMETHING TO YOU THAT CAUSED YOU TO CEASE FROM PRAYING AND TRUSTING IN HIM?

THERE MAY HAVE BEEN SOME THINGS TO TAKE PLACE IN YOUR LIFE, BUT CAN YOU ACTUALLY SAY FOR TRUTH THAT, IT WAS "GOD'S FAULT!! IF SO, WHY???

IS YOUR QUESTION, WHAT IS GOD DOING FOR ME?

THE BODY THAT YOU'RE LIVING IN, WHO GAVE IT TO YOU? HOW IS THE BREATH STAYING IN YOUR LUNGS? WHAT KEEPS THE SIGHT IN YOUR EYES AND THE HEARING IN YOUR EARS? EXACTLY WHAT HAS KEPT THE ABILITY TO WALK IN YOUR LEGS AND THE SWINGING IN YOUR ARMS? WHAT ABOUT THE STRENGTH OF YOUR MUSCLE TISSUE? WHO HAS DONE ALL OF THESE THINGS?

WHEN WAS THE LAST TIME YOU EVEN CONSIDERED THE BENDS OF YOUR ELBOWS AND KNEES? WHAT ABOUT THE OPENING AND CLOSING OF YOUR EYELIDS? ALL OF THESE LITTLE THINGS ARE THOSE KINDS OF THINGS THAT YOU CANNOT DO AND COULD NOT HAVE EVER DONE FOR YOUR OWN SELF!

Can't Get What You Want?

YOU CAN HAVE THINGS, HOWEVER, THERE ARE REQUIREMENTS AND BIBLICAL PRINCIPLES TO BE APPLIED BEFORE YOU GO DEMANDING GOD TO REACH DOWN TO YOUR REQUEST. IF MATERIAL THINGS IS ALL YOU WANT FROM GOD, BUT HE HASN'T GIVEN THEM TO YOU, PERHAPS YOU

SHOULD LOOK A LITTLE DEEPER INTO THE WORD OF GOD.

GOD IS NOT A SLOT MACHINE OR A SANTA CLAUSE. NOT EVEN A SLOT MACHINE YIELDS YOUR IMMEDIATE EXPECTATIONS, JUST BECAUSE YOU PUT A COIN INTO THE MACHINE! YOU MIGHT AS WELL PRAY AND CONTINUE TO PRAISE GOD UNTIL YOU GET AN ANSWER FROM HIM!

GOD HAS ALREADY GIVEN YOU THE ABILITY AND POWER TO DO CERTAIN THINGS FOR YOURSELF AND GOD IS NOT GOING TO FEEL GUILTY ABOUT THOSE THINGS AND CHANGE HIS MIND AND DO THOSE THINGS FOR YOU! IT DOESN'T MAKE GOOD SINCE TO BE ANGRY WITH GOD, SIMPLY BECAUSE YOU'VE FAILED YOURSELF.

MOST POVERTY STRICKEN PEOPLE EXPEND A GREAT BALANCE OF THEIR TIME AND ENERGY IN HOPELESSNESS, PSYCHOLOGICALLY DROWNED IN THE FACT THAT THEY CAN'T HELP THEMSELVES. THEY CAN'T DO IT ON THEIR OWN!

PRAYER, WILL TURN YOUR FOCAL POINT BACK TO THE LORD AND HELP YOU TO KNOW OF YOUR INABILITIES AGAIN, SINCE YOU'VE PROBABLY FORGOTTEN THAT YOU WEREN'T ABLE TO HELP YOUR SELF FROM THE BEGINING.

YOU THAT WON'T PRAY LIKE YOU SHOULD, SUPPOSE GOD WAS JUST LIKE YOU, WHAT SHAPE WOULD YOU BE IN? WHAT IF GOD NEEDED TO DEPEND ON YOU? SUPPOSE HE PRAYED TO YOU INSTEAD? WOULD HE GET HIS PRAYERS ANSWERED? WOULD YOU SUPPLY HIS EVERY NEED?

I WONDER IF HE WOULD SAY THE THINGS ABOUT YOU THAT YOU HAVE SAID ABOUT HIM, WHENEVER YOU WERE DISAPPOINTED WITH HIM? WOULD YOU EVEN FIND HIM WORTHY OF HAVING HIS PRAYERS ANSWERED? THERE HAS BEEN TIMES THAT YOU FELT GOD SHOULD HAVE ANSWERED YOUR PRAYERS, WHEN IN FACT YOU WERE NOT EVEN IN THE RIGHT STANDING WITH HIM.

The Greatest Part Of Prayer; The Answer!

WHENEVER GOD ANSWERS, HE DOES SO FOR THE PURPOSE OF HIS OWN DIVINE INTENTIONS. THROUGH PRAYER WE ARE DEVELOPING A RELATIONSHIP WITH GOD. THERE IS NO GREATER METHOD OF KNOWING THAT GOD IS REAL, THAN TO ENQUIRE OF HIM AND TO GET AN ANSWER.

HOW DO YOU EVEN ASK GOD FOR ANYTHING, WHEN YOU NEVER REALLY INTENDED TO TALK TO HIM, BECAUSE YOU REALLY DON'T BELIEVE THAT HE IS REAL? YOU MAY FEEL THAT YOU WOULD RATHER NOT EVER HEAR THE VOICE OF GOD, IF GOD REALLY TALKS.

IS YOUR ATTITUDE, DON'T TALK TO ME, JUST GIVE TO ME WHAT I WANT?

GOD IS INTERESTED IN YOU, HE DESIRES TO SEE YOU PROSPER THROUGH YOUR RELATIONSHIP WITH HIM. PRAYER IS THE KEY TO RECEIVING EVERYTHING THAT THE LORD HAS FOR YOU. YOU MUST PRAY ACCORDING TO HIS WORD WITH THE RIGHT MOTIVES AND INTENTIONS. GOD PURPOSE FOR INCREASE IS NOT TO ENABLE YOU TO ENGAGE IN MORE SIN AND INIQUITY, THAN YOU DID BEFORE.

WHAT WE DESIRE, WHENEVER WE PRAY SHOULD REFLECT THE ATTITUDE OF THE SAME SPIRIT OF CHRIST. JESUS DESIRED TO BE THE DIRECT REFLECTION TO THE GIVER WHO ANSWERS PRAYER, BEING GOD. DO YOU DESIRE GOD TO BE SEEN IN WHATEVER IT IS YOU GET FROM HIM?

Some People Don't Like It!!!

PRAYER HAS TAKEN ON MANY DIFFERENT ALIENATED FORMS, NOTHING RESEMBLING THE PRAYERFUL MANNER TO WHICH JESUS TAUGHT US (ST. MATTHEW 6: 9-13).

THERE HAS ALWAYS BEEN OPPOSITION TO PRAYER, THOUGH THE REJECTION TO PRAYER WAS NOT NECESSARILY AN ALL OUT WAR LIKE WHAT WE ARE EXPERIENCING THESE DAYS. EXCUSES FOR NOT PRAYING ARE OFTEN GIVEN, WHILE

MANY NEVER SEEM TO REALIZE THE AMPLIFIED ABSENCE OF PRAYER AT LARGE IN THEIR SURROUNDING COMMUNITIES, UNTIL A MAJOR TRAGEDY TAKES PLACE.

PEOPLE ARE OUTRAGED AT THE THOUGHT OF PRAYER, AS IF PRAYER IS GOING TO INFLICT BODILY HARM UPON THEIR PERSON.

SCHOOL OFFICIALS ON ALL LEVELS OFTEN POSE ABSOLUTELY NO RESISTANCE TO TEACHING ALTERNATIVE LIFE-STYLES AND THE GAY AGENDA, AS WELL AS, MANY OTHER SECULARLY PERVERTED TOPICAL MATTERS OF DISCUSSION CONCERNING SEXUALITY. HOWEVER, THEY VIGOROUSLY RESIST OPEN DISCUSSIONS AND CLASSROOM STUDIES THAT PERTAIN TO GOD THE FATHER AND CREATOR, JESUS CHRIST THE ONLY BEGOTTEN SON, AND THE HOLY GHOST.

TEACHINGS OF SUCH BIBLICAL TRUTHS ARE SAID TO BE DISRUPTIVE TO THE FREE THOUGHT-PROCESSES OF YOUNGER PEOPLE AND UNCONSTITUTIONAL. LEGISLATIVE ACTIONS AGAINST PRAYER IN THE SCHOOL, SHOULD NOT HAVE AFFECTED THE HOME, WHICH IS WHERE PRAYER SHOULD BEGIN!

THE BELIEF IS THAT SUCH LIBERATED ATTITUDES ARE HEALTHY FOR YOUTHFUL AND ADOLESCENT MINDS. HOWEVER, THE AUTHORITATIVE INFLUENCE AND POWER OF SOCIETY, HAVE DECIDED THAT YOUNGER PEOPLE ARE TO BE HELD RESPONSIBLE AND SOMETIMES TRIED AS ADULTS FOR UNRESTRAINED DETESTABLE ACTS, WHEN CITED AS PARTAKERS IN UNACCEPTABLE BEHAVIOR.

Pray For The Children!

THE CHILDREN OF TODAY ARE IN NEED OF MUCH PRAYER! EVERY PARENT SHOULD LEAD THEIR OWN CHILDREN IN PRAYER IN THE HOME AND TEACH THEM TO PRAY! IT IS IMPORTANT TO TEACH CHILDREN TO PRAY IN THE CORRECT MANNER, BEGINNING AT THE EARLIEST STAGES OF LEARNING. NEVER DEPEND ON SOMEONE ELSE TO PRAY FOR OR EVEN TO PRAY WITH YOUR OWN CHILDREN.

THE KNOWLEDGE OF THE IN-DEPTH METHODICAL USAGE OF MANY THINGS THAT CONCERNED CHILDREN, MAY HAVE BEEN ABSENT FROM OUR UNDERSTANDING, BEING THAT WE HAD JUST BEEN INTRODUCED TO RAISING CHILDREN AS A PARENT. CONTACT WITH THOSE THINGS, THOUGH FOR THE FIRST TIME, WAS INDEED NECESSARY FOR THE BETTER GOOD OF OUR CHILDREN.

MOST PEOPLE ARE OFTEN SKEPTICAL OF TAKING A CHANCE WITH THINGS THEY ARE UNKNOWLEDGEABLE OF; PERHAPS AS WE MIGHT HAVE BEEN AS PARENTS. HOWEVER, AFTER GIVING ANOTHER THOUGHT, THEY NOW PARTAKE AND PARTICIPATE IN THOSE SAME THINGS THEY WERE PREVIOUSLY AFRAID OF, HAVING DECIDED TO GIVE A CHANCE TO THE UNKNOWN.

We Need More Prayer!*

I CAN REMEMBER LEAVING MY CHILDREN AT THE DAYCARE FOR THE VERY FIRST TIME, NOT REALLY KNOWING ANYTHING ABOUT THE STAFF AND THEIR ABILITY TO CARE FOR CHILDREN, OR THE LEARNING ATMOSPHERE, I SIMPLY TRUSTED BASED ON THE REPORT THAT I HAD RECEIVED FROM ANOTHER SOURCE. EVEN IN A SENSE FEAR, I LEFT MY CHILDREN AT THE DAYCARE. I DID IT AFRAID!

THE SAME OPPORTUNITY IS NEVER GIVEN TO TAKE A CHANCE WITH THE UNKNOWLEDGEABLE APPLICATION OF PRAYER! PEOPLE SIMPLY CHOOSE TO STAY AWAY. JUST IN CASE YOU DIDN'T KNOW, PRAYER IS A SINCERE TALK WITH GOD! PRAYER IS THE HIGHEST ORDER-FORM OF CONTACT IN WHICH WE GET IN TOUCH AND COMMUNICATE WITH OUR GOD.

YOU CAN NEVER PRAY TOO MUCH, SO DON'T EVER LET ANYONE TELL YOU THAT YOU DO! THERE IS NOT A LAW, AS PERTAINING TO THE NUMBER OF TIMES AN INDIVIDUAL MAY GET IN TOUCH WITH GOD, IN THE RUN OF A SINGLE DAY THROUGH PRAYER.

EVERY CHILD OF GOD OUGHT TO PRAY SEVERAL TIMES A DAY, AS DANIEL DID. PRAYER CAUSED DANIEL TO BE

THROWN IN THE LIONS' DEN, BUT, THE STORED UP PRAYERS OF DANIEL, CAUSED THE JAWS OF THE LIONS TO BE SHUT!

IT WAS ALSO PRAYER THAT DELIVERED DANIEL, OUT OF THE LIONS' DEN! DANIEL WASN'T LEFT TO GIVE THE LIONS A CHANCE TO DEVOUR HIM, HE WAS RELEASED!

IF PRAYER WILL GET YOU INTO TROUBLE, PRAYING WILL GET YOU OUT! PRAYER IS NOT TO BE KEPT CON-CEALED BEHIND A WALL OR A CLOSED DOOR LIKE SOME MAY BELIEVE. THE ONLY WAY THAT PEOPLE WILL KNOW WE ARE TRULY ACQUAINTED WITH THE CREATOR OF THE UNIVERSE IS THROUGH PRAYER.

WHENEVER THE QUESTION IS ASKED; "HOW DO YOU KNOW THAT YOU ARE SAVED?" YOU WILL BE EFFEC-TIVE GIVING AN ANSWER, KNOWING THAT YOU HAVE MADE THE CONNECTION WITH GOD THROUGH PRAYER!

IT IS NOT YOU THAT PEOPLE WANT TO KNOW AND NEITHER IS IT YOU THEY WANT TO SEE! THEY WANT TO KNOW GOD AND THEIR DESIRE IS TO SEE HIS HANDY WORKS.

IT IS ALL ABOUT GOD AND IT IS NEVER, EVER ABOUT YOU, AND I CAN'T STATE THIS FACT ENOUGH!!!

> *That I may know him, and the power of his res-*
> *urrection, And the fellowship of his sufferings,*
> *being made conformable unto his death,*
>
> PHILIPPIANS 3:10

Pray For Yourself!

RELATIVE TO WHO YOU MAY HAVE BECOME AS A PER-SON, YOUR FAMILY NAME COULD NEVER BE CITED AS THE REASON THAT YOU DEVELOPED INTO BEING WHO YOU ARE.

SUPPOSE YOU LIVE IN THE BIGGEST HOUSE IN THE COUNTRY, THE HOUSE DOES NOT HAVE THE POWER TO ES-TABLISH YOU; IT MAY DEFINE WHAT YOU HAVE? MONEY OR THE LACK OF MONEY IS REALLY NOT AS IMPORTANT TO YOUR CHARACTER AS MOST PEOPLE WOULD HAVE YOU TO BELIEVE.

PEOPLE DEPEND UPON MATERIALISM AND PROFES-SIONAL CAREERS TO ESTABLISH THE VALIDATED EXISTENCE

OF THEIR LIFE. NATIONAL ACCLAIM AND POPULARITY WILL NOT ADEQUATELY SERVE THE PURPOSE TO ESTABLISH YOU WHENEVER IT MATTERS MOST. PRAYER WILL DO IT! PRAYER WORKS EVERY TIME!

Get Acquainted With Him In Prayer!

PRAYER IS THE ONLY WAY TO BECOME LIKE GOD. PRAYING ENABLES US TO KNOW THE PRESENCE OF GOD THROUGH FAITH. GOD IS AVAILABLE FOR US TO GET IN TOUCH WITH HIM THROUGH PRAYER.

WHENEVER A PERSON PRAYS IN ERROR ON A CONSISTENT BASIS, THEY USUALLY NEVER SEE A NEED TO CHANGE. ONCE YOU HAVE LEARNED TO PRAY RIGHT, YOU NEVER FORGET AND YOU WILL NEVER BE INFLUENCED TO DEVIATE. THERE WILL ALWAYS BE A YEARNING DEEP WITHIN AN INDIVIDUAL, CALLING THEM TO A DEEPER PLACE IN PRAYER.

THE LATE DR. S. E. MITCHELL USED TO SAY; "ANYBODY THAT PRAYS WRONG, CAN'T PRAY RIGHT AND VISE-VERSA", I HAVE FOUND THIS WISDOM TO BE VERY TRUE AND SOUND.

TURN YOUR FAITH LOOSE AND DILIGENTLY SEEK THE FACE OF GOD WITHOUT GIVING UP OR GIVING IN TO THE PRESSURE OF THE WAIT. WAITING PRESSURE, IS OFTEN EQUIVALENT TO <u>WEIGHTED</u> PRESSURE, WHEREAS SITUATIONS BECOME VERY HEAVY OVER AN EXTENDED PERIOD OF TIME.

DON'T EVER THINK THAT GOD HAS DENIED YOU, SIMPLY BECAUSE HE HAS NOT SHOWED UP, WITH YOUR ANSWER. THE ANSWER MAY NOT BE THERE YET, BUT IT'S ON THE WAY. IT IS NOT ABOUT HOW FAST YOU GET THE ANSWER ALWAYS, IT IS HOWEVER, ABOUT KNOWING THAT IT'S COMING. HE IS ON THE WAY TO THE RESCUE, SO WAIT ON HIM!

GOD, HIMSELF; HE DOES NOT HAVE TO COME FROM ANYWHERE, BECAUSE HE IS OMNIPRESENT, MEANING THAT HE IS EVERYWHERE, ALL OF THE TIME, AT EXACTLY THE VERY SAME TIME. YOU REALLY CAN FIND THE LORD, IF YOU WILL SEARCH FOR HIM WITH ALL OF YOUR

HEART.

I Suggest You Consider The Thought!

DON'T WAIT AROUND, SLOWING YOURSELF, BEING HESITANT OF PRAYING. YOU'RE BETTER OFF IF YOU PRAY QUICKLY, WHENEVER THE NEED ARISES. IT IS A GOOD THING TO JUST PRAY, BECAUSE YOU KNOW THE NEED FOR PRAYER IS ALWAYS IN ORDER. NEVER STOP PRAYING FOR YOURSELF, AS WELL AS OTHERS. YOU CAN ACTUALLY PRAY AHEAD OF A PROBLEM OR A SITUATION THAT MAY DEVELOP.

PRAYING AHEAD IS LIKE DEPOSITING MONEY IN THE BANK OR EVEN TO THE LIKES OF BUILDING A STORM SHELTER BEFORE THE STORM! WHENEVER I SAY, PRAY AHEAD, I MEAN TO DEVELOP A LIFE OF PRAYER. PRAY AT EVERY OPPORTUNITY THAT ARISES IN THE RUN OF THE DAY.

PRAYER IN FAITH WILL PLEASE THE LORD. IT IS ALWAYS A GOOD THING TO PRAY TO LIVE A PEACEFUL LIFE IN CHRIST AND TO BE FILLED WITH THE HOLY GHOST, BECAUSE YOU NEED IT.

PRAY TO BE STRONG IN TRYING MOMENTS; THAT YOUR FAITH WILL NOT FAIL YOU. JESUS CHRIST PRAYED AHEAD OF HIS DYING HOUR, THAT HE WOULD FULFILL THE FATHERS PLAN, TO GIVE HIMSELF FOR A PERFECT SACRIFICE. THE TASK AHEAD OF JESUS WAS SO IMPORTANT THAT JESUS DID NOT TAKE A CHANCE ON PUTTING ANY CONFIDENCE IN HIS OWN FLESH.

Settle It On Your Knees![*]

THE ONLY WAY TO TRUST IN THE LORD TOTALLY AND COMPLETELY IS TO PRAY! BE STABLE AND PRAY IN TOTAL FAITH, BELIEVING GOD FOR AN ANSWER. EVERY TIME I PRAY, I ALWAYS EXPECT AN ANSWER FROM THE LORD. IF GOD DON'T ANSWER YOUR PRAYERS, NOBODY ELSE CAN, BECAUSE THERE IS NO ONE ELSE, ANYWHERE, WHO HAS THE POWER TO ANSWER THE PRAYERS THAT

YOU HAVE PRAYED TO THE LORD.

SINCE YOU PRAYED WITH THE LORD IN MIND, DON'T ALLOW ANY OTHER SOURCE OR RESOURCE, TO BE SUBSTITUTED AS A MEANS OF ANSWERING YOUR PRAYERS.

YOU MUST BE ABLE TO SEE A SINGLE TREE, WHILE IT IS YET IN THE MIDST OF THE TREES IN THE FOREST, WHICH MEANS THAT YOU WILL JUST HAVE TO LOOK A LITTLE CLOSER.

IT MAY BE THAT YOU CAN'T SEE THE TREES FOR LOOKING AT THE FOREST. YOU, AND THE REST OF THE PEOPLE, MAKE UP THE TOTAL CONSISTENCY OF THE POPULATION OF THIS WORLD. DON'T THINK THAT GOD IS ONLY INTERESTED IN MEETING THE NEEDS OF THE WORLD IN ITS ENTIRETY, RATHER THAN MEETING YOUR OWN PERSONAL NEEDS. THE HEALTH AND NOURISHMENT OF EVERY SINGLE TREE IN THE FOREST IS EQUALLY NECESSARY TO COMPLETE THE VISIBLE FOLIAGE, AND TO PROVIDE THE NATURAL HABITAT FOR THE EXISTING WILDLIFE IN THE FOREST.

YOU MAY ONLY FEEL THAT YOUR NEEDS WILL BE MET, IF THEY ARE INCLUDED WITHIN THE PRAYER REQUEST THAT HAVE GONE UP BEFORE THE LORD, COLLECTIVELY, FOR THE ENTIRE CHURCH BODY? TO OBSERVE THAT KIND OF AN ATTITUDE TOWARDS PRAYER, IS TRULY SUGGESTIVE THAT YOUR UNDERSTANDING OF GOD AND PRAYING TO HIM, IS TOTALLY OFF! WARPED THINKING ALLEVIATES THE DISTINCT PURPOSE FOR PRAYING.

THERE ARE MANY BOOKS ON THE SUBJECT OF PRAYER AND PRAYING, NEVERTHELESS, SUCH LITERATURE IS NOT NECESSARILY THE *exclusive authority* ON THE SUBJECT OF PRAYER. A LITERARY WORK CAN ONLY BE THE INTERPRETATION OF A PARTICULAR INDIVIDUAL'S PERCEPTION, BASED ON WHAT THEY MAY HAVE BEEN TAUGHT OR THEIR EXPERIENCE ON THE SUBJECT. THE INFORMATION IS NOT NECESSARILY A REVELATION FROM GOD.

THE PROMISED BENEFITS OF PRAYER ARE ONLY REALIZED UPON THE INITIAL DETERMINATION TO BEGIN

PRAYING AND SPONTANEOUSLY ACTING UPON THAT DECISION!

Will You Be Heard Praying?

SOME PEOPLE PREFER TO PRAY IN SILENCE IN THEIR OWN HEART. I BELIEVE SHAMEFULNESS IN THE HEART OF AN INDIVIDUAL WILL NOT ALLOW THEM TO PRAY OUT LOUD, SO THAT OTHERS CAN HEAR THEIR PRAYER. I CAN RELATE TO A SINNER WHO WANTS TO TELL THE LORD ABOUT THEIR SINFULNESS, BUT WOULD PREFER IF NO ONE ELSE HEARD THEIR PRAYER. SIN IS THE CAUSE OF SHAMEFULNESS. SIN IS EMBARRASSING ALL BY ITSELF!

CERTAIN INDIVIDUALS ARE NOT ALWAYS COMFORTABLE WITH THE PRESENT SURROUNDINGS. SOME FEEL THAT PEOPLE WOULD TAKE WHAT THEY HEARD UTTERED FROM THE LIPS OF OTHER PEOPLE DURING PRAYER AND USE THOSE SAME WORDS AGAINST THEM IN A VERY NEGATIVE MANNER. OF COURSE A DESIRE TO PRAY SILENTLY DOES HAVE A PROPER PLACE AND PROPER TIME.

SOME PEOPLE ONLY PRAY OUT ALOUD WHENEVER THEY GET IN TROUBLE, BECAUSE THEY HAVE PERCEIVED THE LORD AS BEING NOTHING MORE THAN A TROUBLE-SHOOTER. AS LONG AS THINGS ARE GOING WELL AND DOING FINE, THE NEED TO PRAY NEVER ARISES. MANY OF THESE SAID INDIVIDUALS ARE REGULAR CHURCH MEMBERS, WHO ARE ALLOWED TO PARTICIPATE IN THE ACTIVITIES OF THE WORSHIP SERVICES.

MOST PEOPLE PRAY ALOUD, SEEKING REMEDIES TO RID THEIR ILLNESS. LET US NOT FORGET THOSE INDIVIDUALS WHO PRAY ALOUD JUST LIKE THE BIBLICAL "PHARISEES", WHOM JESUS REBUKED ON SEVERAL OCCASIONS. THEY PRAYED IN PUBLIC PLACES, SEEKING TO PROVE THAT THEY WERE REALLY IN TOUCH WITH GOD. THEY HAD RELIGION, HOWEVER THEY DID NOT HAVE THE RELATIONSHIP THEY ALWAYS PROJECTED.

SOME PEOPLE WILL PRAY AT THE DROP OF A HAT, AS LONG AS THEY HAVE AN AUDIENCE TO LISTEN TO THEM PRAY.

BEAUTIFUL WORDS DO NOT MAKE PRAYERS, BEAUTIFUL HEARTS DO!!

*Modern Day Pharisee**

I HAVE OBSERVED PEOPLE PRAYING IN CHURCH, AS IF THEY HAD A HAND IN WRITING THE BIBLE. THEY USE EVERY NAME GIVEN TO GOD THAT THEY CAN THINK OF. THEY SPEAK WORDS THAT APPEAL TO THE EMOTIONS OF THE PEOPLE IN ATTENDANCE. THEY PRAY AND THEN GET UP OFF OF THEIR KNEES AND LOOK FOR A PAT ON THE BACK AS IF TO SAY; "WOW, YOU REALLY DID IT!"

HOWEVER, WHAT THEY PROJECTED FROM THEIR DEMEANOR AFTER THE SERVICE ENDED, MADE AN EVEN GREATER STATEMENT, OPPOSING THE FACT THAT THEY EVEN KNOW THE LORD AT ALL.

WHENEVER YOU WILL PRAY OPPOSED TO THOSE WHO WILL NOT PRAY, THE SPOTLIGHT WILL BE CENTERED UPON YOU FOR A LONG TIME TO COME. THOSE INDIVIDUALS WHO HAVE GIVEN THEMSELVES WILLINGLY TO MUCH PRAYER, INDIVIDUALLY AND COLLECTIVELY SET FORTH THE GREATER EXAMPLES OF CHRIST.

THE PRAYING INDIVIDUAL, IS THE SAME INDIVIDUAL WHO WILL BE USED OF GOD IN THE MOST AWESOME WAYS. YOU CAN WITNESS MIRACLES OF HEALING AND RESTORATION, IMMANENTLY FLOWING FROM THE MINISTRY OF THOSE INDIVIDUALS.

THE SAINTS OF OLD WOULD SAY; "EVERY TIME I FEEL THE SPIRIT MOVING IN MY HEART, I WILL PRAY!" I CAN REMEMBER THE SAINTS, UPON ENTERING THE SANCTUARY TO WORSHIP GOD, HOW THEY WOULD COME IN PRAYING AND PRAISING GOD. THOSE DAYS HAVE SLIPPED AWAY FROM OUR EXISTENCE AND UNDERSTANDING. IF WE EVER NEEDED THE LORD BEFORE, WE SURE DO NEED HIM NOW!

THE AVERAGE MEMBER OF THE CHURCH WILL NOT ALLOT PRAYER TIME FOR A SUCCESSFUL SANCTIFIED CHRISTIAN LIFE; RATHER, THEY ARE PREOCCUPIED WITH ATTEMPT-

ING TO WORK FOR THE LORD. THE VERY LEAST IN NUMBERS, OF A CROWD TO ATTEND A SERVICE, ARE THOSE INDIVIDUALS WHO WILL ATTEND A PRAYER MEETING.

Lazy About Prayer?

PEOPLE RUSH OUT TO THE CHURCH TO ENJOY A MUSICAL AND SOMETIMES EVEN TO A REVIVAL OR AN APPRECIATION SERVICE THAT HAS BEEN GIVEN THE PROPER ADVERTISEMENT. THESE SERVICES ARE ALL GOOD, THEY ARE JUST NOT ABLE TO DO FOR YOU, WHAT THE POWER OF PRAYER WILL DO FOR YOU. AN OUNCE OF PRAYER, IS BETTER THAN A POUND OF PREACHING! (DR. S. E. MITCHELL)

THE CHURCH WILL FILL TO CAPACITY FOR A NUMBER OF REASONS. PEOPLE WILL SHOW UP FOR WEDDINGS AND BIZARRE SALES. PEOPLE WILL ALSO CERTAINLY SHOW UP FOR BARBECUE DINNERS, YOUTH MEMBER ACTIVITIES, COUPLES OUTINGS AND SENIOR CITIZEN RETREATS.

MY POINT IS ONLY THAT PEOPLE PREFER RECREATION AND ENTERTAINMENT, OVER AND AGAINST THE NECESSARY APPLICATION TO FAITHFUL PRAYER. IT DOES NOT EVEN MATTER, THAT PARTICIPATION IN THESE ACTIVITIES, WILL NOT ENHANCE SPIRITUAL GROWTH IN THE LEAST POSSIBLE WAY.

PEOPLE WHO PRAY SUFFER PERSECUTION FROM RELIGIOUS PERSONS OF THE COMMUNITY WHO ONLY ATTEND CHURCH EVERY NOW AND THEN. THEY ARE USUALLY QUOTED AS BEING FANATICAL, SUPER-SPIRITUAL OR IT IS SUGGESTED THAT THEY HAVE GONE OFF THE DEEP END! THE MORE SPIRITUAL A PERSON BECOMES, AS A RESULT OF PRAYER, THEY ARE LOOKED UPON AS SOME KIND OF "HOLY FREAK" OR JUST PLAIN OLD WEIRD.

PEOPLE ARE VERY HASTY TO BELIEVE THAT A PERSON CAN BECOME SO HEAVENLY, THAT THEY ARE NO EARTHLY GOOD. THIS IS A SAD EXCUSE TO SHY AWAY FROM PRAYER! GO AHEAD AND PRAY, YOU WILL DISCOVER THAT YOU HAVE THE POWER TO OVERCOME THE RIDICULOUSLY STEREO TYPI-

CAL ATTITUDE AND THE PERSECUTIONS. YOU CAN BECOME SO EARTHLY, THAT YOU ARE NO HEAVENLY GOOD!

Know The Benefit!

PRAYER WILL BUILD YOUR SPIRIT-MAN, LIKE WEIGHT LIFTING AND EXERCISE, BUILDS THE NATURAL BODY. HOW STRONG ARE YOU SPIRITUALLY? WHEN WAS THE LAST TIME YOU CHECKED YOUR STRENGTH THROUGH PRAYER? DON'T YOU THINK THAT IT IS ABOUT TIME, YOU TOOK A PERSONAL EVALUATION OF YOUR SPIRITUAL STATUS?

DON'T EVEN THINK OF LETTING ANYONE ELSE TELL YOU WHERE YOU ARE IN THE LORD. THROUGH PRAYER YOU WILL KNOW EXACTLY WHERE YOU ARE IN THE LORD. PRAYER WILL KEEP YOU HUMBLE AND CARING FOR OTHERS, NO MATTER HOW HIGH YOU MAY GO IN LIFE.

SUCCESSFUL INDIVIDUALS THAT PRAY, NEVER ALLOW THEIR SUCCESS TO BECOME MORE IMPORTANT THAN THEIR PRAYER-LIFE. HEADY AND HIGH-MINDED PEOPLE, WHO ARE FILLED WITH PRIDE, ARE THE GENERAL DEPICTION OF THE PEOPLE WHO SERIOUSLY LACK ADEQUATE, PROPER PRAYER.

I WONDER HOW THE IDEA WAS DEVELOPED THAT BEING SPIRITUAL MEANS THAT AN INDIVIDUAL SHOULD BE POOR OR AT LEAST ONLY AVERAGE, HAVING VERY LITTLE TO SHOW FORTH, IN TERMS OF MATERIALISTIC POSSESSIONS AND FINANCIAL GAIN. NO MATTER WHAT YOUR STATUS IS IN LIFE, YOU NEED MUCH PRAYER. I WAS ALWAYS TAUGHT, THAT PRAYER CHANGES THINGS AND IT CHANGES PEOPLE TOO!

IT'S NOT VERY WISE TO DETERMINE THAT YOU DON'T NEED PRAYER. PRAYER IS THE ONLY ASSURANCE THAT YOU AND I HAVE, TO INSURE US, THAT HEAVEN WILL BE OUR ETERNAL RESTING PLACE WITH THE LORD. DO YOU KNOW JUST HOW MUCH GOD LOVES TO HERE FROM HIS CHILDREN THROUGH PRAYER? GOD DELIGHTS IN HEARING FROM US IN PRAYER.

GOD CREATED AND ESTABLISHED PRAYER FOR US HERE ON THE EARTH, SO THAT WE COULD APPROACH THE

THRONE OF GRACE WITH BOLDNESS.

EVERYDAY OF OUR LIVES WE ARE IN SPIRITUAL WARFARE. IF WE INTEND TO WIN THE WAR, WE NEED JESUS DEEP DOWN WITHIN, AT THE CENTER CORE OF OUR INNERMOST BEING. PRAYER LETS JESUS INTO OUR HEART.

Spill Your Guts!!

WE SPEND A LOT OF TIME SHARING THINGS THAT WE OUGHT TO ONLY BE TELLING GOD. YOU NEVER REALLY KNOW FOR SURE THAT A PERSON SHOULDN'T BE TRUSTED, UNTIL YOU HAVE BEEN BETRAYED. THE DEVASTATION OF BEING DECEIVED BY SOMEONE YOU TRUSTED, MAY HAVE AN ILL-EFFECT ON YOU, IF YOU ARE NOT PRAYERFUL. YOU MAY BE SET BACK FOR QUITE A SPELL.

LIFE IS TOO SHORT TO ALLOW ANYONE TO SEND YOU REELING BACKWARDS. IF YOU KNOW LIKE I DO, YOU WILL ONLY TRUST IN THE LORD JESUS AND TELL HIM WHATEVER IT IS YOU NEED TO TELL SOMEONE.

HE WILL NEVER LET YOU DOWN OR EVER BETRAY YOUR TRUST IN HIM. WHATEVER YOU TELL GOD IN PRAYER, HE WILL NEVER TELL ANOTHER, FOR ANY REASON. YOU NEED TO HAVE FAITH IN THE LORD AND TELL HIM WHAT-EVER YOU NEED. I DO EXPECT THAT YOU ARE AWARE THAT YOU CAN CONFIDE IN THE LORD. GOD NEVER CHANGES! HE IS ALWAYS THE SAME.

> *For my thoughts are not your thoughts, neither are your ways my ways, saith the Lord. For as the heavens are higher than the earth, so are my ways higher than your ways, and my thoughts than your thoughts*   ISAIAH 55:8-9

ISAIAH IS INTENT ON SHOWING US THAT GOD IS NOT LIKE MAN. GOD WILL NEVER, EVER AGAIN BECOME LIKE MAN, AS HIS PURPOSE FOR DOING SO HAS ALREADY BEEN ACCOMPLISHED.

MAN, HOWEVER, WILL CONSISTENTLY BE IN NEED OF BECOMING MORE AND MORE LIKE GOD. WE WILL NEVER

become or ever be a God; contrary to the teaching of the New Age religion, but we can and will become more like the one and only true God.

Whether you know it or not, you can actually tell God everything that is in your heart. Yes! He already knows, but you need to tell Him for yourself. To think that you can hide your inner feelings from the Lord is really outrageous.

God does not have to understand because He already knows, understanding only helps us to know! The things that God knows, understanding itself can't comprehend! God is no wimp, He can stand to hear the most degrading details of your life. God created strength, He does not have to be strong when listening to you. He's God!

Tell God that you have made bad financial investments that left you busted and broke. By all means don't commit suicide to escape your troubles. Perhaps you don't have an education and have not made any efforts to enhance your knowledge, just tell the Lord all about it.

Tell God that you've ruined your life with alcohol, drugs and elicit sex, of all types. As a result of your behavior, none of your family members will have anything to do with you. Don't forget to tell God that you repent for the wrong that you have done and the pain that it caused. You felt you were right, whenever you lied to escape and avoid getting into trouble.

Tell God that you really are guilty of the accusations that have been brought against you and by the way, you really ought to confess your guilt to the Lord.

Tell God that you are prejudice and that there is hatred in your heart for all other persons

ON THE OUTSIDE OF YOUR OWN RACE. IT'S ACCEPTABLE, IF YOU TELL HIM THAT YOU DON'T KNOW HOW IT GOT THERE, AS LONG AS YOU'RE SURE THAT YOU DO NOT KNOW!

STOP TELLING PEOPLE THAT YOU'RE GAY, BECAUSE IT DOESN'T MATTER THAT THERE ARE PEOPLE THAT EMBRACE YOUR ALTERNATIVE PERVERSION, AS MUCH AS IT DOES MAKE A DIFFERENCE TO GOD. TELL HIM ALL ABOUT IT!

THE LORD HAS THE POWER TO FREE YOU FROM THE AWFUL, LIFE-THREATENING GRIP OF HOMOSEXUALITY AND LESBIANISM. IF YOU HAVE ENGAGED YOURSELF IN THE GAY LIFE-STYLE, IT IS TOO LATE TO ATTEMPT AT TRYING TO CONCEAL IT. GOD KNOWS ALL ABOUT IT!

NO NEED TO TRY AND HIDE FROM THE LORD, GET IN A HURRY AND RUN TO HIM, QUICKLY. HE'S WAITING ON YOU TO COME TO HIM.

*Your Pain; His Ears!**

TELL THE LORD ALL ABOUT THE TIMES THAT YOU WERE MOLESTED. TELL HIM HOW YOU WERE RAPED AND SEXUALLY ASSAULTED. TELL GOD HOW YOU EXPERIMENTED WITH MANY THINGS, THRILL SEEKING, TRYING TO FIND REST FOR YOUR WEARY SOUL, BUT YOU FOUND NO REST TO SATISFY YOUR LONGING!

TELL GOD THAT YOU'VE WASTED PRECIOUS TIME SEEKING OTHER SOURCES FOR THE SUPPLY OF YOUR NEEDS.

TELL GOD HOW YOU SET TRAPS AND DUG DITCHES FOR THE MANY DIFFERENT PEOPLE, BECAUSE *they were really living a godly life*, AND YOU THOUGHT THAT THEY NEEDED TO BE TAUGHT A REAL LESSON ABOUT BEING TOO SPIRITUAL.

YOU WANTED THE PEOPLE OF THE LORD TO KNOW THAT THEY WERE NOT BETTER OFF THAN YOU, JUST BECAUSE THEY HAD COME TO THE LIGHT OF THE LORD, WHILE YOU REJECTED HIM.

YOU FELT THE COMPANY OF THE BLOOD-WASHED

BELIEVERS, WAS ACTUALLY BENEATH YOU, DUE TO THE FACT THAT YOU WERE TOO EDUCATED FOR SUCH NONSENSE. GOD WAS TOO SLOW FOR YOU TO WAIT ON HIM, BECAUSE YOU NEEDED TO HAVE YOUR NEEDS MET RIGHT THEN AND THERE.

TELL GOD THAT YOU FOUND BETTER WAYS OF LIVING AND THAT YOU HAVE READ BETTER BOOKS THAN THE HOLY BIBLE. WHILE YOU'RE TELLING HIM THAT, BE SURE TO TELL HIM, THAT YOU NEVER BELIEVED THE BIBLE WAS THE WORD OF GOD ANYWAY! YOU DIDN'T NEED ANYBODY TELLING YOU HOW TO LIVE OR RUN YOUR LIFE.

TELL GOD THAT YOU KNEW A BETTER WAY TO RAISE YOUR CHILDREN, BECAUSE YOU WERE LIVING IN A DIFFERENT DAY. HIS WAYS WERE OUTDATED. TELL GOD THAT YOU LIKE TO GOSSIP AND SPREAD OTHER PEOPLES' BUSINESS ALL OVER THE STREET. WHEN QUESTIONED ABOUT YOUR DEALINGS IN THE MATTER, YOU DENIED EVER HAVING ANYTHING TO DO WITH THEIR PERSONAL BUSINESS BEING IN THE STREET.

WELL, THIS WILL OPEN THE DOOR FOR YOU TO TELL GOD THAT YOU COULD NOT BE TRUSTED, BY ANYONE, ESPECIALLY A CLOSE FRIEND.

PREACHER, TELL GOD HOW YOU COUNSELED A MEMBER OF YOUR CONGREGATION AND BASED YOUR NEXT SERMON ON THE DISCUSSION THAT YOU HAD WITH THAT SAME MEMBER'S TROUBLES.

YOU VOWED TO KEEP THAT MEMBER'S BUSINESS CONFIDENTIAL, YET YOU AIRED THEIR MOST PERSONAL AND PAINFUL MATTERS TO THE CONGREGATION.

YOU MIGHT WANT TO TELL GOD THAT AS THE PASTOR OF THE CONGREGATION, YOU FELT THAT THE LORD WOULD NOT HAVE BEEN INTERESTED IN HEARING THOSE THINGS, SO YOU SHARED THE MATTERS WITH SOMEONE ELSE WHO COULD RELATE.

TELL GOD, HOW YOU RENDERED AID TO A FAMILY IN NEED AND TOLD ABOUT HOW YOU BLESSED THAT FAMILY

EVERYWHERE YOU WENT TO SPEAK.

PASTOR, TELL GOD HOW SUCCESSFUL YOU WERE IN SCATTERING OUT THE FLOCK BECAUSE THEY WERE JUST A BUNCH OF HARDHEADED GOATS WHO WOULD NOT FOLLOW YOUR PROGRAM OR LEADERSHIP.

TELL GOD THAT YOU'VE DISCOVERED SOMETHING IN HIS WORD THAT OTHER PASTORS AND EVANGELISTS HAD NOT YET DISCOVERED, WHICH WAS, CERTAIN PARTS OF THE BIBLE'S SCRIPTURES WERE NOW OBSOLETE, AND CERTAIN PARTS OF THE SCRIPTURE ARE A HINDRANCE TO THE CHURCH OF TODAY. NOT!

Stinking Thinking!

ALSO, TELL GOD, THAT YOU DISCOVERED THAT IF THE PEOPLE WOULD SIMPLY EDUCATE THEMSELVES, THEY COULD LEAD MORE PRODUCTIVE LIVES, NOT HAVING A NEED FOR ANY SIN, SO IN AN EFFORT TO INFLUENCE THEM TO RECEIVE YOUR OWN WAY OF THINKING, YOU DECIDED TO TEACH SECULAR MATTERS RATHER THAN THE *Bible.*

YOU FIGURED OUT, THAT PEOPLE GENERALLY COMMITTED SINS, FOR THE PURPOSE OF SUPPORTING THEMSELVES FINANCIALLY, SOCIOLOGICALLY AND JUST PLAIN AND SIMPLY, BECAUSE THEY DID NOT KNOW ANY BETTER.

 TELL GOD THAT YOU DISCOVERED THAT THE PEOPLE OF THE CHURCH COULD ACTUALLY PAY THEIR BILLS BETTER, IF THEY DID NOT PAY TITHES, "<u>NOT</u>"!

BE SURE TO TELL GOD THAT BECAUSE HE TRUSTED YOU WITH THE CALL OF THE MINISTRY, THAT YOU TOOK IT UPON YOURSELF TO *reinterpret* THE BIBLE FOR YOURSELF. EXPLAIN TO THE LORD HOW YOU CAME TO THE CONCLUSION THAT THERE WAS ACTUALLY NO NEED FOR PEOPLE TO BE CHANGED.

TELL GOD HOW YOU DISCOVERED, THAT YOU THOUGHT THE POWER OF GOD WAS REALLY A THING OF THE PAST. DON'T FORGET TO TELL GOD, THAT YOU DIS-

COVERED HE HAD REALLY CHANGED, AND THAT JUST MAYBE THE PEOPLE OF THE BIBLE AND ALL OF IT'S FOLLOWERS, SORT OF EXAGGERATED THE TRUTH OF THE BIBLE.

The Danger Of Preaching Without A Prayer Life!

BE SURE TO TELL GOD THAT YOU ARE A BETTER POLITICIAN THAN YOU ARE A PASTOR. EXPLAIN TO GOD WHY YOUR SOCIAL STATUS IS GREATER THAN YOUR SPIRITUAL INFLUENCE. PEOPLE WILL SEEK INFORMATION AS TO WHERE TO CAST THEIR BALLOT ON POLITICAL ISSUES. THEY WILL ALSO INQUIRE, HOW THEY MAY BECOME ELIGIBLE FOR REGISTRATION TO VOTE ON THOSE SAME POLITICAL ISSUES, AS WELL AS MANY OTHER POLITICAL AGENDAS.

BUT, FOR A REASON THAT THEY ARE WELL AWARE OF, THEY WILL NEVER CALL ON YOU TO LAY YOUR HANDS ON THEM TO PRAY FOR THEM TO BE HEALED, SET FREE, AND DELIVERED! NEITHER WILL THEY CALL ON YOU TO ANSWER QUESTIONS PERTAINING TO MANY SPIRITUAL MATTERS, BECAUSE THEY DON'T FEEL THAT YOU HAVE AS MUCH SPIRITUAL EXPERIENCE AS THEY DO THEMSELVES.

BE SURE TO ASK THE LORD, IF IT IS YOUR FAULT THAT THE MEMBERS OF YOUR CONGREGATION CONTINUE TO SEEK OTHER SPIRITUAL SOURCES, RATHER THAN SEEKING THE BAPTISM OF THE HOLY GHOST.

EXPLAIN TO GOD, WHY THE STANDARD OF HOLINESS FELL SO DRASTICALLY UNDER THE PASTORAL ADMINISTRATIVE GUIDANCE OF YOUR LEADERSHIP!

PREACHER, YOU ARE NOT THE FIRST TO ALLOW THE STANDARD OF HOLINESS, TO BE COMPROMISED. THE HIGH PRIEST OF ALL THE TRIBES OF ISRAEL, ELI; KNEW THAT HIS OWN SONS DESECRATED THE TEMPLE OF GOD. HE, ALIKE MANY PASTORS AND LEADERS OF THE CHURCH OF TODAY, ONLY MENTIONED HOW AWFUL THEIR BEHAVIOR WAS, DOING NOTHING AT ALL TO BRING THEM UNDER SUBJECTION TO THE WORD AND THE WILL OF THE

Lord.

There are a lot of things that we as people really need to tell the Lord, we need not only to try and justify our action and reactions. Neither do we need to try and wait until we come before the judgment seat of God. We need to start talking to the Lord, right now!

Don't make the mistake, of believing in your mind, that I am suggesting that you have a real gripe-fest with the Lord. I am suggesting to you, that you go to the Lord God in prayer and tell Him that you are weighed in the balance and have found that you are in spiritual error to the word of God!

Don't ignore the fact that you have erred in the word of God. It should not make a difference that you are the leader of the congregation or at the top of the group or class. To be in error and know this to be actually true and do nothing to correct the error or to right the wrong, places your soul in even a more serious, but dangerous state.

Come before the Lord Jesus Christ and express your innermost deep feelings to Him, but remain open for His spiritual interjection, to create the real difference you need to succeed in pleasing him. It is the Lord's will, that we please Him! He's not requiring us to do something that we are not able.

Many people have read the bible from cover to cover; the words of the bible serve their recollection well, only God of the bible has never pricked the hearts of the readers, to activate the word of God to which they have read!

> *And be found in him, not having my own righteousness which is of the law, but that which is through the faith of Christ, the righteousness*

*which is of God by faith: That I may know him,
and the power of his resurrection, and the fellowship of his sufferings, being made conformable unto his death;*   PHILIPPIANS 3:9-10

IF YOUR HEART DOES NOT LINE UP WITH THE WORD OF GOD, THE PRAYER THAT WILL COME OUT YOUR MOUTH WILL BE OUT OF LINE WITH THE WORD OF GOD AS WELL. YOU MAY NOT HAVE BEEN ACQUAINTED WITH THE LORD BEFORE YOU BEGAN TO PRAY; HOWEVER, YOU WILL COME IN CONTACT WITH THE LORD IF YOU WILL CONTINUE TO PRAY IN THE NAME OF JESUS.

Come On Now!

AS A RESULT OF KNOWING THE LORD, WE BECOME MORE ATTUNED TO HEARING THE VOICE OF THE LORD, AND EVEN HEARING THE DIRECT MESSAGES THAT ARE WRITTEN IN THE WORD OF GOD.

THE REAL TRUTH IS THAT, WE HAVE GOT TO KNOW THE LORD AS HE IS TRULY AND NOT RELY ON ONLY WHAT WE THINK OR DESIRE OF HIM TO BE IN OUR OWN MINDS.

THIS IS THE KNOWLEDGE THAT WILL PREVENT US FROM PRAYING IN ERROR TO THE WORD OF GOD! PRAYER WILL KEEP YOU FROM SIN, BUT SIN WILL KEEP YOU FROM PRAYER! SEARCH WITHIN YOURSELF FOR THE REASONS THAT YOU ARE WHERE YOU ARE.

NOW DON'T GO OFF THE DEEP END AND ALLOW YOURSELF TO BELIEVE THAT THE LORD WILL HEAR YOU, WHILE YOU SUGGEST TO HIM, THAT SOMEBODY ELSE DOES NOT DESERVE TO LIVE ANY LONGER, DUE TO THE FACT THAT THEY HAVE RUBBED YOU THE WRONG WAY.

LITERALLY, YOU CAN TELL GOD EVERYTHING! YOU HAD BETTER TELL THE LORD ALL OF THOSE SECRETS, THAT YOU THOUGHT YOU WOULD TAKE TO YOUR GRAVE, BEFORE YOU ACTUALLY DIE! THERE ARE MANY THINGS THAT WOULD NOT BE PROFITABLE FOR ANY BELIEVER, HAVEN NEVER CONFESSED THOSE HIDDEN THINGS TO THE LORD. DON'T BE CAUGHT DEAD WITH THE WRONG THINGS!

Let us therefore come boldly unto the throne of

grace, that we may obtain mercy, and find grace to help in time of need. HEBREWS 4:16

Then said I, Woe is me! For I am undone; because I am a man of unclean lips, and I dwell in the midst of a people of unclean lips: for mine eyes have seen the King, the Lord of host.

ISAIAH 6:5

LISTEN, DON'T BE AFRAID OF APPROACHING THE THRONE OF GRACE, BECAUSE YOU HAVE SINNED, RECOGNIZE YOUR SINFUL STATE AND TAKE IT TO THE LORD IN PRAYER, IMMEDIATELY. IF SIN IS YOUR PROBLEM, ONLY GOD CAN SOLVE YOUR PROBLEM, SO TELL HIM ALL ABOUT THE POSITION THAT YOU ARE IN.

YOU MAY HAVE SOME CONCERNS ABOUT THE CHURCH AS WE KNOW OF IT TODAY, BUT TELL THE LORD WITH AN OPEN HEART, YOU WILL FIND THAT HE KNOWS ALL ABOUT YOUR TRUE CONCERNS.

and him that cometh to me I will in no wise cast out.

ST. JOHN 6:37 B

He Will Not Force You To Come!

THE LORD IS A GENTLEMAN AND IF IT IS NOT YOUR DESIRE TO COME TO HIM IN PRAYER WILLINGLY, HE MOST DEFINITELY WILL NOT FORCE YOU TO COME.

HE IS ACTUALLY AT YOUR DOOR WAITING ON YOU TO OPEN THE DOOR AND LET HIM INTO YOUR HEART. HE WILL NOT BREAK IN LIKE A CRIMINAL, AS THE KNOB TO THE DOOR IS ON THE INSIDE OF YOU. HE IS NOT GOING TO SPEAK AND CAUSE THE DOOR KNOB TO FALL OFF SO THAT THE DOOR WILL SWING WIDE OPEN THE WAY DRACULA DOES IN A HORROR MOVIE.

OPEN YOUR OWN MOUTH IF YOU ARE WILLING TO COME TO HIM ON YOUR OWN. THERE IS NO NEED TO WAIT TO TALK TO HIM. HE KNOWS THE PROBLEMS YOU EXPERIENCED, THAT CAUSED YOU MUCH PAIN AND MENTAL ANGUISH.

THE LORD HAS MORE DETAILED INFORMATION ABOUT WHAT YOU ARE PRESENTLY GOING THROUGH AT

THIS PERIOD AND TIME, THAN YOU. HE KNOWS ABOUT YOUR SLEEPLESSNESS AND ABOUT ALL OF YOUR RESTLESSNESS, AS IT RELATES TO THE PROBLEMS THAT YOU ARE HAVING. THE LORD EVEN KNOWS ABOUT YOUR CHILDREN THAT MAY HAVE BEEN LOCKED AWAY IN JAIL.

THE LORD HAS A LOT MORE TO OFFER YOU THAN ANYONE ELSE YOU MAY HAVE TALKED TO ALREADY. THE LORD HAS THOUGHTS OF PEACE TOWARDS YOU AND NOT EVIL THOUGHTS CONCERNING YOU, TO SHOW YOU THE END TO ALL OF YOUR TROUBLES. *Jeramiah 29:11*

DON'T ALLOW ANYONE TO TELL YOU THAT THE LORD IS THE CAUSE OF ALL OF YOUR TROUBLES. HE MAY HAVE ALLOWED THE TROUBLE, SIMPLY BECAUSE YOU WILL NOT ALLOW HIM TO KEEP YOU AND TO PROTECT YOU FROM THE ATTACK OF THE ADVERSARY.

JESUS CHRIST IS THE WAY OUT! EVERY OTHER PATHWAY THAT YOU TAKE WILL ONLY LEAD YOU AROUND IN A NEVER-ENDING CIRCLE. YOU WILL EVENTUALLY, FIND YOURSELF RIGHT BACK WHERE YOU STARTED, AT THE BEGINNING OF THE TRIAL.

IN CHRIST, WE ALSO HAVE TRIALS AND SOME PROBLEMS, BUT TO OUR OWN ADVANTAGE, WHENEVER WE START OUT AND CONTINUE WITH JESUS, WE END UP WITH JESUS. STARTING OUT ON YOUR OWN, IS NEVER GOING TO BE AS REWARDING, AS TRUSTING IN THE LORD.

Tell Him If You Really Love Him!

TELL GOD THAT YOU THANK HIM FOR JESUS CHRIST OF NAZARETH, THE ANOINTED ONE OF GOD. THANK HIM FOR HEALING YOUR BODY OF THE SICKNESS AND DISEASE THAT HAD TAKEN HOLD OF YOUR BODY. THANK HIM FOR LIFE, AND THAT YOU ARE LIVING AND ALIVE RIGHT NOW.

KEEP THE LINES OF COMMUNICATION OPEN BETWEEN YOURSELF AND THE LORD AT ALL TIMES AND DO NOT ALLOW YOUR RELATIONSHIP TO SLIP OR TO COLLAPSE, UNDER THE WEIGHT OF THE LACK OF EXERCISING THE

NECESSARY VERBAL COMMUNICATION.

TELL GOD THAT YOU NEED HIM TO WALK WITH YOU EVERY STEP OF THE WAY, HOLDING YOUR HAND. PRAY IN YOUR HOME ALWAYS AND PRAY ON YOUR JOB. BEHIND THE STEERING WHEEL OF YOUR CAR, IS AN IDEAL PLACE TO PRAY TO THE LORD. PRAY WHILE YOU TAKE THAT MORNING RUN THROUGH THE NEIGHBORHOOD.

WHENEVER YOUR KNEES HIT THE FLOOR, UPON WAKING UP IN THE MORNING, GO AHEAD AND PRAY, PRAYER WILL MAKE THE DAY PROSPEROUS FOR YOU. AS A MATTER OF THE FACT, YOU OUGHT TO TRY PRAYING WHENEVER YOU AWAKE OUT OF YOUR SLEEP. MANY PEOPLE ARE DREAMERS AND SOME DREAMS ARE DISTURB-ING, SO DON'T JUST GO THROUGH THE RUN OF THE DAY TRYING TO FIGURE OUT THE MEANING OF THOSE PUZ-ZLING DREAMS. TELL THE LORD ALL ABOUT THEM AND BE FINISHED WITH THEM.

> *Casting all your care upon him; for he careth for you.*   I PETER 5:7

TO CAST- <u>IS TO THROW OUT</u>, <u>OR TO THROW FORTH</u>, WHILE RELEASING WHATEVER MAY BE THROWN FROM THE POWER OF YOUR OWN GRIP.

MOST FISHERMEN UNDERSTAND THE ART OF CAST-ING OUT THE FISHING-LINE, WITH A FISHING HOOK AT-TACHED TO THE END OF THE LINE, FOR THE PURPOSE OF REELING THE SAME LINE BACK IN, WHETHER OR NOT A CATCH HAS BEEN ACCOMPLISHED.

WE DO NOT CAST OUR PROBLEMS ON THE LORD IN THIS MANNER, AS IF WE ARE WAITING ON THE RIGHT TIME TO PULL THEM BACK IN TO US. ONCE YOUR CARES HAVE BEEN CAST UPON THE LORD, AT THAT VERY INSTANCE, THEY ARE NO LONGER YOUR CARES, THEY NOW BELONG EXCLU-SIVELY TO THE CARE OF THE LORD. HE KNOWS WHAT TO DO WITH THE PROBLEM AND HE KNOWS HOW TO HANDLE THE SITUATION. HE WILL DO ALL OF THE ABOVE

Just for you!

The Language We Speak*

> And the whole earth was of one language, and of one speech. GENESIS 11:1
> For he that speaketh in an unknown tongue speaketh not unto men, but unto God; for no man understandeth him; howbeit in the spirit he speaketh mysteries. I CORINTHIANS 14:2

Speaking The Same Everywhere!

THE CHURCH AS WE KNOW OF IT TODAY, WOULD BE SO MUCH MORE SUCCESSFUL AND EFFECTIVE IN THE COMMUNITIES IF ALL OF THE PEOPLE THAT CONFESS TO TRULY BEING CHANGED AND WASHED IN THE BLOOD OF JESUS WOULD SPEAK THE SAME LANGUAGE HAVING THE VERY SAME MIND.

ANYONE WHO ATTENDS CHURCH ON A REGULAR BASIS WILL HAVE TO ADMIT THE FACT THAT THERE IS A LOT OF TALKING GOING ON AROUND THE CHURCH ALL OF THE TIME. BUT, THE THINGS THAT ARE ACTUALLY BEING SAID DURING THE WORSHIP SERVICES ARE NOT ALWAYS PRODUCING THE

NEEDED ONENESS IN THE BODY OF CHRIST AT LARGE.

ONE OF THE GREATER ISSUES WE HAVE TAKEN INTO ACCOUNT, IS THE EXTREME LEVEL OF THE CONFUSION THAT HAS BEEN EN-BREAD IN THE MINDS OF THE PEOPLE FROM THE PULPITS.

CERTAIN LEADERS HAVE REJECTED SELECT AREAS OF THE SCRIPTURES, AND ANY TEACHINGS THAT ARE RELATIVE TO AREAS OF THE BIBLE THAT REQUIRE US TO LIVE CLEAN AND SIN-FREE.

THERE IS SUCH A TUG-OF-WAR AMONG THE LEADERS OF THE CHURCHES ALONG DENOMINATIONAL DIVIDES AND ALSO WITHIN THE DENOMINATIONAL SYSTEMS OF THE CHURCHES. MOST OF THE LEADERS WHO OPPOSE THE NEED FOR THE STRICT GUIDELINES OF HOLY LIVING, HAVE BEEN FOUND TO BE FREE-SPIRITED, REBELLIOUS OF THE SCRIPTURE, AND EXTREMELY CARNAL IN THEIR THOUGHT PROCESS.

THERE IS AN EXTREME DIFFERENCE BETWEEN A RELIGIOUS CHURCH; AND A SPIRITUAL CHURCH! HOWEVER, THE MAIN ISSUE THAT SEEMS TO CAUSE THE GREATEST RIPS AND THE UTTERMOST TURMOIL IN THE CHURCHES, IS SPEAKING IN TONGUES!

THERE ARE THINGS THAT ARE ALLOWED TO OCCUR IN A RELIGIOUS SETTING, THAT WOULD NEVER BE ALLOWED TO TAKE PLACE IN A HOLY GHOST; SPIRIT FILLED CHURCH. I HAVE PERSONALLY WITNESSED SOME THINGS IN THE RELIGIOUS CHURCH THAT WOULD SHAME HOLLYWOOD, AND COMEDY CLUBS BASED ON THE THINGS THAT HAVE COME FROM THE MOUTHS OF THE PEOPLE.

I HAVE HEARD A MINISTER CURSE IN THE PULPIT DURING THE DELIVERY OF A PREPARED SERMON, AND EXCUSES WERE MADE FOR THE MINISTER. HOWEVER IN THE SAME CHURCH, I HAVE WITNESSED THE LEADER SILENCE AND HEAVILY CRITICIZE AN INDIVIDUAL FOR SPEAKING IN TONGUES IN THE SANCTUARY OF THAT CHURCH. THE PEOPLE WERE TOLD THAT; "WE DON'T DO THAT HERE!"

A CERTAIN PERCENTAGE OF THE PEOPLE ARE IGNO-
RANT OF THE SCRIPTURES. THEY DON'T HAVE THE UNDER-
STANDING THAT THEY SHOULD HAVE RECEIVED FROM THE
MINISTY OF THE CHURCHES THEY ATTEND AS A MEMBER.

IN AN EFFORT TO BE A SUCCESSFUL MINISTER TO THE
PEOPLE OF GOD, WE HAVE GOT TO BELIEVE THE WHOLE,
ENTIRE BOOK OF THE BIBLE, FROM COVER TO COVER.

I SAT ADJACENT TO A COUPLE OF MINISTERS AT A RES-
TAURANT FOR LUNCH. I OVERHEARD THEM CONVERSING
AND DISPUTING WHETHER OR NOT WE AS THE PEOPLE OF
THE CHURCH AND AS SCHOLARS OF THE BIBLE SHOULD BE-
LIEVE THAT THE BOOK OF JOB & JONAH ARE ACTUALLY TRUE
AND REAL.

THEY WENT ON TO QUOTE A KNOWN PHILOSOPHER
THAT DOES NOT EVEN CONFESS TO BEING A BELIEVER IN
JESUS CHRIST. IT WAS HIS FINDINGS THAT THE THINGS
THAT HAPPENED IN THE BOOK OF JONAH, AND IN THE BOOK
OF JOB; COULD NOT AT ALL HAVE BEEN REAL.

I COULDN'T ALLOW THE OPPORTUNITY TO PASS; I
TOOK IT UPON MYSELF TO INQUIRE WHETHER OR NOT THESE
MEN OF THE CLOTH WERE PASTORS, AND THEY CONFIRMED
TO ME THAT THEY WERE. I ALSO TOOK IT UPON MYSELF TO
INFORM THAT I BELIEVED THE BIBLE'S CANNONIZATION OF
THE SCRIPTURES. I SAID TO THEM; "IF IT'S IN THE BIBLE
IT'S REAL!" GOD ALLOW THE BOOKS OF THE BIBLE TO BE
COMPRISED IN THE MANNER OF WHICH THEY HAVE BEEN
CONFIGURED.

FAR TOO MANY SERMONS OVER THE PULPITS ARE
RELATIVE TO WHAT THE MINISTER DISBELIEVES, WHICH IS
ALSO ENCOURAGING TO THE PEOPLE OF THE CONGREGA-
TION TO DISBELIEVE THE SCRIPTURE.

IT IS HEARTBREAKING THAT MANY OF THE PEOPLE IN
THE CHURCHES AT LARGE, DON'T BELIEVE IN AGREEMENT
AND ONENESS; THE SCRIPTURE. I LISTENED TO A TELEVI-
SION EVANGELIST, AS HE PREACHED TO A CROWD IN EXCESS
OF THOUSANDS OF PEOPLE, THE MAJORITY OF THEM WHITE

PEOPLE. HE SPENT 45 MINUTES ATTEMPTING TO SHOW THEM WHY WE OF ALL DIFFERENT RACES OF PEOPLE SHOULD BE SEPARATED.

HE TOOK SCRIPTURES FROM THE OLD TESTAMENT TO MAKE THE ARGUMENT THAT IT IS GOD'S AGENDA AND PURPOSE FOR EVERY RACE OF PEOPLE TO BE SEGREGATED IN THE COMMUNITY, AND SEPARATED IN THE CHURCH.

MANY PEOPLE LIVE WITH THESE IDEAS IN THEIR MINDS, WHO FEEL THAT SOMEHOW MYSTERIOUSLY, WE ARE ALL GOING TO BE TOGETHER IN HEAVEN, ALTHOUGH PEOPLE ARE DETERMINED TO BELIEVE THAT WE ARE SUPPOSED TO BE SEPARATED; CLAIMING THAT THEY HAVE GOTTEN THEIR INFORMATION FROM THE SAME BIBLE THAT COMMANDS THAT ALL PEOPLE COME TOGETHER AS ONE BODY IN CHRIST.

WHENEVER WE DON'T KNOW THE LETTER OF THE LAWS IN THE LANGUAGE THAT WE SPEAK, WE ARE SEVERELY HINDERED AND AT A DISADVANTAGE TO COMPREHEND THE COMPLETENESS OF THE SPOKEN WORDS, TO DIRECT US TO THE END OF THE PERFORMANCE OF A PARTICULAR TASK.

THE LETTER OF THE LANGUAGE, WOULD BE VERY SIMILAR TO THE LETTER OF THE LAW. THE STATE LEGISLATORS, SPEND TIME CREATING AND WRITING THE DESIRED WORDING FOR THE PROPER MANDATES OF A PARTICULAR LAW, TO BE ACCEPTED INTO STATE LEGISLATION. WHENEVER A LAW IS OFFENDED OR BROKEN, OFTEN THE PERPETRATORS OF THE OFFENSES DID NOT EVEN UNDERSTAND THE LANGUAGE OF THE PARTICULAR LAW THAT HAD BEEN BROKEN IN THE FIRST PLACE.

WHAT MAKES A LAW VALID OR WHAT MAKES A RULE PERMISSIBLE TO THE JUDICIAL SYSTEM, IS THE LANGUAGE STATED IN THE WRITING OF THE CONSTITUTION OF THAT SAME LAW OR RULE. THE STATEMENT; *"Ignorance of the law is no excuse"*, COMES INTO PLAY IN A COURT OF LAW, WHEN A PERSON WHO HAS BROKEN A LAW, STANDS BEFORE THE JUDGE BEING IGNORANT OF THE FACT THAT A CRIME HAD EVEN BEEN COMMITTED.

Most people feel that they should be let off the hook or rather excused, simply because they did not know the language of that particular law.

It does not even matter that the language of the law that had been broken, had recently been changed or that the particular wording of that law had just come into effect. What matters most, is that the officials, who are assigned to enforce the law, knew the language of that law and that they understood it well, in effort to enforce the allowed penalty upon anyone found breaking that law!

It is the responsibility of every individual to learn the language of the laws of the land and the language of the written word of our Lord, and to understand it well.

Far too many people are being left out of the inner-colloquial dialogue of the language of God's people. So, as a result, they are often found complaining and shying away from the people of the Lord, because they are either confused or disbelieving in the power and the necessity of speaking in tongues.

This is how the people of the church often find themselves back in the company of the unsaved individuals who may not even have a mind to turn to the Lord. They have a common understanding about life, but no revelation, as a result of not knowing the language of the word of God.

Language unification was the picture of completeness and whole communication relative to human relations in the livelihood of all people from the beginning of time, unto the Tower of Babel. The total picture relates to a flawless understanding among all people everywhere, of the beginning generations of the world.

Such a statement is not to be received as the

INTENTIONAL CONCLUSIVENESS OF LANGUAGE, RELATIVE TO SPEECH ALONE. TO ENVISION THE TOTAL PICTURE, THE MIND'S EYE SHOULD PERCEIVE THE REALITY OF PERFECT ONENESS OF UNDERSTANDING, WITHOUT THE DISRUPTIVE HINDRANCES THAT ARE SO COMMON TO US TODAY.

IMAGINE EVERY WHERE YOU WENT OVER THE ENTIRE FACE OF THE EARTH, IN EVERY LAND, ON EVERY ISLAND AND OF EVERY RACE AND NATION OF PEOPLE, THE LANGUAGE EVERYONE UNDERSTOOD WAS EXACTLY THE SAME.

EVERYONE, PERCEIVED THINGS THE SAME WAY AND WERE ALL CONFIRMATORY AND CONFORMING TO THEIR FINDINGS, AS A RESULT OF THE SINGLENESS OF THOUGHT.

WORDS, AS WE KNOW OF THEM TODAY, WERE PROBABLY SPOKEN ACCORDING TO THE MEANINGS OF THEIR DEFINITIONS. INSTEAD OF SAYING; "DO", THEY MIGHT HAVE SAID FOR EXAMPLE; "CARRY OUT" OR "PERFORM" THE TASK?

ONE SPEECH ALLOWED GOD'S CHILDREN TO BE GLOBALLY RECOGNIZED AS HUMAN BEINGS OR MANKIND: MEN SPOKE AUDIBLY OUT OF THEIR MOUTHS, LIKE GOD, AND THEY STILL DO TO THIS VERY DAY. MAN HAS ALWAYS BEEN KNOWN FOR HAVING A MOUTH THAT TALKS, AND A LANGUAGE COMMUNICATION OF WORDS AND NOT JUST ANIMATED SOUNDS DEPICTING A CREATED STATUS ABOVE ALL OTHER LIFE-FORMS IN THE EARTH.

UNLIKE TODAY, PEOPLE WERE NOT CATEGORIZED, BY THE MANY DIVERSE LANGUAGE DIALECTS AND BARRIERS, TO AID IN IDENTIFYING THEIR ORIGINS. WHENEVER WE TRAVEL TO OTHER COUNTRIES, PEOPLE OF ALL DIVERSE SKIN PIGMENTATIONS AND HAIR TEXTURES SPEAK THE EXACT SAME LANGUAGE DIALECT, OF THAT PARTICULAR GEOGRAPHICAL REGION!

*From The Beginning**

THE LINGUISTIC ACT OF LANGUAGE ONENESS, WAS SO OUTSTANDING THAT IT WENT BEYOND THE PURPOSEFUL COMPREHENSION OF MANKIND, ALL OVER THE ENTIRE FACE

OF THE EARTH. ONE LORD; ONE LANGUAGE!

PEOPLE WERE NEVER HESITANT TO SPEAK, BECAUSE THEY WERE FEMILIAR, AND EVEN FAMILY TO THE LANGUAGE DIALOGUE, OR THE LINGO. OBVIOUSLY, THEY DID NOT ALL ACQUIRE THE KNOWLEDGE BASE SKILLS TO BUILD A CITY OR A TOWER TO HEAVEN, BUT WHAT THEY DID HAVE WAS A UNIFIED LANGUAGE, WHICH ENABLED THEM TO UNDERSTAND THE LEADER'S SPOKEN WORDS, COMMANDING THEM TO BUILD THE TOWER.

IT IS MY OPINION, AND MY BIBLICAL UNDERSTANDING, THAT THEY RECEIVED INSTRUCTION AS A COMMAND, NOT AS A QUESTION; WHICH WOULD HAVE ONLY HINDERED THEIR PROGRESS!

> *Know ye that the Lord he is God: it is he that hath made us and not we ourselves: We are his people, and the sheep of his pastures.*
>
> PSALMS #100:3

GOD, IS THE ONLY TRUE SOURCE TO BE HELD RESPONSIBLE, FOR SUCH ONENESS OF MIND AMONG MEN. THEREFORE, IT IS NOT GOD'S FAULT THAT MAN CHOSE NOT TO REMAIN IN UNITY AND IN HARMONY WITH ONE ANOTHER.

The Language Did Not Discriminate!

HEAVEN STANDS AND PREVAILS IN TOTAL ONENESS OF LANGUAGE AND SPEECH. TO THIS VERY DAY, WE HAVE NEVER READ THAT THE LANGUAGE OF HEAVEN HAD EVER BEEN CHANGED. THIS GLORIOUSLY UNIFIED LANGUAGE OF HEAVEN, IS THAT OF ADORATION, IN PRAISE AND WORSHIP TO OUR GOD AND YOU CAN BELIEVE THAT THERE IS NO ONE STANDING AROUND BAFFLED AND CONFUSED, BECAUSE THEY DO NOT UNDERSTAND THE DIALOGUE.

HEAVEN'S DIALOGUE DOES NOT ONLY RELATE TO THE INNER KINGDOM OF HEAVEN, OUTSIDE OF THE REALM OF HUMANITY. HEAVEN IS NOT SELFISH, IN TERMS OF THE

RECOGNITION GIVEN TO THINGS THAT ARE RELATIVE TO THE GOD WHO CREATED THEM.

HEAVEN IS SPIRITUALLY ATTUNED TO MAINTAINING THE SOULS THAT HAVE BEEN BORN OF THE SPIRIT OF GOD. THEY DISCUSS THE WILL OF GOD FOR HIS PEOPLE IN THE EARTH AND THESE DISCUSSIONS ARE FREQUENT AND THOROUGH AMONG THE HOST OF HEAVEN.

HEAVEN'S PRIORITIZED AGENDA, ACCORDING TO ITS LANGUAGE DIALOGUE, BESPEAKS OF THE POWERFULLY, BUT YET COMPASSIONATELY SHED BLOOD OF JESUS CHRIST ON THE CROSS, FOR REMISSION OF THE SINS OF THE PEOPLE OF THE EARTH.

HEAVEN'S DISCUSSIONS ARE IN PREPARATION FOR THE IMMINENT RETURN OF CHRIST, TO RECEIVE HIS BRIDE OUT OF THE EARTH.

THE ANGELS QUESTIONED THE STATUS OF MAN IN THE PRESENCE OF GOD. NOT TO SECRETLY OVERTHROW THE KINGDOM OF HEAVEN, BUT, FOR THE PURPOSE OF SEEING MAN THROUGH THE EYES OF GRACE.

> *What is man, that thou art mindful of him? And the son man, that thou visitest him? For thou hast made him a little lower than the angels, and hast crowned him with glory and honor. Thou madest him to have dominion over the works of thy hands; thou hast put all things under his feet.*
>
> PSALMS 8:4-6

HEAVEN IS NOT ON A GLORIOUS TRIP, OUT IN SPACE FLOATING AND ORBITING AROUND THE EARTH, LIKE THE SOLAR SYSTEM. THE GOVERNING SYSTEM TO ESTABLISH ANY ACCEPTABLE MORALITY IN THE EARTH, USED TO BE IN TOUCH WITH HEAVEN.

THE UNSTOPPABLE POWER OF UNITY, AS A RESULT OF IT'S EASY ACCESS THROUGH THE DOORWAY OF UNDERSTANDING, HAD NOW BEEN DISCOVERED IN THE EARTH. HEAVEN KNEW THAT NOTHING WAS IMPOSSIBLE, AS LONG AS MEN WORKED TOGETHER AND KNEW ONE ANOTHER'S LANGUAGE.

When people come into agreement with God, teaching the ways of God's righteous all over the world, will not be so complicated or lacking.

In recent decades past, many astronauts and NASA; reported several successful missions in outerspace, to which they landed, and walked on the moon. America had a fit when Neil Armstrong reported that he had set foot on the moon.

Though the space mission was impressive to the human race, there is an account even more impressive than the trip to the moon, written in the word of God.

Man can say that they went up into the heavens out among the moon and the stars and planets, in the flesh! But, they will never be able to say that they entered into the gates of the Third Heaven, around the throne of God in the presence of all the host of Heaven; in the flesh.

Man almost went to Heaven on their own powerfully unified understanding, but they would have been ungodly men working the common will of their own sinful desires, as if Heaven was in need of their input from an earthly perspective.

If man, would have gotten to the point of reaching Heaven on their own, they would have also foolishly discovered among themselves, that they didn't need to hear from Heaven anymore, because they could hear from each other and accomplish everything that they needed.

Even God, soon realized that man had found the once hidden treasure of His own speech, which was the constructive tools of unity, founded upon the strength of understanding. God saw an ungodly unified influence and an untimely use of the human will, without His consent. Man discovered that they could talk their way into and out of most

ANYTHING!

THE DIVERSIFICATION OF SPEECH AND LANGUAGE HAD TO BE SO BECAUSE OF THE SELFISHNESS AND THE SINFULNESS OF MAN.

ONENESS OF LANGUAGE WAS NOT AN ACCIDENT, AS IF HEAVEN PUSHED THE WRONG BUTTON AND SHUT OFF THE DIVERSIFICATION FORCE FIELD, LIKE SOMETHING THAT MIGHT HAPPEN IN SCIENTIFIC FILM; CAUSING EVERYONE TO SPEAK EXACTLY THE SAME LANGUAGE.

NEITHER, WAS THE CONFOUNDING DIVERSIFICATION OF THE LANGUAGE A MISTAKE, WHICH CAUSED A WIDE SPREAD GLITCH IN THE CONFIGURATIVE FORMAT IN THE ONENESS OF LANGUAGE BARRIER, CAUSING IT TO EXPLODE, SPEWING FRAGMENTS OF VERBAL CONFUSION, SUBVERTING THE HIGH LEVELS OF COMPREHENSION ALL OVER THE EARTH.

GOD SPOKE TO THE UNIFIED LANGUAGE OF MANKIND IN THE EARTH, AND FOR THE FIRST TIME, SINCE THE BEGINNING OF CREATION AND QUICKER THAN AT ONCE, NOBODY ANYWHERE UNDERSTOOD EVERYBODY'S SPEECH ANYMORE. THE UNIFIED LINES OF COMMUNICATION HAD BEEN DISCONNECTED!

OF THE PEOPLE, WHO SPOKE THE SAME LANGUAGE, SOME SPOKE A DIFFERENT DIALECT OF THE SAME SPEECH. OTHERS, DEVELOPED COMPLETELY NEW FOREIGN TONGUES, INSTANTANEOUSLY. THERE WERE PERHAPS SEVERAL INDIVIDUALS WHO STILL UNDERSTOOD EACH OTHER, BUT THERE WERE NOT ENOUGH PEOPLE WHO UNDERSTOOD TO EVEN COMPLETE A FULL DAYS WORK, ON THIS ONCE UNIFIED PROJECT OF BUILDING THE TOWER TO HEAVEN.

NOW, THEIR HARMONIOUSLY UNIFIED CONVERSATIONS, HAD BECOME HORRIFIC BABBLING, NOTHING BUT NOISE. MANKIND, HAS BEEN MAKING NOISE AT EACH OTHER AND EVEN WITH EACH OTHER EVERY SINCE THAT CONFOUNDING DAY, AS A RESULT OF NOT BEING ABLE TO SPEAK ONE ANOTHER'S LANGUAGE.

While we are now confused of speech and disadvantaged to understand foreign tongues, without the aid of an instructional therapist for the comprehension of the many languages of the earth, God is neither confused or colloquially challenged with the earth's multiplicity of languages! He's the master of all languages and the spoken words of everyone, individually!

There's Been A Change Since Then!

Having the diversities of language in the earth for centuries now, we have the development of many more complex dialects of speaking, which has brought about an even greater divide.

The alphabets, for an instance, changed with every language, while the numerical systems in every foreign land, also changed upon the development of many different measurement scales.

Occupational titles, while they might have meant the same thing in definitions, were referred to differently, according to the dialect and the region. They may have even described the performance of exactly the very same job, as pertaining to a particular geographical area.

However, since the tower of Babel, as a result of so many different intellectual interjections, mankind has pulled further and further apart to become enemies. Even more so now that the lack of sin contiousness has crept into the Christian dialogue.

Everyone has been allowed to individually develop their very own ways of thinking about God. The perception of every individual, is often strongly opposed to the next man, as long as Christ has not infiltrated the thought processes of those individuals.

What Are We Really <u>Saying/Seeing?</u>

PERHAPS YOU HAVE BEEN WONDERING, WHAT EVER HAPPENED TO THE PEOPLE OF THE EARTH, IN TERMS OF BEING ABLE TO TALK AND TO UNDERSTAND ONE ANOTHER, SINCE GOD FIRST CREATED US, NOW YOU KNOW.

HAVEN'T YOU EVER WONDERED HOW IT IS THAT PEOPLE READ THE EXACT SAME BIBLE AND FROM THE SAME PASSAGES OF SCRIPTURAL READING, THEY GET MULTIPLES OF DIFFERENT INTERPRETATIONS AND UNDERSTANDINGS?

DENOMINATIONAL PERSUASIONS WITHIN THE CHRISTIAN RELIGION AND OTHER SPIRITUAL MOVEMENTS, WERE STARTED AS A RESULT OF TOO MANY DIFFERENT UNDERSTANDINGS, IN WHICH MAN REFUSED TO COME TOGETHER ON THAT WHICH IS WRONG, OR RIGHT.

OUR UNDERSTANDINGS HAVE CHANGED SO MUCH, THAT OUR VISUAL AND MENTAL, AS WELL AS SPIRITUAL PERCEPTIONS, HAVE DANGEROUSLY SLANTED.

IT'S DISGUSTING TO KNOW THAT SOMEONE ACTUALLY SEES A THING OF BEAUTY IN A PILE OF TRASH OR JUNK, THAT IS FIT FOR NOTHING ELSE BUT LAND FILL BURIAL, UNDERNEATH THE RUBBLE, LEFT TO DECAY. PEOPLE WHO FOCUS ON JUNK, AS IF TO SEE A REAL BEAUTY, DON'T KEEP THEIR FINDINGS TO THEMSELVES.

IT'S NOT A GOOD TO SEE THE ACTUAL BEAUTY OF LIFE AND TO BELIEVE THAT THERE IS STILL AN ALIVE PRESENCE IN A DEAD CORPS, WHEN IN FACT YOU MAY BE ACTUALLY STARING DOWN AT THE DEAD REMAINS IN A COFFIN.

PEOPLE NOW TALK OF BEING SAVED IN CHRIST, YET THEY ARE LIVING UNDER THE BLANKETING PRESENCE OF ALIVE AND ACTIVELY PRACTICAL SINFULNESS, WHERE THERE HAS BEEN ABSOLUTELY NO CHANGE, THEIR CHANGE IS A LIE!

SUCH LANGUAGE USAGE DEPICTS AN ILLUMINATED LIGHT, IN THE MIDST OF DARKNESS AND THE PRESENCE OF DARKNESS IN THE MIDST OF THE LIGHT. NOT!

PEOPLE WILL ATTACH THE WRONG NAME TO THE RIGHT THING AND IN THE PRESENCE OF WHAT IS DETESTABLY WRONG AND UNTRUE; SOME KIND OF THOUGHT PERCEPTION CALLS IT RIGHT, BEFITTING AND/OR EVEN CONDUCIVE.

> *And that ye may put a difference between holy*
> *and unholy, and between unclean and clean.*
> LEVITICUS 10:10

Defining Understanding!

CALL IT WHATEVER IT IS. THERE IS NO ACTUAL ACCEPTANCE IN THE MIDST OF REJECTION. NO MATTER WHAT SCIENTIFIC EXPLANATION IS GIVEN, THERE IS A DIFFERENCE, A NOTABLE DIFFERENCE AND A DIVINE PURPOSE FOR THESE OPPOSITES. NO, NEVER; MEANS YES!

THE TERMINOLOGY OFTEN USED, THAT PROPOSES THAT ALL OPPOSITES ATTRACT, DOES BEAR SOME TRUTH, HOWEVER, THIS IS NOT TRUTHFUL OF EVERY OPPOSITE.

GREASE AND WATER, BEING A LIQUID AND A SOLID, NO MATTER WHAT THE TEMPERAMENT OR THE ADDITIVE, THE TWO WILL NEVER COME TO A COMPLETE POINT OF MIXTURE, WHEREAS THE IDENTITIES OF EACH PART ARE NO LONGER CLEARLY DETECTED. WATER AND FIRE WERE NOT CREATED TO MIX AND THEY NEVER WILL, WOULDN'T YOU AGREE THAT THESE ARE THE OPPOSITES OF EACH OTHER?

A DELUSION OR AN OPTICAL ILLUSION MAY CAUSE ONE TO BELIEVE THAT A MIXTURE HAS OCCURRED, BUT THE ABSENCE OF THE ACTUAL FACTUAL TRUTH TO SUCH FINDINGS IS THAT THESE OPPOSITES DON'T MIX. SCIENTIFIC STUDIES HAVE ONLY SOUGHT TO EXPLAIN THE PATTERNS OF SUCH COMPOSITE BEHAVIOR.

> *O Timothy, keep that which is committed to thy*
> *trust, avoiding profane and vain babblings, and*
> *oppositions <u>of science</u> falsely so called: Which*
> *some professing have erred concerning the faith.*
> *Grace be to you; Amen.* I TIMOTHY 6:20-21

"The Power of Truth!"

*Verily, verily, I say unto thee, we speak that we
do know, and testify that which we have seen;*

ST. JOHN 3:11

KNOWLEDGE ACQUIRED BY WAY OF SOMEONE ELSE'S EXPERIENCES IS ONLY SECOND HAND KNOWLEDGE. IMAGINING THE DESCRIPTIVE STORY TOLD, WHEN SEEN THROUGH THE EYES OF OTHERS IS NOT THE TRUE MEANING OF SEEING. SUCH PRESENTATIONS OF THE TRUTH, FALSIFIES YOUR OWN PERSONAL SPOKEN ACCOUNT OF ANY DETAILS OF THAT TO WHICH YOU PROFESS TO KNOW.

AS A RESULT OF THE TRUTH, WE ARE SAVED, SET FREE, AND DELIVERED; WHICH ONLY SETS US UP FOR THE INTRODUCTION OF THE GREATER MANIFESTATION IN THE SPIRIT. WE HAVE GOT TO EXCEPT THE TRUTH AS IT IS GOING TO OUTLIVE EVERYONE AND EVERYTHING ON THE FACE OF THE EARTH. <u>TRUTH</u>; WILL NEVER LIE.

TRUTH, IS LIKE A RUBBER BALL; THE HARDER YOU THROW IT DOWN TO THE GROUND, THE HIGHER IT WILL RISE BACK UP TO THE SKY. YOU CAN ACTUALLY TRAVEL ON THE VEHICLE OF TRUTH, TO PLACES OF FAVORABLE INFLUENCES, AND HIGH SELF ESTEEM, BY BEING TRUTHFUL EVERYDAY OF YOUR LIFE!

TRUTH BRINGS CHANGE, WHEN INDIVIDUALS IMMERSE THEMSELVES DEEPLY AND REFUSE TO ALLOW THEMSELVES TO ONLY HANG AROUND THE SHALLOW REALMS OF THE EDGE, TO THE LIKES OF PLAYING ON THE BEACH WHILE NEVER GOING OUT INTO THE WATER.

WE NEED TO INGEST HELPFUL MEASURES OF THE TRUTH AND THEN DIGEST TRUTH, NO MATTER HOW HARD IT MAY HAVE BEEN TO SWALLOW. WE'VE GOT TO ALLOW THE TRUTH TO GET DOWN INTO OUR BELLIES, TO TAKE ROOT AND BEGIN TO PRODUCE THE DESIRED EFFECTS OF CHANGE.

NO NEED TO WORRY YOURSELVES RELATIVE TO THE ACTUAL VALIDITY OF SPEAKING IN TONGUES. IF THERE WAS

no truth to the Holy Ghost, we could not receive the in-filling, which give the utterances of the language in the spirit of God.

Is there anyone in your own circle of life who know that you have received the power of God in your life? Are they aware of the fact that the powerful current of the Holy Ghost is alive and actively flowing through you?

I'm sure that your friends and family members know exactly how you talk in the natural. I would think that they know the tone of your voice, and the vernacular that you use to communicate with the people of your own surroundings.

But! Have they ever heard you talk in the spirit of God, whenever you speak the language of His people, in the power of the Holy Ghost? Have they had the opportunity witness your connection with God and the people of God world wide?

"Your Speech Betrayed You!"

There are many different ways of identifying a person. Most identifying measures, if not all of them, are applied to the identification of an individual by someone else, from an outward perspective.

Two people can be unmistakably identical twins, but their spirit and character are individually unique. They look alike, but some how, they act differently. Two people may be similar, but believe me, they are never the same!

Over the telephone, two people may sound exactly alike, however, what is known about the caller or perhaps about the individual who answers the phone, identifies the person on either end of the telephone receiver. In a costume and/or behind a

MASK, SOMETHING ABOUT THE PERSON'S SPEECH OR THEIR VOICE WILL UNMASK THEIR TRUE IDENTITY.

AS BELIEVERS, WE ARE CLEARLY IDENTIFIED BY OUR LANGUAGE AND OUR ACTION OF LOVE. IT IS NOT THAT WE ARE OF A STRANGE OR WEIRD TYPE IN OUR SPIRITUAL NATURE, BUT WE ARE ESPECIALLY UNIQUE WITHIN THE POSTURE OF OUR CHRISTIAN DEMEANOR.

PECULIAR; IS THE GOD GIVEN TITLE TO BELIEVERS. WE THE PEOPLE OF GOD, SHOULD STICK OUT LIKE SORE THUMBS, BECAUSE WE ALLOW OUR LIGHTS TO SHINE BEFORE ALL MEN EVERYWHERE.

What We Say; Is What You Get!

OUR LIGHTS ARE NOT OF THE FLUORESCENCE ILLUMINATION, LIKE THAT OF LIGHT BULBS, BUT IT IS THE LIGHT OF THE GLORIOUS LIFE OF CHRIST, WHICH FILTERS THROUGH THE LANGUAGE OF OUR SPEECH. IT IS NOT JUST ABOUT WHAT WE SAY, IT IS HOWEVER, MORE ABOUT WHAT WE DO ABOUT WHAT WE SAY, THAT WILL HIGHLIGHT OUR DESIRED SYSTEM OF BELIEF.

THE REAL TRUE POWER OF WHAT WE SAY, IS DISPLAYED IN HOW IT EFFECTS OUR OWN LIFE FIRST AND FOREMOST AND THEN HOW IT AFFECTS THE LIVES OF OTHERS. THE CHILDREN OF GOD SIGN THEIR SIGNIFICANT SIGNATURES, IDENTIFYING THEMSELVES BEFORE THE WORLD THROUGH OUR BEHAVIOR, THAT MUST NEVER CONTRADICT OUR CONFESSION OF CHRIST.

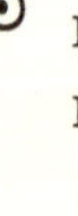

PEOPLE ARE ALWAYS LOOKING FOR SOMETHING IN THE LIFE OF SOMEONE ELSE TO EMULATE. PEOPLE ARE LOOKING FOR WHAT'S REAL, ALTHOUGH THEY ARE CONSISTENTLY LOOKING IN ALL OF THE WRONG PLACES.

YOU WILL OBSERVE VERY SIMILAR BEHAVIOR IN THE PEOPLE OF GOD, EVEN THOUGH THE PEOPLE MAY BE CULTURALLY OPPOSED TO THE PEOPLE THAT YOU MAY BE MOST FAMILIAR WITH PRIOR TO BEING ACQUAINTED WITH THEM.

WHAT WE DO, AS GOD'S PEOPLE, SPEAKS LOUDER,

THAN OUR OWN VERBAL CONVERSATIONS. OUR DAILY LIVES SHOULD ALWAYS LINE UP WITH WHAT WE SAY, EVEN THOUGH THIS IS NOT ALWAYS THE CASE. THERE IS UNBELIEVABLE POWER UNLEASHED, WHENEVER OUR WORD IS FOLLOWED BY NON-CONTRADICTING ACTION.

God' Did It, For A Reason!

EVERY SINCE THE LANGUAGE CHANGED AT THE TOWER OF BABEL, GOD LAUNCHED A SPIRITUAL CAMPAIGN TO REUNITE THE LANGUAGE OF THE PEOPLE OF GOD EVERYWHERE, **ONCE AGAIN TO ONENESS.**

WE NEED ONLY TO ADAPT TO THE IDEAS OF GOD AND TO THINK LIKE HE THINKS. I DO BELIEVE THAT EVERY WORD IN THE BIBLE IS RIGHT AND I DON'T STRUGGLE WITH THE REALITY OF THE BIBLE BEING THE WRITTEN WORD OF GOD.

UNLESS A PERSON COMES TO TERMS WITH BELIEVING THE WORD OF GOD, THEY WILL NEVER BE A <u>DOER</u>, NOR WILL THEY EVER BE A <u>SAYER</u>, OF THE WORD.

THE UNIFICATION OF ANY LANGUAGE, FIRSTLY REQUIRES A SYSTEM OF TOTAL BELIEF AND TRUST. THOSE WHO PARTICIPATED IN CONSTRUCTING THE TOWER OF "BABEL", BELIEVED IN THE TASK. THEY BELIEVED IN EACH OTHER AND THE POWER OF THEIR UNIFIED SPEECH.

THE ACHIEVEMENT OF ONENESS REQUIRES MORE THAN INTELLECTUAL READINESS AND GROUP IDENTIFICATION. BEING CLOSED-OFF TO A PARTICULAR GROUP OR DENOMINATION OF RELIGIOUS PREFERENCES, ONLY INSURES THE PREVENTION OF SUCH ONENESS, AS IS NEEDED IN THE BODY OF CHRIST AT LARGE.

THE BODY OF THE CHURCH IS COMPRISED OF MEMBERS FROM ALL DIVERSE GROUPS OF PEOPLE, THAT BELIEVE IN THE DEATH, BURIAL, AND RESURRECTION OF "JESUS CHRIST OF NAZARETH."

GOD'S PEOPLE ARE FAITHFUL BELIEVERS OF A LIVING HOPE. YOU MIGHT AS WELL GET READY, BECAUSE THERE

WILL BE PEOPLE FROM OTHER DENOMINATIONS, OPPOSITE
OF YOURS, WHO WILL BE THERE IN HEAVEN TOO!

Do, What He Told You To Do!

ONENESS IS TRULY THE EXTRAVAGANTLY PERFECTED
PLAN OF COMMUNICATION FOR GOD'S PEOPLE.

HAVING OBTAINED ONENESS WITH GOD, WE ARE
OFTEN ABSTRACTLY BEING LED BY THE SPIRIT OF GOD, AS
OTHERS FROM PAST TIMES WERE LED BY THE SPIRIT OF THE
LORD. OTHERS, AS WELL AS THE TWELVE SELECTED
APOSTLES OF CHRIST; HEARD THE PROMISE AND BELIEVED
WITH GREAT EXPECTATION. THEY BELIEVED THE PROMISE
AS PROPHESIED BY THE PROPHET JOEL.

> *And it shall come to pass afterward, that I will*
> *pour out my spirit upon all flesh; and your sons*
> *and daughters shall prophesy, your old men*
> *shall dream dreams, and your young men shall*
> *see visions:*
>
> JOEL 2:28

WHENEVER WE ARE GIVEN A WORD OF PROPHECY,
THE MANIFESTATIONS ARE NOT ALWAYS IMMEDIATELY RE-
LEASED TO OUR POSSESSION; THEREFORE, WE JUST HAVE TO
WAIT, PATIENTLY IN FAITH.

MANY YEARS HAD LAPSED, AND THIS PROPHESY OF
THE PROPHET JOEL; SEEMED TO HAVE TAKEN A BACK SEAT
TO MANY OTHER FOLLOWING PROPHESIES THAT WERE SPO-
KEN, BUT, IN DUE TIME THE WORD SPOKE AND IT DID NOT
LIE! THE POWERFUL ENDOWMENT OF THE HOLY GHOST
FELL ON THE DAY OF PENTECOST! *Acts 2:4*

JESUS GAVE INSTRUCTIONS TO THE DISCIPLES, AFTER
HE HAD BEEN RAISED FROM THE GRAVE, WITH ALL POWER
GIVEN UNTO HIM.

> *And, behold, I send the promise of my father*
> *upon you: but tarry ye in the city of Jerusalem,*
> *until ye be endued with power from on high.*
>
> ST. LUKE 24:49

THE LORD HAS GIVEN US INSTRUCTIONS TO FOLLOW ALL THE WAY UP THE ROAD TO RECEIVE-IT BLVD., SO THAT THE BLESSINGS MIGHT FALL ON US, ALIKE. IT IS NOT ENOUGH, TO ONLY RECEIVE INSTRUCTIONS, KNOWING THAT YOU HAVE NO INTENTIONS OF EVER FOLLOWING THEM.

THE APOSTLES WERE WILLING TO FOLLOW THE IN-STRUCTIONS OF THEIR LORD, TO THE VERY END, NO MAT-TER WHERE IT MIGHT HAVE LED THEM.

> *And he led them out as far as to Bethany, and he lifted up his hands, and blessed them. And it came to pass, while he blessed them, he was parted from them, and carried up into heaven. And they worshipped him, and returned to Jerusalem with great joy: And were continually in the temple praising and blessing God. Amen:* ST. LUKE 24:50-53

THEY OBEYED WITH GREAT JOY, ALTHOUGH THERE WERE TIMES THAT THEY COULD NOT EVEN FATHOM HIS REA-SONING!

YOU HAVE GOT TO DEVELOP A LOVE FOR INSTRUC-TION AND LEARN TO FOLLOW. BE HAPPY, TO BE TAUGHT SOMETHING THAT YOU DIDN'T KNOW. MANY PEOPLE ARE OFTEN LED OUT, AWAY FROM THE GENERAL ASSEMBLY OF THE BODY OF BELIEVERS BY THE LORD'S OWN HAND, FOR AN INTENDED PURPOSE, WHICH WILL SOON BE REVEALED, JUST AS SOON AS THAT INDIVIDUAL'S OBEDIENCE HAS BEEN FULFILLED. 

I STRONGLY SUGGEST THAT YOU GO BACK TO THE ORIGINAL INSTRUCTIONS OF THE LORD. THERE, IN THE ORIGINAL INSTRUCTIONS, LIES THE ORIGINAL INTENTIONS AND THE PURPOSE FOR YOUR LIFE. DON'T FORGET THIS!!!

> *Until the day in which he was taken up, after that he through the Holy Ghost had given com-mandment unto the Apostles whom he had chosen:* ACTS 1: 2

OUR OWN ABILITIES TO CHOOSE ARE SO VERY POWERFUL, BUT WHAT IS EVEN MORE POWERFUL THAN THE ABILITY TO CHOOSE, IS THE FACT THAT WE HAVE BEEN SELECTIVELY CHOSEN BY GOD.

THE APOSTLES WERE SELECTIVELY CHOSEN AND HAND PICKED BY JESUS CHRIST, FOR THE DIVINE PROVIDENTIAL PURPOSE OF GOD. EVERYONE THAT IS CALLED AND CHOSEN OF GOD, HAVE BEEN CALLED AND CHOSEN OF A DIVINE PURPOSE.

> *And being assembled together with them, commanded them that they should not depart from Jerusalem, but wait for the promise of the father, which, saith he, ye have heard of me. For John truly baptized with water, but ye shall be baptized with the Holy Ghost not many days hence.*   ACTS 1:4-5

He Promised!

THE HOLY GHOST WAS NEVER INTENDED TO BE DIVIDED FOR THE PURPOSE OF DENOMINATIONAL CHURCH BODY SEPARATIONS! NEITHER WAS THIS ENDOWMENT FOR US TO BE SUPER SPIRITUALLY CHARGED AND HIGH MINDED (*being spiritually puffed up in pride*), AS WE SEE SO OFTEN AMONG THE CHURCHES.

THE LANGUAGE OF THE EARTH WAS NOW TOO CORRUPT AND TOO DETACHED FROM THE SPIRIT OF GOD AND HEAVEN'S LINGUISTIC DIALOGUE. IT WAS BY FAR TOO SINFUL, WICKED AND DETERIORATED, DUE TO THE MAGNITUDE OF THE EVIL INFLUENCES INTERMINGLED INTO THE LANGUAGE OF THE WORLD.

BEARING SO MANY LINGUISTIC FLAWS, SUCH AS CURSING, SWEARING, PROFANITY, FALSE ACCUSATIONS, LYING OBSCENITIES, AND ETC.; THESE UNGODLY ELEMENTS IN THE NATURAL LANGUAGE OF THE EARTH COULD NEVER BE ACCEPTABLE FOR THE USE OF ANY DIVINE PURPOSES.

> *Out of the same mouth proceeded blessing and*
> *cursing. My brethren, these things ought not*
> *so to be.* JAMES 3:10

MAN COUPLED UP WITH THE DEVIL, TO CORRUPT THE ONCE UNIFIED LANGUAGE OF THE EARTH! GOD SOUGHT AND HE CONTINUES TO SEEK, TRUE WORSHIPERS TO WORSHIP HIM IN SPIRIT AND IN TRUTH!

GOD KNEW THAT THERE WOULD BE LIMITED WORSHIP IN THE NATURAL LANGUAGE OF THE EARTH. HE ALSO KNEW THAT BECAUSE OF INDIVIDUALITY, THERE WOULD BE NO COMING TOGETHER IN THE NATURAL, IF ANY CARNAL THINKING MAN HAD ANYTHING TO DO WITH IT. WE WOULD HAVE TO COME TOGETHER SPIRITUALLY!

> *Ye hypocrites, well did Esaias prophesy of you,*
> *saying, This people draweth nigh unto me with*
> *their mouth, and honoureth me with their lips;*
> *but their heart is far from me. But in vain they*
> *do worship me, teaching for doctrine the com-*
> *mandments of men.* ST. MATTHEW 15:7-9

IT TAKES MORE THAN A DESIRE TO TRULY WORSHIP GOD. RELATIVE TO THE CONDITION OF YOUR HEART AT THE TIME OF SPEAKING, WORD DEFINITIONS MAY DEPICT THAT THERE IS A DISCREPANCY IN THE ONENESS OF LANGUAGE AND/OR SPEECH USED.

WE ONLY DISCOVER TOTAL ONENESS AND SPIRITUAL COMPLETENESS BETWEEN GOD AND MANKIND EVERYWHERE, AMONG THOSE PERSONS WHO WILL WORSHIP GOD IN SPIRIT AND IN TRUTH AND IN THE LANGUAGE OF THE HOLY GHOST.

JUST BECAUSE PEOPLE COME TO ASSEMBLE THEMSELVES TO HAVE A CHURCH SERVICE OF SOME SORT, THAT DOES NOT NECESSARILY CONSTITUTE THE FACT THAT THEY HAVE TRULY COME TOGETHER TO WORSHIP GOD, IN SPIRIT AND IN TRUTH!

> *But the hour cometh, and now is, when the true*
> *worshippers shall worship the father in spirit*
> *and in truth: for the father seeketh such to wor-*
> *ship him. God is a spirit: and they that wor-*
> *ship him must worship him in spirit and in*
> *truth.*   ST. JOHN 4:23-24

*Acrobatic Purpose**

TO WORSHIP, OR TO BE A WORSHIPPER, IS NOT TO BE ASCERTAINED IN LIGHT OF BEING A VERB, MEANING SOMETHING YOU DO OR RENDERING A PARTICULAR ACTION, BUT, IT IS TO BE SEEN IN LIGHT OF BEING A NOUN. CHARACTERISTICALLY, OF WHOM YOU HAVE ACTUALLY BECOME.

BOTH SYLLABLES OF THE WORD <u>WORSHIP</u> ARE SIGNIFICANT IN MEANING. FOR AN EXAMPLE: "WÔR" - PRONOUNCED WËR' IS RELATIVE TO THE ENGLISH WORD *were*, WHICH IN DEFINITION MEANS, *to be*. ONE, OF MANY DEFINITION FOR SHIP, IS TO *send or receive*.

THEREFORE THE GREATEST HONOR AND THE MOST SUPREME REVERENCE OF OUR WORSHIP IS SENT OUT FROM US IN THE SPIRIT UP TO GOD; OUR FATHER. OUR TRUE SPIRIT OF WORSHIP IS RECEIVED OF HIM.

REAL, TRUE WORSHIP, IS NOT A PARTICIPATORY COLLECTIVE PRACTICE, WHEREAS, A GROUP OF PEOPLE COME TOGETHER TO PERFORM SOME TYPE OF WORSHIPFUL RITUALISTIC ACT.

BUT, RATHER THE ACTION OF WORSHIP IN ITS TRUEST DEFINITIVE SENSE OF THE MEANING IS; "SPIRITUAL PROJECTION-ISM!" (<u>*not Astrol Projection*</u>) PROJECTION-ISM IS CASTING FORTH OR THROWING FORTH ONES OWN SPIRIT, LITERALLY AND EVEN FIGURATIVELY SPEAKING, <u>**ONLY**</u> IN THE INTENDED DIRECTION OF GOD, FOR THE PURPOSE OF WORSHIPING HIM!

WORSHIP LIFTS OUR SPIRIT TO THE "FATHER'S" SPIRIT, THEREFORE, WE MUST WORSHIP WITH THE PURPOSEFUL INTENTIONS OF TRULY CONNECTING WITH OUR HEAV-

ENLY FATHER. WE MUST NEVER CASUALLY ENTER INTO WORSHIP, AS IF WE ARE DOING GOD A FAVOR. HEREIN, IS WHERE THE ONLY REAL TRUE "HOLY COMMUNION" OF WORSHIP IS REALIZED.

WE MUST PUSH AND PRESS INTO THE PRESENCE OF THE LORD, WITH GREAT DETERMINATION OF BOTH SUCCESSFULLY SENDING AND JOYFULLY RECEIVING THE AWESOMELY SUPER ESSENTIAL PRESENCE OF <u>GOD</u>! HIS PRESENCE IS WHAT IS SO DESPERATELY NEEDED AMONG US, HERE IN THE EARTH.

THIS SPECIAL ENDOWMENT OF THE PROMISE OF GOD, WILL KEEP US IN LINE WITH OUR PURPOSE.

> *But ye shall receive power, after that the Holy Ghost is come upon you; and ye shall be witnesses unto me both in Jerusalem, and in all Judea, and in Samaria, and unto the uttermost part of the earth.* ACTS 1:8

I HEAR JESUS SAYING; THAT ONLY AFTER THE HOLY GHOST IS COME UPON YOU, WILL YOU THEN BE ABLE TO ACHIEVE THE ONLY REAL TRUE SPIRITUAL ONENESS OF LANGUAGE AND SPEECH. THE LANGUAGE THAT YOU'LL SPEAK; WILL BE ONCE AGAIN UNIFIED WITH THE LANGUAGE OF HEAVEN.

> *And they were all filled with the Holy Ghost, and began to speak with other tongues, as the spirit gave them utterance And there were dwelling at Jerusalem Jews, devout men out of every nation under heaven.* ACTS 2: 4-5

NOW!! HERE IT IS! LOOK! THE LANGUAGE OF HIS PEOPLE IS FINALLY RESTORED. HERE THEY ARE BACK TOGETHER AGAIN, BUT FOR THE RIGHT REASON AND WITH THE RIGHT PURPOSE IN MIND, SPEAKING AN "HEAVENLY" LANGUAGE.

GOD STRATEGICALLY PLACED EVERY TONGUE AND EVERY NATION AT THE SAME PLACE ALL OVER AGAIN, JUST

AS THEY WERE WHEN THE LANGUAGES WERE DIVERSIFIED OR CHANGED IF YOU PREFER, AT THE TOWER OF BABEL.

HAS YOUR LANGUAGE BEEN CHANGED AS OF YET, TO THE "HEAVENLY" LANGUAGE? OR RATHER, HAVE YOU RECEIVED THE HOLY GHOST, SINCE YOU BELIEVED? YOU NEED IT!

Speak His Language!!!

SPEAKING WITH UNKNOWN TONGUES AS THE SPIRIT GIVES THE UTTERANCE, IS NOT BABBLING GIBBERISH AND AN UNNECESSARY NOISE, AS SOME SEEM TO ADAMANTLY EMBRACE, BUT IT IS AN "HEAVENLY" LANGUAGE, MUCH MORE BEAUTIFUL AND SWEETER THAN THE LANGUAGE OF WHICH WE ARE SO FAMILIAR.

IT IS THE ULTIMATE LANGUAGE COMMUNICATION BETWEEN GOD AND MAN, BEYOND ANY EARTHLY AND ATMOSPHERIC DISTRACTIONS OR INTERPRETATIONS.

TO BE STUMPED OR CONFUSED, BECAUSE YOU ARE AT A LOSS FOR AN INTERPRETIVE UNDERSTANDING OF THE LANGUAGE ITSELF, IS NO REASON TO BE IN TOTAL REJECTION OF RECEIVING THE HOLY GHOST. GOD, IS THE ONLY ONE WHO NEEDS TO UNDERSTAND YOU, WHENEVER YOU PRAY IN THE SPIRIT AND NOT EVERYONE ELSE.

THE PROBLEM WITH MAN IS THAT WE ALWAYS WANT TO BE IN CONTROL OF UNDERSTANDING EVERYTHING THAT IS RELATING TO US FIRSTLY AND THE AFFAIRS THAT ARE RELATIVE TO EVERYONE ELSE, ESPECIALLY RELATING TO WHATEVER IS SPOKEN OUT OF OTHERS MOUTHS.

DON'T FOCUS ON THE LANGUAGE ITSELF, BUT RATHER FOCUS ON THE PERSON OF THE HOLY GHOST, THAT GIVES YOU THE DIRECT AUTHORITY TO SPEAK THE LANGUAGE ANYWAY!

THIS HEAVENLY LANGUAGE IS INCORRUPTIBLE, BECAUSE IT IS A LANGUAGE THAT THE DEVIL CANNOT UNDERSTAND! HE'S AFRAID OF IT, BECAUSE HE CANNOT HANDLE IT OR EVEN TAMPER WITH IT. IT BEWILDERS THE DEVIL

AND CONFUSES DEMONS. IT BRINGS THE GLORIOUS PRESENCE OF GOD RIGHT DOWN TO US IMMEDIATELY.

THIS HEAVENLY LANGUAGE, IS THE INSIDE ACCESS TO THE VERY THRONE OF GOD. IF YOU REALLY DESIRE TO KNOW THE REAL PURPOSE AND THE VALIDITY OF THE LANGUAGE, WHY DON'T YOU CONSIDER APPROACHING THE THRONE OF GOD, TO ASK HIM DIRECTLY FOR AN ANSWER?

DAVID SAID IN **PSALMS: #27**[TH]; *"to behold the beauty of the Lord and to enquire in his temple."* IT IS A GOOD THING TO DESIRE TO KNOW OF THE THINGS OF THE LORD AND OF COURSE IT IS EVEN A BETTER POSITION FOR YOU TO DESIRE TO ASK GOD FOR YOURSELF!

THERE IS ABSOLUTELY NO REASON TO STAY ON THE OUTSIDE OF THE KNOWLEDGE OF THE WORD OF GOD. YOU CAN HAVE A FULL AND COMPLETE UNDERSTANDING AND AN ILLUMINATED REVELATION OF THE WORD OF GOD DIRECTLY FROM THE LORD.

PRAISE AND WORSHIP IN OUR NATURAL LANGUAGE WILL IN FACT BRING GOD TO US FOR A PERIOD; BUT NOW, BE FILLED WITH THE HOLY GHOST AND BEGIN TO WORSHIP THE LORD IN THE HEAVENLY LANGUAGE, IT WILL TAKE YOU STRAIGHT TO GOD TO BE IN HIS PRESENCE. THE LANGUAGE WE SPEAK IN THE HOLY GHOST IS A ONE-WAY EXPRESS FLIGHT TO THE DESTINATION OF HIS PRESENCE. "HEAVENLY LANGUAGE" WILL TAKE YOU ALL THE WAY UP!

Go ahead, get there!!!

Say It Isn't So!*

> *Blessed are ye, when men shall revile you, and persecute you, and shall say all manner of evil against you falsely, for my sake ,rejoice, and be exceedingly glad; for great is your reward in heaven: for so persecuted they the prophets which were before you.*
> St. Matthew 5:11-12

"Many Untruths, Many False Ideas!"

IT IS VERY SAD AND DISAPPOINTING TO KNOW THAT SO MANY PEOPLE ADHERE TO THE MYTHS ABOUT THE CHURCH AND THE PEOPLE OF GOD. THE ATTITUDE IS THAT OF SAYING; "JUST BECAUSE I'M GOING DOWN IN DESTRUCTION TO SIN, I'M NOT GOING TO HELL BY MYSELF, SOMEBODY ELSE IS GOING DOWN WITH ME!"

MANY WHO REFUSE TO BELIEVE ON THE NAME OF THE LORD, ENGAGE THEMSELVES IN AN ONSLAUGHT OF VERY FRIVOLOUS AND UNFOUNDED ACCUSATIONS AGAINST THE CHURCH, WITH GREAT NEGATIVE INFLUENTIAL INTENTIONS. PEOPLE MANUFACTURE UNTRUTHS ABOUT GOD AND JESUS, WHILE THEY COMPLETELY OVER LOOK THE HOLY GHOST. I WOULD NOT EVEN ATTEMPT TO CHALLENGE THE INNUMERABLE FALLACIES OF THE CHURCH AT LARGE.

MISERABLE PEOPLE WILL TAKE ANYBODY DOWN IN

DISBELIEF AND IN THE DESTRUCTION OF THEIR FAITH, THAT IS ACTUALLY WILLING TO GO DOWN; IF POSSIBLE. YOUR FAITH AND TRUST IN GOD, ARE THE KEYS TO EVERYTHING THAT YOU DESIRE OF HIM.

SATAN'S DESIRE IS NOT FOR THOSE SAME KEYS OF FAITH AND TRUST FOR ANY PURPOSE OF HIS OWN, HE JUST DON'T WANT YOU TO HAVE THEM. OUR FAITH KEYS WON'T HELP SATAN'S SITUATION AT ALL. NOTHING WILL!

We Are Still People!

WE ARE NOT PERFECT BEINGS; HOWEVER, WE ARE TRULY FORGIVEN, AND WASHED IN THE BLOOD OF JESUS CHRIST, WHICH IS GOD'S DIVINELY PERFECTED PLAN.

THE CHANGE WE EXPERIENCE AS BELIEVERS, IS SO POWERFUL THAT UPON ENTERING A ROOM, OUR PRESENCE CAN BE FELT BY ALL PEOPLE. HAVE YOU EVER WALKED INTO A ROOM AND PEOPLE BEGAN TO INQUIRE; "WHO IS THAT?"

IT IS NOT THAT THE PEOPLE ARE NOTICING YOU IN THE NATURAL, BUT RATHER THEIR SPIRITS WERE MADE AWARE OF THE PRESENCE OF ANOTHER INFLUENCE GREATER THAN YOURSELF, THAT WALKED IN WITH YOU. GOD'S PRESENCE STANDS OUT AND EMANATES FROM YOUR PERSON, EVERYWHERE YOU GO.

NONE BELIEVERS ARE OFTEN QUITE UNCOMFORTABLE AND UNABLE TO FIND THEIR ZONE IN YOUR PRESENCE. THE SPIRITS OF MEN AND WOMEN, ALIKE, ARE JUDGED AND SWIFTLY CONDEMNED IN THEIR UNGODLY STATE, UPON YOUR ENTRANCE INTO A ROOM. THEY DON'T WANT TO CHANGE! WE ARE WALKING IN THE BEAUTIFULLY INCORRUPTIBLE LIGHT OF THE LORD.

THERE IS NOTHING AT ALL LOW DOWN, EVER, AT ANY TIME ABOUT CHRIST. NEITHER IS HE UNDERMINING IN HIS WAYS. EVERYTHING ABOUT HIM IS THE NAKED TRUTH.

HAVEN COME UNDER SUCH A HEAVY CONVICTION, THEY MAKE AN ATTEMPT TO REVERSE THE SPOTLIGHT AND TO SHIFT THE ATTENTION FROM THEMSELVES, TO YOU.

> *Who changed the truth of God into a lie, and*
> *worshipped and served the creature more than,*
> *the creator, who is blessed forever. Amen.*
>
> ROMANS 1:25

IT IS MUCH EASIER TO MIX WITH MAN, WHENEVER THERE IS NO CHANGE DESIRED.

I'M APPEALING TO THE FACT THAT JUST BECAUSE AN UNTRUTH IS TOLD, IT DOES NOT MEAN THAT YOU HAVE TO BECOME WHATEVER HAS BEEN SAID ABOUT YOU!

> *And they shall turn away their ears from the*
> *truth, and shall be turned unto fables.*
>
> II TIMOTHY 4:4

PEOPLE JUST DON'T HAVE A DESIRE TO KNOW THE REAL POSITIVE TRUTH ABOUT YOU. EVIL PEOPLE LOVE EVIL THINGS. THEY HAVE ACTUALLY DEVELOPED AN APPETITE FOR HEARING LIES AND MANY TIMES, THEY DO NOT EVEN KNOW WHY.

> *If the world hate you, ye know that it hated me*
> *before it hated you. If ye were of the world, the*
> *world would love his own; but because ye are*
> *not of the world, but I have chosen you out of*
> *the world, therefore the world hateth you.*
>
> ST. JOHN 15:19

SECULAR HUMANIZED INDIVIDUALS; WILL COME AFTER THE CHARACTER OF THE PEOPLE OF THE CHURCH FOR NO APPARENT REASON, OTHER THAN THEIR DESIRE TO DO SO. WE KNOW THE WORLD REJECTED JESUS CHRIST OF NAZARETH, THE MESSIAH. THERE IS A RENEWED HATRED FOR CHRIST JESUS, IN THIS FREE COUNTRY OF THE "U.S.A.", OF WHICH WE LIVE.

IN THESE PRESENT PERILOUS TIMES, MANY IDEOLOGICAL MANIFESTATIONS OF WHATEVER IS CALLED GOD; ARE NOW REARED UP AND OBJECTIVELY POSTURED ON THE DE-

FENSIVE TO OUR LORD JESUS CHRIST. YOU MIGHT JUST BE SHOCKED AND SURPRISED TO REALIZE THAT THE ENEMIES OF THE CAUSE OF CHRIST ARE CLOSER TO YOU THAN YOU THINK.

Satan Doesn't Like You!

WHENEVER YOUR CHARACTER, YOUR BODY, YOUR MARRIAGE, CHILDREN, POSSESSIONS, FINANCES, MINISTRY, OR YOUR INFLUENCES ARE ATTACKED, YOU MAY BE INFLUENCED TO BELIEVE THAT YOU ARE AT FAULT IN SOME WAY OR ANOTHER.

CONTRARY TO WHATEVER YOU MAY HAVE BEEN LED TO BELIEVED, THE ATTACK IS REALLY ABOUT WHO'S YOU ARE AND OF YOUR REPRESENTATION OF HIM RELATIVE TO HIS PURPOSE!

THERE IS THAT SMALL PERCENTAGE OF THE TIME WHERE ONE WILL GIVE IN AND FALL UNDER THE POWER OF SATAN'S ATTACK. EVEN THOUGH HE KNOWS THAT HE CANNOT EVEN STAY TO SET UP RESIDENCE IN YOUR LIFE, HE KEEPS TRYING YOU TO SEE IF YOU ARE GOING TO BE THAT ONE THIS TIME.

SATAN KNOWS THAT A DEFEAT OVER YOU IS NOT NECESSARILY A MATTER OF FACT, BECAUSE IF HE HALF KILLS YOU, HE HAS TRULY LEFT YOU HALF-ALIVE! YOU MAY HAVE BEEN KNOCKED DOWN, BUT YOU WERE NOT KNOCKED OUT!

 GOD EXCLUSIVELY, HAS THE KEY TO LIFE AND DEATH! DON'T EVER WORRY ABOUT THE DEVIL THREATENING TO KILL YOU. HE CAN'T DO IT! WHENEVER HE THREATENS YOU WITH DEATH; "SAY IT ISN'T SO!" CONFESS THE POWER OF LIFE THROUGH CHRIST JESUS AND GET UP ON YOUR FEET AND LIVE! ONLY GOD KNOWS EXCLUSIVELY, WHENEVER THE BREATH OF LIFE WILL LEAVE YOUR BODY.

KNOW THIS! WHEN THE DEVIL JUMPS ON YOU, THE SUPERNATURAL POWER OF GOD, WHICH IS AT WORK CONTINUALLY IN YOU, WILL MAKE HIM JUMP RIGHT BACK OFF OF YOU IF YOU WILL GO AHEAD AND BEGIN TO WORSHIP

GOD IN THE SPIRIT!

EVERY LITTLE BATTLE THAT YOU ENCOUNTER WITH THE DEVIL, YOU MAY NOT WIN, THAT IS NOT WHAT I AM REFERRING TO. I AM SAYING, THAT YOU SHOULD NEVER QUIT RESISTING THE DEVIL. YOU MAY LOSE A BATTLE, BUT BY ALL MEANS, WIN THE WAR!

Be On Guard!

WE ALONE OF OURSELVES, DO NOT POSSESS THE POWER WITHIN OUR OWN FLESH, TO DEFEAT THE DEVIL. ALTHOUGH WE WALK WITH CONFIDENCE, WE ARE NOT THE POWER SOURCE OF OUR OWN KNOWN STRENGTH. WE ARE IN A WAR! THE BATTLE IS ON! IT IS IN THE AIR! DEMON SPIRITS HOVER IN THE AIR, SEEKING A PLACE TO LAND. THEY'RE SEEKING AN OPPORTUNITY TO LOWER THE BOOM, IN THE LIFE OF A BELIEVER SOMEWHERE, IF POSSIBLE.

THE DEVIL WILL EVENTUALLY MOVE SOMEONE, SOME-WHERE, TO OBEY HIM, IT MAY EVEN BE YOUR SPOUSE, OR IT MAY EVEN BE YOU, IF YOU'RE NOT WATCHFUL!

STAY PRAYED UP AND YOU WILL NOT BE ON ALERT, LOOKING FOR THE DEVIL AROUND EVERY CORNER. HE WILL SHOW UP SOMEWHERE, SOMEWAY, WHENEVER YOU LEAST EXPECT IT. JUST KEEP YOUR HAND IN THE CONTROLLER'S HAND, WHICH IS IN THE HAND OF JESUS, WHO ACTUALLY HAS HIS HANDS ON YOU.

> *For though we walk in the flesh, we do not war after the flesh. (For the weapons of our war-fare are not carnal, but mighty through God to the pulling down of strong holds;) Casting down imaginations, and every high thing that exalts itself against the knowledge of God, and bringing into captivity every thought to the obedience of Christ.* II CORINTHIANS 10:3-5

WE LIVE IN A REAL WORLD WHERE WE SOMETIMES ENCOUNTER PEOPLE, WHO GET VIOLENT AND UNREASON-

ABLE WITH US. IF WE ARE NOT WATCHFUL, WE WILL SOME-
TIMES NATURALLY AND PHYSICALLY FIGHT BACK. BUT, THE
WEAPONS OF OUR WARFARE ARE NOT CARNAL; MEANING,
WE DO NOT FIGHT WITH PROFANITY, KNIVES, GUNS, STICKS,
STONES, FISTS, AND FEET.

IT ALSO MEANS THAT IT IS NOT NECCESSARY TO
COUNTER ACT AGAINST THAT SOMEONE ON THE JOB, WHO
HAS SET YOU UP FOR FAILURE. AS A CHILD OF CHRIST, WE
DON'T FIGHT LIKE THE WORLD. HOWEVER, WE DO HAVE
WAR STRATEGIES AGAINST THE ENEMY THAT ARE VERY EF-
FECTIVE. AMEN!

He's Fighting On Your Turf!

THE BATTLEGROUND IS WITHIN YOUR HEAD, RIGHT
BETWEEN YOUR EARS, IN THE INNER-SANCTUM OF YOUR
MIND. NO MATTER WHAT'S BEING DONE, YOU ARE RESPON-
SIBLE AS TO WHETHER YOU COUNTERACT OR REACT. PULL
THE THOUGHT OF ANGER DOWN AND REMAIN IN CONTROL
AND REFUSE TO EVER GIVE THAT MUCH POWER TO ANOTHER
INDIVIDUAL OVER YOURSELF AGAIN.

> *Thy word have I hid in mine heart, that I might
> not sin.*   PSALMS #119:11

✳ THE PEOPLE OF THE CHURCH ARE NOT JUST A
GROUP OF PEOPLE WITH, "THE CAN'T HELP IT'S." DON'T
LET IT BE SAID; THAT, YOU DID IT BEFORE YOU THOUGHT
ABOUT IT, BECAUSE YOU JUST COULDN'T HELP IT!

THE THOUGHT PROCESS OF GOD'S PEOPLE, IS
MORE ACCURATE AND SWIFTER THAN MODERN COM-
PUTERS, WHENEVER IT IS APPLIED TO THE SPIRIT AND
THE WISDOM OF ANY PREVIOUS KNOWLEDGEABLE IN-
PUT OF THE WORD OF GOD.

✳ IT'S BEEN SAID; THAT THE CHURCH IS FILLED
WITH A BUNCH OF SILLY WOMEN WHO CAN'T KEEP THEIR
OWN HUSBANDS AND ON AN AVERAGE, THEY DON'T KEEP

THEIR HOUSES VERY WELL. SOME PEOPLE SAY; THAT CHURCHWOMEN, WHO HAVE HUSBANDS, MANY TIMES HAVE ALL LOST THEIR ATTRACTIVENESS ARE STILL LONELY AND IN NEED OF COMPANIONSHIP.

✳ IT'S BEEN SAID; THAT THE CHURCH IS ONLY A HOUSE OF GOSSIP, A PLACE WHERE YOU CAN GET THE SCOOP. SOME SAY, THE CHURCH, IN MANY PLACES, IS ONLY A FASHION SHOW. I'VE HEARD MANY SINNERS WHO WILL NOT EVEN GO TO CHURCH AT ALL, SAY THAT THE CHURCH IS FULL OF NOTHING BUT HYPOCRITES.

IF IT WERE NOT FOR THE CHURCH, THE HYPO-CRITE WOULD HAVE NO PLACE TO EXIST. THE CHURCH IS THE ONLY REASON THAT A PERSON COULD EVER BE LABELED A HYPOCRITE IN THE FIRST PLACE.

That's, What They Say!!!

✳ PEOPLE SAY THAT ALL THE CHURCH WANTS IS MONEY. YOU THAT ARE READING THIS BOOK; YOU KNOW THAT THE CHURCH CAN NOT OPERATE WITHOUT FINANCES. NOT JUST YOUR PARTICULAR CHURCH, BUT EVERY CHURCH STANDING HAS NEED OF FINANCIAL SUPPORT. THE PEOPLE OF THE CHURCH DON'T SHOW A REASONABLE DISPLAY OF RESPECT FOR ANYONE IN THE MINISTRY THAT DON'T AP-PEAR TO BE FINANCIALLY STABLE.

NEED I REMIND YOU OF THE FACT THAT THIS IS THE DAY OF THE AMERICAN DOLLAR; EVERYBODY EITHER RE-QUIRE IT FOR THE BENEFIT OF SUCCESSFUL BUSINESS PRAC-TICES, OR EVERYBODY IS LIKEWISE SEEKING TO HAVE A HEFTY PROPORTION OF THE AMERICAN FINANCIAL STATUS. WITH-OUT MONEY IN THE WESTERN CIVILIZATION, YOU ARE CON-SIDERED TO BE LESS THAN A RESPECTABLE HUMAN BEING.

THE LATE ROCK & ROLL SINGER; BOBBY WOMACK; WROTE AND PERFORMED A SONG THAT HE RECORDED BACK IN THE SEVENTIES TO THE TITLE OF; "NOBODY WANTS YOU WHEN YOU'RE DOWN AND OUT." THIS IS ALSO TRUE OF

THE CHURCH, WHEREAS, PEOPLE BY THE THOUSANDS WILL FLOCK TO A CHURCH WHERE THE SHEPHERDING LEADER OF THE CONGREGATION APPEAR TO BE PROSPEROUS.

THE AMERICAN MINDSET IS, SHOW ME THE MONEY! PUT UP OR SHUT UP! SO UNTIL YOU CAN BE A MEMBER OF YOUR FAVORITE CLUB AND DRINK ALCOHOL, SMOKE CIGA-RETTES, USE DRUGS, GAMBLE, LIVE IN YOUR HOUSE OR APARTMENT, AND DO EVERYTHING ELSE THAT YOU ENJOY DOING THAT DON'T REQUIRE YOUR MONEY, YOU NEED TO SHUT UP ABOUT THE MONEY IN THE CHURCH AND GET WITH THE PROGRAM.

BY THE WAY, DO YOU KNOW WHERE THE MONEY IS GOING THAT YOU ARE GIVING TO ALL OF OTHER CAUSES THAT ALLOW YOU TO FEEL AS IF YOU ARE A PRODUCTIVE CITIZEN OF THE SOCIETY? HOW VIGOROUS ARE YOU TO DIG OUT THE FACTS ABOUT WHERE THAT MONEY IS GOING? ALL IT IS THAT YOU WANT IS THE PRODUCT THAT YOUR MONEY IS PURCHASING. AS LONG AS YOU HAVE YOUR MERCHANDISE, THEY CAN DO WHATEVER THEY WANT TO DO WITH THE MONEY!

ONCE YOU HAVE GIVEN YOUR MONEY THE CHURCH AND TO THE WORK OF THE KINGDOM OF THE LORD; IT IS NO LONGER YOUR MONEY TO WATCH OVER. THE CHURCH IS NOT AN INVESTMENT CLUB, WHEREAS YOU CAN REACH IN WHENEVER YOU NEED, AND GET THE MONEY THAT YOU HAD GIVEN FREEWILL.

 ✳ THEY SAY THE CHURCH IS ONLY A DATING CLUB. I HAVE HEARD AND SO HAVE YOU; THAT ALL MINISTERS ARE PLAYBOYS! I WONDER HOW WOULD THEY EVEN KNOW, UN-LESS THEY WERE ALL PLAYING WITH THE PLAYBOYS THEM-SELVES?

I believe that you've got to be a player in the game, in order to <u>know</u> the players! Some people are angry that they can't successfully compete with the other known players, who are playing with a particular person they would like to play with!

THOUGH PEOPLE HAVE DONE IT FOR YEARS, THE CHURCH IS THE WRONG PLACE TO GO LOOKING FOR A DATE, OR FOR SOMEBODY TO MARRY. MOST PEOPLE DON'T EVEN COME TO THE CHURCH UNTIL THEY HAVE TOTALLY BLOWN THEIR REPUTED CHARACTER SKETCHES, AND HAVE TRASHED THEIR LIVES TO THE MAXIMUM.

PEOPLE IN THE CHURCH ARE OFTEN SOUGHT OUT LONG BEFORE THEY HAVE SUCCESSFULLY ALLOWED THE LORD TO PUT THE BROKEN PIECES OF THEIR LIVES BACK TOGETHER AGAIN, AFTER ONLY BEING AT THE CHURCH FOR A VERY SHORT WHILE.

MANY OF THEM DON'T EVEN KNOW WHAT THE BIBLE HAS TO SAY ABOUT BEING A DEDICATED SPOUSE TO ANOTHER PERSON BEFORE THEY HAVE BOMBARDED THE PASTOR'S OFFICE TO ASK HIM TO PERFORM A MARRIAGE CEREMONY.

YOU NEED TO SIT YOURSELF DOWN SOMEWHERE AND BE TAUGHT THE WORD OF GOD BEFORE YOU END UP IN A SITUATION SO UNIMAGINABLE, YOU THOUGHT COULD NEVER END UP LIKE THAT IN A LIFE TIME.

✱ SOME SAY THAT THE CHURCH IS ONLY A PLACE FOR THE DOWN TRODDEN AND REJECTED OF LIFE; THOSE INDIVIDUALS THAT HAVE HAD NUMEROUS FAILURES THAT ARE NOW LABELED AS THE SOCIABLY OUTCAST; SUCH AS GAYS, ALCOHOLICS, DRUG ADDICTS, THE POVERTY STRICKEN, THE VERY WEAK AND THE POOR.

HOWEVER, WE DO KNOW THAT PEOPLE WHO MAY HAVE BEEN SLAVES TO SUCH VICES OF THE FLESH CAN BE FOUND AROUND THE CHURCH. 

✱ IT IS NOT WHAT PEOPLE HAVE TO SAY ABOUT YOU THAT IS IMPORTANT, BUT WHAT MATTERS MOST, IS WHAT THE LORD SAYS ABOUT YOU. ✱

YOUR REPUTATION, IS ONLY WHAT OTHER PEOPLE SAY ABOUT YOU. HOWEVER, YOUR TRUE CHARACTER IS WHO YOU REALLY ARE .

Don't Even Think About It!

If you focus on rumors and lies, you will fail to work on your actual character. Stop crying over the lies and stop racking your brain over false rumors. Stop stressing out over ungodly people, who can't see themselves for always looking at you or someone else!

"Say it isn't so", and leave it at that! Stop trying to prove yourself to everyone you know, and be only who you are in the Lord! Be at peace with yourself, for a change of pace.

> *Thou wilt keep him in perfect peace, whose mind is stayed on thee: because he trusteth in him.*
> Isaiah 26:3

Look To Jesus And Keep Your Eyes On Him!

> *Blessed is the man that walketh not in the counsel of the ungodly. Nor standeth in the way of sinners, nor sitteth in the seat of the scornful.*
> Psalms #1:1

The state of being blessed or rather happy, is the very same as knowing who you are and refusing to take down, for any reason or for anybody. <u>You're blessed</u>, being interpreted means that you should be <u>happy</u>. You have every reason to be happy and at peace.

Desiring in your heart, for others to come to know who they are in the Lord, is even more blessed!

Never allow yourself to become uplifted in pride, to the point that you become heady and high minded, once you have discovered that you are blessed! You think that you know it all; you think that you've got it all; You've convinced yourself that you're it! Not! Don't Even Think About It!

> *But his delight is in the law of the Lord; and in*

his law doth he meditate day and night.

PSALMS #1:2

THE LORD HAS GOT EVERYTHING UNDER CONTROL, SO YOU MIGHT AS WELL REJOICE. THE REAL TRUTH IS, WE ENGAGE TO BATTLE WITH THE ENEMY, IN A FIXED FIGHT. THE VERY MOMENT THE FIGHT COMES, FROM THE START, WE ARE DECLARED THE WINNERS. IF YOU LOSE FOCUS, YOU WILL LOSE THE BATTLE, SO STAY WITH THE LORD AND DON'T LOSE YOUR FOCUS ON THE LORD.

For the Lord knoweth the way of the righteous;
But the way of the ungodly shall perish.

PSALMS #1:6

Father Knows Best!!!

THE LORD KNOWS, SO THERE IS NO NEED OF WORRYING ABOUT ANYONE OTHER THAN YOURSELF, REPORTING TO THE LORD ABOUT YOU.

HE KNOWS THAT THE WICKED AND OFTEN THE RELIGIOUSLY MOTIVATED PEOPLE OF THE CHURCH COMMUNITY ARE ANXIOUS TO BEAT THE LIFE OUT OF YOU, BUT ANGELS ARE DISPATCHED TO WATCH OVER YOU AND TO PROTECT YOU. HE PROTECTS THE RELATIONSHIP BETWEEN HIMSELF AND THE BODY OF CHRIST AT LARGE. GOD SMILES ON OBEDIENT PEOPLE; WHILE SIMULTANEOUSLY FROWNING ON THE WICKED.

GOD IS ATTUNED UNTO YOUR BECKONING CALL, HE IS YOUR HELP. THE LORD WILL NEVER GO ON VACATION ON YOU AND FORSAKE YOUR VERY POINT OF NEED, BECAUSE IT DIDN'T APPEAR TO BE IMPORTANT; "{*For the Lord knoweth the way of the righteous*}."

"{*But the way of the ungodly shall perish*}"; THE END OF ALL TROUBLEMAKERS IS SOON DESTRUCTION, IF THEY DO NOT CHANGE THEIR WAYS. THE NOISE AND THE DECEITFULNESS OF THE UNGODLY WON'T GO UNNOTICED.

265

GOD DOES NOT JUST SEE, HE MAKES A DECISION TO JUDGE THE WICKEDNESS IN HIS OWN TIMING.

WICKED UNGODLY PEOPLE DON'T STAND A CHANCE OF GETTING AWAY WITH THE TROUBLE THAT THEY HAVE CAUSED YOU. EVEN IF NO ONE SAW THEM DO THE THINGS THAT THEY DID TO YOU. MY ADVISE TO ALL OF THE DITCH DIGGERS, IS THAT THE DITCHES THEY ARE DIGGING FOR THE CHILDREN OF GOD, ARE MORE THAN LIKELY FOR THEM-SELVES! AND THAT'S NO JOKE!

> *There is a way which seemeth right unto a man,*
> *but the end thereof are the ways of death.*
>
> PROVERBS 14:12

THE WICKED, MAY IN FACT SEEM TO BE RELENT-LESS, WHILE CONTINUING IN THEIR WICKEDNESS, BUT DON'T EVEN FRET OVER IT, GOD IS IN CONTROL AND HE WILL HANDLE THE MATTER, IN DUE TIME.

A PERSON COULD BE DOING WRONG FOR SO LONG, THAT SOMEHOW THEY MIGHT EVEN FORGET THAT WHAT-EVER THEY ARE DOING, IS ACTUALLY WRONG, TO THE POINT THAT THEY BEGIN TO BELIEVE THAT THEY ARE OK' JUST AS THEY ARE!

THERE'S AN ENHANCED DEMONIC DRIVE IN THE BEL-LIES OF EVIL PEOPLE, THAT PUSHES THEM TO ASSURE THE DOWNFALLS AND TO INSURE THE SUCCESS OF THE PITFALLS FOR THE PERSONS OF WHICH THEY HAD BEEN SET. STILL THERE IS NO NEED TO WORRY AS IF YOU HAVE NO HOPE OF OVERCOMING THESE PERILS OF LIFE!

*Inferior Practice Of Choosing**

THERE ARE MANY OTHER CHOSEN SYSTEMS OF BE-LIEF THAT ARE CONTRARY TO THE WORD OF GOD. THE OTHER SYSTEMS ARE MOST DEADLY AND DECEIVING, AS IT RELATES TO THE DESTRUCTIVENESS OF OUR FAITH IN OUR LORD JESUS CHRIST. HOWEVER, THESE BELIEF SYSTEMS AREN'T NEW DISCOVERIES TO THESE LATTER GENERATIONS,

AND THE ALTERNATIVE SYSTEM OF CHOOSING HAS BEEN AROUND ALL OF THE TIME.

PEOPLE MAKE CONSCIOUS CHOICES AND DECISIONS TO EXERCISE AND PRACTICE THESE ALTERNATIVE SUBORDINATE POWER SOURCES, OTHER THAN TO WALK IN THE SUPREME POWER OF THE HOLY GHOST.

THERE IS INADEQUATE REASONING FOR THE USAGE OF SUCH SUBSERVIENT, SUBVERSIVE, AND SUBSTITUTIONAL PRACTICES, IN THE PRESENCE OF SUCH A GREATER GOOD, IN TERMS OF WHATEVER IS ACTUALLY SPIRITUALLY CLEAN. THERE IS A COMMON PREFIX HERE, TO WHICH ALMOST TELLS THE STORY ALL BY ITSELF.

THE PREFIX, <u>SUB</u>; IS INDICATIVE OF SAYING: UNDER, BELOW, DOWN, NEARLY (*almost*), LOWER, OR OF LESS IMPORTANCE.

SUCH PRACTICES ARE FORMED TO SERVE THE PURPOSE OF THE PRACTITIONER WHO HAS FAILED TO REACH THE HIGH STANDARDS OF HOLINESS AND ARE CONVINCED WITHIN THEMSELVES, THAT THEY ARE NOT TO TRY REACHING SUCH UNATTAINABLE STANDARDS OF GODLINESS. THEY SIMPLY REFUSE TO COME UP TO THE CLEAN STANDARDS OF HOLINESS, ON PURPOSE!

GENERALLY, PEOPLE ARE FASCINATED BY THE CONFIDENT EXEMPLIFICATION OF SPIRITUAL AUTHORITY, SUCH AS TO THE LIKENESS OF THAT OF, THE FIVE FOLD MINISTRIES OF THE CHURCH. THE ACTUALITY OF THEIR EXCITEMENT IS FOR THE LIKENESS OF WHAT HAS BEEN CITED AS MINISTERIAL CLEVERNESS.

THIS IS MOST TRUE OF THE FREQUENTING PEERS OF THE ASSEMBLING BODY OF BELIEVERS, WHO COME SEEKING THE SERVICE AND NOT THE SAVIOR! THE HIGHER, ONE APPEARS TO BE RISING, THE MORE INFLUENTIAL THEY SEEM TO BECOME. OFTEN TIMES THIS ATTRACTION IS ONLY POSITIONAL IN RELATION TO TITLES AND IT IS NOT EVEN RELATIVE TO ANY TYPE OF A SPIRITUAL ENDOWMENT, BY WHICH THE LIVES OF THOSE PEERING INDIVIDUALS CAN BE CHANGED!

You Would Think They Really Have It!

THERE ARE INDIVIDUALS OF THE BODY OF CHRIST, WHO PROPOSE TO EXEMPLIFY THAT THEY HAVE BEEN TRULY EMPOWERED TO PRODUCE CHANGE THROUGH THE DIVINE ENDOWMENT OF THE HOLY GHOST. THOSE SELF SAME LEADING PERSONS ARE SOMETIMES REVERED AS A LOWER, FLESHLY, TYPE OF GOD, IN THE PRESENCE OF SOME PEOPLE. IF THE POWER THAT YOU POSSESS IS NOT STRONG ENOUGH TO GET YOU INTO HEAVEN, I WOULD SUGGEST TO YOU THAT YOU THROW THAT POWER DOWN ON THE GROUND AND FORSAKE IT FOREVER!

WHETHER OR NOT THESE PERSONS ARE TRULY BORN OF GOD, THEY OFTEN POSSESS A GIFT THAT IS IN OPERATION.

YOU ARE ACTUALLY GIFTED OF GOD, BEFORE YOU EVER KNOW IT AND EVEN BEFORE YOU HAD EVER BEEN SAVED, SET FREE, AND DELIVERED! YOU KNOW, IT IS TO THE LIKES OF A CAR, THAT HAS GOT A VERY POWERFUL MOTOR AND TRANSMISSION INSTALLED, LONG BEFORE IT HAS EVER BEEN COMPLETED IN THE FACTORY AND DELIVERED TO THE DEALER TO BE SOLD.

SO, IF CERTAIN PEOPLE ARE REAL POWER PACKED, DEVIL DRIVING, DEMON CHASING, HOLY GHOST FILLED WARRIORS IN THE BATTLE OF THE LORD, IT WILL ONLY BE SO, BECAUSE THEY HAVE SURRENDERED THEMSELVES TO THE ONE AND ONLY REAL AND TRUE GOD AND HAVE TOTALLY GIVEN THEIR WILL OVER TO THE LORD.

What's It All About?

WHAT ESTABLISHES THE CONTRASTING DIFFERENCES BETWEEN WHAT IS TRUE AND WHAT IS TO BE KNOWN AS UNREAL, IS THAT THE INTENDED PURPOSE OF THE FALSE IS TO SERVE THE AGENDA WITH MOTIVES TO SPOTLIGHT THE INDIVIDUALS THEMSELVES, AND NEVER TO BRING GLORY TO THE LORD!

MANY PEOPLE ARE DECEIVED, BEING THAT THEIR

268

OWN SOURCE OF INFORMATIVE SUPPLY IS MOST LIKELY INVALID AND SEVERELY UNABLE TO BE UPHELD AS THE TRUTH.

SUCH UNFRUITFUL PRACTICES, UPON THE SCRUTINY OF AN ANALYTICAL EVALUATION, IS ALL ABOUT THE MONEY, BEING THE ACTUAL PURPOSE FOR SUCH INDIVIDUALLY DEGRADING BEHAVIOR, BY WHICH AN INDIVIDUAL WILL HAVE COMPROMISED THEIR OWN INTEGRITY!

TO ALIGN THEIR POCKETS WITH THE MONEY OF ALL OF THE WEAK PEOPLE, WHO ARE IN TOO BIG OF A HURRY TO WAIT ON THE LORD, IS THE MASTER PLAN OF INTENTION. HOWEVER, THEY MAY SURRENDER THEMSELVES TO THE SPIRIT OF GOD, MOMENTARILY, IN A MOMENT OF COMPASSION.

THERE ARE OTHER GROUPS, WHOSE PRACTICES HAVE ABSOLUTELY NOTHING IN ORIGIN AS RELATING TO OUR GOD. DEMONICALLY INFLUENCED, THEY SEEK TO DEFAME THE NAME OF THE LORD, WHILE MANY OF THEM EVEN WORSHIP THE DEVIL (HAVING MANY PRACTICAL FORMS), SEEKING THE POPULARIZATION OF THEIR OWN NAMES.

THESE PERSONS NEVER FEEL INADEQUATE WITHIN THEMSELVES, AS THEY GENERALLY FEEL THEY CAN DO WHATEVER THEY CHOOSE; WHENEVER THEY DESIRE TO AND NO ONE HAS THE RIGHT TO TRY AND STOP THEM!

SUCH EVIL INFLUENCES ARE VERY STRONG AND THEY POSSESS THE POWER TO INCREASE IN STRENGTH, OVER AN EXTENDED PERIOD OF RESIDENCE.

THEY ALSO POSSESS RESULT YIELDING EFFECTS, THAT ARE OBVIOUS IN THE LIVES OF THE PEOPLE THAT CHOOSE TO FOLLOW AFTER SUCH PRACTICES! THE DEVIL'S GIFTS ARE ALSO OPERABLE!

THIS IS THE ENTICING INFLUENCE OF SUCH PERSONS, OVER THE MANY WEAK CHRISTIANS, WHICH WILL NEVER GIVE THEMSELVES OVER TO FAITH-FILLED, SPIRIT-FILLED PRAYER! HOWEVER, BEING EVIL AND TOTALLY UNBELIEVING OF FAITH, THEY DO NOT ACKNOWLEDGE GOD, THEY WANT THEIR'S RIGHT NOW, NO MATTER WHAT IT MIGHT

TAKE OR WHATEVER IT MAY COST SOMEONE ELSE! IMMEDI-
ATE RESULTS, IS WHAT THEY WANT.

They Go Where You Go!

ONE WOULD BELIEVE THAT SUCH PERSONS WEREN'T
MEMBERS OF THE LOCAL CHURCH, BUT THEY ARE MEMBERS
OF CHURCHES EVERYWHERE! SOME OF THESE PERSONS, BE-
LIEVE IT OR NOT, ARE PASTORS AND MEMBERS OF THE
CLERGICAL PLATFORMS, PERHAPS WITHOUT A PASTORAL
CHARGE AND SOME ARE EVEN DEACONS WHO HAVE SLIPPED
THROUGH THE CRACKS, HAVEN ESCAPED THE SCRUTINY OF
PERSONAL EVALUATION AND BIBLICAL EXAMINATION.

MANY ARE CHOIR AND USHER BOARD MEMBERS.
THEY FREQUENT THE PEWS AND LIE ATROCIOUSLY WITH
THEIR ACTIONS, AS IF THEY ARE TRULY, BORN AGAIN BE-
LIEVERS! THEY SHOUT; "AMEN!", OUT LOUD! PAY A TITHE!
GIVE AN OFFERING! THEY EVEN TESTIFY OF THE GOOD-
NESS OF THE LORD! IF WHENEVER AND WHEREVER THEY
ARE ALLOWED TO DO SO, THEY WILL RUN THE AISLES, JUMP
THE PEWS AND EVEN DANCE ON THE CARPET.

THEY HAVE NO FEAR OF THE AVERAGE BELIEVER!
THEY LOOK TO THEMSELVES, MEASURING THEMSELVES BY
THEMSELVES, THEY NEVER REFER TO THE WORD OF GOD
FOR THEIR PROBLEMS BECAUSE THEY BELIEVE THAT WHAT
THEY HAVE SEEN IN THE LIVES OF MANY PROFESSING BE-
LIEVERS IS GREAT LOSS AND DEFEAT.

YOU WILL FIND SUCH PERSONS, FOLLOWING MANY
SIGNS AND WHATEVER THEY WILL CONSIDER TO BE THE
WORKING WONDERS, IN THE MINISTRY OF CERTAIN CHURCH
LEADERS.

FOR THIS CAUSE, THE SO-CALLED SERMONS THAT ARE
SUPPOSED TO BE IN OPPOSITION TO THE UNGODLY, ARE NOT
VERY STRONG PROPONENTS, WHENEVER IT COMES TO BE-
ING A SPIRITUAL THREAT. THROUGH THE WICKED IMAGI-
NATIONS AND EVIL MEDITATIONS OF THE UNGODLY, THEY
ARE ABLE TO HINDER THE PEOPLE OF GOD, BUT NEVER ABLE

TO STOP THE MOVE OF GOD. SO MANY OF THESE WICKED PERSONS WHO CONTINUE TO SHOW UP AT THE HOUSE OF GOD, HAVE ACTUALLY DISCOVERED THAT THEY CANNOT EVEN WIN AGAINST THE POWER OF GOD!

THEY DON'T GO ALONG WITH THE PROGRAM OF THE CHURCH BODY. NEITHER WILL THEY EVER DREAM OF PARTAKING IN THE VISIONS OF THE LEADERSHIP. GENERALLY THEY ARE OUTSPOKEN AT THE WRONG TIME. AS LONG AS THE LEADER DOES NOT PUT THEM IN THEIR PLACE, WHICH IS SOMETIMES OUT OF THE LOCAL CHURCH BODY TO WHICH THEY SEEK TO SUBVERT AS THEY ADAMANTLY REJECT DELIVERANCE AND CONSISTENTLY REMAIN OUT OF ORDER.

ANYBODY EVER SAY TO YOU; "YOU'RE NOT THE PASTOR, AND IF HE DON'T TELL ME, I DON'T HAVE TO LISTEN?" PUT A CHECK IN THAT SPIRIT FROM NOW ON! THESE WICKED PERSONS WILL STAY UP ALL NIGHT LONG CONJURING UP DEMONS, SCHEMING, DIGGING DITCHES, MANUFACTURING LIES, AND MAKING PLANS TO DESTROY THE PEOPLE OF GOD. SAY; "IT ISN'T SO"; SAY; "IT'S NOT YOU", THAT HAD JUST BEEN DESCRIBED.

Say It Isn't You, <u>Or Is It</u>???

PEOPLE DON'T ALWAYS CARE TO RECEIVE THE DIRECT WORD OF WISDOM OR EVEN THE WORD OF KNOWLEDGE, FROM A MINISTER OR FROM THE PROPHET OF GOD. I AM SPEAKING IN REFERENCE TO A DIRECT WORD OF THE DIVINE INFLUENCE BY GOD, HIMSELF!

THE SAME PEOPLE THEMSELVES, SOMEHOW ARE ABLE TO BELIEVE IN A WORD THROUGH THE MEANS OF THE PSYCHIC HOT LINES, PALM READERS OR SPIRITUAL ADVISERS OF ANOTHER SOURCE, OTHER THAN GOD!

PEOPLE READ DAILY HOROSCOPES AND FREQUENT ORIENTAL RESTAURANTS FOR FORTUNE COOKIES, EVEN VISIT PALM READERS AND READERS OF TAROT CARDS, WHERE THEY DO NOT EVEN MIND HANDING OVER THEIR HARD EARNED MONEY AND LEAVING IT BEHIND. NO MATTER OF THE AMOUNT ASKED BY THE PSYCHICS, THEY GIVE IT, WHILE

THE AMOUNT OF MONEY THE CHURCH IS ASKING OF THEM TO CONTRIBUTE, *they are usually outraged!!!!!*

STARGAZERS AND CRYSTAL BALL GAZERS, SEEM TO ALWAYS HOLD ON TO THEIR ATTENTION SPANS, WHILE THE PREACHED WORD OF GOD, SEEMS TO ALWAYS BORE THEM, TO THE POINT THAT THEY BECOME HEAVILY TIRED AND SLEEPY, RIGHT IN THE MIDST OF THE WORSHIP SERVICE.

THE LIST OF SECULAR MAGAZINES AND DAILY NEWSPAPER ARRIVALS TO THE MANY HOMES IN OUR CITIES IS UNREAL. PEOPLE TRUST MUCH MORE IN WHAT MAN HAS TO SAY, THAN GOD, WHO CREATED EVERY MAN, HAS TO SAY THROUGH HIS OWN WORD.

There Is No Comparison To Our God!

THERE IS NO OTHER NAME IN THE COSMOS, GREATER THAN THE NAME OF JESUS CHRIST. NO POWER IS EVER GOING TO BE GREATER THAN THE PRESENT POWER OF THE HOLY GHOST. WHO COULD POSSIBLY BE GREATER THAN OUR GOD, WHO <u>IS</u> ALL, WHO CREATED ALL, WHO KNOWS ALL AND KNOWS EVERYTHING THERE IS TO KNOW ABOUT YOU AND ME AND I REPEAT; "GOD IS!" AND BECAUSE HE IS, WE ARE! YES!!!

IT'S EASIER FOR MOST PEOPLE TO BELIEVE THAT SOMETHING THAT ALREADY EXISTED BECAME SOMETHING ELSE ON ITS OWN, RATHER THAN TO BELIEVE THAT SOMEONE, BEING GOD (ELOHIM) TOOK ABSOLUTELY NOTHING AND MADE EVERYTHING THAT WE DO HAVE TO THIS VERY DAY. THE MIND OF MAN, AS SMART AND INTELLIGENT AS IT IS, IT IS BUT YET FINITE AND LIMITED. BUT, IT DOESN'T GIVE MAN A REASON TO REJECT THE REALITY AND ETERNAL EXISTENCE OF THE INFINITE AND TOTALLY UNRESTRICTED TRUE GOD. LISTEN TO WHAT GOD SAYS OF HIMSELF:

> *And God said unto Moses, I am that I am: and he said, thou shalt say unto the children of Israel, I am hath sent me unto you.* EXODUS 3:14

NOTICE WHAT GOD SAYS TO MOSES HERE. HE COULD HAVE SAID; "TELL THEM THAT I WAS", OR; "TELL

THEM I WILL BE" OR RATHER HE COULD HAVE EVEN GIVEN TO MOSES, ALL OF HIS "*man* GIVEN TITLES." BUT, RATHER HE STATED THE CHARACTER OF HIS EXISTENCE. HE SAID; "I AM." TODAY AND AS LONG AS ETERNITY ROLLS ON, "HE IS FOREVER, I AM", AND HE WILL ALWAYS CONTINUE ON, AND YET REMAIN TO BE KNOWN AS, "I AM."

> *I am Alpha and Omega, the beginning and the*
> *ending, saith the Lord, which is, and which was,*
> *and which is to come, the almighty.*
>
> REVELATION 1:8

THERE IS NO BEGINNING OR AN ENDING TO GOD'S EXISTENCE THAT ANY PERSON ON THE FACE OF THE EARTH HAS EVER BEEN ABLE TO DOCUMENT AND THERE NEVER WILL BE A DAY THAT ANYONE WILL BE ABLE TO LIST ANY SUCH FACT OF KNOWLEDGE.

IT IS AWFULLY AMAZING THAT MANY WHO HAVE AR-GUED THE ACTUAL REALITY OF GOD'S EXISTENCE, DID NOT EVEN HAVE THE POWER OVER THEIR OWN LIVES, TO THE POINT THEY WOULD LIVE AND NEVER EVER HAVE TO DIE AND TO THEIR OWN SURPRISE, **THEY'RE DEAD**!!

THEY SAY THERE IS NO GOD, BUT THEY, WHOMEVER THEY MIGHT BE, CANNOT RECREATE A MAN, OR A BABY WITH-OUT THE AID OF WHATEVER GOD HAS CREATED ALREADY! THEY CAN NOT EVEN START FROM THE GROUND TO PRO-DUCE HUMAN FLESH OR EVEN RECREATE THE DUST OF THE GROUND FOR THAT MATTER! YET THEY WOULD RATHER RE-PLACE GOD AN PLAY THE ROLE THEMSELVES. THEY HAVE LOST THEIR SOBER MINDS!

THOROUGHLY, I'M NOT IMPRESSED WITH SCIENTIFIC CLONING. IT MEANS NOTHING TO ME AND IT SHOULD MEAN NOTHING TO KNOWN BORN AGAIN BLOOD WASHED BELIEV-ERS. A CLONE WILL BE IN NEED OF A SOUL! WHERE WILL IT COME FROM? GOD DOES NOT SEND A LIFE INTO THE WORLD WITHOUT A SOUL! IS ANYONE LAME ENOUGH TO BELIEVE THAT SCIENTIST ARE ABLE TO DUPLICATE A SOUL?

If God didn't give that power to any of the Prophets or the Apostles, or to any other spiritual leaders, whom He knows that He trust to carry the good news of the gospel of Jesus Christ; why would He trust medical-science? *II Timothy 6: 20*

Perhaps God would have given the power to reproduce souls in mankind, to the Prophet Ezekiel in the valley of Dry Bones; recorded in Ezekiel 27:

I believe that God might have shared the mystery of the soul with the prophet, but He never allowed him to handle the souls of man. Satan is the one always seeking to tamper with the souls of man.

There can't be two souls given to one individual who has the very same body; and live to still be the same person that they were before the first soul left the body, else no one would be dead in their graves! All they would need is a new soul and they could be alive again!

As God instructed the prophet to prophecy to the four winds to breath on the slain soldiers, God was simply calling the scattered out souls; the exact souls of every individual soldier that had departed the bodies of these slain, and had already been docked in their space of eternity, to come back, each to its perspective body; and live again.

No Man Can Do It!

Man cannot give a preconceived, unborn, unbirthed individual soul to anyone and neither can he give life, for that matter, to anyone on the face of the earth, simply because we do not have the power within our natural beings to do so!

A soul transplant has never been heard of nor an operation on the soul of any man, ever, by the medical professionals. We have never heard of a

SOUL EXAMINATION IN THE LABORATORIES, BY A MEANS OF ANY SCIENTIFIC EVALUATION THROUGH THE AID OF TELESCOPIC ANALYSIS!

IF YOU, ALIKE MYSELF, BELIEVE THAT WE HAVE A REAL PROBLEM WITH CRACK BABIES, WHOSE MOTHERS SMOKED CRACK COCAINE DURING ANY OR ALL OF A PARTICULAR PART OF THEIR PREGNANCY, THEN JUST WAIT UNTIL THE CLONES HIT THE FACE OF THE EARTH, THAT IS, IF THEY ARE EVER SUCCESSFUL AT ACTUALLY BEING CLONED! IF THEY ARE EVER REALLY ALLOWED TO DO SO, THEY WILL FOR SURE BE, "ZOMBIES!!"

THEY WILL BE WALKING AROUND DEAD ON THE INSIDE, WITHOUT EVEN THE LEAST OF THE NATURAL EMOTIONS, WITHOUT A SOUL HAVEN BEEN PLACED WITHIN THEM BY THE LORD! IT IS A VERY DANGEROUS AND A VERY DEADLY THING, TO PLAY GOD! THE SOUL IS THE SEAT OF EMOTIONS! ASK GOD!!

THERE ARE ATHEISTS WHO TOTALLY REJECT ANY POSSIBLE EXISTENCE OF GOD AND THEN THERE ARE THE PANTHEISTS, WHO BELIEVE THAT ANYTHING AND THAT SOMETIMES EVERYTHING, COULD BE CALLED A GOD. THEY BELIEVE IN A SYSTEM OF RELIGIOUS BELIEFS CALLED POLYTHEISM, WHICH MEANS THAT THERE IS AN ACCEPTANCE OF THE EXISTENCE OF MANY GODS.

THESE PEOPLE REFUSE TO ACKNOWLEDGE THE DEITY OF THE ONE AND THE ONLY TRUE AND LIVING, GOD. TO RECOGNIZE HIM AS GOD, IS TO KNOW HIM FOR WHO HE REALLY IS. WHICH IN TURN REQUIRES WORSHIP AND REVERENCE OF "JESUS CHRIST." 

WHETHER WE WANT TO GIVE GOD THE GLORY THAT IS DUE HIM OR NOT, THE GLORY BELONGS TO GOD. NO NEED IN TAKING THE CREDIT FOR THAT, OF WHICH, ALL HUMAN BEINGS ARE TOTALLY AND ABSOLUTELY INCAPABLE OF DOING.

MAN; WHO CANNOT EVEN TAME THE DEVASTATING WINDS OF A TORNADO AND NEITHER CAN HE UNDERSTAND

THE HORRIFIC DESTRUCTION OF RUSHING FLOODING WATER, NEED MOST DESPERATELY TO LOOK UP TO GOD! MANKIND MUST UNDERSTAND THAT HE IS ABSOLUTELY NO MATCH FOR GOD AND THAT HE COULD NEVER AND HE WILL NEVER, EVEN BECOME EQUAL TO HIS CREATOR. BY THE WAY, JUST WHO CREATED YOU?

<u>GOD IS MY CREATOR</u>!!!

WEATHER DISASTERS, WILL CHANGE THE APPEARANCE OF AN ELEGANT MANSION, TO THAT OF AN IRREGULAR SHAPED BOX OR A PILE OF RUBBLE.

MAKE AN ATTEMPT TO CONTROL THE WEATHER THAT CREATES FOR SOME WHO WERE ONCE FINANCIALLY INDEPENDENT AND SECURE, LEGITIMATE CAUSES FOR BANKRUPTCY, DUE TO GREAT LOSSES. BEFORE AN ATTEMPT IS MADE TO BE GOD YOURSELF OR EVEN CHRIST, WHO DEFIED THE LAWS OF PSYCHICS, AND WALKED ON THE WATER. YOU HAD BETTER TEST YOUR LIMITATIONS, GOD HAS NO LIMITATIONS.

JESUS SPOKE TO THE WIND AND THE SEA IN THE MIDST OF A TERRIBLE STORM. HE SIMPLY, SAID; "PEACE BE STILL" AND THE WIND AND SEA OBEYED HIM. HE DID NOT JUST SPEAK TO THE WAVES ON THE SEA, ELSE HE WOULD HAVE ONLY BEEN SPEAKING TO THE REACTION OF THE SEA TO THE WINDSTORM OUT OVER THE SEA.

BUT JESUS ACTUALLY SPOKE TO THE SEA AND COMMANDED THE SEA TO TAKE HOLD OF ITSELF AND SETTLE DOWN. JESUS REMINDED THE SEA OF THE INITIAL CREATIVE COMMAND IN THE BOOK OF GENESIS. THE WATERS WERE OUT OF CONTROL IN THE BEGINNING UNTIL GOD SPOKE TO THE WATERS AND COMMANDED THEM TO SIT DOWN AND TO BEHAVE.

COMMANDING THE SEA WAS NOT BRAND NEW FOR JESUS CHRIST! NOW! YOU TRY THIS, OF YOUR OWN WILL AND POWER. ***Document the results!***

"SAY IT ISN'T SO", THAT THESE THINGS DON'T DE-

SCRIBE YOU; THAT YOU DO NOT PRACTICE THE DETESTABLE.

You Have To Give It Up!

THE ONLY REAL WAY TO SAY THAT IT ISN'T SO IS TO BE SURE THAT YOU HAVE GIVEN UP ALL THAT WOULD SEPARATE YOU FROM GOD. EVERYTHING!

DON'T SPEND TIME GUESSING OR THINKING TO YOURSELF; "WELL NOBODY KNOWS WHAT I'M DOING AND I'M NOT TRYING TO TELL THEM EITHER." THE FOCUS IS ON YOU! YOUR SOUL IS AT STAKE HERE.

ACCEPT THE TRUTH OF THE WORD OF GOD TOTALLY AND COMPLETELY IN YOUR HEART, THAT YOU MAY KNOW THAT IT ISN'T SO! DARE TO BE DIFFERENT FROM THE TREND OF THE PEOPLE WHO COULD NOT SAY THAT IT ISN'T SO. SEARCH THE SCRIPTURES FOR YOURSELF AND DON'T DEPEND ON SOMEONE ELSE THAT DOESN'T EVEN BELIEVE IN THE BIBLE TO ERRATICATE TO YOU WHAT GOD IS SAYING.

THROUGH REPENTANCE AND FAITH IN THE PRECIOUS BLOOD OF JESUS CHRIST AND BELIEVING IN YOUR OWN HEART THAT GOD HAS RAISED JESUS CHRIST FROM THE DEAD, YOU WILL BE SAVED!!!

Give up to him!

Say Amen!!!

> Else when thou shalt bless with the spirit, how shall he that occupieth the room of the unlearned say amen at thy giving of thanks, seeing he understandeth not what thou sayest.
>
> I CORINTHIANS 14:16
>
> Blessed be the Lord God of Israel from everlasting to everlasting: and let all the people say, amen. Praise ye the Lord.   PSALMS #106:48
>
> For all the promises of God in him are yea, and in him amen, unto the glory of God by us.
>
> I CORINTHIANS 1:20

I Agree!

FROM AS FAR BACK AS ABOUT THE AGE OF 3, I CAN REMEMBER THE VERBALLY UNIFIED RESPONSE TO THE PERSON IN CHARGE OF THE FLOOR SAYING; "EVERYBODY SAY AMEN", AS INSTRUCTED, MOST EVERYBODY WOULD SAY; "AMEN!"

I HAVE ALWAYS RESERVED THE REVERENTIAL RESPECT OF SUBMISSION TO THIS SMALL BUT VERY POWERFUL WORD, DEEP DOWN WITHIN MY INNERMOST BEING.

THE WORD AMEN, IS OFTEN ILL-REPRESENTED, USED OUT OF CONTEXT AND SLUNG AROUND AS IF IT IS OF NO DEFINITIVE IMPORTANCE AT ALL. I DON'T ALWAYS FIND

THE HUMOR IN THE HOLLYWOOD FILM USAGE OF THE WORD. NEITHER AM I ENTERTAINED, WHENEVER CULTURAL ARTS PERFORMERS, MISHANDLE THE USAGE OF THE WORD.

STAND UP COMICS SELDOM DODGE THE MISINTERPRETED USAGE OF THE WORD, AMEN. THIS LITTLE WORD IS EXPLOSIVE AND PACKED WITH POWER.

WHETHER IT IS AS AN INTENTIONAL ACT OR UNINTENTIONAL BLUR, THIS KIND OF A MISHAP JUST SIMPLY SHOULD NOT BE!

Great Meaning; Little Word*

THERE IS MORE MEANING IN THE WORD AMEN, THAN THERE IS IN MOST NAMES AND TITLES THAT ARE FOUND IN A DICTIONARY OR AN ENCYCLOPEDIA. THE WORD AMEN, CARRIES A MORE POWERFUL PUNCH THAN OUR NAMES AND THE NAMES OF OUR CHURCHES.

BECAUSE, TO SAY AMEN, GIVES THE INDICATION THAT AN INDIVIDUAL IS IN TOTAL AGREEMENT WITH THE DEFINITIVE MEANINGFUL PURPOSE OF THE NAME OF A PERSON, A PLACE, OR A THING.

YOUR NAME, MAY HAVE A TRUE MEANINGFUL DEFINITION, BUT IS THERE ANYONE THAT IS IN AGREEMENT WITH THE DEFINITION OF YOUR NAME? IS YOUR CHARACTER EVEN AN AGREEABLE REFLECTION, IN REFERENCE TO THE DEFINITION OF YOUR NAME?

AMEN, ACCORDING TO THE WORLD BOOK, THORNDIKE BARNHART, DICTIONARY AND VINES BIBLE DICTIONARY, IS EQUIVALENT TO SAYING; *"truly* OR *verily."* THIS WORD IS INTENT ON VALIDATING OR GIVING APPROVAL, THE SAME AS TO SAY; "I AGREE! IT IS SO!" ONE IS ACTUALLY TELLING THE SPEAKER OR PERSON IN CHARGE; "I BELIEVE YOU'RE RIGHT!" HOWEVER, VALIDATING OR GIVING APPROVAL, IS A BIT MORE THAN VERBAL ACKNOWLEDGMENTS.

AMEN, ALIKE NITROGLYCERIN, DESTRUCTIVELY MISHANDLING AND MISUSAGE OF SUCH A POWERFUL EX-

PLOSIVE, CAN BE DEADLY, IMMEDIATELY! IT IS ALSO TO THE LIKES OF TNT WITH A SHORT FUSE THAT HAS JUST BEEN LIT! LOOK OUT!!!

TO SAY; "AMEN", STARTS A SPIRITUAL RUMBLING AND SHAKING. IN RETROSPECT, IT MAY ALSO BE THE BEGINNING OF A SPIRITUAL AFFIXATION, IN THE SPIRIT OF THE INDIVIDUAL SPEAKING OR THE LISTENING RESPONDENT.

Thought You Knew!

EVER SAY; "AMEN", AND DIDN'T QUITE KNOW WHAT IT WAS YOU WERE ACTUALLY AGREEING WITH?

THE REAL ISSUE IS THAT YOU WERE NEVER INVOLVED OR CONSUMED, OF THE SUBJECT MATTER TAKING PLACE AT CENTER STAGE. WHILE IT IS IMPORTANT TO BE TAUGHT AND SPIRITUALLY FED, ONE MUST ACTUALLY PAY ATTENTION AND YIELD THEIR PRESENT THOUGHT PROCESS, TO THE RIGHT-OF-WAY OF THE NEW INFORMATION EXITING THE INFORMATION HIGHWAYS, DIRECTED STRAIGHT FOR THEIR EARS.

COMMUNICATION WITH THE TEACHER SHOULD SIGNIFY THAT YOU DO UNDERSTAND, OR AT LEAST THAT YOU RECEIVE THAT WHICH YOU HAVE JUST BEEN TAUGHT.

IT'S NOT A SIN TO BE UNLEARNED OR PRESENTLY IGNORANT OF A FACT; HOWEVER, UNLESS YOU DO LEARN AND BE ENLIGHTENED, YOU WILL REMAIN IN THE SINFUL STATE THAT YOU ARE IN. IGNORANCE, LEADS THE WAY TO A DEEPER AND AN EVEN MORE EXASPERATING, SINFUL STATE OF EXISTENCE.

THERE IS NOTHING WORSE, THAN TO WITNESS UNLEARNED PEOPLE, ATTEMPTING TO TEACH OTHERS, THAT WHICH THEY HAVE NOT YET LEARNED, FOR THE LACK OF TEACHING THEMSELVES!

THE LATE SUPT. L. C. CASTLEBERRY WOULD TEACH US, THAT YOU CAN'T LIVE ABOVE THAT IN WHICH YOU "DO KNOW ALREADY."

How can you agree, if you do not have a prior proven knowledge and an understanding of that which you are making an attempt to agree with? It would be better to just keep silent and to say nothing at all.

If the situations call for you to say something, just say; "I don't know!" You have to acknowledge the fact that you do not know in order to recognize that you need to be taught. Upon hearing, if you discover that you agree, <u>Say So</u>!

Whenever an individual does not verbally respond to the truth, it is easier for the enemy to snatch that truth right away from that individual's thought process.

Figuratively speaking, a strong grasp is placed on the truth whenever you say; "Amen", out of your mouth. A claim is established, as if to say; "This is mine now and you can't have it!" It is also imperative that you know what side of the issues you are standing on, for yourself.

How can one praise the Lord, in whom they do not even agree with or even know? To know and to accept the Lord, is to know and accept His word.

The Holy Bible Is Right!

There is a lot of controversy among the entire religious communities at large, as pertaining to what establishes the exclusive profoundness of the King James Version of the bible, that really allows us to settle our faith upon it's historical actuality and upon the solidarity of its most concrete truths?

It's true, man did write the bible, but, would you have preferred perhaps for an Angelic being

TO HAVE WRITTEN THE BIBLE INSTEAD?

GOD INSPIRED THE VERY MEN, WHO WERE RE-SPONSIBLE FOR THE WRITINGS OF THE 66 BOOKS OF THE BIBLE; TO WRITE ALL THAT IS WRITTEN WITH LOVE, WITH SERIOUSLY COMPASSIONATE FAITH AND WITH THE REVE-LATORY INSIGHT, FROM THE HOLY GHOST! I DON'T HAVE THE ENERGY OR THE TIME TO PROGRESSIVELY ARGUE THIS POINT.

MAN HAS ALSO WRITTEN THE MULTIPLES OF DI-VERSIFIED DICTIONARIES, TO WHICH WE DEFINE WORDS BY THE MULTIPLES OF THOUSANDS, BUT THERE IS NO ALL OUT WAR OVER THE DICTIONARY?

MEN HAVE WRITTEN EVERY OTHER BOOK THERE IS ON THE SHELVES OF EVERY LIBRARY. YOU AND I HAVE NEVER BEEN UP IN OUTER SPACE, BUT WE BELIEVE THAT IT'S UP THERE, SIMPLY BECAUSE WE HAVE READ ABOUT EXTENSIVE SPACE TRAVEL, AND HAVE BELIEVED THE WRITTEN REPORT OF THOSE PERSONS THAT THEY HAVE BEEN UP THERE.

MANY OF US HAVE NEVER EVEN BEEN ABROAD TO FOREIGN COUNTRIES, BUT WE BELIEVE THAT THEY DO EXIST, SIMPLY BECAUSE FOREIGN COUNTRIES HAVE BEEN DRAWN ON A WORLD MAP OR GLOBE OR BECAUSE FOR-EIGN LANDS HAVE BEEN CAPTURED BY THE VISUAL AIDS OF VIDEO TECHNOLOGY.

FAITH IN THE NATURAL THINGS IS EASILY ESTAB-LISHED, BECAUSE OF THE VISUAL AID TO ASSIST IN THE ESTABLISHMENT OF THE CREDIBILITY TO WHAT HAS BEEN SEEN.

YOU'RE RIGHT, IF YOU SAY THAT THE GOD KIND OF FAITH, REQUIRES MUCH MORE THAN YOUR EYESIGHT WILL EVER BE ABLE TO BEHOLD AT FIRST GLANCE. IN LIGHT OF BEING ABLE TO BELIEVE GOD, YOU WILL AC-TUALLY HAVE TO BELIEVE, BEFORE ACTUALLY SEEING, AL-MOST AS IF YOU WERE SLIGHTLY VISUALLY IMPAIRED.

DO YOU REMEMBER HOW THOMAS, ONE OF THE

 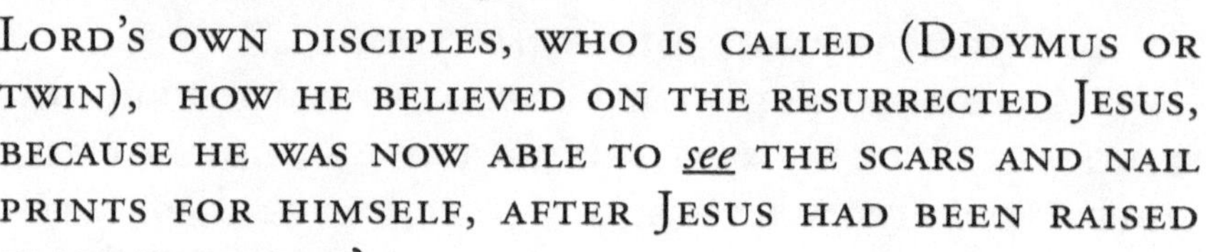

LORD'S OWN DISCIPLES, WHO IS CALLED (DIDYMUS OR TWIN), HOW HE BELIEVED ON THE RESURRECTED JESUS, BECAUSE HE WAS NOW ABLE TO <u>see</u> THE SCARS AND NAIL PRINTS FOR HIMSELF, AFTER JESUS HAD BEEN RAISED FROM THE DEAD?

> *thou hast believed: blessed are they that have not seen, Jesus saith unto him Thomas, because thou hast seen me, and yet have believed.*
>
> ST. JOHN 20:29
>
> *Whom having not seen, ye love; in whom, though now ye see him not, yet believing, ye rejoice with joy unspeakable and full of glory.*
>
> I PETER 1:8

THE REAL SITUATION BEFORE US, IS QUITE VAST IN REPRESENTATION OF THE PEOPLE WHO RESERVE THE VERY SAME IDEALISM TODAY, AS THOMAS. PEOPLE OFTEN SPEAK OF REAL TRUE HAPPINESS, WHO WILL NOT EVEN RECEIVE WHAT THE WORD OF GOD HAS GOT TO SAY, IN RELATION TO THE ONLY BEGOTTEN SON, CHRIST JESUS.

THERE IS GREAT JOY BELIEVING IN JESUS CHRIST, OF WHOM WE HAVE NOT SEEN PHYSICALLY, YET OUR GREATEST EXPECTATION IS TO SEE HIM ONE DAY SOON! I AM TALKING ABOUT, REAL TRUE MAGNIFIED, MULTIPLIED, AMPLIFIED JOY, FULL OF GLORY!

God Glorified It!

AMEN, IS A GOD THING AND ANY GOD THING, IS DEFINITELY A GOOD THING! GOD IS EXALTED AND HIGHLY LIFTED UP, HIGH ABOVE ALL THE HEAVENS AND THE EARTH.

THE PRAISES OF THE LORD, EVEN BEFORE THEY ARE RAISED IN SONG, DURING THE WORSHIPFUL EXPERIENCE OF AN ANOINTED SERVICE, ARE HIGHLY EXALTED.

HIGH, ARE ALL THE THINGS OF GOD, INCLUDING THE WORD AMEN, OF WHICH IS IN GREAT OPPOSITION TO THE LOW DOWN, GROUNDED, AND NON-ELEVATING

UTTERANCES OF THE THOUGHT PROCESSES, WHICH WILL RENDER SAYING AMEN, NONEFFECTIVE.

ANYBODY EVER COME TO YOU, FOLLOWING A WORSHIP SERVICE AND INQUIRE, CONCERNING INFORMATION ABOUT MATTERS, OF WHICH DURING THE WORSHIP SERVICE, YOU INSTANTANEOUSLY GAVE A RAPID RESPONSE TO, BY SHOUTING AMEN?

THOSE PERSONS INQUIRING OF YOU, WERE IMPRESSED TO BELIEVE, THAT YOU ACTUALLY KNEW SOMETHING, BELIEVED SOMETHING, OR EVEN AGREED WITH SOMETHING, TO WHICH THEY DID NOT. IT MEANS MUCH TO FELLOW BROTHERS AND SISTERS IN CHRIST, AS WELL AS TO THE PASTORS, TO HEAR SPONTANEOUS UTTERANCES OF SAYING; "AMEN."

Why Did You Say Amen?

And the four and twenty Elders and the four beast fell down and worshipped God that sat on the throne, saying, Amen; Alleluia:
REVELATION 19:4

I PERSONALLY DO NOT SUGGEST THAT ANYONE SAY; "AMEN", SIMPLY BECAUSE THEY HAVE A DESIRE TO KNOW, BUT RATHER I WOULD RATHER PEOPLE SAID AMEN, BECAUSE THEY ALREADY KNOW AND BELIEVE.

SOME PEOPLE HAVE THE ADEQUATE KNOWLEDGE TO RESPONSIVELY SAY; "AMEN", BUT THEY ADAMANTLY REFUSE TO ACKNOWLEDGE THAT THEY HAVE HEARD THE TRUTH, BY SAYING; "AMEN", FOR THE SAKE OF PRIDE WITHIN THEM!

WHENEVER YOU KNOW THAT WHAT YOU ARE HEARING IS THE TRUTH, FOR CERTAIN, YOU ARE OBLIGATED TO ACKNOWLEDGE THE TRUTH BY SAYING; "AMEN!" SOME MAY FEEL, THAT THE INVOLVEMENT OF ACKNOWLEDGING THE TRUTH BY SAYING; "AMEN", IS A CONTRACT, BINDING THEM TO THE RESPONSIBILITY OF THE TRUTH TO WHICH THEY WERE RESPONSIVE. YOU'RE RIGHT!

However to say nothing at all, does not let you off the hook, in terms of your responsibility to the truth! Every time the truth is told, even the Holy Ghost and the host of Heaven gives a thunderous applause of sanctioning, by saying; "Amen!"

Don't ever allow yourself to believe, that God, the creator of truth, won't know when you have heard the truth. He knows whenever the truth has pricked your heart. Your inner man will leap, as men will do whenever they have been pricked with a sharp stickpin or a sewing needle.

Just as John the Baptist as a baby still in the womb of his mother Elizabeth, leaped for joy at the announcement of the Immaculate conception of Jesus Christ, in the chosen womb of Mary!

No one in the flesh, can see the arousal of your spirit man, without the aid of the Holy Ghost, but God sees everything. Believe that! He saw you!!

Don't Enlist; Into The Silent Army!

Satan is on the lookout, for an army of none acknowledging foot soldiers who refuse to say; "Amen", to the truth. Are you a candidate or prospect? Satan knows who you are and he has been following you very closely, for quite some time now.

Whenever you refused to say; "Amen", it was actually Satan prompting you not to speak. If you lie, curse, swear, profane and blaspheme the Holiness of God, it's OK with Satan, but whatever you do, don't say; "Amen", to the truth of God's word, and don't ever worship God?

Satan is very intrusive to the casual con-

VERSATIONS OF THE PEOPLE OF THE LORD AND HE IS EVEN LISTENING ATTENTIVELY TO THEIR PRAYERS, UNTIL HE REALIZES THAT THE AWESOME PRESENCE OF THE LORD WILL HAVE MANIFESTED, TO INHABIT THE PRAYERFUL ATMOSPHERE.

HE WILL ALWAYS BE TRYING TO FILL YOUR MOUTH WITH ANYTHING AND EVERYTHING OTHER THAN THE TRUTH OF THE WORD OF GOD DURING A PRAYERFUL DIALOGUE.

CONCERNING THE THINGS OF THE LORD, ALL YOU HAVE TO DO IS RECEIVE IT WITH YOUR WHOLE HEART. BUT, YOU WILL HAVE JUSTIFY AND GIVE A VALID REASON FOR ACCEPTING THAT, TO WHICH YOU HAVE EMBRACED IN YOUR OWN HEART KNOWING THAT YOU SHOULD NOT HAVE RECEIVED SUCH A DEVILISH THING!

YOU WOULD NOT WANT GOD TO HOLD YOU ACCOUNTABLE FOR COMPROMISING THE TRUTH. IT WILL NOT BE TAKEN AS A LIGHT THING AND I CAN ASSURE YOU THAT IT WILL NOT BE THE PROPER STATE FOR YOU!

JUST ASK YOURSELF, IF YOU CARE, THAT GOD REALLY CARES ABOUT WHAT YOU BELIEVE? DO YOU EVEN CARE IF GOD TAKES AN INVENTORY OF YOUR FAITH PORTFOLIO? THERE IS A PURPOSE, FOR YOUR VERY PRESENCE, HERE ON THE FACE OF THIS EARTH. YOU ARE NO ACCIDENT!

*Your Entrance**

IT DOESN'T EVEN MATTER HOW YOU CAME ABOUT, YOU WERE NO EXPERIMENT OF SCIENCE OR SOME KIND OF FREAK BIZARRE THING THAT JUST HAPPENED! YOU ARE OF GOD'S OWN DIRECT INTENTION AND PURPOSE HERE IN THE EARTH.

HE KNEW THAT YOU WERE COMING, BEFORE YOU EVER ENTERED YOUR MOTHER'S WOMB, ALTHOUGH YOU MAY NOT HAVE ACTUALLY KNOWN OF WHOM YOUR REAL MOTHER IS OR WAS?

WHENEVER YOU CAME THROUGH THE BIRTH CANAL, IT WAS BECAUSE THE LORD ORDERED YOUR ARRIVAL. ARE YOU EVEN GLAD THAT YOU ARE HERE? YOU COULD BE DEAD AND IN YOUR GRAVE.

SOME PEOPLE, ACT AS IF DEATH DOESN'T REALLY MATTER, UNTIL THEY ACTUALLY BEGIN TO DIE! SO CUT THE ACT AND BE GLAD THAT GOD BROUGHT YOU HERE! BE PROUD TO BE ALIVE AND TO BE NAMED AMONG THE CHILDREN OF THE LORD. THERE IS NO QUESTION AS TO WHETHER OR NOT, THE LORD IS ON OUR SIDE. THE REAL QUESTION IS, WHOSE SIDE ARE YOU ON?

You Should Know!

THERE MAY BE A SHORT SPAN, TO WHICH ONE MAY ACTUALLY BE UNSURE WITHIN THEMSELVES. HOWEVER, UNCERTAINTY AS A WAY OF LIFE, IS TOTALLY UNACCEPTABLE, BECAUSE GOD HATES CONFUSION! WHETHER YOU KNOW OR NOT, THE MORE RAPID A RESPONSE YOU MAKE IN CHOOSING, THE MORE INSISTENT YOU BECOME WITHIN YOUR OWN HEART, ON NOT BEING CONFUSED.

THERE IS FAR TOO MUCH DANGER AT HAND, UPON AN ATTEMPT TO STAY IN THE MIDDLE OF TWO OR MORE ISSUES AT HAND PRESENTLY BEFORE YOU. SOME SAY, WHY CHOOSE, WHY CAN'T I JUST REMAIN OPEN TO EITHER SIDE? I LIKE THE THOUGHT OF BOTH SIDES!

YOU CAN BE ENTICED TO MAKE DECISIONS, HAVING BOTH SIDES OF THE ISSUE EQUALLY IN MIND. SOME PARTICULAR ELEMENTS ON BOTH SIDES OF THE ISSUE, MAY SPARK YOUR INTEREST, BUT DID YOU NOTICE THAT YOU HAD TO EXAMINE ONE SIDE AT A TIME? YOU CANNOT EVEN EXAMINE BOTH SIDES OF A SINGLE ISSUE; SIMULTANEOUSLY, LIKE LOOKING AT BOTH SIDES OF A COIN AT THE SAME TIME.

IT'S LIKE TRYING TO GO BACKWARDS AND FORWARD AT THE SAME TIME. YOU EVER TRY LOVING SOMEONE AND HATING THEM AT THE SAME TIME, SOUNDS RATHER

TWISTED DOESN'T IT? THAT IS EXACTLY WHAT MAKING AN ATTEMPT TO CHOOSE BOTH SIDES OF THE ISSUE WILL DO FOR ANY INDIVIDUAL PERSON. IT WILL CAUSE THEM TO BECOME TWISTED TO THE MAXIMUM.

NOW THERE ARE SOME PEOPLE WHO BELIEVE THEY ARE AT THE VERY CORE OF THE CENTER AND RIGHT IN THE MIDDLE, CONCERNING MULTIPLES OF ISSUES. THEY RESERVE THE OPINION THAT EVERYBODY IS RIGHT IN THEIR OWN WAY. THEY BELIEVE, THAT NOBODY IN THIS WORLD IS ACTUALLY WRONG CONCERNING THEIR OWN IDEALISTIC WAYS OF THINKING.

THEY ALSO BELIEVE AND DO VERBALIZE THE FACT THAT THEY ARE OF THE BELIEF, IN A SYSTEM THAT PROMOTES WHATEVER IS RIGHT FOR THEM, GO WITH YOUR FEELINGS AND TRY EVERYTHING YOU CHOOSE.

THE PROBLEM COMES IN, WHENEVER YOU DISCOVER, THAT MORE THAN TWO OR THREE ISSUES ON EACH SIDE OF THE FENCE, MAY APPEAL TO YOUR DIRECT INTEREST. YOU ARE IN TROUBLE WHEN YOU HAVE DISCOVERED THAT YOU WANT IT ALL! REAL TROUBLE!

MOST INDIVIDUALS ARE BORN WITH TWO EYES, BUT EVEN WITH TWO EYES, ONLY ONE THING CAN BE FOCUSED UPON AT A TIME. THIS IS SO, BECAUSE THE "EYE", AS STATED IN THE WORD OF GOD, MUST BE SINGLE. THE EYE IS ON THE INSIDE OF YOUR SPIRIT, WHERE THE REAL YOU CAN BE FOUND. THE EYE BEING SINGLE, ONLY HAS ONE FOCUS AT A TIME AND THIS IS THE EYE THAT CONTROLS THE TWO EYEBALLS IN THE HEADS OF ALL HUMAN BEINGS. THERE ARE TWO EYES BUT ONLY ONE FOCUS!

THIS IS THE REASON WE HAVE THE SWIVELING AFFECT, FROM THE BASE OF THE SKULL DOWN TO THE TOP CENTER OF THE SHOULDER BLADES. MY FRIEND WE HAVE WHAT IS CALLED A NECK. IN ORDER TO FOCUS ON SOMETHING OTHER THAN WHAT WE HAVE FOCUSED ON ALREADY WE WILL HAVE TO TURN OUR HEADS IN THE DI-

RECTION OF THE NEXT THING TO DIRECT OUR FOCUS.

TELEVISIONS THAT ARE NOW CAPABLE OF RECEIVING SIGNALS FROM THE MANY BROADCASTING NETWORKS ALL OVER THE WORLD, CAN ONLY TUNE IN TO ONE STATION AT A TIME. YOU CAN ONLY TURN TO ONE STATION AT A TIME. THE REMOTE CONTROL WILL NOT EVEN CALL UP MORE THAN ONE STATION. THERE IS NO SUCH THING AS A SIMULTANEOUS CONTROL ON THE TELEVISION.

IF ALL YOU HAVE IN YOUR HOUSE ARE TELEVISIONS BY THE HUNDREDS, YOU COULD ONLY FOCUS AND UNDERSTAND ONE TELEVISION AT A TIME, EVEN IF YOUR TELEVISION HAS GOT THE PICTURE IN PICTURE FEATURE ON THE SCREEN, YOU ARE STILL AT A DISADVANTAGE TO COMPLETELY FOCUS YOUR UNDERSTANDING ON BOTH OR ON ALL PICTURES SIMULTANEOUSLY.

Stand On Your Beliefs!

PEOPLE SAY THAT THEY LOVE THE LORD, BUT SOMEHOW, THEY SEEM TO FIND A SYMPATHETIC INTEREST ALSO IN THE DOCTRINAL BELIEF SYSTEMS OF THE DEVIL AND ALL OF HIS WAYS. SUCH AS HOLLOWEEN AND CASTING EVIL SPELLS OF WITCHCRAFT AND VOODOO.

SUPPOSEDLY SOME DEDICATED TO CHRISTIANITY AND TO THE UP BUILDING OF THE KINGDOM OF GOD, WERE DRIVEN AND ENTICED TO BECOME PERSONALLY ACQUAINTED WITH THE DEVIL. THEY HAVE BEEN TOTALLY DECEIVED INTO BELIEVING THAT THEY ARE YET AS DEDICATED TO THE LORD AS THEY ONCE WERE, BEFORE THEIR EXPLORATIVE EXPEDITION WITH THE DEVIL!

I AM CONCERNED THAT IF WE DON'T SAY SO AND AGREE WITH OUR CHOICE QUICKLY, WE MAY BECOME SUBJECT TO A CHANGE OF HEART, THE DEVIL'S WAY! THERE IS NO TIME TO RELAXED, CONCERNING YOUR CONVICTIONS, TAKING THE DEVIL FOR GRANTED. DON'T BE SO EASILY FOOLED! IT'S THE DEVIL THAT HAS GOT YOU

IN SUCH A LAID BACK MODE, TO THE POINT THAT YOU NEVER FIND IT NECESSARY TO MODIFY YOUR TRUE CONVICTIONS.

TELL SATAN TO LOOSE YOUR MOUTH, IN THE NAME OF JESUS. NOW GO AHEAD RIGHT NOW AND SAY IT WITH CONVICTION, UNDERSTANDING AND THE RIGHT ATTITUDE, SAY; "AMEN!"

ISN'T IT WONDERFUL TO KNOW THAT GOD SAYS TO US, ON OUR BEHALF, WHAT HE DESIRES TO HEAR FROM US IN RESPONSE TO HIS WORD? GOD THE FATHER HAS STILL SAID; "AMEN! LET IT BE SO! I AGREE!" HE SAID; "IT! IS! GOOD!" GOD IS ALWAYS IN AGREEMENT WITH HIMSELF, ARE YOU? GOD IS A GOD OF AGREEMENT.

Agree With God!

THE VERY BEST STATUS OF ANY PERSON, IS TO BE IN AGREEMENT WITH GOD. GOD WAS IN AGREEMENT WITH MANKIND, WHENEVER HE CREATED THEM IN THE BEGINNING OF TIME. GOD'S PURPOSE, SHOULD ALWAYS BE OUR ULTIMATE PURPOSE, IN EFFORT THAT HIS WAYS WOULD FILTER DOWN THROUGH OUR WAYS. HIS AGENDA, SHOULD BE OUR AGENDA. HIS LOVE, OUR LOVE!

NOBODY WOULD EVER HAVE KNOWN WHAT IT WAS THAT GOD WANTED FROM US, HAD HE NOT GIVEN IT TO US FIRST. DO YOU THINK THAT YOU WOULD BE SHARP ENOUGH TO KNOW WHAT GOD WANTED? *I don't think so!*

GOD IS A SPIRIT SO HE CREATED A SPIRIT-BEING, INSIDE OF EVERY MAN ENABLING HIM TO COMMUNICATE TO HIS GOD.

GOD IS LOVE SO HE CREATED LOVE CAPABILITIES IN MAN.

GOD IS ETERNAL SO HE CREATED MAN IN THE SPIRIT, MAKING HIM AN ETERNAL BEING, TO CONNECT WITH HIM FROM IN THE EARTH FROM THE THRONE IN HEAVEN.

GOD IS FAITHFUL SO HE CREATED A FAITH CAPAC-

ITY IN EVERY INDIVIDUAL, WHICH REQUIRES THEM TO MAINTAIN AN UNDIVIDED SYSTEM OF BELIEF, FOR GOD, IN THE PRESENCE OF OTHERS!

GOD IS NOT UNREASONABLE. UNPOPULAR TO CARNAL BELIEF, GOD IS NOT OUT OF TOUCH WITH MAN. GOD ALWAYS DOES HIS PART AND HE WILL ALWAYS DO HIS PART; WE NEED ONLY TO DO OUR PART. HIS PART IS CLEARLY PROVISION, OUR PART IS ACCEPTANCE AND OBEDIENCE!

ALL OF GOD'S PROMISES; FIRSTLY, ARE CERTAINLY TRUE AND IN HIM THEY ARE YES AND IN HIM, THEY ARE AMEN. WHEN WAS THE LAST TIME YOU SEARCHED THE SCRIPTURES TO KNOW THE PROMISES OF GOD?

GOD'S PROMISES, ARE PROVISIONAL GIFTS. HOWEVER, MANY PEOPLE ARE TAUGHT TO SEE THEM AS REWARDS, AS IF THEY HAVE TO RUN THE GAUNTLET OR PERFORM TO AN IMPOSSIBLE CAPACITY, JUST TO RECEIVE THE PROMISES OF GOD.

MANY THEOLOGIANS ARGUE TO THE POINT OF UTTER DISGUST CONCERNING THE PROMISES OF GOD AND THEY NEVER HAVE COME TO A POINT OF AGREEMENT IN THE WORD OF GOD AMONG THEMSELVES.

AGENDA'S AROUND THE CHURCHES TODAY ARE ALL ABOUT QUOTA AND CURRENCY AND NEVER THE PROMISES OF GOD. MAN, AS A RESULT OF HIS OWN GREED, TEND TO CATER TO THE TUNES OF SELFISHNESS AND DIVISION. WHILE THE PEOPLE OF GOD NEVER COME TOGETHER AND THEY ALSO NEVER COME TO A POINT OF KNOWING AND RECEIVING, THE PROMISES OF GOD.

Too Scary!!!

I OFTEN WONDER, WHY SO MANY LEADERS, AROUND THE COUNTRY AND EVEN THE WORLD, ARE SO AFRAID OF TEACHING THE WHOLE UNCUT AND NONE COMPROMISED TRUTH, OF THE WORD OF GOD. IF PEOPLE DON'T KNOW THE PROMISES OF GOD, THEY CAN'T RECEIVE THE PROM-

ises of God. They won't know what to look for in terms of God's desires for His people.

The key is, they are *"In! Him!"* Not around Him or brought by Him. There are promises in the word of God, that are available to everyone of us, who believe the word, right now! All we have to do is apply the principles of the word of God, to the applications of our active faith, which is simply to believe and to receive, and to leave God alone at work, while we wait for the blessing to come, and praise His name.

It's A Working Promise!

The New Standing Generation of the clergy in some instances, NOT ALL OF THEM, seem to believe that they have all of a sudden seen something different in the word of God or perhaps they think that they have discovered something everybody else missed.

Many of these leaders have made the statement, that tithing is now a thing of the past and if you allow some of these new generation leaders, they will tell you, that tithing was not even mentioned in the New Testament of the bible! But, tithing is mentioned in the New Testament. (Matt. 23:23; Luke 18:12; Heb. 7:5)

These same leaders have never found it necessary, to discontinue paying taxes to the state or to cease from gambling in some instances. It is so amazing to me, how certain things of the scriptural writings, seem to have fallen off of the pages, for some so-called believers. There is no way to agree with God and to be in a disagreeable position at the same time. Either you believe God or you do not! AMEN!!!

I have found the problem to be more in the

AREA OF SELFISH EVALUATION AND PERSONAL PERCEP-
TION, THAN A SIMPLE LACK OF UNDERSTANDING. PEOPLE
UNDERSTAND WHATEVER THEY CHOOSE TO UNDERSTAND
AND VICE-VERSA, CONCERNING MISUNDERSTANDING.

MANY PEOPLE HAVE SEEN THE TRUTH, ONE ON
ONE, UP CLOSE AND PERSONAL AND YET THEY REFUSE TO
PARTAKE OF THIS TRUTH CONCERNING *tithing.* THEY SAY;
"THE GOVERNMENT TAKES HIS OFF THE TOP AND I CAN'T
STOP HIM! BUT! I HAVE CONTROL OVER WHERE THE
REST GOES." THE PROBLEM IS THAT THEY HAVE MISSED
THE AWESOME <u>PROMISES OF TITHING</u>. I AM CONVINCED
THAT *"non-tithe payers"* ARE SUFFERING IMMENSELY.

Gotcha!!!

I CAN REMEMBER AS A TEENAGER, THERE WAS A
NONE-TITHE-PAYER AND EVEN NON- MEMBER OF THE
CHURCH, THAT HAD GONE TO THE SERVICE STATION TO
FILL UP THE CAR AT THE GAS PUMP. THE MONEY HE
NORMALLY PAID TO FILL UP THE CAR, HE PAID THAT
AMOUNT.

HOWEVER, THIS PARTICULAR TIME, HE DECIDED
TO GO TO A DIFFERENT STATION, THE FUEL TANK REGIS-
TERED ONLY HALF FULL. THE PUMP REGISTERED THE
RIGHT AMOUNT OF MONEY, ADVERTISING THE EXACT
AMOUNT PER GALLON, AS THE OTHER STATION.

THE FACT OF THIS SITUATION WOULD BE PROVEN,
THAT THE TANK HAD ONLY BEEN HALF FILLED WITH GAS,
UPON RETURNING BACK TO HIS ORIGINAL STATION, HAV-
ING PAID AN AMOUNT OF MONEY THAT SHOULD HAVE
FILLED THE TANK. HE WOULD HAVE BEEN ABLE TO WIT-
NESS THE SAME TANK REGISTER TO BE ONLY HALF FILLED,
FOR THE SAME AMOUNT OF MONEY.

BUT, THE NEXT TIME AT YET ANOTHER STATION,
IT HAPPENED AGAIN. THE AUTOMOBILE, AFTER BEING
CHECKED OUT, DID NOT REVEAL ANY MALFUNCTIONS IN
THE TANK.

It may sound like a mystical plot from the twilight zone or maybe even spooky, if you allow your mind to wonder in such a manner, however, God has got a way of getting His, believe it or not. This story situation actually took place, this statement is no lie, it really did happen!

I can also remember a baby crying and crying and crying; after all efforts to silence the crying were exhausted, we soon discovered that nothing would suffice. Finally the parents of the baby, rushed the baby to the emergency room, for what would turn out to be hours of observation, to which no particular discovery was ever made.

Nothing was wrong, according to the hospital's emergency room professional staff. No insect bites were discovered and there appeared to be no obvious pains that could be pinpointed, no broken bones discovered after careful examination, no air trapped in the stomach, nothing, absolutely nothing, could be pinpointed to have been the cause of this baby's crying.

The baby was finally released from the emergency room, by the clinical staff, to go home. Along with the baby's release from the hospital, an emergency room bill for the services that the baby had received, payable upon receipt, went with them.

Money was spent unintentionally, money that the parents did not even have to spare for such an emergency situation, at that particular time. The examination went well into the night, much sleep was lost; as a result, they would receive absolutely no rest for the following day on the job and still no answer was ever given. Wouldn't you believe that God got His that time?

He Got Me Too!

I HAD BEGUN TO SKIP TITHING OVER AND OVER AGAIN, TIME AFTER TIME, TO WHICH I MADE MANY EXCUSES FOR MY OWN CARELESS BEHAVIOR. I PURCHASED AN ELDORADO CADILLAC BIARRITZ, FROM A PARTICULARLY WELL ACQUAINTED PERSON, THAT I HAD KNOWN FOR QUITE SOME TIME.

TRYING TO DODGE GOD, CONCERNING THE PAYMENT OF YOUR TITHES, WILL KEEP YOU FROM HEARING AND/OR OBEYING THE VOICE OF GOD. THE SPIRIT OF GOD, SPOKE TO ME VERY PLAINLY AND SAID TO ME; *"Do not buy that car!"* I HEARD HIM SAY THAT TO ME VIVIDLY, BUT I WANTED THAT THING BAD AND EVEN MUCH MORE, THAN I EVER WANTED TO PAY TITHES.

AFTER THE CAR HAD BEEN PURCHASED FOR ONLY A SHORT WHILE, I ALLOWED MY YOUNGER SISTER TO DRIVE THE CAR AND THE CAR TOOK A HIT ON THE FREEWAY. DUE TO THE FACT THAT THE FORMER OWNER HAD BEEN PLAYING MECHANIC PREVIOUSLY, BEFORE I PURCHASED THE CAR, THE CAR BEGAN LEAKING GAS UNDER THE HOOD SOON AFTER THE ACCIDENT AND TWO WEEKS LATER THE CAR IGNITED INTO FLAMES AND WAS TOTALED WITHIN 10-15 MIN.

I WAS CAUGHT WITHOUT SUFFICIENT INSURANCE OR RATHER, NOT ENOUGH INSURANCE TO COVER THE FIRE DAMAGES TO THE CAR. THE OTHER DRIVERS, WHO HIT OUR CAR, WERE ALSO COMPLETELY WITHOUT INSURANCE ON THEIR OWN CAR. INSURANCE, WAS NOT REALLY MANDATORY LIKE NOW; AS I REMEMBER THEY WERE SENIOR CITIZENS.

MY WIFE AND I, SOUGHT THE COUNSEL OF AN ATTORNEY. HIS PARALEGAL, MET ME OUT IN THE LOBBY OF HIS OFFICE BUILDING, UPON MY FIRST VISIT. THIS PARALEGAL, TOOK MY CASE AND RAN IT UNDER THE GROUND, CAUSING ME TO LOSE MONEY AND ANY KIND

OF A POTENTIAL VICTORY IN A COURT CASE. WE LOST ALL THE WAY AROUND.

THE CAR WAS SITTING ON THE PARKING LOT OF A BODY REPAIR SHOP, OWNED BY A FRIEND OF MY PERSONAL MECHANIC. IN ORDER, FOR AN INSURANCE ADJUSTER TO COME OUT AND TO INSPECT THE DAMAGES; TO GIVE PROPER ESTIMATION FOR THE REPAIRS, THE CAR HAD TO BE AT A NEUTRAL LOCATION.

THE SHOP OWNER, STRIPPED MY CAR OF THE PARTS THAT WERE NEVER DAMAGED BY THE FIRE OR THE ACCIDENT AND TOOK EVERYTHING THEY WANTED AND PUT THE PARTS ON AN AUTOMOBILE THAT WAS SITTING IN THE BAY FOR REPAIRS.

THE CAR WAS AN OLDSMOBILE, GRAND TORINO, WHICH AT THAT TIME, BOTH CARS HAD EXACTLY THE SAME BODY STYLE. THEY TOOK THE STEERING WHEEL, THE BUMPER, THE RADIO, THE HEAT AND AIR CONDITIONING AND MORE, BECAUSE IT TOOK THE ADJUSTER TOO LONG TO ACTUALLY COME OUT TO THE LOCATION.

THE BUSINESS OWNER, THEN ACQUIRED A MECHANIC'S LIEN AGAINST WHATEVER WAS ACTUALLY LEFT OF MY CAR AND TOWED THE CAR TO BE JUNKED. SO, I KNOW WHAT IT MEANS FOR THE LORD TO ALLOW "<u>THE DEVOURER TO COME IN!</u>"

I COULD GO ON AND ON ABOUT ALL OF MY LOSSES, BEING THAT I HAD TO LEARN THE HARD WAY! JUST IN CASE YOU HAVEN'T BEEN PAYING YOUR TITHES AND PEOPLE HAVE BEEN GETTING OVER ON YOU, YOUR UTILITIES HAVE SKYROCKETED, SICKNESSES MAY HAVE COME OUT OF THE BLUE, MAYBE YOUR HOME BURNED DOWN AND YOU LOST EVERYTHING, YOUR CAR WAS WRECKED WITHOUT INSURANCE, SOMEONE UNEXPECTEDLY CAME ALONG TO DRAG YOU INTO COURT, FOR SOME WILD IDEA, GET THOSE TITHES OUT OF YOUR POSSESSION AND RELEASE THEM TO THE LORD!

> *Ye are cursed with a curse: For ye have robbed*
> *me, even this whole nation bring ye all the tithes*
> *into the storehouse, that there may be meat in*
> *mine house, and prove me now herewith, saith*
> *the Lord of host, if I will not open you the win-*
> *dows of heaven, and pour you out a blessing,*
> *that there shall not be room enough to receive it.*
> *And I will rebuke the Devourer for your sakes,*
> *and he shall not destroy the fruits of your*
> *ground; neither shall your vine cast her fruit*
> *before the time in the field, saith the Lord of host.*
> *And all nations shall call you blessed: For ye*
> *shall be a delightsome land, saith the Lord of*
> *Host.* MALACHI 3:9-12

I Command You, In Jesus Name!

TITHING, IS NOT A LAW OF THE LAND, BUT RATHER IT IS A MANDATE OF LOVE! YOU WON'T GO TO JAIL BECAUSE YOU DO NOT PAY TITHES, LIKE YOU MAY POSSIBLY BE IMPRISONED FOR NOT PAYING TAXES.

THE LORD LOVES YOU. HAVE YOU EVER HEARD THE STATEMENT, "IF YOU TAKE CARE OF GOD'S BUSINESS, HE WILL TAKE CARE OF YOURS?"

THE PROMISES OF GOD ARE GLEEFULLY INCUMBENT UPON THE COMPETENT CHARACTER OF THE INFALLIBLE INTEGRITY OF GOD. NON-TITHING IS CLEARLY ABOUT THE CURSE. HOWEVER TITHING ITSELF, IS ABOUT THE PROMISES OF GOD.

THERE IS A FIVE-PART *promise* INVOLVED IN TITHING. NOTE THIS: 5 IS THE NUMBER OF GOD'S GRACE, HIS UNMERITED FAVOR. SEE IT LIKE THIS. (1) G'-GIVE, (2) R'-RIGHT, (3) A'-AND, (4) C'-COLLECT, (5) E'-EVERYTHING PROMISED; GRACE! ISN'T THAT AWESOME! NOW EXAMINE THE PROMISE:

> PART ONE; *I will open you the windows of*
> *heaven, and pour you out a blessing that there*
> *shall not be room enough to receive.*

IT'S SIMPLE; GOD WILL TAKE YOUR LITTLE BIT AND GIVE YOU A LOT! THIS IS CLEARLY YOUR GREATEST INVESTMENT. WHENEVER YOU GIVE GOD THE SMALL 10%, THAT ALREADY BELONGS TO HIM, THERE IS A PROSPERING, PROTECTIVE ANOINTING THAT IS PLACED OVER THE REMAINING 90% THAT YOU ACTUALLY HAVE LEFT TO WORK WITH!

CAN YOU SEE THAT GOD ALLOWS US TO KEEP THE LARGER PERCENTAGE OF OUR INCREASED EARNINGS AND EVEN AFTER WE ARE ALLOWED TO HOLD ON TO MOST OF OUR MONEY, WE ARE YET EVEN BLESSED WITH MANY MORE GIFTS OF LOVE, FROM THE LORD!

GOD SAID; "I WILL POUR OUT"; NOT, "I WILL HAND OUT!" NEITHER, DID HE SAY; "I WILL GIVE OUT."

THE PICTURE IS TO BE RECEIVED AS A FREE FLOWING RIVER OF BLESSINGS, WITHOUT RESTRAINTS. YES, THAT'S RIGHT, FREE FLOWING, OUT OF THE GOOD AND PLENTEOUS TREASURE OF GOD.

CAN YOU ENVISION A RIVER, OF THE BLESSINGS OF GOD, FLOWING FROM THE THRONE OF GOD, RIGHT TO YOUR PERSONAL POSSESSION? DON'T PICTURE A LAZY RIVER, BUT PICTURE A ROARING RAPID RIVER, FLOWING DOWN A STEEP MOUNTAIN-SIDE. NOTHING CAN STOP THE BLESSINGS FROM COMING RIGHT DOWN TO YOU.

> *The blessing of the Lord, it maketh rich, and he addeth no sorrow with it.* PROVERBS 10:22

CAN YOU SAY; "HE <u>ADDETH</u> NO SORROW WITH IT?" DON'T BE SO FOOLISH, AS TO BE FEARFUL OF THE POURED OUT BLESSINGS OF THE LORD. IT IS GOD'S DELIGHT, TO HONOR HIS OWN PROMISES, TO THEM THAT WILL BELIEVE WITHOUT A DOUBT.

> PART TWO; *and I will rebuke the devourer for your sakes, and he shall not destroy the fruits of your ground.*

HERE, GOD IS SAYING; "AND I WILL TELL THE DEVOURER TO STOP RIGHT THERE IN HIS TRACKS!" HE IS

ALSO SAYING; "THAT'S ENOUGH, YOU'VE DONE ENOUGH DAMAGE!" YOU KNOW HOW IT IS WHEN YOU ARE WORKING AND MAKING AN HONEST LIVING AND THE MONEY IS COMING IN BY HEALTHY PROPORTIONS, BUT YOU CAN'T SEEM TO HOLD ON TO IT?

IT'S AS IF, WHATEVER RECEPTACLE YOU PLACE YOUR MONEY INTO, IT IS FILLED WITH GREAT BIG HOLES. AT TIMES, IT MAY EVEN APPEAR THAT YOU HAVE DEPOSITED YOUR MONEY INTO THE WRONG BANK ACCOUNT. YOU ALMOST CANNOT ACCOUNT FOR WHERE THE MONEY WENT. THE CHECKBOOK, HAS ALL OF A SUDDEN BECOME A RUBBER BOOK. ALL OF THE CHECKS ARE BOUNCING.

REPOSSESSED CARS AND HOMES, ARE NOW A PART OF YOUR EXPERIENCE AND TESTIMONY, AND ALL TYPES OF FINANCIAL LOSSES. YOU SHOULD BE IN A CERTAIN PLACE IN THE COMMUNITY AND EVEN IN THE SOCIETY; FINANCIALLY. BUT, BECAUSE THINGS WILL NOT LEVEL OFF, YOU CANNOT REALLY FIT IN. WORKING TWO JOBS AND A HALF, STILL NEVER BEING ABLE TO CATCH UP.

TOO MANY, UNEXPECTED BREAKDOWNS, THAT COST A BUNDLE, HAVE HAPPEN TO YOU OUT OF THE BLUE. YOU HAVE BEEN SEARCHING HIGH AND LOW SEARCHING FOR THE PROBLEM, FOR A LONG TIME, NOW HERE IT IS. IT'S THAT DEVASTATING "DEVOURER", WREAKING HAVOC AT WILL, ON THE FRUITS OF YOUR GROUNDS. YOUR FRUITS ARE THE MANIFESTATIONS OF YOUR HARD WORK AND LABOR IN FAITH, AND TRUST TO GOD.

> *So shall they fear the name of the Lord from the west, and his glory from the rising of the sun. When the enemy shall come in like a flood, the spirit of the Lord shall lift up a standard against him.* ISAIAH 59:19

THE PROMISE HAS BEEN MADE, GOD WILL DO, WHAT HE SAYS HE WILL DO. I STRONGLY ADMONISH YOU TO TRUST HIM. HOLD ON TO HIS UNCHANGING HAND AND DON'T EVER LET GO. EVERY TIME YOU PAY OR

GIVE WHAT IS REQUIRED, KNOWING THAT IT IS RIGHT FOR YOU TO DO SO, IN YOUR OWN HEART, *you* ARE SETTING A STANDARD FOR THE ENEMY TO YIELD HIMSELF IN RESPECT.

THEREFORE, THE STANDARD TO WHICH THE LORD WILL LIFT UP, IS THE SAME STANDARD TO WHICH YOU WILL HAVE ALREADY ESTABLISHED, AS A RESULT TO YOUR OBEDIENCE TO THE WORD OF GOD.

THE STREET SIGN DOES NOT JUST LEAP INTO ITS PLACE AT THE CORNER OF THE STREET, WHENEVER YOU DRIVE UP, FOR YOU TO STOP THERE; RATHER IT IS ALREADY THERE IN ITS PLACE UPON YOUR APPROACH TO THE CORNER AT THE INTERSECTION, TO WHICH YOU MUST OBEY AND BRING YOUR AUTOMOBILE TO A COMPLETE STOP! AS YOU KNOW, THERE WILL BE PENALTIES, AS A RESULT OF DISREGARDING THE STANDARD SIGN!

WHENEVER WE FAIL TO OBEY THE SET STANDARDS, SUCH AS STOP SIGNS AND YIELD SIGNS AND THE MANY OTHER ROAD SIGNS, THERE IS OFTEN MANY VERY SERIOUS REPERCUSSIONS AND SOMETIMES EVEN FATALITIES, AS A RESULT OF IGNORING THE SIGNS. THE DEVOURER DOES NOT EVEN HAVE A CHOICE AS PERTAINING TO WHETHER OR NOT HE IS GOING TO SHOW REGARDS FOR THE STANDARDS.

PART THREE; *Neither shall your vine cast her fruit before the time in the field.*

YOU SEE, IF SATAN CANNOT CAUSE YOU TO MISS HEARING THE VOICE OF GOD, HE OFTEN TIMES WILL CAUSE YOU TO JUMP OUT AHEAD OF GOD WAITING FOR SOMETHING PREMATURELY TO MANIFEST THAT WON'T, BECAUSE IT'S OUT OF TIMING WITH GOD'S TIMING.

IT'S LIKE TAKING AN EARLIER FLIGHT, BECAUSE YOU ARE OVERLY ANXIOUS TO ARRIVE AT THE INTENDED DESTINATION. AS A RESULT, WHEN YOU REACH YOUR DESTINATION YOU FIND THAT YOU HAVE JUMPED THE GUN AND ARRIVED TOO SOON. YOU WILL NOW HAVE TO WAIT

IN THE AIRPORT, ALL DAY LONG, BECAUSE NO ONE WOULD BE AVAILABLE TO RECEIVE YOU AT THE AIRPORT; EXPECTING THE PREVIOUSLY INTENDED ARRIVAL, OF THE RIGHT PRE-PLANNED FLIGHT.

ON THE SPIRITUAL SIDE, THE ENEMY COULD NOT PREVENT YOUR ACCEPTANCE, TO THE CALL OF GOD ON YOUR LIFE, TO THE MINISTRY. SO HE DELIVERED TO YOU, A READY TO USE PACKAGE OF ZEAL AND ENCOURAGED YOU TO GET STARTED WITHOUT GOD. INSTEAD OF WAITING ON GOD TO ESTABLISH WHO YOU ARE AND TO CULTIVATE THE GIFT OF GOD WORKING IN YOU, YOU END-UP DISQUALIFIED FROM THE RACE, BECAUSE YOU HAVE JUMPED THE GUN.

YOU LEAPED OUT OF THE STARTING BLOCKS AND TOOK OFF RUNNING BEFORE THE ACTUAL START OF YOUR RACE; HEADED IN THE DIRECTION OF THE WRONG FINISHING LINE. THE TRUTH IS THAT, GOD IS IN CONTROL AND HE KNOWS WHEN YOU ARE READY. HE WILL TELL ALL OF US, WHAT, HOW AND WHEN TO SAY WHAT IS NEEDED.

YOU AND EVERYONE ELSE ALIKE, HAS GOT THEIR VERY OWN SEASON TO BLOOM IN DUE TIME. GOD KNOWS WHERE HE IS TAKING YOU. GOD IS A GOD OF TIMING.

DON'T LET THE ENEMY TALK IN YOUR EAR ABOUT YOUR AGE AND ABOUT THE MANY PEOPLE WHO ARE ACTUALLY YOUNGER THAN YOU ARE, HOW THEY ARE GOING ON AND FLOURISHING AHEAD OF YOU. EVERYTHING THAT LOOKS WONDERFUL, IS NOT NECESSARILY AS WONDERFUL AS IT MAY SEEM.

SOMETIMES, IT MAY EVEN APPEAR AS THOUGH OTHERS ARE WHERE YOU REALLY WANT TO BE. THEY MAY HAVE GOTTEN THERE A LITTLE QUICKER THAN YOURSELF, BUT YOU NEED TO READ BETWEEN THE LINES OF LIFE. YOU HAVE TO BOTH SELL OUT TO THE WILL OF GOD AND WAIT ON HIS DIVINE PROVIDENCE, OR YOU WILL SELL OUT TO THE DEVIL OF THIS WORLD AND DO

WHATEVER IT TAKES TO GET WHERE YOU WANT TO GO.

> *I returned, and saw under the sun, that the race is not to the swift, nor the battle to the strong, neither yet bread to the wise, nor yet riches to men of understanding, nor yet favor to men of skill; but time and chance happeneth to them all. For man also knoweth not his time: as the fishes that are taken in an evil net, and as the birds that are caught in the snare; so are the sons of men snared in an evil time, when it falleth suddenly upon them.* ECCLESIASTES 9:11-12

BY ALL MEANS, RECEIVE THE PROMISE AND WATCH THE FRUIT OF YOUR VINE YIELD THEMSELVES AT THE PROPER APPOINTED TIME. YOU WILL BE BLESSED.

PART FOUR; *And all nations shall call you blessed:*

> *This is the Lord's doing; it is marvelous in our eyes.* PSALMS #118: 23

THE COUNTRY ADVERTISED A COMMERCIAL ABOUT BASKETBALL'S GREATEST; MICHAEL JORDAN. "WANT TO BE LIKE MIKE?"

TRUTH IS, IT IS REALLY NOT MIKE THAT YOU REALLY WANT TO BE LIKE. NOT ENOUGH BELIEVERS, WILL TAKE THE INITIATIVE, TO INVOKE THE MANIFESTATIONS OF THE PROMISES OF GOD, THROUGH THEIR OBEDIENCE TO THE WORD, IN AN EFFORT THAT GOD MIGHT SHOW JUST WHAT IT IS THAT HE WILL DO FOR HIS PEOPLE, WHENEVER THEY WILL TRUST IN HIM!

IF OTHERS, EVER GET AN OPPORTUNITY TO SEE THE AWESOME BENEFITS OF TITHING, THEY THEMSELVES WILL BECOME FAITHFUL, PROSPERING TITHERS. THERE ARE TOO MANY PEOPLE THAT ARE FORCED INTO TITHING AGAINST THEIR OWN WILL. THEY ARE DOUBTFUL, RESENTFUL AND BEGRUDGING, AS PERTAINING TO THE VERY IDEA OF PAYING TITHES, HOWEVER, MANY OF THEM TITHE ANYWAY. PERHAPS YOUR QUESTION IS, WHAT'S WRONG

AND YOU MIGHT SAY; "I'M DOING THE RIGHT THING, WHY AM I NOT GETTING THE RIGHT RESULTS?"

HERE'S WHY: IF TITHING; FIRSTLY, DOES NOT COME FROM YOUR HEART, BECAUSE YOU LOVE GOD AND APPRECIATE GOD'S DAILY PROVISION FOR YOUR LIVELY HOOD, AND IF YOU ARE RESENTFUL FOR EVEN THE LITTLE AMOUNT OF MONEY THAT YOU ARE GIVING FOR THE ON-GOING WORK OF THE KINGDOM OF GOD, YOU ARE DOING THE RIGHT THING IN THE WRONG ATTITUDE AND SPIRIT OF YOUR MIND!

TITHING MUST BE DONE IN THE RIGHT SPIRIT AND MOTIVE, WITH THE RIGHT INTENTIONS. GOD IS LOOKING RIGHT AT YOU, WHENEVER YOU SIT AND ATTEMPT TO COUNT THE NUMBER OF TITHE PAYERS IN ANY GIVEN SERVICE, TITHING. NOT KNOWING THE EXACT AMOUNT OF THE GIFT OF EACH TITHE, YOU STILL WILL ATTEMPT AT MAKING AN ASSESSMENT OF THE AMOUNT RECEIVED. RULING OUT A NEED TO GIVE YOUR OWN TITHES.

IT'S AN INDIVIDUAL AFFAIR! YOU NEED NOT TO WORRY ABOUT THE NEXT PERSON, JUST DO YOUR PART, AS YOU ARE THE ONLY ONE WHO CAN RECEIVE YOUR BLESSING WITH YOUR NAME ON IT. SO GET YOUR BLESSING!

DO IT RIGHT AND WATCH THE PEOPLE EVERY-WHERE, MARVEL AT GOD WORKING ON YOUR BEHALF. PERHAPS YOU MAY HAVE DISCOVERED, THAT YOU REALLY DO NEED MORE BLESSINGS IN YOUR OWN LIFE, IF SUCH BE THE CASE, YOU NEED TO GIVE GOD A RAISE, AS HE MAY IN FACT NEED MORE TO WORK WITH FROM YOU, ON YOUR BEHALF, IN AN EFFORT TO ALLOW, THE "MORE", THAT YOU NEED.

INSTEAD OF TEN PERCENT, GIVE GOD FIFTEEN PER-CENT OR EVEN AS MUCH AS YOU CAN. FAITH IN GOD WILL NOT FAIL YOU! IF YOU INCREASE GOD, HE WILL INCREASE YOU. WHENEVER YOU PAY GOD WHAT IS DUE, HE WILL PAY YOU IN RETURN. YOU CANNOT BEAT GOD

GIVING, HOWEVER, YOU CAN NEVER BEAT HIM TAKING AWAY!

> *Cast thy bread upon the waters: for thou shalt*
> *find it after many days.*   ECCLESIASTES 11:1

We Need To Line-Up With The Word Of God!

WHENEVER WE ALIGN OURSELVES WITH THE WORD OF GOD, WE SET OURSELVES UP FOR THE BLESSINGS. GOD GIVES TO US MANY TIMES, OVER AND OVER, BEFORE WE EVEN ASK. GOD PAYS US HANDSOMELY, EVEN WHEN WE DO NOT PHYSICALLY WORK FOR IT. HE SENDS THE ANOINTING UPON OUR LIVES. HE HEALS OUR BODIES WITHOUT MEDICINE OR EVEN DOCTORS. HE WILL PUT US IN HIGHLY RESPECTED JOB POSITIONS, TO WHICH OTHERS BELIEVE THAT THEY ACTUALLY DESERVE!

DON'T EVEN FLINCH AT THE JEALOUSY OF OTHER PEOPLE AROUND YOU, IF THEY DO NOT UNDERSTAND THAT YOU ARE JUST BEING BLESSED! HE IS ABLE! GOD CAN DO AND WILL DO THE IMPOSSIBLE FOR THEM THAT BELIEVE THE PROMISE.

ABRAHAM TITHED TEN PERCENT OF EVERYTHING HE HAD TO MELCHIZEDEK, AND GOD INCREASED ABRAHAM SO, THAT HE IMPUTED ABRAHAM'S OBEDIENCE FOR RIGHTEOUSNESS AND HE BECAME THE FRIEND OF GOD. EVEN TO THE POINT THAT WE STILL ADMIRE THE ACCOMPLISHMENTS OF ABRAHAM.

PART FIVE; *For ye shall be a delightsome land.*

> *His Lord said unto him, well done, thou good*
> *and faithful servant: thou hast been faithful over*
> *a few things, I will make thee ruler over many*
> *things. Enter thou into the joy of thy Lord.*
>   ST. MATTHEW 25:21

> *These things have I spoken unto you, that my*
> *joy might remain in you, and that your joy*
> *might be full.*   ST. JOHN 15:11

> *Hither to have ye asked nothing in my name;*

ask and ye shall receive, that your joy may be full.　　　　　　　　　　St. John 16:24

For the kingdom of God is not meat and drink; but righteousness, and peace, and joy in the Holy Ghost.　　　　　　　　　　Romans 14:17

Now the God of hope fill you with all joy and peace in believing, that ye may abound in hope, through the power of the Holy Ghost.
　　　　　　　　　　Romans 15:13

You have not even witnessed real joy, until you have been a personal recipient of the "fullness of joy." Having the "fullness of joy", in itself, is not to be measured by worldly possessions or bank accounts. That is, *able and flourishing bank accounts*.

Joy is not measured by social status, nor is it measured by immeasurable popularity. Joy has nothing to do with the sometimes fake outburst-like put-on that take place in a crowd.

Joy is not a thing of the surface, at all. Joy is intangible. YOU CANNOT TOUCH MY JOY. Joy is not visible to the naked eye. Although others appear to have joy; even you yourself may at times exemplify an outward display of an inward joy; however, you and the Lord only know the truth, pertaining to whether or not your joy is real and if your joy is full.

This, my friend, is the one element in which people are seeking. Oh! The power of possessing joy!

No person in their right mind, would ever have a since of admiration for sour, frowning, mean, totally unreasonable and irrational people. Such people, usually are not generally well thought of people, neither good company to spend time around.

HOWEVER, "JOY-F<u>ULL</u>-NESS" IS ATTRACTIVE. THERE IS AN INESCAPABLE MAGNETISM ASSOCIATED WITH JOYFULNESS. JOY FLOWS FROM DEEP DOWN WITHIN THE INNERMOST PART OF THE BELLY OF AN INDIVIDUAL, WHOSE DETERMINATION IS NOTHING OTHER THAN TO OBEY THE WORD OF GOD.

HAVE YOU EVER BEEN SO FULL OF JOY, THAT YOU COULD NOT EXPLAIN IT IF YOU TRIED? POWERFUL ISN'T IT?

AS A RESULT OF OBEYING THE VOICE OF GOD AND RECEIVING THE PROMISE OF HIS WORD, YOU KNOW JOY. WHETHER PEOPLE UNDERSTAND IT OR NOT, THEY WILL BE ABLE TO OBSERVE THE JOYOUSNESS ABOUT YOU.

JOYFUL PEOPLE ARE VERY BENEFICIAL, THROUGH THEIR EXAMPLES OF LIVING AND SHARING. THEY ARE MUCH TO BE DESIRED. THEY OFTEN EXPERIENCE TRIALS WITHOUT OTHERS EVEN KNOWING.

BECAUSE, WE GLORIFY GOD, GOD GLORIFIES US, WITH GLORIFIED BLESSINGS FROM ON HIGH. EVERY PROMISE IN THE BIBLE IS TRUE! NOT ONE OF THEM IS FALSE, OUTDATED, INVALID OR EVEN DONE AWAY WITH.

ALWAYS BELIEVE GOD. KNOW THAT GOD BELIEVES YOU. OUR RELATIONSHIP WITH GOD IN SOME ASPECTS, IS RETROACTIVE. WHENEVER WE ACT UPON THE WORD OF GOD; GOD IN RETURN WILL ACT UPON OUR FAITH IN HIM.

> *But, without faith it is impossible to please him: for he that cometh to God must believe that he is, and that he is a rewarder of them that diligently seek him.* HEBREWS 11:6

Believe it to the very end until it manifest!!!

Now! Say!! Amen!!!

Victorious And Proud!!!

> And he answered and said unto them, I tell you that if these should hold their peace the stones would immediately cry out.   St. Luke 19:40

I Won't Be Silent!

YOU WILL NEVER BE THE SAME AGAIN, SO YOU SHOULD EXPECT NOTHING LESS THAN TO WALK IN TOTAL VICTORY AND THE NEWNESS OF LIFE IN CHRIST JESUS.

BE COMPLETELY CONFIDENT IN THE FACT THAT YOU ARE TOTALLY CONVINCED OF YOUR DELIVERANCE, WITH THE EVIDENCE OF TRUTH TO FOLLOW YOUR CLAIM THAT THE LORD HAS INDEED LAID HIS HAND ON YOU.

BE PERFECTLY SURE THAT THINGS HAVE CHANGED IN YOUR LIFE THAT WOULD HAVE TAKEN YOU TO HELL, HAD THEY REMAINED THE SAME.

THE ONLY REASONABLE PURPOSE FOR LOOKING BACK ON LIFE IN THE PAST WITHOUT CHRIST, IS FOR THE SAKE OF REMEMBERING JUST HOW WONDERFUL IT IS TO EXPERIENCE THE POWERFUL HAND OF MERCY AND DELIVERANCE.

WHAT SHOULD BE MOST MEMORABLE, IS THE ACTUAL MOMENT THE POWER OF GOD MADE IT'S ENTRANCE INTO OUR LIVES, BROKE THE CHAINS OF BONDAGE AND SET US FREE! I WILL ALWAYS REMEMBER, THE DAY THE LIGHT OF THE LORD, DISPELLED THE DARKNESS OF MY PAST AND RELEASED THE PADLOCK OF GUILT, THAT HAD MY DUNGEON SECURED!

SO MANY PEOPLE HAVE BEEN ADVISED OF MY PAST GUILT OF SINNING AND SHAME, AND THEY VOWED AND MADE UNCANNY ATTEMPTS TO HOLD ME HOSTAGE TO THE NEGATIVE REPORTS TO WHICH THEY HAD HEARD AND BELIEVED, VOWING ALSO TO NEVER LET ME GO FREE!

JESUS REACHED INTO THE DARKNESS AND PULLED ALL OF US OUT, WHO WANTED TO COME OUT; STEPPED INTO OUR LIVES AND SEVERED THE TIES TO THOSE WRONG PERSONS WHO HAD A HAND IN THE DESTRUCTION OF OUR LIFE AND REBUKED THE BAD NEWS OF OUR PAST REPUTATION, DELIVERED US TO THE LIGHT OF HIS WORD, ALL IN THE PRESENCE OF OUR ENEMIES.

DELIVERANCE DIDN'T COME TO US IN SECRET, THEREFORE WE CAN'T AFFORD TO BE SILENT ABOUT WHAT THE LORD HAS DONE IN OUR LIVES.

You've Been Changed!!!

NOW THAT YOUR LIFE HAS BEEN CHANGED PERMANENTLY, YOU DON'T HAVE TIME TO WASTE, REFLECTING BACK ON THE PAST, STILL FEELING GUILTY AND CRINGING AT EVERY SINFUL MEMORY. IT'S REALLY OVER NOW?

YOU HAVE ACCEPTED THE WORD OF THE LORD AND HAVE FINALLY SURRENDERED, RECEIVING CHRIST INTO YOUR HEART, CONFESSING WITH YOUR MOUTH, UNTO REPENTANCE.

THERE SHOULD BE NO DESIRE TO EVER BE ASSOCIATED WITH THE WORKS OF DARKNESS EVER AGAIN. WHEN AN INDIVIDUAL HAS NO MORE GANG ACTIVITY OR ANY MAFIA ASSOCIATION, THERE WILL BE NO MORE DRUG ABUSE,

WHETHER THEY ARE ILLEGAL OR PRESCRIPTION DRUGS, IT IS ONLY OBVIOUS THAT THERE HAS INDEED BEEN A CHANGE.

NO MORE DRUG DEALING, NOT A WHORE OR A WHORE MONGER, NO LONGER A PROSTITUTE, NO LONGER A PIMP, NO LONGER A STREET HUSTLER, DISHONEST AS A WAY OF LIFE, NO MORE ROBBERY OR BURGLARY THAT WILL EVER BE A PART OF THE FUTURE, BECAUSE JESUS HAS MADE A CHANGE.

THERE USE TO BE A TIME, WHEN YOU WERE NEVER TO BE TRUSTED IN THE GATHERING OF A HOLY GHOST FILLED WORSHIP SERVICE, BECAUSE SOMEBODY WAS GOING TO LOSE A PURSE OR SOMETHING OF VALUE. NOW THAT THERE IS TRUE DELIVERANCE, YOU COULD WORK AT THE MINT OR A BANK, OR ANYWHERE THERE IS LOOSE MERCHANDISE AVAILABLE, BECAUSE, THERE IS JUST NO MORE DESIRE TO STEAL, EVER.

NOW, YOU WOULD MUCH RATHER GIVE THAN TO TAKE ANYTHING THAT DID NOT BELONG TO YOU.

YOU WILL WALK INTO A DEPARTMENT STORE NOW AND GLADLY PAY FOR WHATEVER YOU WANT, WITHOUT ANY HESITATION. YOUR EYES ARE NO LONGER SEARCHING FOR SOMEONE ELSE'S BLANK CHECK, TO ILLEGALLY FORGE, FOR THE PURPOSE OF FINANCING YOUR OWN ADDICTIVE LIFE-STYLE OF DRUGS, ALCOHOL AND WAYWARD LIVING.

YOU ARE NO LONGER A CONSPIRATOR, IN THE LIVES OF THE BROTHERS AND SISTERS, OF THE BODY OF CHRIST. IT DOESN'T EVEN MATTER, IF YOU KNOW THAT THE PASTOR OF YOUR OWN LOCAL CHURCH FAMILY, IS INVOLVED IN THE CONSPIRACY OF ANOTHER PERSON OF THE BODY OF CHRIST, YOU ARE NOT MAKING AN ATTEMPT TO BE A PART OF THE CONSPIRACY, BECAUSE YOU KNOW THAT IT IS WRONG AND DISPLEASING IN THE SIGHT OF THE LORD.

NO MORE LOAN SHARKING! THE BIBLE SPEAKS VERY STERNLY, AS PERTAINING TO PUTTING YOUR MONEY TO USURY, LETTING SOMEONE HAVE YOUR MONEY, IN AN EFFORT TO EXERCISE A FORM OF CONTROL OVER THEM, BY DEMANDING MORE MONEY IN RETURN FOR THE LOAN THAT

YOU GAVE THEM.

People Won't Forget!

MANY OF YOUR OWN IMMEDIATE FAMILY MEMBERS WON'T BELIEVE OR EVEN EMBRACE THE REALITY OF YOUR DELIVERANCE. THAT IS NO REASON, TO GO BACK INTO THE PATTERNS OF YOUR FORMER BEHAVIOR. GO ON FORWARD WITH THE BELIEVERS WHO ARE SHOUTING THE VICTORY IN JESUS WITH YOU AND LET THAT DO!

THE VERY PEOPLE, WHO COULD NOT DELIVER YOU IN THE FIRST PLACE, ARE THE SAME PERSONS WHO ARE TRYING TO KEEP YOU UNDER THE BONDAGE OF YOUR PAST, TRYING TO CREATE ALL OF THE POSSIBLE HELL AND CONTINUAL DAMNATION FOR YOU, RIGHT HERE ON EARTH. SO, WHOMEVER IT MAY BE THAT CANNOT SEEM TO GET WITH YOUR DELIVERANCE, DON'T EVEN MATTER!

PEOPLE LISTEN AND PAY STRICT ATTENTION WHEN THEY SHOULDN'T, TO THE SPOKEN WORDS OF THOSE PERSONS WHO COULD NOT EVEN SAVE THEIR OWN SOUL FROM HELL; WHILE THEY VERBALLY DESTROY THE CHARACTER OF ANOTHER INDIVIDUAL IN THE BODY OF CHRIST.

FOR A WHILE, IT SEEMED AS IF YOU WERE RUNNING THROUGH LIFE, FLEEING THE PRESENCE OF OUR ENEMIES, BUT GETTING ABSOLUTELY NOWHERE! YOU MAY HAVE EVEN THOUGH THAT YOU WERE INDEED IN A HIDING PLACE, BUT SEEMING AS IF, YOU WERE NEVER HIDDEN.

NOW, DEATH AND EVIL, ARE NO LONGER GAINING GROUND ON YOU, NO MATTER HOW YOU MAKE AN ATTEMPT TO ESCAPE. EVERY DEMON SPIRIT THAT WAS CAST OUT OF YOUR POSSESSED SOUL, HATES THE VERY TRUTH OF THE FACT THAT YOU'VE BEEN SET FREE.

THE DARKNESS OF YOUR PAST HAS DISSIPATED, BECAUSE THE LIGHT OF THE LORD HAS COME INTO YOUR OWN PERSONAL EXISTENCE. YOU FEEL AS LIGHT AS A FEATHER, BECAUSE ALL OF YOUR HEAVY BURDENS HAVE BEEN LIFTED.

FEAR HAS NOW BEEN ARRESTED. JESUS HAS CAPTURED

YOUR FEAR. SAY IT LOUD!! I'M SAVED!!!

Now Go Ahead, Exhale!!!

FINALLY; YOU FEEL GOOD ABOUT YOURSELF. YOU'VE LOOKED INTO THE MIRROR AND YOU LIKED WHAT YOU SAW! YOU HAVE NOTICED THAT YOU ARE NOT THE WEAKLING THAT YOU USE TO BE. NOW, YOU CAN "SAY; <u>NO!</u>"

YOU'RE READY TO GO, SO GO AHEAD AND SHOUT THE VICTORY IN JESUS CHRIST. GOD TOOK THE MESS OF OUR LIVES AND GAVE US HIS BEST, IN THE PERSON OF CHRIST JESUS. NOBODY IS EVEN MAD ABOUT THIS BUT THE DEVIL. GO AHEAD AND DANCE ON THE DEVIL'S HEAD! YOU DESERVE TO HAVE A HOLY GHOST FIT.

THE REAL TRUTH IS, 97% OF VICTORIOUS PEOPLE IN CHRIST, HAVE SPENT MANY YEARS FAILING, WHILE ON THEIR WAY TO BEING MADE VICTORIOUS. THEY DIDN'T GET TO THE POINT AND PLACE OF VICTORY, OVER NIGHT. MANY, BARE THE WOUNDS AND SCARS OF HAVING BEEN IN MANY FIERCE HARD BATTLES WITH THE ENEMY. YOU HAVE THE VICTORY NOW, SO IT'S OK TO TELL WHERE THE LORD BROUGHT YOU FROM AND NOT BE ASHAMED.

WHERE YOU ARE IN CHRIST NOW, IS A GREAT THING TO BE PROUD OF. IT REALLY DOESN'T MATTER, THAT YOU HAVE NOT BEEN THERE FOR VERY LONG. THE FACT THAT YOU MAY HAVE JUST RECEIVED SALVATION AND THAT THE LEVEL OF YOUR WORD KNOWLEDGE IS VERY LOW, SHOULD NEVER HINDER YOU FROM PRAISING "GOD', REJOICE ANYWAY! STAY WITH THE CHURCH. LOOK UP AND SHOUT; "I'VE GOT THE VICTORY!"

THE MORE YOU CONFESS IT, THE MORE YOU WILL REALIZE THE POWERFUL TRANSFORMATION THAT HAS TAKEN PLACE IN YOUR OWN LIFE.

RECEIVING A BIRTHDAY AND A CHRISTMAS GIFT IS ALWAYS EXCITING, AND I WOULD EXPECT THAT THE EXCITEMENT OF THE WEDDING DAY MUST HAVE BEEN RECORD BREAKING FOR MANY.

Graduation from high school, college, the armed force academy and the many other accomplishments may have brought great self-esteem.

None of the above mentioned accomplishments compare to what God has done for you. If at anytime you have ever expressed excitement over anything, you ought to really be going on and up about what Christ has done.

Have you ever lost yourself in the praise and worship of the Lord? You should experience such a time, as to be lost in His presence. "Get Lost"!!!

Do What Counts!

People don't know what we've been through, just to get where we are in the Anointing. Most of us, have had to come through the devil's troops. It has actually taken years to come to the point of really and truly surrendering to the will of God.

Just to look at people, you wouldn't know the intense struggles that they had encountered, on their way to being made victorious.

Many people have had to dig themselves out of the deep pit to which they themselves had actually dug for other people.

Others had fallen prey to alcoholism and drug addiction; while being embarrassed knowing that they were the topic of much negative rhetorical discussion, which brought about a deeper hardening of their heart, to affixed a greater addictive hold on their lives.

They're Not Better Than You !!

People mock and poke fun at the inability of an alcoholic or a drug addict, because they cannot maintain themselves in an orderly manner before the public, being that they are out of control.

314

PEOPLE DON'T USUALLY REALIZE THE GREATER DAMAGE THAT IS ACTUALLY CAUSED BY THE REJECTION AND THE INTENSE MOCKERY.

MOST PERSONS, IN WHATEVER THEIR STATE, HAVE EVEN WALKED AWAY FROM CERTAIN CHURCHES ACTUALLY FEELING WORSE UPON LEAVING, THAN THEY DID WHENEVER THEY ARRIVED. INSTEAD OF BEING HELPED, THEY WERE SOMETIMES RE-INJURED AND STABBED IN AN ALREADY OPEN WOUND, FIGURATIVELY SPEAKING.

SELF-RIGHTEOUS, RELIGIOUSLY PREPARED PEOPLE IN MANY OF THE ORGANIZED DENOMINATIONAL CHURCHES, HAVE A WAY OF TELLING OTHERS; IF YOU WERE LIKE ME, YOU WOULDN'T BE IN THAT PREDICAMENT.

THE PROBLEMATIC VISITOR HAS BEEN SUBJECT TO ALMOST BEING LEFT OUT IN THE VESTIBULE OR OUT ON THE FRONT PORCH, OF THE CHURCH. I'M SPEAKING ONLY OF THOSE INDIVIDUALS WHO REALLY WERE SEEKING HELP, AND FOR WHATEVER THE REASON, THEY FELT THAT GOD MIGHT HEAR THE PRAYERS OF THE PEOPLE AT THE CHURCH, WHILE HE MIGHT NOT HEAR THEIR OWN PRAYERS, BEING THAT THEY ARE YET A SINNER!

THEY PROBABLY WOULD PRAY FOR THEMSELVES, IF THEY COULD STAY SOBER LONG ENOUGH, KEEPING THE HYPODERMIC NEEDLES OUT OF THEIR ARMS OR THROWING DOWN THEIR CRACK PIPE AND REFUSING TO SUCK ON THE FORTY OUNCE BOTTLE OF BEER.

THEY HAD EVENTUALLY COME TO THE REALITY THAT THEY COULD NOT HELP THEMSELVES. THE PEOPLE OF GOD HARDLY EVER SEEM TO HEAR THE OUTCRIES FOR HELP, FROM THE MANY HURTING PEOPLE OF THE WORLD, AS THEY SHOULD. CERTAINLY AFTER HAVING BEEN BORN AGAIN, WE SHOULD BE MORE ATTENTIVE TO THE CRIES OF OTHERS.

The Wrong, Long Journey!

PEOPLE, BY THE SCORES, HAVE COME FROM A MULTIPLICITY OF ABUSES. THE ABUSE FOR SOME PEOPLE ACTU-

ALLY BEGAN IN THE MOTHER'S WOMB. THE IMPREGNATED WOMAN, WHO WOULD NOT EVEN THINK OF GETTING AN ABORTION, IS ALSO IN TOTAL REJECTION TO THE IDEA OF BEING PREGNANT, AND SHE HAS NEVER HAD THE DESIRE TO BE A MOTHER! SHE IS IN A REAL DILEMMA, SHE'S CONFUSED!

PERHAPS THE WRONG MAN HAS FATHERED HER BABY AND ALREADY SHE'S LEFT ALONE TO PROVIDE FOR HER COMING CHILD AND OTHER CHILDREN OR ANOTHER CHILD. THE WAY HAS ALREADY BEEN HARD FOR HER, AND SHE DID NOT USE GOOD JUDGMENT OR EVEN EXERCISE GOOD WISDOM IN TERMS OF THE CHOICE THAT SHE MADE.

SO NOW, THE CHILD WILL CATCH IT, BEING AN ALIVE MEMORY OF A BAD DECISION OF THE PAST, FOR THE REST OF ITS LIFE, UNLESS GOD INTERVENES! CRADLE ABUSE MAY BE THE INEVITABLE. THE CHILD MAY BE LEFT TO CRY FOR EXTENDED PERIODS OF TIME. LEFT HUNGRY AND NEGLECTED OR EVEN LEFT ON THE DOORSTEP OF A STRANGER. IT WAS NOT THE CHILD'S FAULT.

SO MANY BABIES ARE PLACED IN A TRASH DUMPSTER OR SIMPLY WRAPPED IN A TOWEL AND LEFT OUTDOORS TO BE DISCOVERED BY ANY WONDERING STRANGER OR A DOG. OTHERS WERE GIVEN UP FOR ADOPTION; THE BEAT GOES ON.

MANY CHILDREN HAVE SUFFERED VIOLENT PHYSICAL ATTACKS, WHEREAS, PARENTS OR GUARDIANS TOOK OUT ALL OF THEIR FRUSTRATIONS ON THEM. BEATING THEM, WITH ANY NUMBER OF UNTHINKABLE OBJECTS, UNTIL THE PARENTS WERE SATISFIED. CHILDREN HAVE BEEN PUNCHED, KICKED, THROWN AROUND, BURNED, CUT WITH RAZOR BLADES, KNIVES AND EVEN PRICKED WITH SHARP OBJECTS. EVEN TODAY WE HEAR OF MANY RIDICULOUSLY HORRENDOUS STORIES OF ABUSE.

Thank God You Made It!

IT ALWAYS TEARS MY HEART, WHENEVER I MINISTER

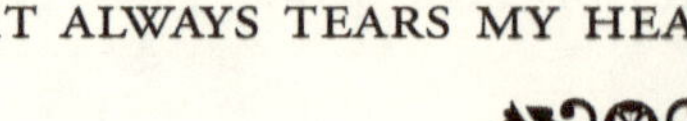

TO A PERSON WHO HAS BEEN SEXUALLY MOLESTED AS A CHILD, BY A FATHER OR AN UNCLE OR SOME OTHER FAMILY MEMBER, A NEIGHBOR, OR WHOMEVER! EVEN THE MOLESTERS THEMSELVES NEED TO COME TO JESUS IN A HURRY, TO REPENT AND BE VICTORIOUSLY SET FREE, *or burn in Hell eternally!*

PEOPLE, WHOSE LIVES HAVE BEEN SHATTERED FOR DECADES AS A RESULT OF HAVING BEEN ABUSED, ARE OFTEN THE NEWLY DEVELOPED ABUSERS, ACTUALLY REPLAYING THEIR OWN TRAUMA ON ANOTHER PERSON.

I HAVE SUFFERED ABUSE AS A CHILD, AS A TEEN, AND EVEN AS AN ADULT, ALTHOUGH NONE OF MY ABUSE HAS EVER BEEN SEXUAL, IT HAS ALWAYS BEEN PAINFUL TO ME, AND MOST OFTEN IT OCCURED IN THE CHURCH. IN MOST CASES, THE ADVISE FROM THE AVERAGE PERSON OF SOCIETY AND IN THE CHURCH, HAD BEEN FOR ME TO JUST GET OVER IT!

PERHAPS IF THE SITUATIONS WERE ANIMATED EVENTS OF TRAUMA, THAT WERE ONLY FICTITIOUS OCCURRENCES IN THE LIVES OF PEOPLE, IT WOULDN'T BE SO HARD TO GET OVER IT!

BUT, REAL LIFE TRAUMATIC EXPERIENCES THAT HAPPEN WITHOUT A REASONABLE EXPLANATION, IIAS A PAINFULLY LASTING EFFECT, THAT LINGERS ON AND ON WITHOUT THE NECESSARY AID OF COUNSEL AND THE ADMINISTERING OF HEALING TO RID THE INFFLICTION OF PAIN PREVENTING TO EROTION OF THE NATURAL ABILITY TO FEEL.

MANY FATHERS TEACH IN ERROR OR EITHER THEY FAIL ALL TOGETHER, TO TEACH THEIR SONS, THE GRAVE NECESSITY OF PROPER SEXUAL BEHAVIOR, WHICH SHOULD BEGIN AS SOON AS THE CHILD DISCOVERS THAT HE IS A BOY, IN MY OWN OPINION. MANY YOUNG CHILDREN, BEING THE YOUNGER BROTHER, HAVE BEEN THE TARGET OF THEIR OLDER SIBLING'S SEXUAL CURIOSITY. IT IS PSYCHOLOGICALLY DEBILITATING TO THE YOUNG CHILD.

I HAVE BEEN INFORMED OF A MOTHER, WHO HAD GOTTEN INTO BED TO HAVE SEX WITH HER OWN SON. SUCH

AN ATROCIOUS ACT CARRIED OUT ON A YOUNG MAN, WILL CAUSE THE YOUNG MAN TO HAVE A VERY SERIOUSLY SLANTED PERSPECTIVE VIEWPOINT OF WOMEN, EVERYWHERE, UNTIL DELIVERANCE COMES.

WE ARE WELL ACQUAINTED WITH THE PSYCHOLOGICAL DAMAGE THAT HAS BEEN CAUSED IN MANY YOUNG WOMEN.

YES IT'S TRUE; PEOPLE REALLY EXPERIENCE SUCH ENTANGLEMENTS OF THE FLESH, BUT, THE SAME TYPES OF PEOPLE ALSO EXPERIENCE FREEDOM IN JESUS CHRIST. THEY HAVE A REASON AND A RIGHT, TO PRAISE THE LORD. BE ADVISED: GOD IS DELIVERING EVERYDAY!

MANY ABUSE VICTIMS, THROUGH CHRIST CAN NOW SAY; "I'M FREE", "I'VE GOT THE VICTORY!"

NO MORE SHAME ATTACHED TO ME AND NEITHER IS THERE ANY MORE PAIN, I'M NOT THE SAME AND JESUS DID IT.

THEN, THERE ARE THOSE PEOPLE, WHO HAVE BEEN ABUSED BY SOCIETY. THEY HAVE BEEN VICTIMIZED BY THE IDEOLOGY OF SECULAR HUMANISM. THE POWER HAS BEEN TAKEN FROM THE PARENT/PARENTS OF THE HOUSEHOLD, PREVENTING THE PHYSICAL CHASTISEMENT OF THE CHILDREN OF THE FAMILY, WHICH IS NOW A FORM OF ABUSE, THEY SAY.

SOCIAL SCIENCE, HAS BEEN UNSUCCESSFUL IN RANDOMLY WEAVING THROUGH THE COMMUNITIES TARGETING ALL ABUSIVE SITUATIONS, SO THEY BELIEVED THAT IF THEY PENALIZE ALL FAMILY HOUSEHOLDS, THEY MIGHT DETER THE OPPORTUNITY FOR CHILD ABUSE.

NOBODY CAN TEACH, CORRECT AND TRAIN A CHILD/ CHILDREN, LIKE THE PARENTS WHO LOVE THEIR CHILDREN OR TRULY LOVING GUARDIANS WHO RAISE CHILDREN AS THEIR OWN. DON'T EVER ALLOW YOURSELF TO BELIEVE, THAT A PARENT WHO SPANKS HIS OR HER CHILD, IS GOING TO ABUSE THE CHILD.

TIME-OUT IN A CORNER, JUST SIMPLY WILL NOT WORK

IN MANY CASES, WHERE TRUE DISCIPLINARY CORRECTIVE ACTIONS SHOULD BE TAKEN. CHILD WELFARE, EMPLOYEES FOR THE STATE NEED JOBS, *so in my own opinion*, THEY COME UP WITH ALL TYPES OF ALTERNATE DISCIPLINARY METHODS OF CHASTISING CHILDREN FOR THE WRONG THEY DO, OTHER THAN SPANKING THE CHILD, IN AN EFFORT TO MEASURE OUT THE FULL EXTENT OF THE LAW FOR A PARENT WHO CONDUCT THEIR PRACTICAL PARENTING SKILLS, CONTRARY TO THE MANDATES OF THE STATE.

MANY CHILD WELFARE EMPLOYEES DO NOT EVEN HAVE ANY CHILDREN THEMSELVES.

CHILD PROTECTIVE SERVICES, ON MANY OCCASIONS HAVE DRAGGED THE WRONG PEOPLE INTO COURT. TAKING THEM OFF OF THEIR JOBS, CAUSING FINANCIAL LOSSES AND STIFF FINANCIAL PENALTIES, SEVERELY AFFECTING HOUSEHOLDS, ONLY TO DISCOVER, THAT THE ABUSE CHARGES WILL HAVE TO BE DROPPED.

THE PARENTS ARE NOT GUILTY OF ANY ABUSE. THEY ONLY LOVE THEIR CHILDREN ENOUGH TO CORRECT THE WRONG THEIR CHILD HAD COMMITTED.

> *He that spareth his rod hateht his son: but he*
> *that loveth him chasteneth him betimes.*
>
> PROVERBS 13:24

WHENEVER SOCIETY INTERVENES OR INTERRUPTS THE NATURAL RECOURSE OF THE HOME, THEY ARE SENDING THE WRONG MESSAGE, POSSIBLY IMPLYING THAT THE POLICE ACTUALLY NEED MORE WORK OR THAT THE PENITENTIARY IS REALLY NOT FULL ENOUGH YET. SOCIETY SEEMS TO SEND THE MESSAGE THAT THEY NEED MORE YOUNG GRAVES IN THE CEMETERY, THE EMERGENCY ROOMS ARE NOT REALLY BUSY ENOUGH, AS WELL AS NOT ENOUGH WHEEL CHAIRS BEING SOLD, FOR LACK OF DISCIPLINE.

NOT ENOUGH BANKS, GROCERY STORES, CONVENIENCE STORES AND FINANCIAL INSTITUTIONS BEING ROBBED. NOT ENOUGH AUTOMOBILES BEING STOLEN OR

CAR-JACKED IN THE BROAD OPEN DAYLIGHT.

SOCIETY'S MESSAGE IS THAT WE NEED MORE BAD NEWS TO REPORT. WE NEED MORE NEGATIVE IMAGES FOR THE NEWSPAPER AND RAP MUSIC. WE NEED MORE RAPIST; WE NEED MORE CONVICTED FELONS ON DEATH ROW. WE NEED MORE EXTORTIONISTS AND THE BEAT GOES ON. THE BOTTOM LINE IS, THAT IF PARENTS ARE NOT IN CONTROL, MORE YOUNG PEOPLE BY THE SCORES ARE BEING RAISED UP OUT OF CONTROL.

SOCIETY'S SOCIAL IMPACT, IS NEVER TO BE IMPLEMENTED AS THE PARENTING AUTHORITY OF ANY CHILDREN. THE PARENTS KNOW THE INTENDED DIRECTION THAT THEY DESIRE FOR THEIR OWN CHILDREN! WHENEVER ANY PERSON IS OUT OF CONTROL, GENERALLY THEY ARE OUT OF CONTROL EVERYWHERE THEY GO.

ASK THE ELEMENTARY, JUNIOR HIGH AND EVEN SENIOR HIGH SCHOOL TEACHERS ABOUT THE CONTROL STATUS OF THE CHILDREN, WHOSE PARENTS SEEM TO BE LACKING IN THE AREAS OF DISCIPLINE. DON'T EVEN THINK ABOUT ASKING SUNDAY SCHOOL TEACHERS.

A Narrow Escape!

JUDGES HAVE HELD MANY IN CONTEMPT OF COURT, SENDING THEM TO JAIL AND ATTACHING STIFF FINES, DUE TO THE FACT THAT THEY FAIL TO CONTROL THEMSELVES, WHILE LACKING PROPER RESPECT FOR THE VOICE OF AUTHORITY FROM THE BENCH IN THE COURTROOM.

SOME WHO HAVE LIVED OUT OF CONTROL WHILE FREE IN SOCIETY, WERE ALSO FORTUNATE ENOUGH TO MAKE IT THROUGH THE UNFORTUNATE OBSTACLES OF HAVING BEEN INCARCERATED IN PRISON SEVERAL TIMES AS A RESULT OF THEIR OUTRAGEOUS BEHAVIOR, BOTH MALE AND FEMALE ALIKE.

SOME ONLY CONTINUED IN THE SAME DIRECTION OF CRIME, TO BECOME HABITUAL CRIMINALS AND REPEAT OFFENDERS. TERRIBLE DISDAIN HAS BEEN ATTACHED TO THEIR

CHARACTER, WHICH HAS RUINED THE FAVORABLENESS OF THEIR NAME. THEY ARE CONSIDERED TO BE PUBLIC EMBARRASSMENTS AND HAVE BEEN WRITTEN OFF AS NEVER POSSIBLY BEING PRODUCTIVE TO THE SOCIETY.

THE POLICE AND THE JUDICIAL SYSTEM ARE ACQUAINTED WITH THEM, BY THEIR PERSONAL NAMES. THEY KNOW THEIR CRIMINAL, HISTORICAL RECORD, BY MEMORY.

IT'S FAIR TO SAY, THAT THE CRIMINALS HAVE BEEN THE CAUSE OF THEIR OWN PAIN, THEY HAVE DONE IT TO THEMSELVES. <u>BUT</u>!! <u>GOD</u>!!! IN HIS INFINITE WISDOM, KNOWING EVERYTHING THERE IS TO KNOW, PROVIDED A WAY OF ESCAPE.

SOMEBODY ESCAPED THROUGH HEARING THE WORD OF GOD ON THE TELEVISION OR THE RADIO, WHILE OTHERS MAY HAVE HEARD THE WORD THROUGH PRISON MINISTRIES. OTHERS WERE WITNESSED TO, ONE ON ONE, BY ANOTHER BELIEVER.

SOME PEOPLE SIMPLY WENT TO CHURCH. SOME PEOPLE RECEIVED THE WORD OF LIFE BEING MINISTERED, AT A FUNERAL. THE STREET EVANGELIST CAUGHT THE ATTENTION OF SOME. SOME PEOPLE FELL UNDER CONVICTION DURING SERVICES AT THE TENT MEETING.

SOME PEOPLE HAD ALREADY HEARD THE WORD YEARS AGO AS CHILDREN, THEY KNEW RIGHT FROM WRONG. THEY FINALLY MADE A DECISION TO TURN TO THE POWER OF JESUS CHRIST, WHOSE POWER IS GREATER THAN THE RIPPING TERRIBLE POWER OF SIN.

WHATEVER THE CASE AND HOWEVER YOU CAME TO CHRIST, THE FACT IS THAT YOU ARE NOW VICTORIOUSLY CHANGED! SAY IT LOUD! I'VE GOT THE VICTORY!

Grown-Up Troubles!

THE HEREAFTER EXPERIENCE, IS HOWEVER THE ULTIMATE PROMISE TO EVERY BELIEVER. IN ORDER TO LIVE IN TOTAL VICTORY, THEREAFTER, YOU MUST KNOW AND POSSESS TOTAL VICTORY HERE, RIGHT NOW. IT IS POSSIBLE!

To be victorious, is to be a conqueror and an overcomer. Before anything could ever be overcome, one would have had to overcome the powerful struggle within themselves.

Self, is the number one enemy, whether people will admit this or not! While many people came to the Lord to be saved, the truth is that they never actually released themselves and all of the damage that only self can in fact do.

Many had adult experiences, in which they never thought they would come out of. Far too many people, entertain the wild notion of knowing freedom from the very bondage of sin and self, only after death has rent the soul from the body. They actually believe that they will never be free from bondage, in this life.

Many have overcome stress, strain and worry. Anxiety has been a tough hurdle for many who are truly born again and in a hurry to get busy for the Lord.

Upon the discovery of the benefits of salvation, they found the strength through Christ Jesus, to finally let go of the terror of their past.

After searching extensively for the base root cause of their problems, they finally came to realize that they needed to forgive themselves, as well as others and be delivered.

Many had to overcome the stubborn willingness to hold on to very deep seated, low down and envious grudges against others, that had remained hidden within their hearts for many years.

Adults, usually have the terrible problem of resistance, as it relates to submitting to authority. Once a person realizes, that they have reached the legal age of accountability, according to the law everywhere, they know that they have now reached

ADULTHOOD!

SOMEBODY IS, AND WILL ALWAYS BE GIVING YOU INSTRUCTIONS EVERYWHERE YOU GO IN ONE WAY OR ANOTHER, THAT YOU MUST SUBMIT TO, IN RESPECT OF PROPER AUTHORITY. THROUGH CHRIST, MANY PEOPLE OF WHICH WERE OF A REBELLIOUS NATURE, HAVE LEARNED TO FOLLOW AND TO OBEY LEADERSHIP.

QUITE A NUMBER OF PEOPLE HAVE BEEN FREED FROM OTHER'S OPINIONS, LIKES, DISLIKES, FAILURES, FRAILTIES, INCONSISTENCIES, WRATH, ENVY, STRIFE, LYING, CHEATING, EVEN OTHER PEOPLE'S PERSPECTIVES ABOUT GOD, JESUS, AND THE HOLY GHOST. THEY HAVE ACTUALLY EVEN OVERCOME BEING FEARFUL AND FAITHLESS, IN THE EXPRESSION OF THEIR WALK WITH THE LORD.

I HAVE MET SCORES OF PEOPLE, WHO HAVE BEEN DELIVERED FROM THE VERY INFLUENTIAL, BUT, VERY DANGEROUSLY GRIPPING HOLD OF OTHER RELIGIOUS PEOPLE.

MANY PEOPLE ARE NOW DELIVERED FROM WHAT WOULD BE REFERRED TO AS, "<u>MAN</u>-<u>MADE</u>" RELIGION. THEY BELIEVE THAT THEY WERE NO LONGER JUST RELIGIOUSLY REPETITIVE, WHILE THEY ATTEND CHURCH SERVICES WHENEVER THEY ARE SUPPOSED TO, THEY JUST DO NOT MIX WITH OTHER DENOMINATIONAL PERSUASIONS OR CONGREGATIONS, BECAUSE THEY ONLY BELIEVE IN THEIR OWN PASTOR AND MEMBERSHIP BODY. BUT GUESS WHAT,

THAT'S <u>BEING RELIGIOU</u>S TOO!

BUT OF COURSE, THIS IS ONLY A TIP OF ALL THE ISSUES THAT MAKE RELIGION AS DESTRUCTIVE TO THE BODY OF CHRIST AS IT IS. RELIGION GOES MUCH DEEPER THAN WHATEVER I HAVE PURPOSEFULLY MENTIONED. IN MANY INSTANCES, RELIGION IS A FAMILY PRACTICE THAT HAS BEEN IN PLACE FOR A CENTURY OR BETTER. THE NEED TO OVERCOME RELIGION, WOULD BE FOR THE FACT OF NOT BEING ABLE TO INTIMATELY KNOW CHRIST, FOR THE RELIGIOUS, RITUALISTIC PRACTICES, AND CERTAIN CHURCH CUSTOMS IN THE FAMILY.

Christ's truest essence, has a need to transcend the customary practical walls of religion. The purest form of religion, is yet not as powerful or even as authentic, as the lowest level of salvation! Religion will show you the visible church and it practices, however, salvation on the other hand will show you Christ and the finished work of the cross of Calvary.

You need to know the resurrection power of God, by which Christ Jesus was raised from the dead! Victory is in Jesus!

Many people, have overcome being divorced, after being married for only a short time and in some cases the marriages had lasted for a number of years. Death of a spouse; has been the devastation for those who had wrapped their entire world's existence into that spouse.

Many overcame loneliness, desiring the companionship of a significant individual; as Jesus fills the emptiness. Many have stepped out of being discouraged, into encouragement. Had it not been for the Lord , they never would have been able to continue on in life, without their loved one.

Some people have overcome on the spot job terminations, which actually effected the continuation of their career.

 Many have overcome multiple sicknesses, and terminal diseases, which was supposed to have been absolutely no cure, however they got up off of their sick beds, by the grace of God.

Heart attacks, strokes, aneurysms, diabetes, high and low blood pressure, of which were all possibly deadly by a very high percentage, but the victorious victims were able to walk away alive, glory to God!

Many people have overcome the real bondage

OF POVERTY AND BEING DOWNRIGHT POOR, TO THE POINT THAT THEY SOMETIMES DID NOT EVEN HAVE A PLACE TO LIVE. THEIR BANK ACCOUNTS WERE ALL BOTTOMED OUT, AFTER A PERIOD OF BEING JOBLESS AND WITHOUT ANY TYPE OF AN INCOME AT ALL, LEAVING THEM UNABLE TO PAY UTILITIES. THERE WAS NO FOOD IN THE HOUSE AND NOWHERE TO GET ANY MONEY TO BUY FOOD.

Where Did You Come From??

FOR CERTAIN, MANY PEOPLE LITERALLY CAME TO THE LIGHT, THAT WERE ON THE DARKER SIDE OF LIFE. COMING UP FROM THE UNDERGROUND RANKS OF SPIRITUALISM. THEY WERE UNDER THE SPIRITUAL BONDAGE TO THAT OF WITCHCRAFT, WIZARDRY, SORCERY, BLACK MAGIC, VOODOO, DEMONOLOGY AND SATANISM.

MANY PEOPLE HAD BEEN INDUCTED AND INTRODUCED TO SUCH SPIRITUAL DEGRADATION, AT VERY INNOCENTLY YOUNG TENDER AGES AS CHILDREN AND HAD EVEN BECOME WELL VERSED PRACTITIONERS OF THESE EVIL WORKS OF DARKNESS BY THE TIME THEY HAD REACHED THEIR TEENS. HOWEVER AS AN ADULT, THEY WERE ABLE TO EXERCISE A STRONGER WILL TO RENOUNCE ALL OF THE DEMONIC INFLUENCES OF THEIR UPBRINGING.

MANY HACE COME ON OVER TO THE LORD'S SIDE, TO WALK IN THE HIGH CALLING OF GOD, BEING SERIOUSLY ANOINTED. NOW, ANYONE WHO SEES THEIR OWN REFLECTION IN WHAT YOU MAY HAVE READ, SHOULD DEFINITELY BE PROUD AND NOT ASHAMED. THE DEVIL DIDN'T LET YOU HAVE THE VICTORY IN JESUS, GOD DELIVERED YOU FROM THE DARK POWERS OF THE UNDERWORLD!

YOU'VE GOT TO DECLARE YOUR VICTORY IN THE DEVIL'S FACE. DON'T WAIT UNTIL YOU FEEL THAT THE DEVIL IS OUT OF SIGHT AND MAYBE TOO FAR AWAY TO CAUSE YOU ANY HARM, GO AHEAD, DECLARE YOUR VICTORY AND PRAISE THE NAME OF THE LORD. THE LORD DELIVERED YOU IN THE DEVIL'S PRESENCE!

Whenever you begin to praise the Lord, the devil will back out from your immediate presence, taking his hands off of your possessions, allowing you to realize, that you *can* lose sight of the devil's presence on purpose.

Make The Devil Mad!!!

If you really love Jesus Christ, the devil is already mad at you, for that matter alone. If you ever really make the devil mad, you have made the Lord glad.

It may be that you have witnessed the fierce evil attacks of Satan's wrath, upon those individuals, who leave his utter darkness and anger him, by turning to the Lord;

All you need to do, to paralyze the devil, is shout the victory, like you intend to keep the victory that you now have. Every time the devil tells you that you do not have the victory, don't argue with the devil, just go ahead, shout the victory anyway. Leap for joy. Clap your hands. Then out of your own mouth, "Say it loud! I've got the victory!"

You are proud because Jesus is the light! The light has power over the darkness. Whenever the light comes on or comes in, darkness from every angle has to flee.

> *In him was life; and the life was the light of men. And the light shineth in darkness; and the darkness comprehended it not.*
>
> St. John 1:4-5

Listen, there is no debate over the incomprehensible powerlessness of the darkness, underneath the power of the light of the Lord.

How could there be any resistance, when darkness does not even know what the argument is about or even understand where to begin or what

THE TOTAL OUTCOME WILL BE, BECAUSE IT DIDN'T KNOW WHAT TO EXPECT AS A RESULT OF THE ARGUMENT?

WHY WOULD YOU ENGAGE IN AN ARGUMENT, FOR NO REASON AT ALL? THERE'S AN INSURMOUNTABLE MEASUREMENT OF STRESS ADDED TO AN INDIVIDUAL, WHENEVER THERE IS EVEN A LEGITIMATELY REASONABLE PURPOSE FOR AN ARGUMENT.

SO I WOULD SUGGEST THAT YOU WOULD REFRAIN FROM WASTING PRECIOUS VALUABLE TIME, OVER A WORTHLESS ARGUMENT THAT WILL NOT BE BENEFICIAL TO EITHER PARTY INVOLVED!

Here's How It All Went Down!

THE LIGHT, SO AWESOME AND POWERFUL, IS AN ELEMENT AND THE SOURCE OF THE HEAT PRODUCTION IN ITSELF.

THE DARKNESS IS A LOITERING PLACE FOR COLD TEMPERATURES, EVEN DOWN TO FREEZING. IN THE WINTER MONTHS THE LATER IT GETS IN THE EVENING, THE DARKER THE NIGHT FALLS, THE TEMPERATURES DROP EVEN LOWER.

THE MICROWAVE LIKE, POWERFUL ABILITY OF THE LIGHT, WAS THEN AND STILL IS TO THIS DAY, JUST TOO MUCH FOR THE DARKNESS TO CONTEND WITH.

DARKNESS WOULD HAVE STRUCK A BLOW IN REJECTION AND IN RETALIATION, TO BEING OVERTAKEN OF THE LIGHT, HAD IT BEEN ABLE TO DEFINE THE POWERFUL PURPOSE AND DEFYING AGENDA OF THE LIGHT, LEAPING FROM IT'S ORIGIN, TO IT'S DESTINY IN AN IMMEASURABLE RATE OF SPEED.

COMMANDING THE DARKNESS TO MOVE, THE LIGHT MOVED FROM IT'S ORIGINAL PURPOSE, TO ITS EXPECTED FULFILLMENT, SO INSTANTANEOUSLY THAT THE DARKNESS BLACKED-OUT AND RELINQUISHED ITS STAND, HAVEN BEEN DOMINANT FOR AN UNKNOWN PERIOD OF TIME, WHICH DID NOT MATTER TO THE LIGHT.

DARKNESS WAS HIT ON EVERY SIDE, SO QUICKLY, THAT IT HAD NO TIME TO RESIST, FIGHT BACK, TAKE A STAND OR EVEN DO NOTHING AT ALL. ALL OF A SUDDEN, DARKNESS WAS ABSOLUTELY WIPED OUT AND IT IS STILL THAT WAY TO-DAY. LITERALLY, FIGURATIVELY, MENTALLY, SPIRITUALLY, SOCIALLY AND HABITUALLY, WHENEVER THE LIGHT COMES IN, DARKNESS CAN NOT STAND. DARKNESS IS POWERFUL, FOR ONLY AS LONG AS YOU ALLOW IT OR UNTIL THE LIGHT MOVES IN.

Light Is Just Like God

HAVE YOU EVER HEARD THE STATEMENT, WHICH SAYS; "THAT, DONE IN THE DARK, WILL SOON COME TO THE LIGHT?"

SETUPS AND TRAPS ARE EXPOSED IN THE DEFENSE OF THE BELIEVERS, WHENEVER THE CULPRIT OF THE TRAPS AND SETUPS ARE TAKEN OF THE VICES THEMSELVES. THERE IS NO QUESTION WHO HAS TRULY BEEN EXPOSED AND THAT THE TRUTH HAS FINALLY SURFACED FROM BENEATH THE BLANKET OF DECEPTION, THAT COVERED IT BY LIES.

AS SOON AS THE LIGHT OF THE TRUTH HAS BEEN SHED UPON THE HEARING EARS, THAT HAVE ALREADY HEARD THE UNTRUTH, THE LIES AND RUMORS THAT ARE GOING AROUND, *are* NULLIFIED.

WHENEVER THE LIGHT IS TURNED ON, SPIDERS, COCKROACHES, RATS, RODENTS, SNAKES, BUGS AND ALL OF THE SORTS, RUN FOR THE COVER OF ANOTHER DARK PLACE TO HIDE.

THEY RUN FOR CRACKS, DITCHES, HOLES, PITS, ETC. THEY SEEK TO HIDE UNDERNEATH A ROCK, A PLANK OR WHATEVER IS AVAILABLE. THEY SEEK A REFUGE AWAY FROM THE LIGHT, TO A COLD DARK PLACE. WE HAVE VICTORY OVER THESE CREEPY, CRAWLING, CREATURES OF THE DARK, THROUGH THE LIGHT! EVEN THE *two legged dwellers of the dark*, CAN'T HIDE EITHER!

THERE ARE MANY PEOPLE WHO WILL SAY; "I AM WALK-

ING IN THE LIGHT"; HOWEVER, THEY LIKE TO PLAY IN THE COLD DARK PLACES OF LIFE, AWAY FROM ANY TRACE OF THE LIGHT, OF THE LORD! SERIOUSLY DABBLING WITH ALL SORTS OF LOW-DOWN THINGS, OF THE DARK. CHILDREN OF THE LIGHT, AT ALL COST, SHOULD NOT PLAY IN THE DARK. SOMETIMES IT IS VIEWED AS A HARMLESS GESTURE OR JUST AN EXPERIMENTAL OR RECREATIONAL THING TO DO.

WHATEVER THE CASE, THE INHABITANTS OF THE DARK, WHO INTEND TO BE TOTALLY OUT OF THE PRESENCE OF ANY LIGHT, ARE THERE.

IT IS NEVER THE INTENTIONAL PRACTICE FOR DARK DWELLERS THEMSELVES TO BE EXPOSED TO THE LIGHT. BUT, WHILE THEY WERE MOVING FROM ONE DARK PLACE OR SITUATION, TO ANOTHER, THEY HAD TO PASS THROUGH THE LIGHT. THEIR EXPOSURE WAS ACTUALLY NO ACCIDENT TO THOSE PERSONS OF WHOM THEY WERE EXPOSED.

THE INHABITANTS OF THE DARKNESS, ARE DEADLY, BOTH NATURALLY AND SPIRITUALLY, BOTH TEMPORALLY AND ETERNALLY. SO PLEASE, AS YOU ARE WALKING IN THE VICTORIOUS LIGHT OF THE LORD, STAY IN THE PRESENCE OF THE LORD AND CONTINUE TO WALK IN THE LIGHT!

GOD SHINNED THE POWER OF THE GLORIOUS LIGHT AND EXPOSED THE DARKNESS AND THEN TOLD US EXACTLY WHAT IT WAS THAT WE WERE LOOKING AT AND CALLED IT BY IT'S NAME, *"Darkness."* BUT, YOU MUST REMEMBER THAT THE DARKNESS COMPREHENDED NOT, THE LIGHT OF THE LORD. THEREFORE THE DARKNESS WAS DISORIENTED AND DISPELLED, AND WITHOUT ANY HESITATION, THE DARKNESS DISSIPATED.

TO SAY IT BEST, IN A WAY THAT YOU WOULD ALWAYS REMEMBER, THE DARKNESS ALWAYS MOVES, AT THE WILL OF THE LIGHT. WHENEVER LIGHT COMMANDS, THE DARKNESS OBEYS. HAVING YIELDED YOURSELF TO THE AWESOME OMNIPOTENT POWER OF THE LIGHT, THE MASTER OF THE DARKNESS, HAS BEEN RENDERED POWERLESS AGAINST YOU, SO WALK OUT INTO FREEDOM WITH AN ATTITUDE OF GRATITUDE!

Stop Fooling Yourself!!

It is contrary to being victorious, to move from a dark place, to only continue desperately longing for the places of which you may have just left, lingering around in the darkness of your own thinking.

You can't live and walk in the light, but think in the darkness of sinful idealism all of the time, professing to being victoriously changed. Since your mind has got to change, such a description should be the exact case scenario to inform that you really did not come out of the darkness at all!

The attitude and spirit of your demeanor, may suggest to others that you have possibly given up on the power of the light, or developed a sense of rejection to the light!

No matter where you go or however you walk, in terms of your posture, you are still walking in darkness. Come on, into the light, heart first, with your head up and see your ways amended.

> *And this is the condemnation, that light is come into the world, and men loved darkness rather than light, because their deeds were evil. For every one that doeth evil hateth the light, neither cometh to the light, lest his deeds should be reproved. But he that doeth truth cometh to the light, that his deeds may be made manifest, that they are wrought in God.*
>
> St. John 3:19-21

Jesus has illuminated the pathways of your life. Being the power source, He has made you and myself alike, the reflecting factors of that same glorious light.

Now, you and I will be the only light sometimes that other men and women of the darkness will ever see. Shinning, is what lights are supposed

TO DO. ACCORDING TO THE SCRIPTURE, THE LIGHT IS SHOWN THROUGH OUR DEEDS.

Let your light so shine before men, that they may see your good works, and glorify your father which is in heaven. ST. MATTHEW 5:16

OUR VERY LIVES, SHOULD BECOME MIRROR IMAGES OF THE FATHERS LIGHT, WITHIN OUR SOULS. GENERALLY, THE LIGHT OF THE LORD CAN BE SEEN IN THE EYES OF THE TRUE BORN-AGAIN-BELIEVERS, EVERYWHERE. THE TERRIBLE SCARS OF YOUR PAST, DOES NOT EVEN MATTER, BECAUSE THE LORD WILL TURN YOUR "*scars* INTO *stars*" AND YOUR "*story* INTO *glory!*"

PEOPLE WILL OFTEN ACT, AS IF THEY DON'T SEE OR RATHER AS IF THEY CAN'T SEE THE LIGHT INSIDE OF YOU, BUT IN REALITY THEY SEE THE LIGHT! LIGHT, IS SO POWERFUL, THAT MANY VISUALLY IMPAIRED PEOPLE, CAN DISCERN FLASHES AND SPARKLES OF THE LIGHT. SO, DON'T QUESTION WITHIN YOUR OWNSELF, WHETHER OR NOT OTHERS SEE YOUR LIGHT; IF INDEED THE LIGHT OF THE LORD IS TRULY SHINNING THROUGH YOU.

GOD HAS PREORDAINED, THAT MEN EVERYWHERE, WOULD SEE THE LIGHT OF THE LORD, BY THE FRUIT OF OUR DEEDS, THAT ARE A REFLECTION OF THE EXPRESSED IMAGE OF THE LOVE OF CHRIST.

Follow Instructions!

DON'T TAKE OTHERS FOR GRANTED, BECAUSE THEY TAKE YOU FOR GRANTED. STATE YOUR GODLY PRESENCE, IN THEIR PRESENCE. THE LIGHT OF YOUR VICTORY, WILL PIERCE RIGHT THROUGH THE MOST OBSCURE DARKNESS, SHINNING BRIGHTLY THROUGH, TO LIGHT YOUR WAY. EVEN THROUGH DARKNESS SO BLACK THAT NOTHING OF ANY IMAGE CAN BE VISUALIZED.

DON'T EVEN THINK ABOUT GIVING A ROCK A CHANCE TO TAKE YOUR PLACE IN GIVING GOD THE PRAISE. SINCE THE VICTORY HAS BEEN ESTABLISHED IN YOUR LIFE, WALK

VICTORIOUSLY. TALK VICTORY. SHOUT, BECAUSE OF VICTORY, DANCE, AND RUN FOR THE VICTORY AND LEAP FOR JOY BY ALL MEANS! GET EXCITED!!

VICTORY IS VICTORY AND IT IS IRREVERSIBLE. DO NOT ALLOW THE MEMORY OF THE VICTORY, YOU POSSESS, TO SLIP AWAY FROM YOUR MEMORY. HOLD ON TIGHT TO YOUR VICTORY. TELL IT EVERYWHERE YOU GO.

VICTORY IS NOT MEANT TO BE A PEAK EXPERIENCE, ONLY MOMENTARILY. NEITHER, IS IT MEANT TO BE A TEMPORARY STATE OF EXISTENCE. HOWEVER, WHATEVER THE STATE, TO WHICH YOU HAVE BEEN MADE VICTORIOUS, VICTORY SHOULD BE AN INDEFINITE STATE OF EXISTENCE. BY ALL MEANS, DON'T GIVE YOUR VICTORY AWAY.

I'M NOT MAKING REFERENCE TO VICTORY, AS THE WORLD KNOWS VICTORY, AS IN A BOXING MATCH OR A SPORTING EVENT.

OTHERS, MAY SEE VICTORY, ONLY IN THE LIGHT OF POLITICS, HAVING WON THE ELECTION. THE BIG PROBLEM IS OFTEN, THE TECHNICALITY OF THE WIN, WHICH ENABLES THE VICTORY TO BE SOMETIMES OVER TURNED. THIS IS A PITIFUL STATE OF VICTORY. WHO WANTS TO BE UNSURE ABOUT THE VICTORY THAT IS OBTAINED?

I WOULD NOT EVEN THINK ABOUT BEING UNSURE OR EVEN INSECURE ABOUT MY VICTORY. IN SOCIETY, YOU HAVE TO CONTINUE WINNING, HAVING VICTORIES FREE OF ANY CONTROVERSY, IN ORDER TO BE A REAL WINNER. HOWEVER, ON THE LORD'S SIDE, VICTORY WAS OBTAINED BY YOUR ACCEPTANCE OF THE DEATH, BURIAL, AND THE RESURRECTION OF CHRIST JESUS, AND THE VICTORIOUSLY FINISHED WORK OF "CALVARY."

THEREFORE, VICTORY IS NOT SOMETHING TO BE ACHIEVED OR WORKED FOR. THERE IS NO TASK OR PERFORMANCE TO BE RENDERED. THE MOST STRENUOUS EFFORT APPLIED IN BEING VICTORIOUS, IS BELIEVING AND RECEIVING! FEAR AND UNBELIEF, WILL NULLIFY THE POWER AND THE REALITY OF YOUR VICTORY. WALK IN THE VIC-

TORY, AND DON'T EVER BE ASHAMED!

It's Desirable!

GOD HAS SO DESIGNED, THAT GREAT ADMIRATION, BE ATTACHED TO YOUR VICTORY. OTHERS WANT IT, BUT DON'T ALWAYS KNOW HOW TO OBTAIN THE VICTORY, THAT THEY SEEM TO SO DESPERATELY DESIRE. BEING THE REPRESENTATIVE AMBASSADORS THAT WE ARE FOR THE LORD, WE ARE TO DIRECT THEM TO THE SOURCE AND THE LIFELINE OF THE VICTORY WE POSSESS, WHICH IS CHRIST.

DO YOU REMEMBER HOW GOD GAVE DAVID THE VICTORY IN SECRET OVER A FEROCIOUS LION AND A VISCOUS BEAR, TO DELIVER ONE OF THE SHEEP, DAVID SLEW THEM BOTH.

DAVID SHARED HIS VICTORIES WITH PEOPLE WHO REALLY MATTERED MOST. DAVID'S PREVIOUSLY PAST VICTORIES WERE OF GREAT MEANINGFUL RELEVANCE IN ESSENCE TO THE PRESENT TASK, WHICH WAS SET BEFORE OF HIM.

WITHOUT THOSE VICTORIES, KING SAUL WOULD NOT HAVE OBTAINED CONFIDENCE IN THE SHEPHERD BOY. DAVID SLEW THE PHILISTINE GIANT, NAMED GOLIATH. IT SEEMED IMPOSSIBLE; HOWEVER, THROUGH EARLIER VICTORIES, DAVID WAS PREPARED FOR THIS UNUSUALLY, VICTORIOUS ACCOMPLISHMENT.

THE PEOPLE OF ISRAEL CHANTED OF DAVID'S VICTORY IN THE STREETS, OF THE CITY. ALL OF THE BATTLES, TO WHICH GOD HAS BROUGHT YOU THROUGH, ARE SETUPS FOR GREATER VICTORIES, THAT WILL ESTABLISH YOU TO THOSE PEOPLE WHO KNOW YOU BEST. THROUGH YOUR VICTORY, PEOPLE WILL GIVE YOU THE RESPECT THAT IS DUE YOU. VICTORY WILL OPEN THE DOOR TO GREAT REWARDS. OH! YES!

YOU DO WANT VICTORY!

THE LORD WILL CAUSE GREAT MEN TO RECOGNIZE YOUR SUCCESS. BUT, NOT ONLY THEM, THERE ARE PEOPLE OF ALL WALKS OF LIFE, WHO NEED TO SET THEIR FOCUS ON

THE VICTORY OF YOUR SUCCESSFUL LIFE. WHENEVER WE DECLARE THE VICTORY, WE ARE SAYING; "OH!, TASTE AND SEE THAT THE LORD IS GOOD!

OH! GIVE THANKS UNTO THE LORD FOR HE IS GOOD! AND HIS MERCY ENDURES FOREVER!!"

YOU SHOULD BE PROUD TO TELL SOMEONE; "THANK GOD! I MADE IT!!!

THEY SAID, I WOULDN'T MAKE IT. BUT, I MADE IT. THEY SAID, I WOULDN'T SURVIVE THE STORM, BUT I MADE IT. THEY SAID, I'D NEVER BE ANYTHING, BUT, LOOK AT ME NOW!!

I'VE KNOWN ABASEMENT, NOW I AM EXALTED OF THE LORD. HE HAS LIFTED ME. VICTORY IS WONDERFUL! I'M BEING HOISTED TO A NEW HEIGHT IN THE LORD.

"I'm a winner!!!"

16

Word up

Joyful Noise Worship*

> *O come, let us sing unto the Lord: let us make a joyful noise to the rock of our salvation. Let us come before his presence with thanksgiving, and make a joyful noise unto him with Psalms*
>
> PSALMS #94:1-2
>
> *Make a joyful noise unto the Lord, all ye lands. Serve the Lord with gladness: come before his presence with singing*
>
> PSALMS #100:1-2

Mentioning Verbally, Motioning Physically*

IMAGINE A SPORTING EVENT IN A LARGE STADIUM OR IN AN AUDITORIUM WHERE MULTIPLES OF CONVERSATIONS ARE GOING ON, PEOPLE ARE TALKING EVERYWHERE, BUT YOU ARE UNABLE TO CLEARLY UNDERSTAND OR TO MAKE SENSE OF NOT EVEN JUST ONE OF THE CONVERSATIONS GOING ON BECAUSE THE NOISE FACTOR WAS SO HIGH?

WHEN PEOPLE BEGIN TO TALK, IF THE NOISE FACTOR IS ALREADY HIGH THEY FEEL IT NECESSARY TO RAISE THE VOLUMES OF THEIR OWN SPEECH IN EFFORT TO BE HEARD SPEAKING, THEY BELIEVE?

THERE MAY HAVE BEEN MULTIPLES OF LEGITIMATELY NECESSARY CONVERSATIONS GOING ON, HOWEVER DUE TO

THE VAST NUMBER OF TALKERS, IT SOUNDED AS IF IT WERE ONLY A GIGANTIC MASS OF CONFUSED NOISE!

WE COULD SEE LIPS MOVING, HEADS NODDING, HANDS GESTURING, AND BODIES IN MOTION, BUT THE NUMBER OF PEOPLE CONTRIBUTING TO THE NOISE FACTOR IS SO HIGH THAT ALL WE GET FROM THE CROWD IS CONFUSION.

NO NONSENSE NOISE IS WHAT WE GET FROM SUCH A HUGE CONGLOMERATE OF TALKING MOUTHS. SOUND SPEWED OUT INTO EVERY DIRECTION WITH NO MEANINGFUL POINT OF DIRECTION, IS DEFINITELY NERVE RACKING!

CONFUSION IS CREATED WHENEVER EVERYBODY FEELS THAT THEY HAVE TO TALK AT THE SAME TIME. NOT EVEN TWO PEOPLE CAN SUCCESSFULLY TALK AT THE SAME TIME.

SINGING TOGETHER WORKS, ONLY IF WE ALL SING THE SAME SONG IN THE SAME KEY! ELSE, AGAIN WE ONLY CREATE UNNECESSARY NOISE! IF TWO OR THREE PEOPLE STARTED OUT AT THE VERY SAME TIME SINGING A COMPLETE STANZA OF TOTALLY DIFFERENT SONGS; THERE WOULD BE NERVE RACKING NOISE CREATED, EVEN IF THEY WERE ALL IN THE SAME KEY?

UNITY AS WELL AS CLARITY AND EXACT LANGUAGE AND SPEECH, OR DICTION AND LYRICS IF YOU PREFER, IS EXTREMELY IMPORTANT WHENEVER A GROUP OF PEOPLE ENDEAVOR TO SING A SONG TOGETHER.

YOU COULD ACTUALLY HAVE THE RIGHT TUNE OR TONE, APPLIED TO THE WRONG DICTION AND STILL BE OUT OF TUNE, FOR FAILURE TO SAY EXACTLY WHAT YOU ARE SINGING. THERE IS SO MANY DIVERSE FACTORS THAT CREATE A SENSE OF UNNECESSARY NOISE.

THE DIFFERENT GENERATIONS OF NOISE TONES THAT ARE HELPFUL TO OUR LIVES DAILY ARE INNUMERABLE. IT IS NECESSARY THAT NO TWO NOISE FACTORS ARE TO BE EXACTLY ALIKE WHICH HELPS TO CREATE AN EVEN LESSER POSSIBILITY OF CONFUSION.

Make The Right Noise!

Noise is never to be misplaced as it has been, often times. Noise is a response to a particular happening, an event or a certain circumstance. In other words noise should always be made for a reason, or for a specific purpose.

The noise of the crowd in attendance for a musical or a stage play, will make a statement, pertaining to whether or not they are favorably entertained with what is taking place.

Just imagine the extreme boredom of a sporting event, if the crowd made absolutely no noise, at all! You could only imagine the small number of people upon leaving the sporting event, that would say that they had indeed been favorably amused. Spectators make noise to show their involved interest during those events.

Have you ever observed the noise of the crowd, whenever one of the officials in charge, makes a bad call during a sporting event? Most everyone other than them self, thought that it was a bad call.

How about that boxing match, whereas, your favorite boxer is showing themselves most confident and very strong and it even looks as if they may win the fight. There is much excitement both in the boxing arena and in the living rooms, of the many people watching.

There are many levels of excitement, because of the many different types of people to excite. It really does not require much effort to excite most people.

What excites one individual does not necessarily move the next person or even most everyone. For some people, it would almost take a nuclear

EXPLOSION TO AROUSE THEM (FIGURATIVELY SPEAKING); THEY JUST SIMPLY ARE NOT GOING TO BE MOVED WITH MUCH EXCITEMENT.

OTHERS, WHO HAVE BECOME NEGATIVELY AFFIXED OVER A PERIOD OF TIME AS A RESULT OF BITTER EXPERIENCES, HAVE BECOME EMOTIONALLY DESENSITIZED, BEING FILLED WITH STUBBORNNESS AND REBELLION, THEY ARE UNABLE TO DISPLAY ANY MOVEMENT OF EXCITEMENT.

AS A RULE, THE SONG OF THE LIVES OF SOME PEOPLE OUGHT TO BE; "I SHALL NOT, BE MOVED!"

FEW PEOPLE ACTUALLY LIVE EVENLY, ON A TEMPERAMENT THAT CONTROLS WHAT AROUSES THEM AND WHATEVER IT TAKES TO ACTUALLY DEPRESS THEM. THEY OBSERVE EXCITEMENT AT THE RIGHT TIMES AND NEVER SEEM TO DISPLACE EXCITEMENT AT THE WRONG SETTINGS.

THE ONLY PROBLEM WITH THESE INDIVIDUALS, IS THAT THEY MAY BE TOO EVENLY TEMPERATE, MISSING THE POINT AND TIME OF WHEN OR WHEN NOT TO BE EXCITED. WHEN EVERYONE SHOULD HAVE BEEN EXCITED, THEY SEEM TO HAVE BEEN ON ANOTHER PLANET SOMEWHERE, THEY MISSED THE PUNCH-LINE!

On The Funny Side!

SOME INDIVIDUALS ALWAYS DO THINGS THAT ENABLE THEMSELVES AND OTHERS AS WELL, TO GET A LAUGH. THEY ARE ALWAYS LOOKING FOR THE PARTY. THEY NEVER SETTLE FOR ANYTHING OTHER THAN REAL FUN. THEY ARE GENUINELY FUN LOVING, TO MOST PEOPLE THEY ARE CONSIDERED TO BE JOKERS AND TRICKSTERS, ALIKE JACOB WHOSE NAME MEANT *supplanter* OR *trickster*.

THEY HAVE NO PROBLEM WITH NOISE, AT ALL, DUE TO THE FACT THAT THEY ARE USUALLY LOUD AND NOISY!

SOME PEOPLE SAY THAT THEY CAN'T STAND TO BE IN THE COMPANY OF CHILDREN, BECAUSE CHILDREN ARE TOO NOISY. THE NOISE OF A CHILD IS NECESSARY BEGINNING AT THE STAGES OF INFANCY, UP UNTO ADOLESCENCE, AND

EVEN ON THROUGHOUT THEIR TEENAGE YEARS. GENERALLY, WHENEVER A CHILD IS TOO QUIET, SOME FORM OF UNDERDEVELOPMENT HAS TAKEN PLACE ON THE INSIDE.

MOST RATIONALLY THINKING MATURE INDIVIDUALS EMBRACE THE JOY AND LAUGHTER OF A CHILD. I ENJOY SEEING HAPPY CHILDREN APPEAR TO BE HAVING A GOOD CHILDHOOD. ONLY PEOPLE THAT HAVE FORGOTTEN THAT THEY WERE ONCE A CHILD, OR PEOPLE THAT HAD A WRECKED CHILDHOOD CAN'T APPRECIATE THE JOYFUL LAUGHTER OF CHILDREN.

PERHAPS YOUR CHILDHOOD WAS NOT AS EXCITING AS YOU WOULD LIKE FOR IT TO HAVE BEEN? BUT DON'T ROB OTHER CHILDREN, BY NOT ALLOWING THEM TO EXPRESS THEIR JOY, LET THEM MAKE NOISE! IT WILL BE NECESSARY, IN THEIR FUTURE, AS RATIONAL THINKING ADULTS. YOUR PLACE, AS THE ADULT, IS TO LEAD AND TO GUIDE CHILDREN, INSTRUCTING THEM WHEN AND WHERE TO MAKE NOISE.

THE CHILDREN ARE THE CHURCH OF TODAY, IN TRAINING TO BE THE LEADERS OF THE CHURCH OF TOMORROW!! MY REAL FOCUS IS TO THE ATTENTION OF THE MORE MATURE INDIVIDUAL.

Silence; Don't Make A Move!

VOCAL NOISE, AND THE MOVEMENT OF NOISE MAKING INDIVIDUALS, IS DESPISED AND SUPPRESSED BY MANY AUTHORITATIVE FIGURES OF SOME CHURCHES BECAUSE IT SEEMS TO CAUSE THEM TO BECOME RATHER UNNERVED.

LOTS OF PEOPLE WOULD PREFER TO SEE THE PEOPLE OF THE CHURCH SHUT UP, SIT DOWN AND BE STILL. PEOPLE OUGHT TO PRAISE AND THANK GOD FOR ALL THAT HE HAS DONE FOR US, WE SHOULD GO FORTH IN THE DANCE BEFORE THE LORD! WE CAN'T AFFORD TO SIT DOWN AND SHUT UP IN THE CHURCH.

AS THE PASTOR OF THE CHURCH, YOU MAY READILY SAY THAT ALL OF THE ABOVE MENTIONED BEHAVIOR OF THE

PEOPLE, OF THE CHURCH, HAS TO BE CONTROLLED!!

BUT!!! IF YOU ARE TOO CONTROLLING, YOU MAY HAVE ALREADY NOTICED THAT PEOPLE ONLY GO FORTH AT YOUR WORD AND NOT AT THE WORD OF GOD OR AT THE COMMAND OF THE SPIRIT OF THE LORD, OR IN OTHER WORDS, THEY ONLY MOVE FOR YOU!

YOU MAY BE EXTREMELY OVERWHELMED WITH THE IDEA OF MOVING THE PEOPLE, BUT THAT'S NOT AS GOOD FOR YOU AS YOU THINK!

MOVEMENT MAKES A SOUND ALL BY ITSELF, SO LET THE LORD MOVE YOU AS WELL! THE SCRIPTURE INSTRUCTS US THAT BODILY EXERCISE PROFITS LITTLE, BUT WHILE IT MAY ONLY BE LITTLE BENEFIT TO THE SPIRITUAL WELFARE OF AN INDIVIDUAL, THERE IS YET A BENEFIT!

GAME OFFICIALS AND TELEVISION TALK SHOW HOST, DO NOT FORCE THE ISSUE OF QUIETNESS DURING THE TAPING OF THOSE SHOWS, AS MANY LEADERS OF THE LOCAL CHURCH BODIES, SOMETIMES DO. WHY WOULD ANYONE WANT TO CREATE SUCH A HUSH IN THE SPIRIT OF THE CHURCH?

IT IS FAR BEYOND MY UNDERSTANDING, CONCERNING THE SERIOUS DESIRE OF THE QUIETNESS THAT IS PREFERRED DURING THE WORSHIP SERVICE, ON A CONSISTENT BASIS. IN SOME CHURCH SETTINGS, AN USHER OR A DEACON {*bouncer*} MIGHT ESCORT AN INDIVIDUAL FROM THE SANCTUARY, OF THAT PARTICULAR WORSHIP SERVICE.

Pastor? Or Police?

PERHAPS YOU MIGHT SAY THAT YOUR PASTOR DOES NOT UNDERSTAND ALL OF THE NOISE AND THE EXCITEMENT. YOU'RE IN THE WRONG PLACE TO WORSHIP, IF YOU CAN'T FREELY GIVE GOD PRAISE AND GLORY. BECAUSE YOU AND I WE NEED THE PRACTISE; HEAVERN WON'T BE SILENT!

PEOPLE DON'T LIKE BEING ARRESTED WHEN THEY ARE GUILTY OF COMMITTING A SERIOUS CRIME, SO BY ALL MEANS DON'T ARREST THE PEOPLE OF THE CHURCH WHENEVER

THEY BEGIN TO GIVE GOD THE PRAISE.

PRAISING GOD IS NOT ABOUT YOUR BLOODLINE, FRIENDSHIP OR THE BUDDY SYSTEM. THE CHURCH YOU ARE PRESENTLY ATTENDING AT THIS TIME, IS NOT THE ONLY CHURCH IN THE WORLD! SOMETIMES YOU HAVE TO LITERALLY STAND ALONE AND GET OUT FROM AMONG THE FAMILIAR SURROUNDINGS IN ORDER TO GIVE GOD THE PRAISE.

YOU MIGHT FEEL AS IF YOUR RIGHTS HAVE BEEN TAKEN AWAY, BY WAY OF THE AUTHORITATIVE FIGURE IN CHARGE, WELL JUST REMEMBER THAT IF YOU KNOW YOUR RIGHTS, KEEP IN MIND ALL OF YOUR <u>REASONS</u> TO PRAISE THE LORD.

I WOULD NEVER STAY IN A PLACE WHERE I WAS FORBIDDEN TO PRAISE THE LORD AND COMMANDED TO KEEP SILENT, KNOWING THAT I HAD THE ABILITY TO MAKE A CONSCIENCE DECISION TO GO WHERE I COULD BE FREE TO GLORIFY THE LORD.

IT DOES NOT MAKE GOOD-GOD-SENSE TO DRIVE ALL THE WAY ACROSS TOWN, TO ATTEND A WORSHIP SERVICE AND NOT WORSHIP.

PRAISE AND WORSHIP MUST BE AN ACT OF CHOICE, YOUR OWN CHOICE AT YOUR OWN WILL. YOU SHOULD ALWAYS BE DETERMINED TO SAY LIKE DAVID; *"I <u>will</u> bless the Lord at all times!"*

WHENEVER YOUR MIND IS MADE UP, NOTHING CAN STOP YOU AND NOTHING WILL STOP YOU, FROM PRAISING THE LORD.

THE WORD OF GOD INSTRUCTS US TO DO EVERYTHING, DECENTLY AND IN ORDER; HOWEVER, I AM APPEALING TO THOSE THAT WILL NOT DO ANYTHING AT ALL! YOU HAVE NO MOTIVATION TO PRAISE THE LORD. NOTHING EVER MOVES YOU TO BE EXCITED ABOUT THE LORD.

LUCIFER, WAS THE CHIEF WORSHIPPER IN HEAVEN BEFORE THE THRONE OF GOD. IN HIS BODY WERE CONSTRUCTED INSTRUMENTS AND ORGANS. THEREFORE, WHENEVER HE MOVED, HE PLAYED A TUNE OR RATHER HE OF-

FERED WORSHIP. LUCIFER WAS A WALKING SYMPHONY ALL BY HIMSELF, TO WHICH WAS VERY PLEASURABLE AND WORSHIPFUL TO OUR GOD IN HEAVEN.

WHENEVER IT IS ULTIMATELY YOUR DESIRE THAT THE PEOPLE OF THE LORD KEEP SILENT AND BE STILL IN WORSHIP, PERHAPS IT IS THE SPIRIT OF SATAN, THAT YOU HAVE TAKEN UPON YOURSELF.

SATAN CAN NO LONGER MOVE HIMSELF TO THE PLEASURE OF THE LORD IN WORSHIP. SO NOW, IT IS ALSO SATAN'S DESIRE FOR PEOPLE NOT TO PLEASE THE LORD IN PRAISE AND WORSHIP, EITHER. SATAN HIMSELF, WOULD DEFINITELY LIKE TO SEE THE PEOPLE OF THE LORD, "SHUT UP AND SIT DOWN!"

Just Or Joyful ?

IF THERE IS A VOID IN THE NOISE OF THE WORSHIPFUL EXPRESSION, TO WHICH YOU ARE RESPONSIBLE, YOU SHOULD BE ADVISED OF THE ABSENCE OF THE JOY OF THE LORD!

NOISE, AND I DON'T MEAN *justified* NOISE, I MEAN PURPOSELESS NOISE, IS REALLY A WAIST OF EVERY BODY'S TIME. MANY PEOPLE OF THE CHURCH TODAY, ALLOW THEMSELVES TO BELIEVE THAT THEY ARE REALLY HAVING CHURCH, BECAUSE OF THE EXTREME NOISE FACTOR ALONE.

I BELIEVE THAT WE OUGHT TO MAKE SOME NOISE; BUT, I DON'T BELIEVE THAT IT OUGHT TO BE JUST NOISE ALONE. THE ENEMY KNOWS, WHENEVER THERE IS A REAL MEANING TO THE NOISE THAT IS COMING FROM THE CHURCH BECAUSE HE KNOWS THE SPIRIT OF THE LORD, FOR SURE!

WOULDN'T YOU BELIEVE THAT YOUR ENEMY KNEW, WHENEVER THE SPIRIT OF THE LORD, IS IN THE NOISE THAT IS COMING FROM YOU? WELL, HE DOES KNOW AND HE KNOWS EVEN MORE SO, WHENEVER THE PRESENCE OF GOD IS NOT THERE!

IT IS POSSIBLE TO MAKE, THE RIGHT NOISE, AT THE

WRONG TIME OR IN THE WRONG PLACE, AND FOR ALL THE WRONG REASONS, RENDERING THE NOISE OF THE CHURCH OF GOD, NULL AND VOID.

BEING OUT OF ORDER, RELATIVE TO THE POSITIONAL LINAGE OF AUTHORITY TO THE SET "ANGEL" IN THE HOUSE OF WORSHIP, WILL NULLIFY THE WORSHIP THAT IS SENT UP BEFORE THE LORD. MISGUIDED PURPOSES AND WRONG MOTIVATIONS, WILL KILL THE JOY OF YOUR JOYFUL NOISE AND REVOKE THE POWER OF YOUR VICTORIOUS EXPRESSION!

The Wrong Noise Is Serious Trouble!

THE ISRAELITES AND THE PHILISTINES, WOULD OFTEN ENGAGE INTO BATTLE ON OCCASIONS WITH EACH OTHER, AS WELL AS WITH MANY OTHER NATIONS AND TRIBES OF PEOPLE. THE NOISE CREATED BY THE ISRAELITES, ON THE BATTLEFIELD, SIGNIFIED THAT THE PRESENCE OF THE LORD WAS IN THE MIDST OF THE CAMP WITH THEM, OR WAS IT?

THE ISRAELITES TOOK IT UPON THEMSELVES TO FETCH THE ARC OF THE COVENANT OF GOD, TO WHICH THEY WERE TO NEVER HAVE HANDLED WITH THEIR OWN HANDS, THEY GOT OUT OF LINE WITH THE COVENANT OF GOD. THEY MADE A DECISION TO TAKE THE ARC OUT TO BATTLE, AGAINST THE PHILISTINES.

THE PRESSURE OF THE DEFEAT WAS UPON THE ISRAELITES AND THEY FELT THEY WOULD HELP THE LORD, BY HELPING THEMSELVES TO WHAT THEY FELT WOULD BETTER DETERMINE THE OUTCOME OF THE BATTLE. WELL, THE CHILDREN OF ISRAEL, WENT FORTH WITH THE SHOUT OF A GREAT NOISE.

And when the "Philistines" heard the noise of the shout, they said, what meaneth the noise of this great shout in the camp of the Hebrews? And they understood that the Ark of the Lord was come into the camp.   I SAMUEL 3:6

Never attempt to take the noise, which has been truly ordained of the Lord, to a place where the Lord has not ordained and provided for you to carry on such a factor, like to your job or to the hospital, the grocery store, and in many instances out in the midst of your neighborhood.

Though you have been ordained to take the ministry to the street, you need to use good wisdom in your manner of ministry. Besides, what is it that you believe that the Lord is using to save the people of your church surroundings; is it the noise of your church atmosphere, or is it the power of the word of God being delivered?

Your city ordinance will permit you to take the worshipful expression of your desired manner of praise and worship with all of the instruments and the noise of the shouts of the people who participate to certain places in the city.

Don't be a hard headed Israelite; and go out there on the street without the proper permission, of which respect and obedience to the laws of the land is also a part of being a true worshipper.

There are some things the Lord is not going to ordain for you to carry out. There is a reason that the Lord has anointed certain individuals to be in the forefront of the ministry, so get out of  the way if you are not that one ordained to be the leader.

The Philistines became rather suspicious of the noise being made in the camp of the Israelites. They wanted to know the validity and the purpose for the noise.

People of today are curious to know the purpose for the noise that we are making in the church! The Philistines decided to go over and to investigate the reason for the noise for themselves, while

MOST PEOPLE OF TODAY REMAIN CURIOUS.

THE ISRAELITES WERE IN BIG TROUBLE, WHENEVER THE SPIES FROM THE ENEMY'S CAMP CAME OVER TO INVESTIGATE THE NOISE AND DISCOVERED THAT IT WAS JUST NOISE ALONE, EMPTY LOUD NOISE!

YOU WILL LIKEWISE STAND A CHANCE OF BEING IN SERIOUS TROUBLE, WHENEVER THE ENEMY WILL COME CLOSER, TO SEE IF THE NOISE THAT YOU ARE MAKING HAS ANY REAL PURPOSE. BE REAL IN THE MIDST OF YOUR EXPRESSION. DON'T JUST KEEP UP RELIGIOUS NOISE BECAUSE YOU HAVE BEEN ALLOWED TO DO SO, WHENEVER THE PEOPLE COME IN FOR A CLOSER LOOK, THEY OUGHT TO FIND THE PRESENCE OF THE LORD.

> *And the Philistines were afraid, for they said, God is come into the camp. And they said, Woe unto us! For there hath not been such a thing heretofore . Woe unto us! Who shall deliver us out of the hand of these mighty Gods? These are the Gods that smote the Egyptians with all the plagues in the wilderness. Be strong, and quit yourselves like men, O ye Philistines, that ye be not servants unto the Hebrews, as they have been to you: quit yourselves like men, and fight. And the Philistines fought, And Israel was smitten, and they fled every man into his tent: and there was a very great slaughter; for there fell of Israel thirty thousand footman. And the ark of God was taken;*
> I SAMUEL 3:7-11

ISRAEL KNEW THAT THEY DID NOT HAVE THE COVENANT HAND OF BLESSING, BECAUSE THEY HAD NOT EVEN SOUGHT THE COUNCIL OF THE HIGH PRIEST OF GOD, TO RECEIVE THE BLESSING OF THE LORD.

THIS BIBLE ILLUSTRATION REVEALS, THAT THE ISRAELITES HAD THEIR ENEMY FOOLED AND EVEN FRIGHTENED FOR A WHILE. BUT, THEY HAD NOTHING TO SHOW FOR THE PURPOSE OF THE NOISE THEY HAD BEEN MAKING AND

 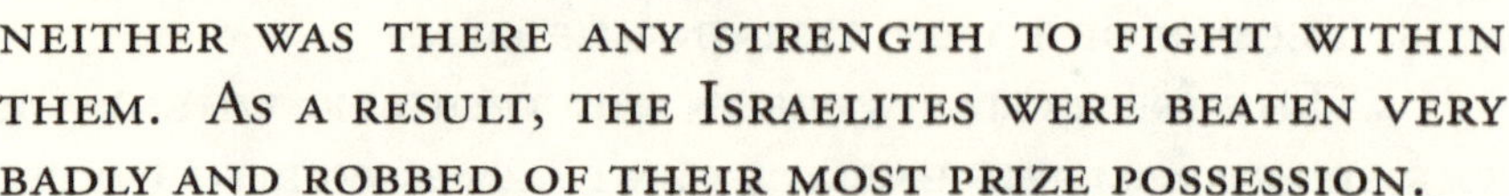

NEITHER WAS THERE ANY STRENGTH TO FIGHT WITHIN THEM. AS A RESULT, THE ISRAELITES WERE BEATEN VERY BADLY AND ROBBED OF THEIR MOST PRIZE POSSESSION.

ON THE OTHER HAND; JOSHUA AND THE ARMIES OF ISRAEL AND JUDAH, SHOUTED AT THE BATTLE OF JERICHO, AND THE WALLS CAME TUMBLING DOWN; SINKING INTO THE EARTH.

JEHOSHAPHAT SENT OUT THE ARMIES OF JUDAH FIRST, TO PRAISE THE LORD IN SONG, ON THE BATTLEFIELD, AND GOD SET AMBUSHMENTS AGAINST THE ENEMY, AND THEY TURNED ON EACH OTHER AND BEGAN TO KILL ONE ANOTHER UNTIL EVERY ONE OF THEM HAD BEEN SLAIN.

THE RIGHT NOISE PAID THE RIGHT PRICE THIS TIME, ON BOTH OCCASION.

Can You Afford Just Noise?

JUST NOISE, IS OFTEN VERY EXPENSIVE AND SOONER OR LATER THE BILL HAS GOT TO BE PAID! TO THE LIKES OF THE BOY WHO ALWAYS CRIED WOLF, BRINGING MUCH EX-CITEMENT TO THE PEOPLE OF THE VILLAGE, NOT REALIZ-ING THAT ONE DAY THE WOLF WOULD ACTUALLY COME AND AT THE EXPENSE OF HIS OWN PREVIOUS NOISY DECEPTION, NONE OF THE PEOPLE CAME TO SAVE HIM!

YOU WILL END UP PAYING AN UNINTENTIONALLY LARGE SUM FOR PRETENDING! THE ENEMY DISCOVERED THAT THE CHILDREN OF ISRAEL WERE ONLY FAKING THE VICTORY. DON'T EVER ALLOW YOURSELF TO BE CAUGHT FAKING THE VICTORY! IT IS NOT NECESSARY TO BE A FAKE!

NOT ONLY WERE THE ISRAELITE'S EXPOSED TO THEIR ENEMY AND HUMILIATED, THEY WERE ALSO MADE TO FES-TER IN THE MESS THAT THEY HAD JUST MADE, BECAUSE OF JUST NOISE.

THE ARK OF THE COVENANT OF GOD, HAD BEEN TAKEN BY THE PHILISTINES. IT IS ALWAYS A BAD THING, WHENEVER THE ENEMY WILL HAVE RUN OFF WITH YOUR STUFF!

To allow the Anointing to be tampered with or even tainted, because you are only making noise for no reason at all, is going to be your detriment.

Some people say in the worship service; "**Well let's just praise the Lord.**" However, all that seems to emanate from people is, just noise! My friend if you are going to praise Him, you must speak His name! You cannot praise Him and never direct your praise to Him, by never speaking His almighty name.

The Spirit In Your Music!

I have spent a great deal of my life in the choir, both in the church and in high school, in different community choirs, state choirs and national choirs. There is almost nothing more beautiful, than a well-trained choir that knows how to deliver the message of the songs they sing.

The right conviction, coupled with the anointing, will send the song right to the exact place, in the heart of every listener.

There are many vocalist who are really capable singers, the only problem is that there is absolutely no anointing in their singing!

After a while, their singing begins to sound like nothing more than noise. Whenever they sing, it has the tendacy to aggravate and even agitate the spirit, within a spirit filled individual.

Some musicians are not even close to being as skilled as they ought to be. They never play any beautiful melodies, being that they are so unskillful, all they are able to do is make noise!!

The unskillful musicians, will be allowed to express whatever it is they are to be able to drastically express musically upon the instrument. Whenever a skilled anointed musician would begin to play skillfully upon the instrument, they are asked to

347

STOP PLAYING IMMEDIATELY.

I HAVE QUESTIONED MYSELF, TO SEE IF I COULD FIGURE OUT WHETHER OR NOT SOME PEOPLE JUST SERIOUSLY PREFER TO ONLY HEAR, JUST NOISE! DEAD NOISE!

> *Sing onto him a new song; Play skillfully with a loud noise.* PSALMS #33:3

OTHER MUSICIANS THAT ARE EXTREMELY SKILLFUL TO PLAY UPON THE INSTRUMENTS, HAVE THE NERVE TO ALSO LACK THE ANOINTING, WHICH HINDERS THE ABILITY FOR THEIR MUSIC TO MINISTER IN THE EARS OF THE LISTENERS.

I KNOW VERY SKILLFUL MUSICIANS WHO ARE PROFESSIONAL AT ENTERTAINING AN AUDIENCE, WHO ARE RATHER STUMPED AT THE FACT THAT THEY CAN'T SEEM TO MOVE THE PEOPLE OF THE CHURCH, SO AS A RESULT THEY ARE LED TO BELIEVE THAT THE CHURCH DOESN'T PREFER THEIR SKILLFUL MANNER OF PLAYING DURING WORSHIP.

YOUR PROFESSIONAL SKILLS ALONG, DOES NOT CONSTITUTE THE FACT THAT YOUR MUSIC BELONGS IN THE WORSHIP SERVICE. WITHOUT THE ANOINTING, OR THE SPIRIT OF THE LORD IF YOU PREFER, YOUR MUSICAL EXPRESSION IS LIKEWISE A DEAD ISSUE AS IT RELATES TO WORSHIP. YOU NEED TO BE MINDFUL OF YOUR MUSICAL OFFERING TO THE LORD, TO NEVER OFFER A DEAD SOUND.

SATAN HIMSELF, MAY BE THE DRIVING FORCE BEHIND YOUR EMPTY MOTIVATIONS, WHENEVER YOU GO FORTH WITHOUT THE PRESENCE OF THE LORD.

Noisy Everywhere Else!

PERHAPS YOU ARE ONE OF THOSE PEOPLE WHO ALWAYS COMPLAIN THAT THE MUSIC IS <u>TOO LOUD</u>?

AS A RESULT, YOU'VE STOPPED BEING FAITHFUL TO ATTEND WORSHIP SERVICES LIKE YOU USE TO, BECAUSE NO ONE IS LISTENING TO YOU, CONCERNING THE VOLUME LEVELS IN THE CHURCH.

WHY IS IT THAT ONLY IN THE CHURCH, EVERYTHING IS ALWAYS TOO LOUD?

VERBALLY, PEOPLE ARE SO LOUD THEMSELVES, THAT THEIR LAUGHTER ALMOST APPEARS AS IF THEY COULD BLOW THE HAIR RIGHT OFF THE TOP OF YOUR HEAD (FIGURATIVELY SPEAKING).

PEOPLE MAKE NOISE, INTENTIONALLY AND ALSO UN-INTENTIONALLY, DURING WORSHIP. EITHER CASE SCENARIO, COULD BE AS DISASTROUS AS THE OTHER.

AS A RESULT OF FAILING TO BEHAVE THEMSELVES DURING WORSHIP, WHENEVER PEOPLE LEAVE THE CHURCH SANCTUARY, THEY DON'T KNOW THE PROPER CONDUCT THAT ALLOWS THEM TO BE SEPARATED FROM THE CONDUCTIVITY OF THE ACTUAL CONTRASTING SOCIETAL BEHAVIOR OF THE WORLD. YOUR IN-HOUSE CONDUCT, INSIDE OF THE CHURCH, IS ONE OF THE MORE POWERFUL GUIDING AIDS, TO HELP YOU CONDUCT YOURSELF ALONG YOUR WAY THROUGH YOUR LIFE DAILY.

CONDUCT, IN THE PROPER MANNER DURING WOR-SHIP, IS NOT AN ASSURANCE OF THE FACT THAT YOU WILL LEAD A GODLY LIFE.

HOWEVER, SUCH BEHAVIOR COULD HAVE THE POWER TO ESTABLISH A REASONABLE EXPLANATION, FOR WHICH YOU CONDUCT YOURSELF, IN A GODLY MANNER AT ALL TIMES, TO THEM THAT WILL ASK.

THERE WILL ALWAYS BE SOMEONE THAT WILL WANT TO HEAR YOUR REASONING, FOR THE MANNER OF WHICH YOU CARRY YOURSELF, IN YOUR DAILY WALK WITH THE LORD.

WHAT WOULD YOU TELL AN INDIVIDUAL WHO WILL ASK YOU, A REASON OF YOUR WALK WITH THE LORD, IF YOU ARE ALWAYS OUT OF CONTROL OR OUT OF SYNC WITH THE WORSHIP OF THE LORD?

WILL YOU ONLY BEGIN TO MAKE A LOT OF NOISE AND ACT AS IF YOU ARE VERY EXCITED ABOUT THE LORD, ONLY TO ALLOW THE ENEMY TO COME IN FOR A CLOSER LOOK?

OR, WILL YOU HONESTLY TELL THEM THAT IT IS AGAINST YOUR BETTER JUDGMENT TO BELIEVE THAT WILL-FULLY AND JOYFULLY EXPRESSING YOURSELF, IN THE CHURCH

DURING WORSHIP, IS WRONG, SO THAT'S WHY YOU ARE OUT OF SYNC?

Or, WOULD YOU TELL THEM THAT EVERYTHING THAT YOU HAVE BEEN DOING IN THE SANCTUARY OF THE CHURCH, HAS NOT AT ALL BEEN REAL, YOU'VE ONLY BEEN GOING ALONG WITH THE EXPECTED BEHAVIOR OF THE PEOPLE OF THE CHURCH?

DURING THE SERVICES OF CHURCHES EVERYWHERE, THERE ARE A LOT OF PRAISES BEING VERBALIZED THAT ARE NOT EVEN FROM THE HEART OF MOST INDIVIDUALS! STATEMENTS OF ADORATION AND GLORY ARE SOMETIMES VERY LOUDLY VERBALIZED, TO THE POINT OF SHOUTING, OFTEN AT THE WRONG TIMES, DROWNING OUT THE MESSAGE OF THE GOSPEL.

THE LORD IMPRESSED UPON ME TO DELIVER A MESSAGE, FOR THE SAKE OF PEOPLE WHO RAISE THE NOISE DURING THE SERMON, BUT WERE HARDLY EVER FOUND PRAISING THE LORD AND WORSHIPING IN HIS PRESENCE.

THE TITLE OF THAT MESSAGE WAS; "SOUNDING GOOD, BUT! SAYING NOTHING."

I'D OBSERVED PEOPLE GETTING EXCITED OVER SERMONS THAT DIDN'T ADMONISH HOLINESS OR ENCOURAGE PEOPLE TO TURN TO CHRIST AND BE SAVED. PEOPLE ONLY GOT EXCITED ABOUT THE SOUND OF THE PREACHER'S VOICE! I LIKE TO SAY, CONCERNING SERMONS THAT DON'T EDIFY CHRIST; *"Sounds good, but not Sound Doctrine?"*

People Lose The Fire!

 WE ARE TOO SILENT DURING THE PRAISE AND WORSHIP SEGMENT OF THE SERVICES, WHICH MATTERS THE MOST! BECAUSE, PEOPLE HAVE A TENDANCY TO BE ENTERTAINED; THEY GET LOST IN LISTENING TO THE MELODIOUS VOICES, AND SKILLFUL MUSICIANSHIP OF THE BAND. PEOPLE FAIL TO GET INVOLVED IN WORSHIP AS A PARTICIPATOR, THEY CHOOSE TO BE A SPECTATOR!

PEOPLE USUALLY DON'T GENERATE A LOT OF NOISE, WHENEVER A STRONG SOUND DOCTRINAL MESSAGE OF THE

GOSPEL IS GOING FORTH.

THE LATE DR. S. E. MITCHELL, ONE OF THE GREATEST GOSPEL PREACHERS OF THE C.O.G.I.C CHURCHES, WHO LEFT US SEVERAL YEARS AGO TO BE IN THE PRESENCE OF THE LORD, WOULD BEGIN TO PREACH STRONG SOUND DOCTRINAL MESSAGES OF DELIVERANCE, AND ALL OF SUDDEN, A *Holy* HUSH WOULD APPEAR TO COME OVER THE SANCTUARY.

CERTAIN PEOPLE, WHO HAD JUST FINISHED DANCING IN THE AISLES, WOULD SEEM TO BECOME PARALYZED AND MUTED! THEIR LOUD MOUTHS, WOULD SUDDENLY BECOME SILENT, AS IF THEIR TONGUES HAD BEEN MYSTERIOUSLY SEVERED, RIGHT BEFORE THE PEOPLE OF THE LORD! THOSE WHO APPEARED TO HAVE BEEN ON FIRE FOR THE LORD, ACTED AS IF THEY HAD BEEN DOUSED WITH A BUCKET OF WATER.

SUCH A LOSS OF FIRE AND EMOTIONAL DISPLAY, WOULD BE MORE EXPECTED BEHAVIOR FOR UNSAVED PEOPLE WHO FREQUENT THE CHURCH, BUT HAVE NOT MADE A DECISION TO TURN THEIR LIVES OVER TO THE LORD.

PEOPLE SAY THAT THEY ARE TOO AFRAID TO TAKE THE WORSHIP OF THE LORD TO THE PEOPLE OUT THERE ON THE STREETS; BUT, WHENEVER THE PEOPLE OUT THERE ON THOSE STREETS COME IN TO OUR WORSHIP SERVICES, THE PEOPLE OF THE CHURCH, DROP THE BALL AND CHOKE-UP ON THE INSIDE OF THE SANCTUARY AS WELL!

WHAT ARE YOU AFRAID OF?

QUESTION, WHO IS GREATER THAN THE LORD?

ANSWER, ABSOLUTELY NO ONE IS GREATER THAN THE LORD JESUS CHRIST!

JOYFULLY BUBBLING OVER IN WORSHIP SERVICES, SHOULD NOT ONLY BE AN APPEARANCE. JOY SHOULD BE GLORIOUSLY FLOWING OUT EVEN AS PEOPLE LEAVE THE SANCTUARY OF THE CHURCH, TO BE SPREAD THROUGHOUT THE COMMUNITY IN EVERY WAY POSSIBLE!

THERE ARE PERSONS THAT CAN'T KEEP THEIR SEAT

AND THEY DON'T HOLD THEIR PEACE IN THE WORSHIP SERVICE, THEY ARE ALWAYS OUT OF CONTROL.

THEY WILL TELL YOU THE LORD HAS BEEN GOOD TO THEM AND THEY CAN'T HOLD THEIR PEACE. NO ONE SHOULD HOLD THEIR PEACE, AS IF THEY ARE LOOKING FOR SOMETHING TO LAND IN THE SANCTUARY FROM OUTER SPACE TO AWAKEN THEM.

OUT-OF-CONTROL PEOPLE REFUSE TO CONDUCT THEMSELVES IN AN ORDERLY MANNER, DISRESPECTING THE AUTHORITY OF THE HOUSE OF GOD, AND CONSISTENTLY DISRUPTING THE FLOW OF THE WORSHIP SERVICE.

SILENCE MAY BE GOLDEN; BUT, SILENCE AS A WAY OF PUBLIC WORSHIP, IS LIKE GOLD THAT HAS TARNISHED AND GONE BAD! TRUE WORSHIPPERS SHOULD ALWAYS GO DEEPER INTO THE WORSHIP OF THE LORD. I BELONG TO THE NOISY CREW AND IF YOU THINK FOR ONE MOMENT THAT I'M ASHAMED OF IT, YOU ARE WRONG.

Give God What He Wants!

WHY SHOULD THE CHURCH BE ASHAMED OF THE JOY OF THE LORD. WHENEVER YOU ENTER TO WORSHIP THE LORD, IF YOUR ARMS AND HANDS ARE NOT BROKEN OR PHYSICALLY DEFORMED AND HANDICAPPED, CLAP YOUR HANDS AND LIFT THEM HIGH FOR THE LORD, LIFTING UP HOLY HANDS.

THERE ARE PEOPLE WHO WOULD LOVE TO BE ABLE TO CLAP THEIR HANDS AND LIFT THEM HIGH IN REVERENCE TO THE LORD.

WHEEL CHAIRS AND CRUTCHES, FOR THE PHYSICALLY HANDICAPPED AND DEBILITATED, SHOULD WARRANT THE SERIOUSNESS OF OUR RELENTLESS, RESPECTFUL CARE, THAT IS GIVEN TO SUCH CONDITIONS. BUT WE SHOULD NEVER OFFER PITY IN THE PLACE OF OFFERING PRAISE, AS THOSE CONDITIONS ARE NEVER TO BE A REAL HINDRANCE TO GIVING PRAISE AND WORSHIP TO THE LORD, FOR THOSE INDIVIDUALS.

WHAT ABOUT YOUR LEGS, ARE YOU ABLE TO GO FORTH AND PRAISE THE LORD? WHEN WAS THE LAST TIME THAT

YOU WENT FORTH IN DANCE BEFORE THE LORD, TO GIVE HIM THE GLORY? IF YOUR BODY IS IN GOOD SHAPE, THEN EXACTLY WHAT IS YOUR PROBLEM, OTHER THAN THE DEVIL?

YOUR HEART PROBLEM MAY ACTUALLY GET BETTER IF YOU WILL GET RADICAL FOR THE LORD. GET ON UP AND PRAISE THE LORD!

WE HAVE EVERY REASON THAT WE CAN THINK OF AND EVERY REASON THAT WE CAN'T THINK OF, TO GIVE GOD THE GLORY, THE HONOR AND THE PRAISE. WE PRAISE HIM FOR WHAT HE HAS DONE FOR US, BUT WE WORSHIP HIM FOR WHO HE IS, THROUGHOUT ALL ETERNITY. COME ON, LET'S MAKE A JOYFUL NOISE UNTO THE LORD, IN THE SANCTUARY. IN THE CONGREGATION OF THE RIGHTEOUS, WE NEED TO LIFT THE "NAME OF JESUS" HIGH.

THESE DAYS, WE NEED TO PRAISE GOD IN EVERY POSSIBLE MANNER OF SAINTLY EXPRESSION. IF YOU ARE HAPPY AND YOU KNOW IT, CLAP YOUR HANDS, STOMP YOUR FEET, AND SHOUT FOR JOY.

WHENEVER YOU COME INTO THE HOUSE OF THE LORD, YOU SHOULD COME PREPARED TO RAISE THE PRAISE AS HIGH AS IT CAN GO! ALWAYS REMEMBER THAT THERE IS A RAISE IN THE PRAISE! LET THE PRAISE RING OUT OF YOUR MOUTH.

GIVE GOD THE GLORY SO THAT HE CAN GET THE GLORY OUT OF YOUR LIFE. IF YOU PRAISE THE LORD, HE WILL BLESS YOU AND PRAISE YOU BEFORE THE FATHER IN HEAVEN. IF YOU MAGNIFY THE LORD, HE WILL IN TURN MAGNIFY YOU. OH CLAP YOUR HANDS ALL OF YOU PEOPLE, SHOUT TO GOD WITH THE "VOICE OF TRIUMPH"; SHOUT TO GOD AND GIVE HIM THE PRAISE. *Psalms 47: 1*

Watch Yourself!

BE CAREFUL NOT TO ALLOW YOURSELF TO BECOME AFFIXED INTO AN AREA OF SILENCE, DURING WORSHIP. IT'S UP TO YOU TO BE RESPONSIVE IN THE WORSHIP SERVICE OF THE LORD.

MAYBE YOU HOLD YOUR PEACE IN WORSHIP BECAUSE

THE SITUATIONS IN YOUR LIFE ARE STILL THE SAME? YOU DON'T HAVE TO WAIT UNTIL THE SMOKE CLEARS OR UNTIL THE RUMBLING AND THE SHAKING SETTLES OR EVEN UNTIL ALL OF YOUR ENEMIES HAVE CHANGED THEIR MINDS AND HAVE DECIDED TO BECOME YOUR FRIEND. MANY YEARS AGO, SINGER, SONGWRITER "WALTER HAWKINS" WROTE A SONG THAT SAYS; "DON'T WAIT TILL' THE BATTLE IS OVER, SHOUT NOW!!!

WORSHIP IN THE MIDST OF THE BATTLE, BECAUSE WE ARE ALREADY CONQUERS AND WINNERS, EVEN BEFORE THE LOSER OF THE BATTLE GOES DOWN. IN GOOD TIMES AND BAD TIMES, WHENEVER YOU ARE UP OR DOWN, YOU STILL HAVE A RIGHT TO PRAISE THE LORD. PERHAPS YOU'VE BEEN SICK AND HAVE NOT BEEN FEELING WELL, PRAISING GOD IS NOT ABOUT A FEELING ANYWAY, IT'S ABOUT <u>FAITH</u>!!!

Do What You Know To Do!

WHENEVER YOU GET UP OUT OF YOUR BED, ON A DAY OF WORSHIP AND PREPARE YOURSELF TO GO TO THE HOUSE OF THE LORD, MAKE UP YOUR MIND BEFORE YOU EVER LEAVE THE HOUSE THAT YOU ARE GOING TO PRAISE THE LORD.

TAKE YOUR HEADACHES AND BACKACHES, HEART-ACHES, FRUSTRATIONS, DISAPPOINTMENTS, UPSETS AND LETDOWNS WITH YOU TO CHURCH. IF YOU TAKE THESE THINGS TO THE HOUSE OF WORSHIP WITH YOU, BE SURE TO ADMONISH ALL OF THE LOAD AND THE EXCESS BAGGAGE THAT YOU ARE GOING TO PRAISE THE LORD, TOO!

DEAD WEIGHT IS HEAVY, SO DON'T ALLOW DEAD WEIGHT TO JUST HANG ON TO YOU IN SERVICE, BUT RATHER SPRING UP THE LIFE OF YOUR PRAISE AND ALLOW THE LIFE OF THE SPIRIT TO BE RELEASED AND REJECT THE POSSIBIL-ITY OF THE DEATH OF YOUR PRAISE AND WORSHIP!

IF PEOPLE CAN PRAISE GOD FROM A WHEELCHAIR WITH AMPUTATED LIMBS, CERTAINLY YOU AND I CAN PRAISE THE LORD HAVING ALL OF OUR LIMBS INTACT! I HAVE SEEN PEOPLE PRAISE THE LORD WITH AN OXYGEN TANK ATTACHED

TO THEM, IN ORDER TO BREATHE, (MY FATHER WAS ONE OF THOSE LIKE PERSONS).

PEOPLE PRAISE THE LORD, DURING THE FUNERAL OF THEIR DEARLY DEPARTED LOVED ONE. THERE IS JUST NO REASON TO KEEP SILENT AND NOT GIVE GOD THE GLORY.

SOME SAY, THAT THEY ARE JUST NOT VERY EMOTIONAL PEOPLE, THIS IS THE REASON THEY NEVER MOVE OR CLAP THEIR HANDS IN THE HOUSE OF THE LORD. I WONDER WHY THESE SAME UNEMOTIONAL PEOPLE, GET SO EXCITED ABOUT SO MANY OTHER OUTDOOR AND INDOOR ACTIVITIES ALIKE.

YOU JUST LET ONE OF THESE UNEMOTIONAL PEOPLE WIN THE LOTTERY, THEY SEEM TO COME UP WITH EMOTIONS FROM SOMEWHERE. THEIR SHOES SEEM TO GET HAPPY AND THEIR BODIES GO OUT OF CONTROL.

NEVERTHELESS, PEOPLE WOULD RATHER <u>RE</u>-<u>CREATE</u> THE THINGS THAT ARE IMPORTANT, RATHER THAN TO ACCEPT WHAT THE WORD OF GOD SAYS IS IMPORTANT TO EVERY BELIEVER, WHICH IS TO GIVE GOD THE GLORY OF PRAISE AND WORSHIP.

PEOPLE ARE ALWAYS LOOKING FOR SOMETHING, OTHER THAN THE LORD TO FULFILL THEM, EVEN IF WHATEVER THEY FIND TO INDULGE THEMSELVES IN, BRINGS DEGRADATION AND SHAME.

It not too late to get started;

Make A Joyful Noise!

Finally Speaking!*

> Finally, my brethren, be strong in the Lord, and in the power of his might.　　　EPHESIANS 6:10
>
> This book of the law shall not depart out of thy mouth; but thou shalt meditate therein day and night, that thou mayest observe to do according to all that is written therein: for then thou shalt make thy way prosperous, and then thou shalt have good success.　　　JOSHUA 1:8

Yea! Your Mouth!

YOUR VOICE, YIELDED TO THE LORD, IS THE MOST POWERFUL ORIFICE, AMONG THE SPEAKING PEOPLE OF THE EARTH, IF YOU WOULD TAKE THE INITIATIVE TO SPEAK UP AND TO SPEAK OUT WITH AUTHORITY. HOWEVER, YOU HAVE GOT TO BE SKILLFUL AT USING YOU ABILITY TO SPEAK.

AUTHORITY IS NOT THE THING TO BE DESIRED WHEN SPEAKING FORTH TO ANY LISTENING PERSON OR GROUP OF PEOPLE, BECAUSE IT'S TOO LATE TO DISCOVER THAT YOU

ARE LACKING THE NECESSARY AUTHORITY RIGHT IN THE MIDDLE OF A SENTENCE OR A THOUGHT.

WHILE MOST PEOPLE WHO DESIRE TO BE AUTHORITATIVE, DO GIVE SOME THOUGHT TO THE THINGS THAT THEY WILL SAY, MY ENCOURAGEMENT HAS BEEN TO NUDGE THEM TO GIVE EVEN GREATER THOUGHT TO WHAT THEY ARE THINKING ABOUT SAYING BEFORE THEY MAKE THE UNRECOVERABLE MISTAKE OF SAYING THE WRONG THINGS!

IF YOU ARE FAULTY AND NEGATIVE IN YOUR OWN PERSONALIZED MANNER OF MANEUVERING THOUGHTS THROUGH YOUR MIND AS YOU PROCESS DATA IMPUTE, YOU WILL FIND YOURSELF TO BE VERBALLY DAMAGING TO MOST OF THE PEOPLE THAT YOU COME INTO CONTACT WITH.

LOTS OF PEOPLE MAKE UP IN THEIR MINDS TO JUST GO AHEAD AND SAY WHAT IT IS THEY DESIRE TO SAY. TO THE LIKES OF AN INDIVIDUAL WHO MAKES UP IN THEIR MIND TO PULL THE TRIGGER OF A LOADED SAWED-OFF, DOUBLE-BARREL SHOT GUN, WITHOUT LOOKING. AFTER THE SHOTS HAVE BEEN FIRED, THEY WILL TAKE THE TIME TO SURVEY THE AREA TO SEE IF THE BULLETS OR THE SHOTGUN PELLETS HAVE ACCURATELY HIT THE TARGET; OR ELSE, OH WELL!

PEOPLE LACK THE FEELING OF RESPONSIBILITY FOR THE DAMAGE CAUSED TO OTHER INDIVIDUALS WHENEVER THEY LET GO OF THEIR OWN SPOKEN WORDS IN THE PRESENCE OF PEOPLE WHETHER THE STATEMENTS ARE DIRECTED TO THE PEOPLE THAT ARE STANDING CLOSE BY, OR TO SOMEONE ELSE JUST A SHORT DISTANCE AWAY. NEVERTHELESS, SOMEBODY'S GOING TO GET TONGUE-LASHED!

NO DOUBT ABOUT IT; THEY KNEW THAT THEY HAD LIVE AMMUNITION, AND A WORKING SHOTGUN. WHAT THEY DIDN'T HAVE WAS A WORKING KNOWLEDGE OF THE SKILLS TO PROPERLY HANDLE THE SHOTGUN. THE MENTALITY IS TO SHOOT FIRST AND TALK ABOUT IT LATER; IF THERE IS ANYONE LEFT STANDING TO TALK!

PEOPLE KNOW THAT THEY HAVE THE FIRST AMEND-

MENT RIGHT TO SAY WHATEVER THEY CHOOSE TO SAY OUT OF THEIR MOUTHS, SO THEY TAKE ADVANTAGE OF EVERY OPPORTUNITY TO DO JUST THAT. THEIR CHILDREN ARE TAUGHT TO DO LIKEWISE, NO MATTER WHAT.

I HAVE BEEN IN THE COMPANY OF SOME PEOPLE WHO'S MOUTHS OUGHT TO BE SHUT TIGHT AND SOWN TOGETHER TO PREVENT THEM FROM CAUSING THE HEARTACHE AND THE PAIN THAT THEY HAVE CAUSED OTHER PEOPLE IN THE PAST WITH THE HORRIBLE WORDS THAT CAME OUT OF THEIR MOUTHS.

SOME PEOPLE ARE SO VULGAR THAT IT WILL MAKE YOU ALMOST WANT TO THROW-UP! THE FILTH THAT IS SPEWED OUT OF THE MOUTH OF SOME PEOPLE WILL GIVE YOU A HEADACHE!

WE HAVE NO CONTROL OVER WHATEVER COMES OUT OF THE MOUTHS OF OTHER PEOPLE. ALTHOUGH WE ARE OFTEN DEVASTATED AND AT OTHER TIMES WE ARE THOROUGHLY EMBARRASSED AT WHAT HAS COME FROM THE MOUTHS OF OTHER PEOPLE, WE ARE NOT RESPONSIBLE FOR WHAT THEY SAID.

WE ARE TAKEN FAST BECAUSE MANY OF THE PEOPLE WHO ARE OUT OF CONTROL, ARE ALSO PEOPLE WHO CONFESS TO BEING BORN AGAIN BLOOD WASHED BELIEVERS; IN CHRIST JESUS. IT REALLY DOESN'T MATTER WHERE THEY MIGHT BE, THEY APPEAR TO BE TOTALLY DISREGARDING OF THE FACT THAT THEY HAVE FAILED TO EXEMPLIFY THAT THERE HAS BEEN A CHANGE IN THEIR LIVES, THROUGH THEIR CONVERSATIONS.

AS BELIEVERS, WE COME UNDER SUCH GRUELING AND DEGRADING CRITICISM FROM THE PEOPLE OF THE COMMUNITY, AND FROM THE SOCIETY OF WHICH WE LIVE, THAT IT CAN CAUSE LIVING HOLY TO BECOME A VERY LONELY LIFE TO LIVE. AS A RESULT, MANY BELIEVERS WILL ALLOW THEIR SPEECH TO BE COMPROMISED IN ORDER TO RELAY THE MESSAGE TO OTHER PEOPLE THAT THEY ARE STILL DOWN TO EARTH.

 # Conclusion*

PEOPLE WANT YOU TO LIGHTEN-UP ON YOUR SPEECH AS IT RELATES TO SPEAKING THE WORD OF GOD, SIMPLY BECAUSE THEY DON'T WANT THE PRESSURE OF CHANGING THE WAY THAT THEY LIVE, COMING OUT OF YOUR MOUTH. AS A MATTER OF THE FACT, THE ARE SUBTLY WORKING ON YOU TO REVERSE YOUR CHANGE IF IT IS POSSIBLE.

IT IS EASY TO BELIEVE THAT OTHERS ARE UNDERSTANDING OF YOU WHILE YOU COMPROMISE YOUR SELF, SO THAT THEY WILL BE COMFORTABLE IN YOUR COMPANY, BUT THEY ARE DECEIVING YOU, THEY DON'T UNDERSTAND YOU AT ALL! WHENEVER THEY GET A CHANCE, THEY WILL REMIND YOU OF HOW YOU SHOULD HAVE CONDUCTED YOURSELF IN THEIR PRESENCE, BUT INSTEAD, YOU LOWERED YOUR CHRISTIAN STANDARDS.

BELIEVE ME; PEOPLE WON'T FORGET THE FACT THEY HAD THE OPPORTUNITY TO SEE THE MORE HUMAN SIDE OF YOU, OR TO HEAR THE MORE HUMANISTIC LIKE VERNACULAR COMING FROM YOUR MOUTH. YOU'RE SUPPOSED TO BE A CHILD OF THE LORD! THEY DON'T MIND TELLING YOU THAT!

MOST OF US WERE TAUGHT THAT YOU ONLY GET ONE OPPORTUNITY TO MAKE A FIRST IMPRESSION. THIS IS THE THING: YOUR FIRST IMPRESSION MAY BE TO THAT SOMEONE THAT YOU ALREADY KNOW AND ARE WELL ACQUAINTED WITH FOR QUITE SOME TIME NOW. IT MAY BE THAT YOU NEED TO MAKE A FIRST IMPRESSION OF THE CHANGE THAT IS IN YOUR LIFE NOW SINCE YOU MET JESUS!

IT DOESN'T MATTER THAT PEOPLE ARE WITNESSES TO THE FACT THAT THEY SAW SOMEONE ELSE AGGRAVATING YOU AND PUSHING YOU TO THE LIMIT, WHAT THEY ARE FOREVER GOING TO REMEMBER IS THAT FACT THAT YOU DO NOT VERBALLY HANDLE THE SITUATION IN THE WAY OF THE WORD OF THE LORD.

AS A CONFESSING BELIEVER IN JESUS CHRIST; PEOPLE WOULD RATHER HEAR YOU QUOTE SCRIPTURES OR SAY NOTHING AT ALL, BEFORE THEY HEAR YOU LOSE IT AND BEGIN TO

CURSE BACK. IT DOESN'T EVEN MATTER TO MOST PEOPLE IF YOU NEVER REMOVED YOURSELF FROM THE SITUATION AS LONG AS YOU HELD ON TO YOUR INTEGRITY AND THE CONFESSION OF YOUR FAITH IN GOD.

PEOPLE KNOW WHEN THE DEVIL IS DOGGING YOUR TRAIL, THEY DON'T WANT TO SEE YOU BEGIN TO ACT LIKE THE DEVIL AND THEY NEVER WANT TO HEAR THE DEVIL'S LANGUAGE COMING OUT OF YOUR MOUTH.

THEY MAY NOT BE READY FOR THE CHANGE THAT THEY ARE AWARE OF THAT THEY DESPERATELY NEED. HOWEVER, KNOWING THAT YOU HAVE BEEN CHANGED, THOSE SAME PEOPLE ARE REALLY LOOKING FOR SOMEONE TO LOOK TO IN THE FUTURE WHEN THE FEEL THEY MIGHT BE READY TO MAKE THAT CHANGE.

WHO WE ARE VERBALLY, DETERMINES WHO WE ARE SPIRITUALLY AS WELL. THERE IS ABSOLUTELY NO WAY TO BE LIKE GOD AND TALK LIKE THE DEVIL EVERYDAY OF YOUR LIFE.

DON'T YOU REMEMBER HOW PETER DENIED THE LORD. PETER WAS WARMING HIS HAND BY THE ENEMIES FIRE, WHEN ONE OF THE WOMEN STANDING BYE NOTICED HIM. SHE TOLD THE OTHERS STANDING AROUND DISCUSSING THE LORD'S CAPTURE, THAT PETER WAS ONE OF THE LORD'S DISCIPLES.

PETER KNEW THAT HE WAS THE LORD'S DISCIPLE BETTER THAN ANYONE ELSE COULD HAVE KNOWN. AS HE BEGAN TO DENY THE LORD, THE KEY STATEMENT TO ME WAS WHEN THE WOMAN SAID TO PETER; I KNOW THAT YOU ARE INDEED ONE OF THE LORD'S DISCIPLES, BECAUSE THE WAY YOU TALK BETRAYS YOUR HIDDEN IDENTITY.

YOU TALK JUST LIKE JESUS!

PETER WAS DETERMINED TO SAVE HIS OWN LIFE AND TO AVOID BEING CRUCIFIED ALSO, SO HE CHANGED THE WAY HE TALKED AND THE BIBLE SAID THAT HE BEGAN TO SWEAR. TO BRING IT UP TO DATE, PETER BEGAN TO USE PROFANITY JUST LIKE THE UNBELIEVERS OF HIS TIME.

YOU MIGHT JUST WANT TO MAKE A MENTAL NOTE OF

# *Conclusion**

THE FACT THAT JUST BECAUSE PETER STARTING TALKING OUT OF CHARACTER TO HIS DISCIPLESHIP, IT DIDN'T ALLOW HIM TO BE LEFT ALONE TO CONTINUE WARMING BY THE ENEMIES FIRE. HE STILL HAD TO FLEE FOR HIS LIFE AND GET AWAY FROM THE ANGRY MOB OF JESUS HATERS.

THOUGH THE COCK CREW AND PETER WAS REMINDED OF THE WORDS THE LORD JESUS HAD SPOKEN TO HIM, HOW THAT HE WOULD DENY THE LORD THREE TIMES, HE WAS ALSO FORCED TO REALIZE THE ERROR OF HIS SPEECH.

HE KNEW THAT HE HADN'T SPOKEN THE TRUTH, BECAUSE HE HAD GONE OUT OF HIS WAY TO CONVINCE JESUS HOW MUCH HE LOVED HIM AND THAT HE WOULD NEVER ALLOW ANYTHING TO HAPPEN TO HIM, AND HE ALSO VERBALLY TURNED HIS BACK WHEN FACED WITH THE CRISIS OF BEING HATED LIKE THE LORD.

IT'S TIME THAT WE MAKE UP OUR MINDS AS TO WHETHER WE WANT TO BE ACCEPTED BY THE PEOPLE OF THE SOCIETY, OR WHETHER WE ARE TRUE IN OUR HEARTS WHEN WE SAY THAT WE HAVE ACCEPTED THE LORD AS OUR SAVIOR!

HOW WOULD YOU FAIR, IF YOU WERE CONFRONTED IN THE LIKE MANNER AS PETER, WHERE PEOPLE WERE IN THE SPIRIT OF DOING SOMETHING TERRIBLE TO YOU BECAUSE YOU TALK LIKE THE LORD? IS THERE ENOUGH EVIDENCE TO CONVICT YOU, OR TO VALIDATE THE CAUSE OF THE JESUS HATERS AGAINST YOU?

IT'S NEVER OUR WORDS VERSUS THE WRITTEN WORDS OF THE BIBLE; AS IF OUR OPINION OF THE WORD OF GOD HAS TO BE IMPUTED BEFORE THE SPOKEN WORD WILL HAVE ANY SIGNIFICANCE.

YOU SHOULD BE CONVICTED AND CONVINCED THAT THE WORD OF GOD IS RIGHT ALL BY ITSELF, BEFORE EVER ATTEMPTING TO SPEAK PUBLICLY BEFORE ANY AUDIENCE, OR EVEN PRIVATE, FOR THAT MATTER.

PEOPLE WOULD HAVE TO BE EQUALLY AS GREAT AS GOD, OR ABSOLUTELY GREATER IN ORDER TO ESTABLISH ANY

 # Conclusion*

CREDENCE TO THE WORD OF GOD.

THE ABSOLUTE WORD OF GOD IS IMMOVABLY SETTLED ETERNALLY IN HEAVEN. NO ONE COULD EVER UPROOT THE PILLARS AND THE FOUNDATION OF HEAVEN, THEREFORE IT IS FOREVER IMPOSSIBLE TO REMOVE THE FOUNDING ESTABLISHMENT OF THE WORD OF GOD!

Working, A Working Mouth!*

WHAT DIFFERENCE DOES IT MAKE TO HAVE A PARTICULAR TOOL FOR SPEAKING, SUCH AS THE MOUTH AND BE TOTALLY DEPRAVED OF UNDERSTANDING THE PROPER USAGE AND THE PURPOSE FOR PERSONALLY POSSESSING THE TOOL IN THE FIRST PLACE?

I TOOK IT UPON MYSELF TO ENCOURAGE THE ENHANCEMENT OF KNOWLEDGE, RELATIVE TO AN EXCELLENT INSTRUCTIONAL GUIDE FOR SPEAKING.

THE POWER TO POSSESS THE WEALTH OF THIS WORLD IS OFTEN HIDDEN WITHIN THE SECRET OF CONFIGURATIVE, PROPERLY PLACED WORDS.

NOT JUST THE WORDS THAT HAVE BEEN SECRETLY IMPUTED INTO THE THINKING CAPACITY OF A PERSON'S MIND, BECAUSE MOST PEOPLE ARE CAPABLE OF THINKING THE RIGHT WORDS THAT THEY OUGHT TO SAY. BUT, SOMEHOW THEY SEEM TO FAIL AT PUTTING THE PROPER WORDS OF THEIR OWN ORIGINATED THOUGHTS INTO SENTENCES AND IMPORTANT PHRASAL VERBALIZATIONS THAT PRODUCE THE DESIRED RESULTS OF THEIR FAITH.

THE CONCEALED COMBINATION OF A BANK VAULT, IS NOT DISCOVERED THROUGH POINTING THE BARREL OF A HIGH POWERED WEAPON AT A BANK TELLER. IT IS FAVORABLY REVEALED TO BANK EMPLOYEES AS A RESULT OF THE TRUST THAT HAS BEEN ESTABLISHED BY WAY OF INTELLIGENTLY SPEAKING FORTH, TO PROVE THAT AN INDIVIDUAL IS CAPABLE OF HANDLING SUCH AN EXCLUSIVE WEALTH OF INFORMATION.

IT'S PROPER TO THINK THAT EDUCATION WOULD BE THE ULTIMATE ANSWER TO BEING INDIGENT OF WORD PLACEMENT, BUT DON'T OVERLOOK THE FACT THAT TOO

 # Conclusion*

MANY PEOPLE HAVE EMERGED FROM INSTITUTIONS OF LEARNING, ONLY TO REVEAL THAT THEY HAD FAILED AT BEING PROPERLY EDUCATED!

THE EDUCATION NEEDED TO BE A SPOKESPERSON FOR THE LORD USUALLY CAN NEVER BE FOUND IN THE CLASSROOM OF A LEARNING INSTITUTION. THE UNDERSTANDING COMES ONLY FROM THE LORD AND THE WRITTEN WORD OF GOD.

MANY PEOPLE BELIEVE THAT THEY HAVE CHOSEN THE WINNING SIDE, HOWEVER, THEY HAVE NOT YET MASTERED THE ART OF WINNING.

IT IS IMPERATIVE TO PAY ATTENTION TO THE INSTRUCTION THAT TEACHES US HOW TO WIN AND ADHERE TO THAT SAME WINNING VERNACULAR TO ESTABLISH PROPER COMMUNICATION TO THE WIN SEEKERS IN THE WORLD, KNOWING THAT THE WINNING SIDE IS THE ONLY SIDE TO BE ON.

THE KNOWLEDGE OF MANUAL MANIPULATION SKILLS, IS NOT THE TOTAL CONFIGURATION NECESSARY THAT ESTABLISHES THE ACTUALITY OF THE WIN. IT IS EQUALLY AS IMPORTANT TO VERBALLY ARTICULATE AND TO DEFINITIVELY ENUNCIATE YOUR SKILLS, AS WELL AS IT IS TO PHYSICALLY MANIPULATE WITH YOUR HANDS; PUTTING THE SKILLS INTO ACTION.

WHEN YOU CAN'T SAY WHAT IT IS THAT YOU DO, THE GREATER CHANCE IS THAT YOU REALLY DON'T KNOW WHAT YOU'RE DOING, RELATIVE TO THE CHOICES, OF YOUR OWN CHOSEN ACTIONS!

THE SPORT OF BOXING, AS BRUTAL AS IT IS, HAS CONSISTENTLY YIELDED CHAMPIONS, WHO COULD NOT EVEN DESCRIBE THE STRATEGY OF THEIR WIN VERBALLY. ALL THEY KNOW, IS THAT THEY STEPPED INTO THE RING AND BEAT THE LIVING DAYLIGHTS OUT OF THEIR OPPONENT. THEY RECEIVED THE TITLE BELT, LOOKING FORWARD TO THE VERY NEXT OPPORTUNITY TO REPEAT THE TRAGEDY ALL OVER AGAIN, JUST AS ILLITERATE AS BEFORE.

Conclusion*

NO MATTER WHAT SPORT HAS BEEN CHOSEN, THERE ARE MANUALS TO BE STUDIED, FOR THE VERY PURPOSE OF BEING CAPABLE OF SAYING IT, AS WELL AS DOING IT.

WE OFTEN CRINGE WITHIN OURSELVES AND CRITICIZE AN ATHLETE, WHO HAS VERBALLY DESTROYED THEIR OWN IMAGE, THROUGH THE PROJECTION OF ILLITERACY, WHILE BEING INTERVIEWED?

MANY SHADE-TREE MECHANICS HAVE THE SKILL TO MAKE AN AUTOMOBILE HUM AND PURR; BUT SADLY, THEY DON'T HAVE THE VERBAL SKILLS, TO PUT INTO WORDS WHAT THEY HAVE DONE TO REPAIR THE AUTOMOBILE.

THEY HAVE VERY CREATIVE MINDS, THAT ALLOWS THEM TO DO MANY INCREDIBLE THINGS, BUT THEY DON'T HAVE THE NECESSARY SKILLFUL MECHANICAL DIALOGUE, NECESSARY TO SHARE THEIR SKILLS, AND TO ENHANCE THE FUTURE GROWTH OF OTHERS.

THE RESUME, OF ALL PAST EMPLOYMENT OPPORTUNITIES ALONE, DOES NOT INSURE THAT THE POSITION OF THE NEXT JOB WILL BE YOURS. THE INDIVIDUAL WHO HAS THE CAPABILITY TO VERBALLY DIALOGUE THE ACTUALITY OF THEIR EXPERIENCES, WILL USUALLY MORE ASSUREDLY TAKE THE POSSESSION OF THEIR NEXT JOB POSITION.

SIMPLY KNOWING WHAT AN INTERVIEWER IS EXPECTING TO HEAR AND KNOWING HOW TO ARTICULATE THE SAME INFORMATION AT THE TIME OF INTERVIEWING, WILL ALWAYS BE A MAJOR BENEFIT.

THE WORLD IS NOT CONQUERED THROUGH THE AID OF FIGHTING AND WARS ALONE, AS IT MAY APPEAR, AND NEITHER IS THE WORLD TAKEN FOR A POSSESSION BY MONEY ALONE.

THE CONQUERING FACTOR IS DISCOVERED THROUGH THE POWER OF WORDS PROPERLY PLACED AND THE TIMELY RELEASE OF A CHARISMATIC PRESENTATION; TAKING THE VAST LISTENING AUDIENCES OF THE WORLD CAPTIVE, ONE BY ONE; ALMOST AS IF TO MAKE HOSTAGES AND PRISONERS OF THE LISTENING EARS.

Conclusion*

People, who are usually in a big hurry, to say it "best" and to make it very plain, usually don't! Effective talking is never done in a hurry, it takes time to deliver flawless messages that are plainly understood.

Fast talkers are those individuals who are usually at a lost to care for use of the necessary words to establish reliability between themselves and the listeners because they have other interest.

Don't allow yourself to believe that it is OK to aimlessly speak into the wind for no reason at all, just because you have a mouth and a platform.

Christianity has been so compromised; many people are talking, but refusing to walk the walk of their talk! As a result, it is not always easy to know who's, who? Many act the part, but were never truly converted from the inside out.

It is no longer obvious in this present day, as to where the church stands on many issues that would clearly indicate its positional strength. Many spiritual leaders have fallen prey to plain old ungodly sinful talking.

Refusing to speak out against the ungodliness of this demonically influenced society, they frequently talk of sexual scandals and financial scams of the clergy that have ripped right through the heart of the church.

The politician like demeanor of spiritual leaders and perpetrators of fraudulent behavior, have infiltrated the characteristics of these speaking Generals, that lead the congregations. This has openly hampered the compassionate repose of the local church body, disabling the changing effectiveness of the church in the community.

More of the church's influence should have entered into the world by now; however, because

Conclusion*

THE MESSAGE OF THE CHURCH HAS BEEN ALTERED, NOW EVEN IN THESE DAYS OF THE HIP-HOP CRAZE, MORE OF THE WORLD'S INFLUENCE HAS ENTERED INTO THE CHURCH.

THE PEOPLE OF THE CHURCH ARE FEARFUL AND OFTEN TOO ASHAMED, TO STAND AGAINST EVERYTHING AND EVERYONE THAT MOVES IN THE OPPOSITE DIRECTION OF THE MOVEMENT OF THE CHURCH.

THE GOD FEARING, HOLY GHOST FILLED MEMBERS OF THE CHURCH, ARE SO BUSY, PURPOSEFULLY SEPARATING THEMSELVES FROM THE PEOPLE OF THE WORLD, THAT THEY HAVE FORGOTTEN THEIR PURPOSE FOR BEING HERE IN THE FIRST PLACE.

THE NON-CHURCHED INDIVIDUAL DOES NOT HAVE A PROBLEM SAYING TO THE MEMBER OF THE LOCAL CHURCH; "MOST OF YOU IN THE CHURCH ARE NOT EVEN REAL."

BUT, THE CHURCH MEMBER WILL NOT ALWAYS TELL THE NON-CHURCHED INDIVIDUAL THAT; *"All* OF YOU OUTSIDE OF THE SALVATION OF CHRIST ARE REALLY LOST, IN NEED OF HELP FAST, BECAUSE YOU ARE *all* ON YOUR WAY TO HELL!"

THE CHURCH IS OFTEN TAUGHT TO BE SENSITIVE TO THE ISSUES OF THE PEOPLE OF THE WORLD, SO SINNERS OFTEN BELIEVE THAT THE CHURCH SHOULDN'T HURT ANYBODY'S FEELINGS, WHILE PREACHING OR TEACHING THE WORD OF GOD.

THIS IS A VERY SORRY ATTITUDE AND FOR CERTAIN, YOU ARE NOT A SUCCESSFUL WITNESS FOR THE LORD IF THIS IS WHAT YOU BELIEVE.

THE WORLD IS NOT VERY SENSITIVE ABOUT THE FEELINGS OF THE CHURCH?

WHATEVER THEY WILL DO OR SAY, WILL NOT BE HIDDEN FROM THE PEOPLE OF THE CHURCH! THEY DON'T EVEN CARE, AND THEY FEEL THAT IT IS YOUR FAULT IF YOU GET IN THEIR WAY AND BECOME EXPOSED TO THEIR WRONG DOINGS!

PEOPLE DRIVE UP ON THE CHURCH CAMPUS, WITH

 # *Conclusion**

CAR WINDOWS DOWN AND THEIR STEREOS BLARING AND EVEN BLASTING THE SECULAR RADIO TUNES AND SMOKING CIGARETTES! HOW DISRESPECTFUL!!! I DON'T THINK THAT THIS BEHAVIOR DEPICTS ANY SENSITIVITY TOWARDS THE CHURCH. <u>DO YOU</u>???

LET ME ENCOURAGE YOU TO STOP WALKING ON THE DELICATE EGG SHELLS OF LIFE THROUGH SILENCE AND PUT YOUR FEET ON THE GROUND AND WALK TALL AND WALK SOLIDLY IN THE PRESENCE OF EVERY DISRESPECTFUL, UNGODLY AND UNCARING PERSON ON THE FACE OF THE EARTH AND SAY SOMETHING!

DON'T GO AROUND ANSWERING ANY DUMB AND UNNECESSARILY DEGRADING QUESTIONS ABOUT THE CHURCH AND YOUR SALVATION.

BE HUMBLE; NOT AN HUMILIATED DOORMAT THAT PEOPLE SEEK TO WALK ON, SIMPLY BECAUSE YOU ARE A PART OF THE CHURCH.

> *Whosoever therefore shall be ashamed of me and of my words in this adulterous and sinful generation; of him also shall the son of man be ashamed, when he cometh in the glory of his father with the holy angels.*   ST. MARK 8 :38

WE HAVE ABSOLUTELY NOTHING TO BE ASHAMED OF, AS THE CHILDREN OF THE LORD. PEOPLE WILL ALWAYS REMEMBER, WAY BACK WHEN YOU WERE NOT YET DELIVERED AND LIVING FOR THE LORD. BUT, MY SUGGESTION TO YOU,  IS LEAVE THEM WAY BACK THERE, RUMBLING THROUGH THE TRASH AND THE FILTHY RUBBLE OF YOUR PAST.

YOU WOULD BE BETTER OFF, IF YOU GO WITH THE PEOPLE, WHO HAVE DECIDED TO GO WITH THE LORD, AND LEARN TO SPEAK THE SAME LANGUAGE THAT THEY SPEAK.

ONLY THOSE INDIVIDUALS, WHO WANT TO NULLIFY THE SPEAKING AUTHORITY THAT YOU POSSESS IN CHRIST JESUS RIGHT NOW, ARE ALWAYS FINDING IT NECESSARY, FOR SOME UNKNOWN PURPOSE TO YOU, TO CONSISTENTLY REFLECT ON YOUR UNSAVED PAST.

Conclusion*

PEOPLE OF THE SAME ACCORD OF FAITH IN GOD, AS YOU ARE, WILL NEVER SEEK TO DERAIL YOU OR TO OVERTHROW YOU AND KNOCK YOU OFF YOUR MISSION.

DON'T ALLOW THE JOY OF YOUR SALVATION, TO BE WRAPPED UP IN THE APPROVAL OF ANYONE ELSE SIGNIFICANT, OTHER THAN JESUS CHRIST. "JESUS IS THE JOY OF MY SALVATION", LET HIM BE YOURS TOO!

NO ONE CAN TRULY SAY THAT THEY HAVE GOOD WISDOM, WITHOUT GOD. GOD GIVES US ALL OF THE WISDOM THAT WE WILL EVER NEED AND THEN SOME! I CAN'T NEGLECT TO TELL YOU THAT YOU SHOULD NEVER BE FOUND SPEAKING WITHOUT WISDOM.

THERE'S NOT A TEXTBOOK ON THE SUBJECT OF WISDOM ANYWHERE, TO WHICH YOU CAN BE TRULY TAUGHT OR EVEN MADE KNOWLEDGEABLE CONCERNING THE USAGE OF WISDOM, OTHER THAN THE KING JAMES VERSION OF THE HOLY BIBLE.

TO KNOW WISDOM, IS TO EXPERIENCE WISDOM. TO EXPERIENCE WISDOM, IS TO APPLY WISDOM TO YOUR LIFE, DAILY. OF COURSE, WISDOM IS HANDED DOWN TO YOU, STRAIGHT FROM THE FATHER'S OWN HAND, FROM SITUATION TO SITUATION.

> *If any of you lack wisdom, let him ask of God,*
> *that giveth to all men liberally, and upbraideth*
> *not; and it shall be given him.*   JAMES 1: 5

I LIKE TO THINK OF WISDOM AS, WISE- DOMINION OR RULER-SHIP OR RATHER IN SIMPLER TERMS, HOLY AND DIVINELY GUIDED DOMINATING AUTHORITY.

WISDOM - IS THE INSTRUCTIONAL GUIDE TO OUR EARTHLY DOMINATION THAT ALLOWS US TO BE IN CONTROL OF OUR OWN LIVES WHILE AT THE SAME TIME KEEPING IN MIND THAT WE ARE NOT OUR OWN, WE BELONG TO THE LORD, AND WE WILLFULLY GIVE HIM THE CONTROL OF OUR LIVES.

Conclusion*

Some really think of themselves as wise; but, they never ever seem to exercise wisdom at all. You can speak at the right time, but say the wrong thing, now is that wisdom? Wisdom will inform you, that it's the right time to keep silent and it will even instruct you of the wrong that you are doing by saying nothing at all.

Some situations that you have gone through, where you said the wrong thing and things blew up out of control, were only opportunities to show you the need to seek the Lord for wisdom. If it happened to you once, it can happen again and again, without wisdom.

Exalting and magnifying God, will always escalate the heightened intensified awareness of the entrance of God's glory. However, it is of no consequence to know these things if you are too afraid of offending those who disregard the same systems of belief that you do, or if you are too insecure to allow yourself to be used of the Lord.

It is foolish to try and convince others of your opinions or your convictions, who have already clearly expressed to you that they don't except or respect your point of view.

A sure way to know a fool, is to recognize that they hold no regard or reverential esteem for the truth at anytime, simply because the truth really has not found it's way into the thought process of that individual, in an effort to reach their own heart.

You may not be a fool, but it is very foolish to bring false railing accusations, against another person, knowing that the accusations are truly false!

It is not very healthy, for your own spirit being or your character disposition, to tell that, you <u>do</u> know out of your mouth, to everyone that will

370

 Conclusion*

LISTEN. <u>SHUT</u> UP!!

Most things that you know for truth should be kept on the inside unless the Lord instructs you to say it. Whose business is it that you know the things that you know? People don't know the things that you know often because, it was never intended or ordained for them to know!

Give thorough examination to whatever you have received as the truth, before you repeat whatever you have heard!

Many people have already experienced the law of reciprocity, even before reading this book. They were being blessed with the imminent return of the verbal seeds they had sown previously.

We've been instructed to strengthen others, once we have been individually strengthened ourselves.

It is our divine heritage to speak, so that we might see the glory of God manifested in the earth. Whenever I say; "might", it is not to be ascertained, that I am suggesting maybe or probably that it will happen. I'm speaking in terms of the immeasurable unrestricted power of God.

Nothing or no one can stop the power of God at any given time or place in the cosmos. Things are not going to be evidently manifested, until we make up our minds to speak the word of God. We will see things and know things as the Lord has intended from the beginning.

It's hard to get people to keep the devil's name out of their mouths. Praising and magnifying the devil increases his power over our lives.

Whatever the devil tells you, you can bank on the fact that it's a lie. The devil plays for keeps and whenever he has an opportunity to get his hands on you, he will not let go of you very easily!

Conclusion*

You have never heard of the devil seeking a change and you never will hear of the devil seeking any kind of a change that would put him in better standing of any kind with the Lord! It's not possible!

You shouldn't be afraid to be identified with the people of the Lord everywhere, being a born again believer.

If you are born of the spirit of God, then how is it that you are able to deny the powerful manifestation of the in-filling of the Holy Ghost? The bible teaches us that there is only One Lord, One faith and One baptism!

There is one spirit of the Lord, as He Himself is one Lord! You need the Holy Ghost to live on the inside of you, for the purpose of keeping you unto the day of redemption and to seriously empower your life in Jesus Christ!

Don't go through life looking for somebody to give you a word, at every open church door. You do not even know whether or not the individual, giving you the spoken word, actually even knows the Lord!

Don't allow anyone who refuses to get excited about the Lord, to dampen your joy, by always criticizing your expressions of praise and worship, criticizing your manner of dancing in the spirit or shouting and leaping for joy! I've been there.

A senior individual of the church, literally stopped me once, from praising the Lord and said that all of my bodily exercise only made mockery of God.

No one else ever told me of that same thing, of course I was too young to realize that her opinions of my praise to the Lord was not the opinion of the entire church body at that particular time

 # Conclusion*

OF MY YOUNG LIFE.

THE WORDS THAT SHE SPOKE TO ME SIMPLY ROCKED MY WORLD AND I ALLOWED IT TO PULL THE PLUG ON MY PRAISE, AS IF SHE WAS THE LORD'S VERY OWN PERSONAL QUALITY CONTROL SPOKESPERSON, WATCHING OVER MY PRAISE.

SINCE THAT TIME, I HAVE FOUND THAT GOD CONTINUALLY GIVES HIS ANGELS CHARGE OVER US TO KEEP US IN ALL OF OUR WAYS.

SINCE THE ANGELS OF THE LORD ARE WATCHING OVER US, THERE IS NO NEED TO WORRY OURSELVES WITH RELIGIOUSLY MOTIVATED BUSYBODIES, WHO ARE ALWAYS LOOKING FOR SOMEONE IN THE CHURCH TO CONTROL.

Word Up;

"It's Got To Come Out Of Your Mouth!"

BLESS EVERY READER OF THIS BOOK,

OH LORD,   *in the name of Jesus!!!*

Conclusion*

For speaking engagements, and for more information on
WET Publishing, co. Please write:

PASTOR WILLIAM THOMPSON JR.
Founder/President
P.O. BOX 51092
Fort Worth, Texas 76105

Additional copies of this book and other book titles
coming soon at your local bookstore.

www.ingramcontent.com/pod-product-compliance
Lightning Source LLC
Chambersburg PA
CBHW032040050726
47590CB00001B/71